BLACK WOMEN IN
UNITED STATES HISTORY

Editor

DARLENE CLARK HINE

Associate Editors

ELSA BARKLEY BROWN

TIFFANY R.L. PATTERSON

LILLIAN S. WILLIAMS

Research Assistant

EARNESTINE JENKINS

A CARLSON PUBLISHING SERIES

See the end of the fourth volume of this title for a comprehensive guide to this sixteen-volume series.

Black Women in American History

FROM COLONIAL TIMES THROUGH THE NINETEENTH CENTURY

Edited with a Preface by Darlene Clark Hine

IN FOUR VOLUMES

Volume Three

CARLSON
Publishing Inc

BROOKLYN, NEW YORK 1990

See the end of the fourth volume of this title for a comprehensive guide to the sixteen-volume series of which this title is Volumes One through Four.

Library of Congress Cataloging-in-Publication Data

Black women in American history : from colonial times through the
   nineteenth century / edited with a preface by Darlene Clark Hine.
        p.   cm. — (Black Women in United States history ; v. 1-4)
   Includes bibliographical references.
   ISBN 0-926019-14-7 (set)
   1. Afro-American women—history. I. Hine, Darlene Clark.
II. Series: Black women in United States history ; v. 1, etc.
E185.86.B543 vol. 1-4
973'.0496073 s—dc20
[973'.0496073022]
[B]   90-1390

Case design: Allison Lew

The index to this book was created using NL Cindex, a scholarly indexing program from the Newberry Library.

Printed on acid-free, 250-year-life paper.

Manufactured in the United States of America.

Contents of the Set

Volume One

Volume Two

Volume Three

Volume Four

Black Women
in American History

"MY MOTHER WAS MUCH OF A WOMAN": BLACK WOMEN, WORK, AND THE FAMILY UNDER SLAVERY

JACQUELINE JONES

"Ah was born back due in slavery," says Nanny to her grand-daughter in Zora Neale Hurston's novel, *Their Eyes Were Watching God,* "so it wasn't for me to fulfill my dreams of whut a woman oughta be and to do." Nanny had never confused the degrading regimen of slavery with her own desires as they related to work, love, and motherhood: "Ah didn't want to be used for a work-ox and a brood-sow and Ah didn't want mah daughter used dat way neither. It sho wasn't mah will for things to happen lak they did." Throughout her life, she had sustained a silent faith in herself and her sisters that was permitted no expression within the spiritual void of bondage: "Ah wanted to preach a great sermon about colored women sittin' on high, but they wasn't no pulpit for me," she grieved.[1]

Nanny's lament offers a challenge to the historian who seeks to understand American slave women — their unfulfilled dreams as well as their day-in, day-out experiences. Despite recent scholarly interest in the relationship between women's work and family life on the one hand and Afro-American culture on the other, a systematic analysis of the roles of slave women is lacking. In her pioneering article entitled "Reflections on the Black Woman's Role in the Community of Slaves" (published over a decade ago), Angela Davis made a crucial distinction between the work that women were forced to perform for a master and the domestic labor that they provided for their own families. But her emphasis on the political implications of nurturing under slavery has not received the in-depth consideration it deserves.[2]

For example, a few scholars have explored the roles of the bondwoman as devoted wife and mother, physically powerful

Feminist Studies 8, no. 2 (Summer 1982). © 1982 by Feminist Studies, Inc.

fieldworker, and rebellious servant. Herbert G. Gutman has il-
luminated the strength of kin ties within the slave community,
and Eugene D. Genovese has furthered our understanding of
black-white, male-female relations on the antebellum plantation.
However, most historians continue to rely on the gender-neutral
term "slave" — which invariably connotes "male" — and race
supersedes sex as the focal point of their discussions. Consequently, questions related to the sexual division of labor under slavery
and the way in which task assignments in the fields, the "Big
House," and the slave quarters shaped the experiences of black
women have largely gone unanswered — and unasked.[3]

738

Moreover, historians primarily concerned with the status of
American women have examined the effects of patriarchy on
various classes and ethnic groups over time; in the process they
have highlighted variations on the theme of women's distinctive
work patterns as determined by changing economic conditions,
combined with traditional cultural assumptions about women's
domestic responsibilities. Yet within the context of current
feminist scholarship, slave women as a group remain for the most
part neglected, perhaps because they existed outside the
mainstream of the industrial revolution and (together with their
menfolk) had few opportunities to put into practice their own
ideas about appropriate work for women and men. According to
this view, slave women were something of a historical aberration,
a "special case" that has little relevance to current theoretical and
methodological perspectives on women's work.[4]

The purpose of this article is to suggest that the burdens
shouldered by slave women actually represented in extreme form
the dual nature of all women's labor within a patriarchal,
capitalist society: the production of goods and services and the
reproduction and care of members of a future work force. The
antebellum plantation brought into focus the interaction between
notions of women *qua* "equal" workers and women *qua* unequal
reproducers; hence a slaveowner just as "naturally" put his bondwomen to work chopping cotton as washing, ironing, or cooking. Furthermore, in seeking to maximize the productivity of his
entire labor force while reserving certain domestic tasks for
women exclusively, the master demonstrated how patriarchal
and capitalist assumptions concerning women's work could rein-
force one another. The "peculiar institution" thus involved forms
of oppression against women that were unique manifestations of
a more universal condition. The following discussion focuses on

female slaves in the American rural South between 1830 and 1860
— cotton boom years that laid bare the economic and social
underpinnings of slavery and indeed all of American society.[5]

Under slavery, blacks' attempts to maintain the integrity of
family life amounted to a political act of protest, and herein lies a
central irony in the history of slave women. In defiance of their
owners' tendencies to ignore gender differences in making work
assignments in the fields, the slaves whenever possible adhered to
a strict division of labor within their own households and communities. This impulse was exhibited most dramatically in patterns of black family and economic life after emancipation. Consequently, the family, often considered by feminists to be a source
(or at least a vehicle) of women's subservience, played a key role
in the freed people's struggle to resist racial and gender oppression, for black women's full attention to the duties of
motherhood deprived whites of their power over these women
as field laborers and domestic servants.[6]

739

Interviewed by a Federal Writers Project (FWP) worker in
1937, Hannah Davidson spoke reluctantly of her experiences as a
slave in Kentucky: "The things that my sister May and I suffered
were so terrible . . . . It is best not to have such things in our
memory." During the course of the interview, she stressed that
unremitting toil had been the hallmark of her life under bondage.
"Work, work, work," she said; it had consumed all her days
(from dawn until midnight) and all her years (she was only eight
when she began minding her master's children and helping the
older women with their spinning). "I been so exhausted working,
I was like an inchworm crawling along a roof. I worked till I
thought another lick would kill me." On Sundays, "the only time
they had to themselves," women washed clothes, and some of
the men tended their small tobacco patches. As a child she loved
to play in the haystack, but that was possible only on "Sunday
evening, after work."[7]

American slavery was an economic and political system by
which a group of whites extracted as much labor as possible from
blacks through the use or threat of force. A slaveowner thus
replaced any traditional division of labor that might have existed
among blacks before enslavement with a work structure of his
own choosing. All slaves were barred by law from owning pro-

perty or acquiring literacy skills, and although the system played favorites with a few, black females and males were equal in the sense that neither sex wielded economic power over the other. Hence property relations — "the basic determinant of the sexual division of labor and of the sexual order" within most societies[8] — did not affect male-female interaction among the slaves themselves. To a considerable extent, the types of jobs slaves did, and the amount and regularity of labor they were forced to devote to such jobs, were all dictated by the master.

740

For these reasons the definition of slave women's work is problematical. If work is any activity that leads either directly or indirectly to the production of marketable goods, then slave women did nothing *but* work.[9] Even their efforts to care for themselves and their families helped to maintain the owner's work force, and to enhance its overall productivity. Tasks performed within the family context — childcare, cooking, and washing clothes, for example — were distinct from labor carried out under the lash in the field or under the mistress's watchful eye in the Big House. Still, these forms of nurture contributed to the health and welfare of the slave population, thereby increasing the actual value of the master's property (that is, slaves as both strong workers and "marketable commodities"). White men warned prospective mothers that they wanted neither "runts" nor girls born on their plantations, and slave women understood that their owner's economic self-interest affected even the most intimate family ties. Of the pregnant bondwomen on her husband's expansive Butlers Island (Georgia) rice plantation, Fanny Kemble observed, "they have all of them a most distinct and perfect knowledge of their value to their owners as property," and she recoiled at their obsequious profession obviously intended to delight her: "Missus, tho' we no able to work, we make little niggers for Massa." One North Carolina slave woman, the mother of fifteen children, used to carry her youngest with her to the field each day, and "when it get hungry she just slip it around in front and feed it and go right on picking or hoeing. . . ," symbolizing in one deft motion the equal significance of the productive and reproductive functions to her owner.[10]

It is possible to divide the daily work routine of slave women into three discrete types of activity. These involved the production of goods and services for different groups and individuals, and included women's labor that directly benefited first, their families, second, other members of the slave community, and third, their owners. Although the master served as the ultimate regulator of all three types of work, he did not subject certain duties related to personal sustenance (that is, those carried out in the slave quarters) to the same scrutiny that characterized fieldwork or domestic service.

The rhythm of the planting-weeding-harvesting cycle shaped the lives of almost all American slaves, 95 percent of whom lived in rural areas. This cycle dictated a common work routine for slaves throughout the South, though the staple crop varied from tobacco in the Upper South to rice on the Georgia and South Carolina Sea Islands, sugar in Louisiana, and the "king" of all agricultural products, cotton, in the broad swath of "Black Belt" that dominated the whole region. Of almost four million slaves, about one-half labored on farms with holdings of twenty slaves or more; one-quarter endured bondage with at least fifty other people on the same plantation. In its most basic form, a life of slavery meant working the soil with other blacks at a pace calculated to reap the largest harvest for a white master.[11]

741

In his efforts to wrench as much field labor as possible from female slaves without injuring their capacity to bear children, the master made "a noble admission of female equality," observed one abolitionist sympathizer with bitter irony. Slaveholders had little use for sentimental platitudes about the delicacy of the female constitution when it came to grading their "hands" according to physical strength and endurance. Judged on the basis of a standard set by a healthy adult man, most women probably ranked as three-quarter hands; yet there were enough women like Susan Mabry of Virginia, who could pick four or five hundred pounds of cotton a day (one hundred and fifty to two hundred pounds was considered respectable for an average worker), to remove from a master's mind all doubts about the ability of a strong, healthy, woman fieldworker. As a result, he conveniently discarded his time-honored Anglo-Saxon notions about the types of work best suited for women, thereby producing many "dreary scenes" like the one described by northern journalist Frederick Law Olmsted: during winter preparation of rice fields on a Sea Island plantation, a group of black women, "armed with axes, shovels and hoes . . . all slopping about in the black, unctuous mire at the bottom of the ditches." Although pregnant and nursing women suffered from temporary lapses in productivity, most slaveholders apparently agreed with the (in Olmsted's words) "well-known, intelligent, and benevolent" Mississippi planter who declared that "labor is conducive to health; a healthy woman will rear most children." In essence, the quest for an "efficient" agricultural work force led slaveowners to downplay gender differences in assigning adults to field labor.[12]

Dressed in coarse osnaburg gowns; their skirts "reefed up with a cord drawn tightly around the body, a little above the hips" (the traditional "second belt"); long sleeves pushed above the elbows and kerchiefs on their heads, female field hands were a common sight throughout the antebellum South. Together with their fathers, husbands, brothers, and sons, black women were roused at four A.M. and spent up to fourteen hours a day toiling out of doors, often under a blazing sun. In the cotton belt they plowed fields; dropped seed; and hoed, picked, ginned, and sorted cotton. On farms in Virginia, North Carolina, Kentucky, and Tennessee, women hoed tobacco; laid worm fences; and threshed, raked, and bound wheat. For those on the Sea Islands and in coastal areas, rice culture included raking and burning the stubble from the previous year's crop; ditching; sowing seed; plowing, listing, and hoeing fields; and harvesting, stacking, and threshing the rice. In the bayou region of Louisiana, women planted sugarcane cuttings, plowed, and helped to harvest and gin the cane. During the winter, they performed a myriad of tasks necessary on nineteenth-century farms of all kinds: repairing roads, pitching hay, burning brush, and setting up post and rail fences. Like Sara Colquitt of Alabama, most adult females "worked in de fields every day from 'fore daylight to almost plumb dark." During the busy harvest season, everyone was forced to labor up to sixteen hours at a time — after sunset by the light of candles or burning pine knots. Miscellaneous chores occupied women and men around outbuildings regularly and indoors on rainy days. Slaves of both sexes watered the horses, fed the chickens, and slopped the hogs. Together they ginned cotton, ground hominy, shelled corn and peas, and milled flour.[13]

Work assignments for women and men differed according to the size of a plantation and its degree of specialization. For example, on one Virginia wheat farm, the men scythed and cradled the grain, women raked and bound it into sheaves which children then gathered and stacked. Thomas Couper, a wealthy Sea Island planter, divided his slaves according to sex and employed men exclusively in ditching and women in moting and sorting cotton. Within the two gender groups, he further classified hands according to individual strength so that during the sugarcane harvest

742

three "gangs" of women stripped blades (medium-level task), cut them (hardest), and bound and carried them (easiest). However, because cotton served as the basis of the southern agricultural system, distinct patterns of female work usually transcended local and regional differences in labor-force management. Stated simply, most women spent a good deal of their lives plowing, hoeing, and picking cotton. In the fields, the notion of a distinctive "women's work" vanished as slaveholders realized that "women can do plowing very well and full well with the hoes and equal to men at picking."[14]

To harness a double team of mules or oxen and steer a heavy wooden plow was no mean feat for any person, and yet a "substantial minority" of slave women mastered these rigorous activities. White women and men from the North and South marvelled at the skill and strength of female plow hands. Emily Burke of eastern Georgia saw women and men "promiscuously run their ploughs side by side, and day after day. . . and as far as I was able to learn, the part the women sustained in this masculine employment, was quite as efficient as that of the more athletic sex." In his travels through Mississippi, Olmsted watched as women "twitched their plows around on the headland, jerking their reins, and yelling to their mules, with apparent ease, energy, and rapidity." He saw no indication that "their sex unfitted them for the occupation."[15]

743

On another estate in the Mississippi Valley, Olmsted observed forty of the "largest and strongest" women he had ever seen; they "carried themselves loftily, each having a hoe over the shoulder, and walking with a free, powerful swing, like *chasseurs* on the march." In preparing fields for planting, and in keeping grass from strangling the crop, women as well as men blistered their hands with the clumsy hoe characteristic of southern agriculture. "Hammered out of pig iron, broad like a shovel," these "slave-time hoes" withstood most forms of abuse (destruction of farm implements constituted an integral part of resistance to forced labor). Recalled one former slave of the tool that also served as pick, spade, and gravedigger: "Dey make 'em heavy so dey fall hard, but de bigges' trouble was liftin' dem up." Hoeing was backbreaking labor, but the versatility of the tool and its importance to cotton cultivation meant that the majority of female hands used it a good part of the year.[16]

The cotton-picking season usually began in late July or early August and continued without interruption until the end of

December. Thus for up to five months annually, every available man, woman, and child was engaged in a type of work that was strenuous and "tedious from its sameness." Each picker carried a bag fastened by a strap around her neck and deposited the cotton in it as she made her way down the row, at the end of which she emptied the bag's contents into a basket. Picking cotton required endurance and agility as much as physical strength, and women frequently won regional and interfarm competitions conducted during the year. Pregnant and nursing women usually ranked as half-hands and were required to pick an amount less than the "average" one hundred and fifty or so pounds per day.[17]

Slaveholders often reserved the tasks that demanded sheer muscle power for men exclusively. These included clearing the land of trees, rolling logs, and chopping and hauling wood. However, plantation exigencies sometimes mandated women's labor in this area, too; in general, the smaller the farm, the more arduous and varied was women's fieldwork. Lizzie Atkins, who lived on a twenty-five-acre Texas plantation with only three other slaves, remembered working "until slam dark every day"; she helped to clear land, cut wood, and tend the livestock in addition to her other duties of hoeing corn, spinning thread, sewing clothes, cooking, washing dishes, and grinding corn. One Texas farmer, who had his female slaves haul logs and plow with oxen, even made them wear breeches, thus minimizing outward differences between the sexes. Still, FWP interviews with former slaves indicate that blacks considered certain jobs uncharacteristic of bondwomen. Recalled Louise Terrell of her days on a farm near Jackson, Mississippi: "The women had to split rails all day long, just like the men." Nancy Boudry of Georgia said she used to "split wood jus' like a man." Elderly women reminisced about their mothers and grandmothers with a mixture of pride and wonder. Mary Frances Webb declared of her slave grandmother, "in the winter she sawed and cut cord wood just like a man. She said it didn't hurt her as she was strong as an ox." Janie Scott's description of her mother implied the extent of the older woman's emotional as well as physical strength: she was "strong and could roll and cut logs like a man, and was much of a woman."[18]

Very few women served as skilled artisans or mechanics; on large estates, men invariably filled the positions of carpenter, cooper, wheelwright, tanner, blacksmith, and shoemaker. At first it seems ironic that masters would utilize women fully as field

744

laborers, but reserve most of the skilled occupations that required manual dexterity for men. Here the high cost of specialized and extensive training proved crucial in determining the division of labor; although women were capable of learning these skills, their work lives were frequently interrupted by childbearing and nursing; a female blacksmith might not be able to provide the regular service required on a plantation. Too, masters frequently "hired out" mechanics and artisans to work for other employers during the winter, and women's domestic responsibilities were deemed too important to permit protracted absences from the quarters. However, many young girls learned to spin thread and weave cloth because these tasks could occupy them during confinement.[19]

745

The drive for cotton profits induced slaveowners to squeeze every bit of strength from black women as a group. According to the estimates of Roger L. Ransom and Richard Sutch, in the 1850s at least 90 percent of all female slaves over sixteen years of age labored more than 261 days per year, eleven to thirteen hours each day. Few overseers or masters had any patience with women whose movements in the field were persistently "clumsy, awkward, gross, [and] elephantine" for whatever reasons — malnutrition, exhaustion, recalcitrance. As Hannah Davidson said: "If you had something to do, you did it or got whipped." The enforced pace of work more nearly resembled that of a factory than a farm; Kemble referred to female field hands as "human hoeing machines." The bitter memories of former slaves merely suggest the extent to which the physical strength of women was exploited. Eliza Scantling of South Carolina, only sixteen years old at the end of the Civil War, plowed with a mule during the coldest months of the year: "Sometimes me hands get so cold I jes' cry." Matilda Perry of Virginia "Use to wuk fum sun to sun in dat ole terbaccy field. Wuk till my back felt lak it ready to pop in two."[20]

At times a woman would rebel in a manner commensurate with the work demands imposed upon her. "She'd git stubborn like a mule and quit." Or she took her hoe and knocked the overseer "plum down" and "chopped him right across his head." When masters and drivers "got rough on her, she got rough on them, and ran away in the woods." She cursed the man who insisted he "owned" her so that he beat her "till she fell" and left her broken body to serve as a warning to the others: "Dat's what you git effen you sass me." Indeed, in the severity of punishment meted

out to slaves, little distinction was made between the sexes: "Beat
women! Why sure he [master] beat women. Beat women jes' lak
men." A systematic survey of the FWP slave narrative collection
reveals that women were more likely than men to engage in "verbal confrontations and striking the master but not running away,"
probably because of their family and childcare responsibilities.[21]

746

Family members who perceived their mothers or sisters as particularly weak and vulnerable in the fields conspired to lessen
their work load. Frank Bell and his four brothers, slaves on a
Virginia wheat farm, followed his parents down the long rows of
grain during the harvest season. "In dat way one could help de
other when dey got behind. All of us would pitch in and help
Momma who warn't very strong." The overseer discouraged
families from working together because he believed "dey ain't
gonna work as fast as when dey all mixed up," but the black
driver, Bell's uncle, "always looked out for his kinfolk, especially
my mother." James Taliaferro told of his father, who counted the
corn rows marked out for Aunt Rebecca ("a short-talking woman
that ole Marsa didn't like") and told her that her assignment was
almost double that given to the other women. Rebecca indignant-
ly confronted the master, who relented by reducing her task, but
not before he threatened to sell James's father for his meddling.
On another plantation, the hands surreptitiously added handfuls
of cotton to the basket of a young woman who "was small and
just couldn't get her proper amount."[22]

No slave women exercised authority over slave men as part of
their work routine, but it is uncertain whether this practice
reflected the sensibilities of the slaveowners or of the slaves
themselves. Women were assigned to teach children simple tasks
in the house and field and to supervise other women in various
facets of household industry. A master might "let [a woman] off
fo' de buryings 'cause she know how to manage de other niggahs
and keep dem quiet at de funerls," but he would not install her as
a driver over people in the field. Many strong-willed women
demonstrated that they commanded respect among males as well
as females, but more often than not masters perceived this as a
negative quality to be suppressed. One Louisiana slaveholder
complained bitterly about a particularly "rascally set of old
negroes" — "the better you treat them the worst they are." He
had no difficulty pinpointing the cause of the trouble, for "Big
Lucy, the leader, corrupts every young negro in her power." On
other plantations, women were held responsible for instigating all

sorts of undesirable behavior among their husbands and brothers and sisters. On Charles Colcock Jones's Georgia plantation, the slave Cash gave up going to prayer meeting and started swearing as soon as he married Phoebe, well-known for her truculence. Apparently few masters attempted to co-opt high-spirited women by offering them positions of formal power over black men.[23]

In terms of labor-force management, southern slaveowners walked a fine line between making use of the physical strength of women as productive workers and protecting their investment in women as childbearers. These two objectives — one focused on immediate profit returns and the other on long-term economic considerations — at times clashed, because women who spent long hours picking cotton, toiling in the fields with heavy iron hoes, and walking several miles a day sustained damage to their reproductive systems immediately before and after giving birth. For financial reasons, slaveholders might have "regarded pregnancy as almost holy," in the words of one medical historian. But they frequently suspected their bondwomen (like "the most insufferable liar" Nora) of shamming illness — "play [ing] the lady at your expense," as one Virginia planter put it. These fears help to account for the reckless brutality with which owners forced women to work in the fields during and after pregnancy.[24]

747

Work in the soil thus represented the chief lot of all slaves, female and male. In the Big House, a division of labor based on both gender and age became more apparent, reflecting slaveowners' assumptions about the nature of domestic service. Although women predominated as household workers, few devoted their energies full time to this kind of labor; the size of the plantation determined the degree to which the tasks of cleaning, laundering, caring for the master's children, cooking, and ironing were specialized. According to Eugene Genovese, as few as 5 percent of all antebellum adult slaves served in the elite corps of house servants trained for specific duties. Of course, during the harvest season all slaves, including those in the house, went to the fields to make obeisance to King Cotton. Thus the lines between domestic service and fieldwork blurred during the day and during the lives of slave women. Many continued to live in the slave quarters, but rose early in the morning to perform various chores for the mistress — "up wid de fust light to draw water and help as a house girl" — before heading for the field. James Claiborne's mother "wuked in de fiel' some, an' aroun' de house sometimes .

. . ." Young girls tended babies and waited on tables until they were sent outside — "mos' soon's" they could work — and returned to the house years later, too frail to hoe weeds, but still able to cook and sew. The circle of women's domestic work went unbroken from day to day and from generation to generation.[25]

Just as southern white men scorned manual labor as the proper sphere of slaves, so their wives strove (often unsuccessfully) to lead a life of leisure within their own homes. Those duties necessary to maintain the health, comfort, and daily welfare of white slaveholders were considered less women's work than black women's and black children's work. Slave mistresses supervised the whole operation, but the sheer magnitude of labor involved in keeping all slaves and whites fed and clothed (with different standards set according to race, of course) meant that black women had to supply the elbow grease. For most slaves, housework involved hard, steady, often strenuous labor as they juggled the demands made by the mistress and other members of the master's family. Mingo White of Alabama never forgot that his slave mother had shouldered a work load "too heavy for any one person." She served as personal maid to the master's daughter, cooked for all the hands on the plantation, carded cotton, spun a daily quota of thread, wove and dyed cloth. Every Wednesday she carried the white family's laundry three-quarters of a mile to a creek, where she beat each garment with a wooden paddle. Ironing consumed the rest of her day. Like the lowliest field hand, she felt the lash if any tasks went undone.[26]

Although mistresses found that their husbands commandeered most bondwomen for fieldwork during the better part of the day, they discovered in black children an acceptable alternative source of labor. Girls were favored for domestic service, but a child's sex played only a secondary role in determining household assignments. On smaller holdings especially, the demands of housework, like cotton cultivation, admitted of no finely honed division of labor. Indeed, until puberty, girls and boys shared a great deal in terms of dress and work. All children wore a "split-tail shirt," a knee-length smock slit up the sides: "Boys and gals all dress jes' alike . . . . They call it a shirt iffen a boy wear it and call it a dress iffen the gal wear it." At the age of six or so, many received assignments around the barnyard or in the Big House from one or more members of the master's family. Mr. and Mrs. Alex Smith, who grew up together, remembered performing different tasks. As a girl she helped to spin thread and pick seeds from cotton and

748

cockle burrs from wool. He chopped wood, carried water, hoed weeds, tended the cows, and picked bugs from tobacco plants. However, slave narratives contain descriptions of both girls and boys elsewhere doing each of these things.[27]

Between the ages of six and twelve, black girls and boys followed the mistress's directions in filling woodboxes with kindling, lighting fires in chilly bedrooms in the morning and evening, making beds, washing and ironing clothes, parching coffee, polishing shoes, and stoking fires while the white family slept at night. They fetched water and milk from the springhouse and meat from the smokehouse. Three times a day they set the table, helped to prepare and serve meals, "minded flies" with peacock feather brushes, passed the salt and pepper on command and washed the dishes. They swept, polished, and dusted, served drinks and fanned overheated visitors. Mistresses entrusted to the care of those who were little more than babies themselves the bathing, diapering, dressing, grooming, and entertaining of white infants. In the barnyard black children gathered eggs, plucked chickens, drove cows to and from the stable and "tended the gaps" (opened and closed gates). (In the fields they acted as human scarecrows, toted water to the hands, and hauled shocks of corn together.) It was no wonder that Mary Ella Grandberry, a slave child grown old, "disremember[ed] ever playin' lack chilluns do today."[28]

749

In only a few tasks did a sexual division of labor exist among children. Masters always chose boys to accompany them on hunting trips and to serve as their personal valets. Little girls learned how to sew, to milk cows and churn butter, and to attend to the personal needs of their mistresses. As tiny ladies-in-waiting, they did the bidding of fastidious white women and of girls not much older than they. Cicely Cawthon, age six when the Civil War began, called herself the mistress's "little keeper"; "I stayed around, and waited on her, handed her water, fanned her, kept the flies off her, pulled up her pillow, and done anything she'd tell me to do." Martha Showvely recounted a nightly ritual with her Virginia mistress. After she finished her regular work around the house, the young girl would go to the woman's bedroom, bow to her, wait for acknowledgment, and then scurry around as ordered, lowering the shades, filling the water pitcher, arranging towels on the washstand, or "anything else" that struck the woman's fancy. Mary Woodward, only eleven in 1865, was taught to comb her mistress's hair, lace her corset, and arrange her hoop skirts. At the end of the toilet Mary was supposed to say, "You is served, mistress!" Recalled the former slave, "Her lak them little words at de last."[29]

Sexual exploitation of female servants of all ages (described in graphic detail by Harriet Jacobs in Lydia Maria Child's *Incidents in the Life of a Slave Girl*) predictably antagonized white women. Jealousy over their husbands' real or suspected infidelities resulted in a propensity for spontaneous violence among many. Husbands who flaunted their adventures in the slave quarters increased the chance that their wives would attack a specific woman or her offspring. Sarah Wilson remembered being "picked on" by the mistress, who chafed under her husband's taunts; he would say, "'Let her alone, she got big, big blood in her,' and then laugh."[30]

A divorce petition filed with the Virginia legislature in 1848 included a witness's testimony that the master in question one morning told his slave favorite to sit down at the breakfast table "to which Mrs. N [his wife] objected, saying. . . that she (Mrs. N.) would have her severely punished." Her husband replied "that in that event he would visit her (Mrs. N.) with a like punishment. Mrs. N. then burst into tears and asked if it was not too much for her to stand." This husband went to extreme lengths to remind his spouse of slave-mistress Mary Chesnut's observation that "there is no slave, after all, like a wife." In the black woman the mistress saw not only the source of her own degradation, she saw herself — a woman without rights, subject to the impulses of an arrogant husband-master.[31]

To punish black women for minor offenses, mistresses were likely to attack with any weapon available — a fork, butcher knife, knitting needle, pan of boiling water. Some of the most barbaric forms of punishment resulting in the mutilation and permanent scarring of female servants were devised by white mistresses in the heat of passion. As a group they received well-deserved notoriety for the "veritable terror" they unleashed upon black women in the Big House.[32]

Interviews with former slaves suggest that the advantages of domestic service (over fieldwork) for women have been exaggerated in accounts written by whites. Carrying wood and water, preparing three full meals a day over a smoky fireplace or pressing damp clothes with a hot iron rivaled cotton picking as backbreaking labor. Always "on call," women servants often had to snatch a bite to eat whenever they could, remain standing in the presence of whites, and sleep on the floor at the foot of their mistress's bed (increasing the chances that they would sooner or later be bribed, seduced, or forced into sexual relations with the master). To peel potatoes with a sharp knife, build a fire, or carry a heavy load of laundry down a steep flight of stairs required skills and dexterity not always possessed by little girls and boys, and injuries were common. Chastisement for minor infractions came with swift severity; cooks who burned the bread and children who stole cookies or fell asleep while singing to the baby suffered every conceivable form of physical abuse, from jabs with pins to beatings that left them disfigured for life. The master's house offered no shelter from the most brutal manifestations of slavery.[33]

751

For any one or all of these reasons, black women might prefer fieldwork to housework. During his visit to a rice plantation in 1853, Olmsted noted that hands "accustomed to the comparatively unconstrained life of the negro-settlement detest the close control and careful movements required of the house servants." Marriage could be both a means and an incentive to escape a willful mistress. Jessie Sparrow's mother wed at age thirteen in order "to go outer de big house. Dat how come she to marry so soon. . . ." Claude Wilson recalled many years later that "his mother was very rebellious toward her duties and constantly harassed the 'Missus' about letting her work in the fields with her husband until finally she was permitted to make the change from the house to the fields to be near her man." Other women, denied an alternative, explored the range of their own emotional resources in attempting to resist petty tyranny; their "sassiness" rubbed raw the nerves of mistresses already harried and highstrung. A few servants simply withdrew into a shell of "melancholy and timidity."[34]

The dual status of a bondwoman — a slave and a female — afforded her master a certain degree of flexibility in formulating her work assignments. When he needed a field hand, her status as an able-bodied slave took precedence over gender considerations, and she was forced to toil alongside her menfolk. At the same time, the master's belief that most forms of domestic service required the attentions of a female reinforced among slave women the traditional role of woman as household worker.

The authority of the master in enforcing a sexual division of labor was absolute, but at times individual women could influence his decisions to some extent. In certain cases, a woman's preferences for either fieldwork or domestic service worked to her advantage. For example, the rebelliousness of Claude Wilson's mother prompted her removal from the Big House to the field, a change she desired. Similarly, masters might promise a woman an opportunity to do a kind of work she preferred as a reward for her cooperation and diligence. On the other hand, a slave's misbehavior might cause her to lose a position she had come to value; more than one prized cook or maid was exiled to the fields for "sassing" the mistress or stealing. A system of rewards and punishments thus depended on the preferences of individual slaves, and a servant determined to make life miserable for the family in the Big House might get her way in any case.[35]

752

In the field and Big House, black women worked under the close supervision of whites (the master, overseer, or mistress) at a forced pace. The slaves derived few, if any, tangible benefits from their labor to increase staple-crop profits and to render the white family comfortable (at least in physical terms). However, their efforts to provide for their own health and welfare often took place apart from whites, with a rhythm more in tune with community and family life. For slave women, these responsibilities, although physically arduous, offered a degree of personal fulfillment. As Martha Colquitt remarked of her slave grandmother and mother who stayed up late to knit and sew clothes "for us chillun": "Dey done it 'cause dey wanted to. Dey wuz workin' for deyselves den." Slave women deprived of the ability to cook for their own kinfolk or discipline their own children felt a keen sense of loss; family responsibilities revealed the limited extent to which black women (and men) could control their own lives. Furthermore, a strict sexual division of labor in the quarters openly challenged the master's opportunistic approach to slave women's work.[36]

A number of activities were carried out either communally or centrally for the whole plantation by older women. On smaller farms, for example, a cook and her assistants might prepare one or all of the meals for the other slaves each day except Sunday. Similarly, an elderly woman, with the help of children too young to work in the fields, often was assigned charge of a nursery in the quarters, where mothers left their babies during the day. To keep any number of little ones happy and out of trouble for up to twelve to fourteen hours at a time taxed the patience of the most kindly souls. Slave children grew up with a mixture of affection and fear for the "grandmothers" who had dished out the licks along with the cornbread and clabber. Other grannies usurped the position of the white physician (he rarely appeared in any case); they "brewed medicines for every ailment," gave cloves and whiskey to ease the pain of childbirth, and prescribed potions for the lovesick. Even a child forced to partake of "Stinkin' Jacob tea" or a concoction of "turpentine an' castor oil an' Jerusalem oak" (for worms) would assert years later that "Gran'mammy was a great doctor," surely a testimony to her respected position within the slave community, if not to the delectability of her remedies.[37]

On many plantations, it was the custom to release adult women from fieldwork early on Saturday so that they could do their week's washing. Whether laundering was done in old wooden tubs, iron pots, or a nearby creek with batten sticks, wooden paddles, or washboards, it was a time-consuming and difficult chore. Yet this ancient form of women's work provided opportunities for socializing "whilst de 'omans leaned over de tubs washin' and a-singin' dem old songs." Mary Frances Webb remembered wash day — "a regular picnic" — with some fondness; it was a time for women "to spend the day together," out of the sight and earshot of whites.[38]

753

Much of the work black women did for the slave community resembled the colonial system of household industry. Well into the nineteenth century throughout the South, slave women continued to spin thread, weave and dye cloth, sew clothes, make soap and candles, prepare and preserve foods, churn butter, and grow food for the family table. Slave women mastered all these tasks with the aid of primitive equipment and skills passed on from grandmothers. Many years later, blacks of both sexes exclaimed over their slave mothers' ability to prepare clothing dye from various combinations of tree bark and leaves, soil and berries; make soap out of ashes and animal skins; and fashion bottle lamps from string and tallow. Because of their lack of time and materials, black women only rarely found in these activities an outlet for creative expression, but they did take pride in their resourcefulness and produced articles of value to the community as a whole.[39]

Black women's work in home textile production illustrates the ironies of community labor under slavery, for the threads of cotton and wool bound them together in both bondage and sisterhood. Masters (or mistresses) imposed rigid spinning and weaving quotas on women who worked in the fields all day. For example, many were forced to spin one "cut" (about three hundred yards) of thread nightly, or four to five cuts during rainy days or in the winter. Women of all ages worked together and children of both sexes helped to tease and card wool, pick up the loom shuttles, and knit. In the flickering candlelight, the whirr of the spinning wheel and the clackety-clack of the loom played a seductive lullabye, drawing those who were already "mighty tired" away from their assigned tasks.[40]

As the "head spinner" on a Virginia plantation, Bob Ellis's mother was often sent home from fieldwork early to prepare materials for the night's work; "She had to portion out de cotton dey was gonna spin an' see dat each got a fair share." Later that evening, after supper, as she moved around the dusty loom room to check on the progress of the other women, she would sing:

> Keep yo' eye on de sun,
> See how she run
> Don't let her catch you with you work undone,
> I'm a trouble, I'm a trouble,
> Trouble don' las' always.

With her song of urgency and promise she coaxed her sisters to finish their work so they could return home by sundown: "Dat made de women all speed up so dey could finish fo' dark catch 'em, 'cause it mighty hard handlin' dat cotton thread by fire-light."[41]

In the quarters, group work melded into family responsibilities, for the communal spirit was but a manifestation of primary kin relationships. Here it is possible only to outline the social dynamics of the slave household. The significance of the family in relation to the sexual division of labor under slavery cannot be overestimated; out of the mother-father, wife-husband nexus sprang the slaves' beliefs about what women and men should be and do. Ultimately, the practical application of those beliefs (in the words of Genovese) "provided a weapon for joint resistance to dehumanization."[42]

The two-parent, nuclear family was the typical form of slave cohabitation regardless of the location, size, or economy of a plantation; the nature of its ownership; or the age of its slave community. Because of the omnipresent threat of forced separation by sale, gift, or bequest, this family was not "stable." Yet, in the absence of such separations, unions between husbands and wives and parents and children often endured for many years. Marital customs, particularly exogamy, and the practice of naming children after the mother's or father's relatives (the most common pattern was to name a boy after a male relative) revealed the strong sense of kinship among slaves. Households tended to be large; Herbert G. Gutman found families with eight living children to be quite common. Out of economic considerations, a master would encourage his work force to reproduce itself, but the slaves welcomed each new birth primarily as "a social and familial fact." A web of human emotions spun by close family ties — affection, dignity, love — brought slaves together in a world apart from whites.[43]

In their own cabins, the blacks maintained a traditional division of labor between the sexes. Like women in almost all cultures, slave women had both a biological and a social "destiny." As part of their childbearing role, they assumed primary responsibility for childcare (when a husband and wife lived on separate plantations, the children remained with their mother and belonged to her master). Women also performed operations related to daily household maintenance — cooking, cleaning, tending fires, sewing and patching clothes.[44]

Fathers shared the obligations of family life with their wives. In denying slaves the right to own property, make a living for themselves, participate in public life, or protect their children, the institution of bondage deprived black men of access to the patriarchy in the larger economic and political sense. But at home women and men worked together to support the father's role as provider and protector. In the evenings and on Sundays, men collected firewood; made shoes; wove baskets; constructed beds, tables, and chairs; and carved butter paddles, ax handles, and animal traps. Other family members appreciated a father's skills; recalled Molly Ammonds, "My pappy make all de funiture dat went in our house an' it were might' good funiture too," and Pauline Johnson echoed, "De furn'chure was ho-mek, but my daddy mek it good an' stout." Husbands provided necessary supplements to the family diet by hunting and trapping quails, possums, turkeys, rabbits, squirrels, and raccoons, and by fishing. They often assumed responsibility for cultivating the tiny household garden plots allotted to families by the master. Some craftsmen, like Bill Austin's father, received goods or small sums of money in return for their work on nearby estates; Jack Austin, "regarded as a fairly good carpenter, mason, and bricklayer," was paid in " hams, bits of cornmeal, cloth for dresses for his wife and children, and other small gifts; these he either used for his small family or bartered with other slaves."[45]

These familial duties also applied to men who lived apart from their wives and children even though they were usually allowed to visit only on Saturday night and Sunday. Lucinda Miller's family "never had any sugar, and only got coffee when her father would bring it to her mother" during his visits. The father of Hannah Chapman was sold to a nearby planter when she was very small. Because "he missed us and us longed for him," she said many years later, he tried to visit his family under the cover of darkness whenever possible. She noted, "Us would gather 'round him an' crawl up in his lap, tickled slap to death, but he give us dese pleasures at painful risk." If the master should happen to discover him, "Us could track him de nex' day by de blood stains," she remembered.[46]

Hannah McFarland of South Carolina well remembered the time when the local slave patrol attempted to whip her mother, "but my papa sho' stopped dat," she said proudly. Whether or not he was made to suffer for his courage is unknown; however, the primary literature of slavery is replete with accounts of slave husbands who intervened, at the risk of their own lives, to save wives and children from violence at the hands of white men. More often, however, fathers had to show their compassion in less dramatic (though no less revealing) ways. On a Florida plantation, the Minus children often rose in the morning to find still warm in the fireplace the potatoes "which their father had thoughtfully roasted and which [they] readily consumed." Margrett Nickerson recalled how her father would tenderly bind up the wounds inflicted on her by a maniacal overseer; in later years, her crippled legs preserved the memory of a father's sorrow intermingled with her own suffering.[47]

The more freedom the slaves had in determining their own activities the more clearly emerged a distinct division of labor between the sexes. During community festivities like log rollings, rail splittings, wood choppings, and corn shuckings, men performed the prescribed labor while women cooked the meals. At times, male participants willingly "worked all night," for, in the words of one former slave, "we had the 'Heavenly Banners' (women and whiskey) by us." A limited amount of primary evidence indicates that men actively scorned women's work, especially cooking, housecleaning, sewing, washing clothes, and intimate forms of childcare (like bathing children and picking lice out of their hair). Some slaveholders devised forms of public humiliation that capitalized on men's attempts to avoid these tasks. One Louisiana cotton planter punished slave men by forcing them to wash clothes (he also made chronic offenders wear women's dresses). In *This Species of Property*, Leslie Howard Owens remarks of men so treated, "So great was their shame before their fellows that many ran off and suffered the lash on their backs rather than submit to the discipline. Men clearly viewed certain chores as women's tasks, and female slaves largely respected the distinction."[48]

The values and customs of the slave community played a predominant role in structuring work patterns among women and men within the quarters in general and the family in particular. Yet slaveholders affected the division of labor in the quarters in several ways; for example, they took women and girls out of the fields early on Saturdays to wash the clothes, and they enforced certain task assignments related to the production of household goods. An understanding of the social significance of the sexual division of labor requires at least brief mention of West African cultural preferences and the ways in which the American system of slavery disrupted or sustained traditional (African) patterns of women's work. Here it is important to keep in mind two points. First, cotton did not emerge as the South's primary staple crop until the late eighteenth century (the first slaves on the North American continent toiled in tobacco, rice, indigo, and corn fields); and second, regardless of the system of task assignments imposed upon antebellum blacks, the grueling pace of forced labor represented a cruel break from the past for people who had followed age-old customs related to subsistence agriculture.[49]

Though dimmed by time and necessity, the outlines of African work patterns endured among the slaves. As members of traditional agricultural societies, African women played a major role in producing the family's food as well as in providing basic household services. The sexual division of labor was more often determined by a woman's childcare and domestic reponsibilities than by any presumed physical weakness. She might engage in heavy, monotonous fieldwork (in some tribes) as long as she could make provisions for nursing her baby; that often meant keeping an infant with her in the field. She cultivated a kitchen garden that yielded a variety of vegetables consumed by the family or sold at market, and she usually milked the cows and churned butter.[50]

West Africans in general brought with them competencies and

757

knowledge that slaveowners readily exploited. Certain tribes were familiar with rice, cotton, and indigo cultivation. Many black women had had experience spinning thread, weaving cloth, and sewing clothes. Moreover, slaves often used techniques and tools handed down from their ancestors — in the method of planting, hoeing, and pounding rice, for example. Whites frequently commented on the ability of slave women to balance heavy and unwieldy loads on their heads, an African trait.[51]

758

The primary difficulty in generalizing about African women's part in agriculture stems from the fact that members of West African tribes captured for the North American slave trade came from different hoe-culture economies. Within the geographically limited Niger Delta region, for example, women and men of the Ibo tribe worked together in planting, weeding, and harvesting, but female members of another prominent group, the Yoruba, helped only with harvest. In general, throughout most of sub-Saharan Africa (and particularly on the west coast) women had primary responsibility for tilling (though not clearing) the soil and cultivating the crops; perhaps this tradition, combined with work patterns established by white masters in this country, reinforced the blacks' beliefs that cutting trees and rolling logs was "men's work." In any case it is clear that African women often did fieldwork. But because the sexual division of labor varied according to tribe, it is impossible to state with any precision the effect of the African heritage on the slaves' perceptions of women's agricultural work.[52]

The West African tradition of respect for one's elders found new meaning among American slaves; for most women, old age brought increased influence within the slave community even as their economic value to the master declined. Owners, fearful lest women escape from "earning their salt" once they became too infirm to go to the field, set them to work at other tasks — knitting, cooking, spinning, weaving, dairying, washing, ironing, caring for the children. (Elderly men worked as gardeners, wagoners, carters, and stocktenders.) But the imperatives of the southern economic system sometimes compelled slaveowners to extract from feeble women what field labor they could. In other cases they reduced the material provisions of the elderly — housing and allowances of food and clothing — in proportion to their decreased productivity.[53]

The overwhelming youth of the general slave population between 1830 and 1860 (more than one-half of all slaves were under twenty years of age) meant that most plantations had only a few old persons — the 10 percent over fifty years of age considered elderly. These slaves served as a repository of history and folklore for the others. Harriet Ware, a northern teacher assigned to the South Carolina Sea Islands, reported in 1862, "'Learning' with these people I find means a knowledge of medicine, and a person is valued accordingly." Many older women practiced "medicine" in the broadest sense in their combined role of midwife, root doctor, healer, and conjurer. They guarded ancient secrets about herbs and other forms of plant life. In their interpretation of dreams and strange occurrences, they brought the real world closer to the supernatural realm and offered spiritual guidance to the ill, the troubled, and the lovelorn.[54]

For slaves in the late antebellum period, these revered (and sometimes feared) women served as a tangible link with the African past. Interviewed by an FWP worker in 1937, a Mississippi-born former slave, James Brittian, recalled his own "grandma Aunt Mary" who had lived for 110 years. A "Molly Gasca [Madagascar?] negro," she was plagued by a jealous mistress because of her striking physical appearance; "Her hair it was fine as silk and hung down below her waist." Ned Chaney's African-born Granny Silla (she was the oldest person anyone knew, he thought) commanded respect among the other slaves by virtue of her advanced age and her remarkable healing powers: "Ever'body set a heap of sto' by her. I reckon, because she done 'cumullated so much knowledge an' because her head were so white." When Granny Silla died, her "little bags" of mysterious substances were buried with her because no one else knew how to use them. Yet Chaney's description of his own mother, a midwife and herb doctor, indicates that she too eventually assumed a position of at least informal authority within the community.[55]

As a little girl in Georgia, Mary Colbert adored her grandmother, a strong field hand, "smart as a whip." "I used to tell my mother that I wished I was named Hannah for her, and so Mother called me Mary Hannah," she recalled. Amanda Harris, interviewed in Virginia when she was ninety years old, looked back to the decade before the war when her grandmother was still alive: "Used to see her puffin' on dat ole pipe o' her'n, an' one day I ast her what fun she got outen it. 'Tain't no fun, chile,' she tole me. 'But it's a pow'ful lot o' easment. Smoke away trouble, darter. Blow ole trouble an' worry 'way in smoke.'" Amanda started smoking a pipe shortly before her grandmother died, and in 1937 she declared, "Now dat I'm ole as she was I know what she mean." In the quiet dignity of their own lives, these grandmothers preserved the past for future generations of Afro-American women.[56]

Within well-defined limits, the slaves created — or preserved — an explicit sexual division of labor based on their own preferences. Wives and husbands and mothers and fathers had reciprocal obligations toward one another. Together they worked to preserve the integrity of the family. Having laid to rest once and for all the myth of the slave matriarchy, some historians suggest that relations between the sexes approximated "a healthy sexual equality."[57] Without private property, slave men lacked the means to achieve economic superiority over their wives, one of the major sources of inequality in the ("free") sexual order. But if female and male slaves shared duties related to household maintenance and community survival, they were nonetheless reduced to a state of powerlessness that rendered virtually meaningless the concept of equality as it applies to marital relations.

Developments during the turbulent postwar years, when the chains of bondage were loosened but not destroyed, made clear the significance of black women's work in supporting the southern staple-crop economy. They also revealed the connection between patterns of women's work and black family life — a connection that had, at least to some degree, remained latent under slavery. Black women did their part in helping to provide for their families after the war. Female household heads had a particularly difficult time, for under the "free labor" system, a mother working alone rarely earned enough to support small children who were themselves too little to make any money. Relatives in a better financial situation often "adopted" these children, or took the whole family under their care.[58]

After the war, black women continued to serve as domestic servants, but large numbers stopped going to the fields altogether, or agreed to work only in harvest time. Indeed, from all over the South came reports that "the negro women are now almost wholly withdrawn from field labor." Ransom and Sutch, in their study of the economic consequences of emancipation, estimate that between one-third and one-half of all the women who worked in the fields under slavery provided proportionately less agricultural labor in the 1870s. This decline in overall female productivity was the result of two factors: many wives stayed home, and the ones who did continue to labor in the fields (like black men) put in shorter hours and fewer days each year than they had as slaves.

760

Crop output in many locales dropped accordingly, and white landowners lamented their loss, "for women were as efficient as men in working and picking cotton."[59]

In their speculation about the sources of this "evil of female loaferism," whites offered a number of theories, from the pernicious influence of northern schoolteachers to the inherent laziness of the black race. Actually, black women and men responded to freedom in a manner consistent with preferences that had been thwarted during slavery. Husbands sought to protect their wives from the sexual abuse and physical punishment that continued to prevail under the wage system of agricultural labor. Wives wanted to remain at home with their children, as befitted free and freed women; many continued to contribute to the family welfare by taking in washing or raising chickens.[60]

761

By 1867, freed people who wanted to assert control over their own productive energies had reached what some historians term a "compromise" with white landowners anxious to duplicate antebellum crop levels. This "compromise" came in the form of the sharecropping system, a family organization of labor that represented both a radical departure from collective or "gang" work characteristic of slavery and a rejection of the wage economy so integral to the (North's) fledgling industrial revolution. Freed families moved out of the old slave quarters into cabins scattered around a white man's plantation; they received "furnishings" (tools and seed) and agreed to pay the landlord a share of the crop — usually one-half of all the cotton they produced — in return for the use of the land and modest dwelling. Under this arrangement, black husbands assumed primary responsibility for crop management, and their wives devoted as much attention as possible to their roles as mothers and homemakers. During the particularly busy planting or harvesting seasons, a woman would join her husband and children at work in the field. In this way she could keep an eye on her offspring and still put to use her considerable strength and skills unmolested by white men.[61]

The Reconstruction South was not the best of all worlds in which to foster a new order between the races — or the sexes. Faced with persistent economic exploitation and political subservience within white-dominated society, black men sought to assert their authority as protectors of their communities and families. Outwardly, they placed a premium on closing ranks at home. This impulse was institutionalized in the freed people's churches ("Wives submit yourselves to your husbands" was the text of more than one postbellum sermon) and political organizations. One searches in vain for evidence of female participants in the many black conventions and meetings during this period, although this was perhaps in part attributable to the fact that women did not have the right to vote. Black women remained militantly outspoken in defense of their families and property rights, but they lacked a formal power base within their own communities. And in an atmosphere fraught with sexual violence, where freedwomen remained at the mercy of white men and where "the mere suggestion" that a black man was attracted to a white woman was "enough to hang him," a black husband's resentment might continue to manifest itself in his relations with those closest to him. A Sea Island slave folktale offered the lesson that "God had nebber made a woman for the head of a man." In the struggle against white racism this often meant that black women were denied the equality with their men to which their labor — not to mention justice — entitled them.[62]

762

The sexual division of labor under slavery actually assumed two forms — one system of work forced upon slaves by masters who valued women only as work-oxen and brood-sows, and the other initiated by the slaves themselves in the quarters. Only the profit motive accorded a measure of consistency to the slaveholder's decisions concerning female work assignments; he sought to exploit his "hands" efficiently, and either invoked or repudiated traditional notions of women's work to suit his own purposes. In this respect, his decision-making process represented in microcosm the shifting priorities of the larger society, wherein different groups of women were alternately defined primarily as producers or as reproducers according to the fluctuating labor demands of the capitalist economy.[63]

Within their own communities, the slaves attempted to make work choices based on their African heritage as it applied to the American experience. Their well-defined sexual division of labor contrasted with the calculated self-interest of slaveowners. Slave women were allowed to fulfill their duties as wives and mothers only insofar as these responsibilities did not conflict with their masters' demands for field or domestic labor. As sharecroppers, freed people sought to institutionalize their resistance to the whites' conviction that black women should be servants or cotton pickers first, and family members only incidentally. In working together as a unit, black parents and children made an explicit political statement to the effect that their own priorities were inimical to those of white landowners.

To a considerable extent, the freed family's own patriarchal tendencies — fathers took care of "public" negotiations with the white landlord while mothers assumed primary responsibility for childcare — resulted from the black man's desire to protect his household in the midst of a violently racist society. The 763 postbellum black nuclear family never duplicated exactly the functions of the white middle-class model, which (beginning in the late eighteenth century) drew an increasingly rigid distinction between masculine and feminine spheres of activity characteristic of commercial-industrial capitalism. Clearly, the peculiar southern way of life suggests that an analysis of black women's oppression should focus not so much on the family as on the dynamics of racial prejudice. However, black women and men in the long run paid a high price for their allegiance to a patriarchal family structure, and it is important not to romanticize this arrangement as it affected the status and opportunities of women, even within the confines of black community life. Women continued to wield informal influence in their roles as herb doctors and "grannies," but men held all positions of formal political and religious authority. Ultimately, black people's "preferences" in the postwar period took shape within two overlapping caste systems — one based on race, the other on gender. Former slaves were "free" only in the sense that they created their own forms of masculine authority as a counter to poverty and racism.

The story of slave women's work encapsulates an important part of American history. For here in naked form, stripped free of the pieties often used in describing white women and free workers at the time, were the forces that shaped patriarchal capitalism — exploitation of the most vulnerable members of society, and a contempt for women that knew no ethical or physical bounds. And yet, slave women demonstrated "true womanhood" in its truest sense. Like Janie Scott's mother who was "much of a woman," they revealed a physical and emotional strength that transcended gender and preached a great sermon about the human spirit.

NOTES

The author would like to acknowledge the helpful suggestions and comments provided by Rosalind Petchesky and other members of the *Feminist Studies* editorial board and by Michael P. Johnson. Research for this project (part of a full-length study of black women, work, and the family in America, 1830-1980) was funded by a grant from the National Endowment for the Humanities.

[1]Zora N. Hurston, *Their Eyes Were Watching God* (London: J.M. Dent and Sons, 1938), pp. 31-32. Novelist, folklorist, and anthropologist, Hurston (born 1901, died 1960) had collected a massive amount of primary data on the culture and folklore of Afro-Americans before she began work on *Their Eyes Were Watching God*. In 1938 she served as supervisor of the Negro Unit of the Florida Federal Writers Project which compiled interviews with former slaves. Her various writings are finally receiving long-overdue literary attention and critical acclaim. See Robert E. Hemenway, *Zora Neale Hurston: A Literary Biography* (Urbana: University of Illinois Press, 1977); and a recent anthology: Zora N. Hurston, *I Love Myself When I Am Laughing. . . And Then Again When I Am Looking Mean And Impressive*, ed. Alice Walker (Old Westbury, N.Y.: Feminist Press, 1980).

[2]Angela Davis, "Reflections on the Black Woman's Role in the Community of Slaves," *The Black Scholar* 3 (December 1971): 3-15. For other works that focus on slave women, see Mary Ellen Obitko, "'Custodians of a House of Resistance': Black Women Respond to Slavery," in *Women and Men: The Consequences of Power*, ed. Dana V. Hiller and Robin Ann Sheets (Cincinnati: Office of Women's Studies, University of Cincinnati, 1977), pp. 256-59; Deborah G. White, "Ain't I A Woman? Female Slaves in the Antebellum South" (Ph.D. dissertation, University of Illinois-Chicago Circle, 1979). White's work examines several important themes related to slave women's work and family life, but her study lacks a coherent theoretical framework. She asserts that slave women gained considerable "self-confidence" because they achieved "equality" with men of their race, and even suggests that emancipation resulted in a "loss" of women's "equality"; freedom amounted to "a decline in the status of black women" (p. 51). When used in this context, the concepts of equality and status lose all meaning and relevance to the complex issues involved; White's argument obscures the subtleties of black female-male relations under bondage and after emancipation.

The volume edited by Gerda Lerner, *Black Women in White America: A Documentary History* (New York: Randam House, 1972), includes material on the history of slave women.

[3]Herbert G. Gutman, *The Black Family in Slavery and Freedom, 1750-1925* (New York: Pantheon Books, 1976); Eugene D. Genovese, *Roll, Jordan, Roll: The World the Slaves Made* (New York: Randam House, 1974); Leslie Howard Owens, *This Species of Property: Slave Life and Culture in the Old South* (New York: Oxford University Press, 1976); John D. Blassingame, *The Slave Community: Plantation Life in the Old South* (New York: Oxford University Press, 1972); Paul A. David et al., *Reckoning With Slavery: A Critical Study in the Quantitative History of American Negro Slavery* (New York: Oxford University Press, 1976); Paul D. Escott, *Slavery Remembered: A Record of Twentieth-Century Slave Narratives* (Chapel Hill: University of North Carolina Press, 1978).

In some specialized studies, women are largely excluded from the general analysis and discussed only in brief sections under the heading "Women and Children." See, for example, Robert S. Starobin, *Industrial Slavery in the Old South* (New York: Oxford University Press, 1970); and Todd L. Savitt, *Medicine and Slavery: The Diseases and*

Health Care of Blacks in Antebellum Virginia (Urbana: University of Illinois Press, 1978).

⁴For examples of studies of specific groups of women and the relationship between their work and family life, see Nancy F. Cott, *The Bonds of Womanhood: 'Woman's Sphere' in New England, 1780-1835* (New Haven: Yale University Press, 1977); Thomas Dublin, *Women at Work: The Transformation of Work and Community in Lowell, Massachusetts, 1826-1860* (New York: Columbia University Press, 1979); Milton Cantor and Bruce Laurie, eds., *Class, Sex, and the Woman Worker* (Westport, Conn.: Greenwood Press, 1977); Virginia Yans McLaughlin, "Patterns of Work and Family Organization: Buffalo's Italians," *Journal of Interdisciplinary History* 2 (Autumn 1971): 297-314; Leslie Woodcock Tentler, *Wage-Earning Women: Industrial Work and Family Life in the United States, 1900-1930* (New York: Oxford University Press, 1979).

General overviews and theoretical formulations that fail to take into account the experiences of slave women include Patricia Branca, "A New Perspective on Women's Work: A Comparative Typology," *Journal of Social History* 9 (Winter 1975): 129-53; W. Elliot Brownlee, "Household Values, Women's Work, and Economic Growth, 1800-1930," *Journal of Economic History* 39 (March 1979): 199-209; Maurine Weiner Greenwald, "Historians and the Working-Class Woman in America," *International Labor and Working-Class History*, no. 14/15 (Spring 1979): 23-32; Alice Kessler-Harris, "Women, Work, and the Social Order," in *Liberating Women's History: Theoretical and Critical Essays*, ed. Berenice A. Carroll (Urbana: University of Illinois Press, 1976), pp. 330-43.

⁵On women's "productive-reproductive" functions and the relationship between patriarchy and capitalism, see Joan Kelly, "The Doubled Vision of Feminist Theory: A Postscript to the 'Women and Power' Conference," *Feminist Studies* 5 (Spring 1979): 216-27; Heidi Hartmann, "Capitalism, Patriarchy, and Job Segregation by Sex," and Zillah Eisenstein, "Developing a Theory of Capitalist Patriarchy and Socialist Feminism," and "Some Notes on the Relations of Capitalist Patriarchy," in *Capitalist Patriarchy and the Case for Socialist Feminism*, ed. Zillah R. Eisenstein (New York: Monthly Review Press, 1979); Annette Kuhn and AnnMarie Wolpe, "Feminism and Materialism" and Veronica Beechey, "Women and Production: A Critical Analysis of Some Sociological Theories of Women's Work," both in *Feminism and Materialism: Women and Modes of Production*, ed. Annette Kuhn and AnnMarie Wolpe (London: Routledge and Kegan Paul, 1978).

Several scholars argue that the last three decades of the antebellum period constituted a distinct phase in the history of slavery. Improved textile machinery and a rise in world demand for cotton led to a tremendous growth in the American slave economy, especially in the Lower South. A marked increase in slave mortality rates and family breakups (a consequence of forced migration from Upper to Lower South), and a slight decline in female fertility rates indicate the heightened demands made upon slave labor during the years 1830-60. See David, et al., *Reckoning With Slavery*, pp. 99, 356-57; Jack Erickson Eblen, "New Estimates of the Vital Rates of the United States Black Population During the Nineteenth Century," *Demography* 11 (May 1974): 307-13.

⁶For example, see Kelly, "Doubled Vision," pp. 217-18, and Eisenstein, "Relations of Capitalist Patriarchy," pp. 48-52, on the regressive implications of family life for women. But Davis notes that the slave woman's "survival-oriented activities were themselves a form of resistance" ("Reflections on the Black Woman's Role," p.7).

⁷Interviews with former slaves have been published in various forms, including George P. Rawick, ed., *The American Slave: A Composite Autobiography*, 41 vols., Series 1 and 2, supp. Series 1 and 2 (Westport Conn.: Greenwood Press, 1972, 1978, 1979); Social Science Institute, Fisk University, *Unwritten History of Slavery:*

Autobiographical Accounts of Negro Ex-Slaves (Washington, D.C.: Microcards Editions, 1968); Charles L. Perdue, Jr., Thomas E. Borden, and Robert K. Phillips, *Weevils in the Wheat: Interviews with Virginia Ex-Slaves* (Charlottesville: University Press of Virginia, 1976); John B. Cade, "Out of the Mouths of Ex-Slaves," *Journal of Negro History* 20 (July 1935): 294-337.

The narratives as a historical source are evaluated in Escott, *Slavery Remembered,* pp. 3-18 ("the slave narratives offer the best evidence we will ever have on the feelings and attitudes of America's slaves . . ."); Martia Graham Goodson, "An Introductory Essay and Subject Index to Selected Interviews from the Slave Narrative Collection" (Ph.D. dissertation, Union Graduate School, 1977); and C. Vann Woodward, "History from Slave Sources," *American Historical Review* 79 (April 1974): 470-81.

The Davidson quotation is from Rawick, ed., *American Slave,* Ohio Narrs., Series 1, vol. 16, pp. 26-29. Hereafter, all references to this collection will include the name of the state, series number, volume, and page numbers. The other major source of slave interview material taken from the FWP collection for this paper — Perdue, et al. — will be referred to as *Weevils in the Wheat.*

⁸Joan Kelly-Gadol, "The Social Relations of the Sexes: Methodological Implications of Women's History," *Signs* 1 (Summer 1976): 809-10, 819.

⁹For discussions of women's work and the inadequacy of male-biased economic and social-scientific theory to define and analyze it, see Joan Acker, "Issues in the Sociological Study of Women's Work," in *Working Women: Theories and Facts in Perspective,* ed., Ann H. Stromberg and Shirley Harkess (Palo Alto, Calif.: Mayfield Publishing Co. 1978), pp. 134-61; and Judith K. Brown, "A Note on the Division of Labor by Sex," *American Anthropologist* 72 (October 1970): 1073-78.

¹⁰Miss. Narrs., supp. Series 1, pt. 2, vol. 7, p. 350; Okla. Narrs., supp. Series 1, vol. 12, p. 110; Davis, "Reflections on the Black Woman's Role," p. 8; Frances Anne Kemble, *Journal of A Residence on a Georgian Plantation in 1838-1839* (London: Longman, Green, 1863), pp. 60, 92.

¹¹Owens, *This Species of Property,* pp. 8-20.

¹²Kemble, *Journal of a Residence,* p. 28; Lewis Cecil Gray, *History of Agriculture in the Southern United States,* vol. 1 (Washington, D.C.: Carnegie Institution, 1933), pp. 533-548; *Weevils in the Wheat,* p. 199; Fla. Narrs., Series 1, vol. 17, p. 305; Charles S. Sydnor, *Slavery in Mississippi* (Gloucester, Mass.: P. Smith, 1965), p. 20; Frederick Law Olmsted, *A Journey in the Seaboard Slave States* (New York: Dix and Edwards, 1856), p. 470; Frederick Law Olmsted, *A Journey in the Back Country* (New York: Mason Brothers, 1860), p.59.

¹³Olmsted, *A Journey in the Seaboard Slave States,* p. 387; Ala. Narrs., Series 1, vol. 6, p. 87. Work descriptions were gleaned from the FWP slave narrative collection (*American Slave* and *Weevils in the Wheat*) and Gray, *History of Agriculture.* Goodson ("Introductory Essay") has indexed a sample of the interviews with women by subject (for example, "candlemaking," "carding wool," "field work," "splitting rails.").

For pictures of early twentieth-century black women of St. Helena's Islands, South Carolina, wearing the second belt, see photographs in Edith M. Dabbs, *Face of an Island: Leigh Richmond Miner's Photographs of St. Helena's Island* (New York: Grossman, 1971). The caption of one photo entitled "Woman with Hoe" reads: "Adelaide Washington sets off for her day's work in the field. The second belt or cord tied around the hips lifted all her garments a little and protected the long skirts from both early morning dew and contact with the dirt . . . . [according to] an African superstition . . . the second cord also gave the wearer extra strength" (no pp.). Olmsted, *Slave States,* p. 387, includes a sketch of this form of dress.

[14]*Weevils in the Wheat,* p. 26; Gary, *History of Agriculture,* p. 251; planter quoted in Owens, *This Species of Property,* p. 39.

[15]Genovese, *Roll, Jordan, Roll,* p. 495; Burke quoted in Gray, *History of Agriculture,* p. 549; Olmsted, *A Journey in the Back Country,* p. 81. For former slaves' descriptions of women who plowed, see Okla. Narrs., Series 1, vol. 7, p. 314; Fla. Narrs., Series 1, vol. 17, p. 33.

[16]Olmsted quoted in Sydnor, *Slavery in Mississippi,* p. 68; *Weevils in the Wheat,* p. 77. Of the women who worked in the South Carolina Sea Islands cotton fields, Harriet Ware (a northern teacher) wrote, "they walk off with their heavy hoes on their shoulders, as free, strong, and graceful as possible." Elizabeth Ware Pearson, ed., *Letters from Port Royal Written at the Time of the Civil War* (Boston: W.B. Clarke, 1906), p. 52.

[17]Stuart Bruchey, ed., *Cotton and the Growth of the American Economy: 1790-1860* (New York: Harcourt, Brace & World, 1967), p. 174. See the documents under the heading "Making Cotton" and "The Routine of the Cotton Year," pp. 171-80. For examples of outstanding female pickers see Ala. Narrs., Series 1, vol 6, p. 275 ("Oncet I won a contest wid a man an' made 480 pounds."); *Weevils in the Wheat,* p. 199.

767

[18]Texas Narrs., supp. Series 2, pt. 1, vol. 2, pp. 93-94; Miss. Narrs., supp. Series 1, pt. 1, vol. 6, pp. 235-36, and pt. 2, vol. 7, p. 404; Tex. Narrs., Series 1, pt. 3, vol. 5, p. 231; Ind. Narrs., Series 1, vol. 6, p. 25; Ga. Narrs., Series 1, pt. 1, vol. 12, p. 113; Okla. Narrs., Series 1, vol. 7, p. 314; Ala. Narrs., Series 1, vol. 6, p. 338.

[19]For a general discussion of slave artisans in the South see Gray, *History of Agriculture,* pp. 548, 565-67; Sydnor, *Slavery in Mississippi,* p. 9. Roger L. Ransom and Richard Sutch, in *One Kind of Freedom: The Economic Consequences of Emancipation* (Cambridge: Cambridge University Press, 1977), discuss "Occupational Distribution of Southern Blacks: 1860, 1870, 1890" in app. B, pp. 220-31. The works of Starobin *(Industrial Slavery),* and James H. Brewer, *The Confederate Negro: Virginia's Craftsmen and Military Laborers, 1861-1865* (Durham: Duke University Press, 1969), focus almost exclusively on male slaves. See also Herbert Gutman and Richard Sutch, "Victorians All? The Sexual Mores and Conduct of Slaves and their Masters," in David, et al., *Reckoning With Slavery,* p. 160; Gutman, *Black Family,* pp. 599-600. The "hiring out" of men and children frequently disrupted family life.

[20]Ransom and Sutch, *One Kind of Freedom,* p. 233; Olmsted, *Slave States,* p. 388; Ohio Narrs., Series 1, vol. 16, p. 28; Kemble, *Journal,* p. 121; S.C. Narrs., Series 1, pt. 4, vol. 3, p. 78; *Weevils in the Wheat,* pp. 223-24. Genovese describes the plantation system as a "halfway house between peasant and factory cultures" *(Roll, Jordan, Roll,* p. 286). For further discussion of the grueling pace of fieldwork see Herbert G. Gutman and Richard Sutch, "Sambo Makes Good, or Were Slaves Imbued with the Protestant Work Ethic?" in David, et al., *Reckoning With Slavery,* pp. 55-93.

[21]Ala. Narrs., Series 1, vol. 6, p. 46; Fla. Narrs., Series 1, vol. 17, p. 185; *Weevils in the Wheat,* pp. 259, 216; Va. Narrs., Series 1, vol. 16, p. 51; Escott, *Slavery Remembered,* pp. 86-93. Escott includes an extensive discussion of resistance as revealed in the FWP slave narrative collection and provides data on the age, sex, and marital status of resisters and the purposes and forms of resistance. Gutman argues that the "typical runaway" was a male, aged sixteen to thirty-five years *(Black Family,* pp. 264-65). See also Obitko, "Custodians of a House of Resistance,"; Owens, *This Species of Property,* pp. 38, 88, 95.

[22]*Weevils in the Wheat,* pp. 26, 282, 157. According to Gutman, plantation work patterns "apparently failed to take into account enlarged slave kin groups, and further study may show that a central tension between slaves and their owners had its origins

in the separation of work and kinship obligations" *(Black Family, p. 209.).*

[23]Fla. Narrs., Series 1, vol. 17, p. 191; Bennet H. Barrow quoted in Gutman, *Black Family,* p.263; Robert S. Starobin, ed., *Blacks in Bondage: Letters of American Slaves* (New York: New Viewpoints, 1974), p. 54.

In his recent study, *The Slave Drivers: Black Agricultural Labor Supervisors in the Antebellum South* (Westport, Conn.: Greenwood Press, 1979), William L. Van DeBurg examines the anomalous position of black (male) drivers in relation to the rest of the slave community.

[24]Savitt, *Medicine and Slavery,* pp. 115-20; planter quoted in Owens, *This Species of Property,* pp. 38-40; planter quoted in Olmsted, *A Journey in the Seaboard Slave States,* p. 190; Kemble, *Journal of a Residence,* p. 121. Cf. White, "Ain't I A Woman?" pp. 77-86, 101, 155-60.

[25]Genovese, *Roll, Jordan, Roll,* pp. 328, 340; Ala, Narrs., Series 1, vol. 6, p. 273; Miss. Narrs., supp. Series 1, pt. 2, vol. 7, p. 400; Tex. Narrs., Series 1, pt. 3, vol. 5, p. 45. Recent historians have emphasized that the distinction between housework and fieldwork was not always meaningful in terms of shaping a slave's personality and self-perception or defining her or his status. See Owens, *This Species of Property,* p. 113; Escott, *Slavery Remembered,* pp. 59-60.

[26]Ala. Narrs., Series 1, vol. 6, pp. 416-17. In her study of slave mistresses, Anne Firor Scott gives an accurate description of their numerous supervisory duties, but she ignores that most of the actual manual labor was performed by slave women. See *The Southern Lady: From Pedestal to Politics, 1830-1930* (Chicago: University of Chicago Press, 1970), p.31.

[27]Tex. Narrs., Series 1, pt. 4, vol. 5, p. 11; Ind. Narrs., Series 1, vol. 6, p. 83. See also Miss. Narrs., supp. Series 1, pt. 1, vol. 6, pp. 54-55, 216, 257, 365, 380-81.

[28]The FWP slave narrative collection provides these examples of children's work, and many more. Ala. Narrs., Series 1, vol. 6, p. 157; Genovese, *Roll, Jordan, Roll,* pp. 502-19; Owens, *This Species of Property,* p. 202.

In early adolescence (ages ten to fourteen), a child would normally join the regular work force as a half-hand. At that time (or perhaps before), she or he received adult clothing. This *ritè de passage* apparently made more of an impression on boys than girls, probably because pants offered more of a contrast to the infant's smock than did a dress. Willis Cofer attested to the significance of the change: "Boys jes' wore shirts what looked lak dresses 'til dey wuz 12 years old and big enough to wuk in de field . . . and all de boys wuz mighty proud when dey got big enough to wear pants and go to wuk in de fields wid grown folkses. When a boy got to be man enough to wear pants, he drawed rations and quit eatin' out of de trough [in the nursery]." Ga. Narrs., Series 1, pt. 1, vol. 12, p. 203. For other examples of the significance of change from adults' to children's clothing, see Tex. Narrs., Series 1, pt. 3, vol. 5, pp. 211, 275; p. 4, pp. 109-110; Ga. Narrs., Series 1, pt. 1, vol. 12, p. 277; Genovese, *Roll, Jordan, Roll,* p. 505.

[29]Ga. Narrs., supp. Series 1, pt. 1, vol. 3, p. 185; *Weevils in the Wheat,* pp. 264-65; S.C. Narrs., Series 1, pt. 4, vol. 3, p. 257.

[30]Okla. Narrs., Series 1, vol. 7, p. 347; White "Ain't I A Woman?" pp. 210-15; L. Maria Child, ed., *Incidents in the Life of a Slave Girl, Written By Herself* (Boston: L. Maria Child, 1861).

[31]James Hugo Johnston, *Race Relations in Virginia and Miscegenation in the South, 1776-1860* (Amherst: University of Massachusetts Press, 1970), p. 247; Mary Boykin Chesnut, *A Diary From Dixie,* ed. Ben Ames Williams (Cambridge, Mass.: Harvard University Press, 1980), p. 49.

³²Fla. Narrs., Series 1, vol. 17, p. 35. For specific incidents illustrating these points, see *Weevils in the Wheat*, pp. 63, 199; Okla. Narrs., Series 1, vol. 7, pp. 135, 165-66; Tenn. Narrs., Series 1, vol. 16, p. 14. Slave punishment in general is discussed in Escott, *Slavery Remembered*, pp. 42-46; Owens, *This Species of Property*, p. 88; Savitt, *Slavery and Medicine*, pp. 65-69; Gutman and Sutch, "Sambo Makes Good," pp. 55-93; Frederick Douglass, *Narrative of the Life of Frederick Douglass, An American Slave* (Cambridge: Harvard University Press, 1960), pp. 60-61. These examples indicate that Anne Firor Scott is a bit sanguine in suggesting that although southern women were sensitive to the "depravity" of their husbands, "It may be significant that they did not blame black women, who might have provided convenient scapegoats. The blame was squarely placed on men." See Anne Firor Scott, "Women's Perspectives on the Patriarchy in the 1850s," *Journal of American History* 61 (June 1974): 52-64.

³³Genovese, *Roll, Jordan, Roll*, pp. 333-38. See, for example, the document entitled "A Seamstress is Punished" in Lerner, ed., *Black Women in White America*, pp. 18-19.

³⁴Olmsted, *A Journey in the Seaboard Slave States*, p. 421; S.C. Narrs., Series 1, pt. 4, vol. 3, p. 126; Fla. Narrs., Series 1, vol. 14, p. 356; Escott, *Slavery Remembered*, p. 64; Kemble, *Journal of a Residence*, p. 98; Genovese, *Roll, Jordan, Roll*, pp. 346-47.

³⁵Fla. Narrs., Series 1, vol. 17, p. 356; Gutman and Sutch, "Sambo Makes Good," p. 74; Kemble, *Journal of a Residence*, p. 153; Gray, *History of Agriculture*, p. 553; Owens, *This Species of Property*, p. 113.

³⁶Ga. Narrs., Series 1, pt. 1, vol. 12, p. 243; Davis, "Reflections on the Black Woman's Role," pp. 4-7. For general discussions of women's work as it related to slave communal life see also Owens, *This Species of Property*, pp. 23, 225; and White, "Ain't I A Woman?." Polly Cancer recalled that, when she was growing up on a Mississippi plantation, the master "wudn't let de mammies whip dey own chillun [or "do dey own cookin"] . . . , ef he cum 'cross a 'ooman whuppin' her chile he'd say, 'Git 'way 'ooman; dats my bizness . . . .'" Miss. Narrs., supp. Series 1, pt. 2, vol. 7, pp. 340-41.

³⁷Gray, *History of Agriculture*, p. 563; Olmsted, *A Journey in the Seaboard Slave States*, pp. 424-25, 697-98; Owens, *This Species of Property*, p. 47; Fla. Narrs., Series 1, vol. 17, p. 175; Ala. Narrs., Series 1, vol. 6, p. 216; Miss. Narrs., supp. Series 1, pt. 1, vol. 6, pp. 10, 23, 25, 123; Ga. Narrs., supp. Series 1, pt. 1, vol. 3, p. 27. Savitt *(Slavery and Medicine)* includes a section on "Black Medicine" (pp. 171-84) and confirms Rebecca Hook's recollection that "on the plantation, the doctor was not nearly as popular as the 'granny' or midwife." Fla. Narrs., Series 1, vol. 17, p. 175.

³⁸Ga. Narrs., Series 1, pt. 1, vol. 12, p. 70; Okla. Narrs., Series 1, vol. 7, pp. 314-15; White, "Ain't I A Woman?" pp. 22-23; Tex. Narrs., Series 2, pt. 1, vol. 2, p. 98.

³⁹The FWP slave narrative collection contains many descriptions of slaves engaged in household industry. Alice Morse Earle details comparable techniques used by white women in colonial New England in *Home Life in Colonial Days* (New York: MacMillan Co., 1935).

⁴⁰See, for example, S.C. Narrs., Series 1, pt. 3, vol. 3, pp. 15, 218, 236; Tex. Narrs., Series 1, pt. 3, vol. 5, pp. 20, 89, 108, 114, 171, 188, 220; Miss. Narrs., supp. Series 1, pt. 1, vol. 6, p. 36.

⁴¹*Weevils in the Wheat*, pp. 88-89. George White of Lynchburg reported that his mother sang a similar version of this song to women while they were spinning (p. 309).

⁴²Genovese, *Roll, Jordan, Roll*, p. 319.

⁴³Gutman, *Black Family*, p. 75. Escott points out that masters and slaves lived in "different worlds" *(Slavery Remembered*, p. 20). This paragraph briefly summarizes Gutman's pioneering work.

⁴⁴Davis, "Reflections on the Black Woman's Role," p. 7.

⁴⁵Ala. Narrs., Series 1, vol. 6, p. 9; Tex. Narrs., supp. Series 2, pt. 5, vol. 6, pp. 2036-37; Fla. Narrs., Series 1, vol. 17, pp. 22-23; White, "Ain't I A Woman?," pp. 30-31, 65.

⁴⁶Gutman, *Black Family*, pp. 142, 67-68, 267-78; Genovese, *Roll, Jordan, Roll*, pp. 318, 482-94; S.C. Narrs., Series 1, pt. 3, vol. 3, p. 192; Miss. Nars., supp. Series 1, pt. 2, vol. 7, pp. 380-81.

⁴⁷Okla. Narrs., Series 1, vol. 7, p. 210; Escott, *Slavery Remembered*, pp. 49-57, 87; Owens, *This Species of Property*, p. 201.

⁴⁸Gutman and Sutch, "Sambo Makes Good," p. 63; Owens, *This Species of Property*, p. 195; Miss. Narrs., supp. Series 1, pt. 1, vol. 6, pp. 59-60. For mention of corn shuckings in particular, see Genovese, *Roll, Jordan, Roll*, p. 318; Miss. Narrs., Series 1, vol. 7, p. 6; Okla. Narrs., Series 1, vol. 7, p. 230. In the context of traditional female-male roles, what Genovese calls the "curious sexual division of labor" that marked these festivities was not "curious" at all (p. 318).

⁴⁹Unfortunately, much of the data about pre colonial African work patterns must be extrapolated from recent findings of anthropologists. The author benefited from conversations with Dr. M. Jean Hay of the Boston University African Studies Center concerning women's work in precolonial Africa and methodological problems in studying this subject.

⁵⁰For a theoretical formulation of the sexual division of labor in preindustrial societies, see Brown, "A Note on the Division of Labor By Sex."

⁵¹Peter Wood, *Black Majority: Negroes in Colonial South Carolina From 1670 Through the Stono Rebellion* (New York: Alfred A. Knopf, 1974), pp. 59-62; P.C. Lloyd, "Osi fakunde of Ijebu," in *Africa Remembered: Narratives by West Africans from the Era of the Slave Trade*, ed. Philip D. Curtin (Madison: University of Wisconsin Press, 1967), p. 263; Marguerite Dupire, "The Position of Women in a Pastoral Society," in *Women of Tropical Africa*, ed. Denise Paulme (Berkeley: University of California Press, 1963), pp. 76-80; Olaudah Equiano, "The Life of Olaudah Equiano or Gustavus Vassa the African Written By Himself," in *Great Slave Narratives*, ed. Arna Bontemps (Boston: Beacon Press, 1969), pp. 7-10; Kemble, *Journal of a Residence*, p. 42; Pearson, ed., *Letters from Port Royal*, pp. 58, 106.

⁵²Melville J. Herskovits, *The Myth of the Negro Past* (New York: Harper & Bros., 1941), pp. 33-85; Wood, *Black Majority*, pp. 179, 250; Hermann Baumann, "The Division of Work According to Sex in African Hoe Culture," *Africa* 1 (July 1928): 289-319. On the role of women in hoe agriculture, see also Leith Mullings, "Women and Economic Change in Africa," in *Women in Africa: Studies in Social and Economic Change*, ed. Nancy J. Hafkin and Edna G. Bay (Stanford: Stanford University Press, 1976), pp. 239-64; Sylvia Leith-Ross, *African Women: A Study of the Ibo of Nigeria* (New York: Frederick A. Praeger, 1965), pp. 84-91; Ester Boserup, *Woman's Role in Economic Development* (New York: St. Martin's Press, 1970), pp. 156-36; Jack Goody and Joan Buckley, "Inheritance and Women's Labour in Africa," *Africa* 63 (April 1973): 108-21. No tribes in precolonial Africa used the plow.

⁵³Olmsted, *A Journey in the Seaboard Slave States*, p. 433; Gray, *History of Agriculture*, p. 548; Kemble, *Journal of a Residence*, pp. 164, 247; Douglass, *Narrative*, pp. 76-78. According to Genovese, the ability of these elderly slaves "to live decently and with self-respect depended primarily on the support of their younger fellow slaves" *(Roll, Jordan, Roll*, p. 523); White "Ain't I A Woman?" p. 49; Miss. Narrs., supp. Series 1, pt. 1, vol. 6, p. 242.

⁵⁴Eblen, "New Estimates," p. 306; Pearson, ed. *Letters from Port Royal*, p. 25;

770

Genovese, *Roll, Jordan, Roll,* pp. 522-23; Eliza F. Andrews, *The War-Time Journal of a Georgia Girl, 1864-1865* (New York: D. Appleton & Co., 1908), p. 101; Escott, *Slavery Remembered,* pp., 108-09; Owens, *This Species of Property,* p. 140; Gutman, *Black Family,* p. 218. For specific examples, see Ala. Narrs., supp. Series 1, pt. 1, vol. 6, p. 217; pt. 2, vol. 7, pp. 369-73. See also White, "Ain't I A Woman?" pp. 107-112.

⁵⁵Miss. Narrs., Supp. Series 1, pt. 1, Vol. 6, p. 217; pt. 2, Vol. 7, pp. 369-73. See also White, "Ain't I A Woman?" pp. 107-112.

⁵⁶Ga. Narrs., Series 1, pt. 1, vol. 12, p. 214; *Weevils in the Wheat,* p. 128

⁵⁷Genovese, *Roll, Jordan, Roll,* p. 500. See also White, "Ain't I A Woman?" pp. 3-20, 51-54; and Davis, "Reflections on the Black Woman's Role," p. 7.

⁵⁸This section summarizes material in an essay by the author entitled "Freed Women?: Black Women, Work, and the Family During the Civil War and Reconstruction," Wellesley Center for Research on Women Working Paper No. 61 (Wellesley, Mass., 1980). "'My Mother'" and "Freed Women" constitute the first two chapters of a book on Afro-American women, work, and the family, 1830-1980 (forthcoming).

⁵⁹Robert Somers, *The Southern States Since the War, 1870-1* (London: MacMillan & Co., 1871), p. 59; Ransom and Sutch, *One Kind of Freedom,* p. 233; Francis W. Loring and C.F. Atkinson, *Cotton Culture and the South Considered with Reference to Emigration* (Boston: A. Williams, 1869), pp. 4-23. Other primary works that include relevant information are Frances Butler Leigh, *Ten Years on a Georgia Plantation Since the War* (London: R. Bentley, 1883); Charles Nordhoff, *The Cotton States in the Spring and Summer of 1875* (New York: D. Appleton & Co., 1876); George Campbell, *White and Black: The Outcome of a Visit to the United States* (London: Chatto and Windus, 1879).

⁶⁰Freedmen's Bureau official quoted in Gutman, *Black Family,* p. 167.

⁶¹The transition from wage labor to the sharecropping system is examined in Ralph Shlomowitz, "The Origins of Southern Sharecropping," *Agricultural History* 53 (July 1979): 557-75, and his "The Transition From Slave to Freedman Labor Arrangements in Southern Agriculture, 1865-1870," *Journal of Economic History* 39 (March 1979): 333-36; Jay R. Mandle, *The Roots of Black Poverty: The Southern Plantation Economy After the Civil War* (Durham, N.C.,: Duke University Press, 1978); Joseph D. Reid, Jr., "White Land, Black Labor, and Agricultural Stagnation: The Causes and Effects of Sharecropping in the Postbellum South," *Explorations in Economic History* 16 (January 1979): 31-55; Ransom and Sutch, *One Kind of Freedom.*
Jonathan Wiener suggests that blacks' rejection of gang labor and preference for family share units "represented a move away from classic capitalist organizations." See "Class Structure and Economic Development in the American South, 1865-1955," *American Historical Review* 84 (October 1979): 984.

⁶²Elizabeth Hyde Botume, *First Days Amongst the Contrabands* (Boston: Lee & Shepard, 1893), p. 166; Campbell, *White and Black,* pp. 172, 344, 364; tale entitled "De Tiger an' de Nyung Lady" quoted in Owens, *This Species of Property,* p. 144. See Leon Litwack, *Been in the Storm So Long: The Aftermath of Slavery* (New York: Alfred A. Knopf, 1979), pp. 502-56, for a detailed discussion of various freedmen's conventions held throughout the South.

⁶³For an analysis of the ways in which the household responsibilities of women are defined and redefined to alter the supply of available wage-earners, see Louise A. Tilly and Joan Scott, *Women, Work, and Family* (New York: Holt, Rinehart & Winston, 1978).

771

THE FIRST NEGRO TEACHER IN LITTLE ROCK

By
CLARA B. KENNAN
Little Rock, Arkansas

I

The first Negro ever employed as a teacher by the Little Rock Public School Board is living today. In her life span of almost a century, she has witnessed tremendous changes in the fortunes of her race. She says, "The Lord hath done great things for us, whereof we are glad." But those who know her are aware that Charlotte Andrews Stephens herself has been a strong ally of the Lord in this matter.

773

In the spring of 1869, just a year after Little Rock set up its public school system, Lottie Andrews, age fifteen, was chosen as the brightest pupil in the Negro school to finish out the term for a white teacher of the school who had become ill. Charlotte Andrews Stephens retired in 1939. After she had taught in Little Rock for seventy consecutive years.

Thirty years as an elementary teacher, with sometimes as many as ninety children in her room at one time; thirty more years as a high school teacher; ten years as teaching librarian in high school and junior college—thus was her service apportioned. One can imagine how many lives her tutelage has touched. She is said by one of her distinguished former students, Dr. William Pickens, to have taught and inspired with self respect more boys and girls in her long and fruitful career than any other teacher he has ever met, and he has met many in his long life as an educator. He adds, "She probably influenced more children and young people for good than any other teacher in the south in the last three-quarters of a century."

That is high praise. But good is a very general term and Charlotte Stephens' influence has had a more specific flavor. In the first place, she loved learning and acquired as much of it as possible early in life at Oberlin College, and later by whatever means presented itself in Little Rock. Then she had the knack of explaining the English langauge to children so that it made sense to them. In other words,

Originally published in *The Arkansas Historical Quarterly*, Vol. IX (Spring 1950).

when she taught, the children learned. Always fair minded, she recognized the worth and dignity of the individual, whether he was a little Negro beginner or a white supervisor. A white reporter once said, "Her diction is that of a person of highest culture and refinement, and one need only to converse with her for a few minutes to become aware of her keen, trained intellect and to realize that here is one of the outstanding women of the Negro race."

William Grant Still, a former student of hers and composer of the music for the New York produced opera *Troubled Island*, remembers her air of kindly maternal understanding. "Her personality was definitely one congenial to the development of the higher things in life," he says. "All her efforts were directed toward bringing out the good qualities of every individual without regard to race."

774

This ability to cross over racial lines with her understanding and sympathies made her invaluable in twilight decades of racal inequalities. Always she taught her people to strive for better things. Always she seemed to understand the administrative difficulties faced by the school superintendent in his efforts to deal fairly with the Negroes. She was consistently fair minded, and she held the respect and confidence of both races. "She was almost as much help to the whites as she was to the Negroes," said a former supervisor. Even today, when she comments on the times, she says, "I esteem it a wonderful and happy experience to have seen and been a part of the marvelous growth, expansion, and development of our schools, both white and colored."

When a new Negro elementary school was to be named, in 1910, it was a negro who proposed that it be named for her. The white board agreed and so her name won the toss over that of Booker T. Washington, who had to wait for another school. Of Little Rock's thirty-two public schools today, the Charlotte Stephens school remains the only one named for a woman.

It has been forty years since the original Charlotte Stephens school was built, and it is worn out. Now under construction to replace it is an ultra-modern functional brick costing nearly $125,000.00. But the woman whose name this new building will carry on is not worn out. At ninety-six, she has lost much of her faculties of sight and hearing, but she is physically active for an old person, and her intellect, her spirit, her social consciousness are as strong as ever. Today she is still a charter and life member of her State Teachers' Association, a member of the Methodist church, the O E S, the N A A C P, the Phyllis Wheatley branch of the Y W C A, the Sunshine Charity Club (an affiliate of the National Federation of Women's Clubs, colored), and a helper, as she is able, of the civic, charitable, and cultural organizations of her people.

775

What are the antecedents of this remarkable woman? And what early experiences gave drive and direction to her long life?

II

Charlotte Andrews was born of slave parents in Little Rock on May 9, 1854. Her father was William Wallace Andrews. In 1821, when he was four years old, he and his mother were brought to Little Rock by their master, Colonel Chester Ashley (afterward Senator Ashley). Mrs. Ashley is said to have been very fond of the young son of her personal maid. She taught him to read, and the boy proved an apt pupil. As he grew up, he developed a deep religious feeling and a great thirst for knowledge. The Ashleys had a good library, and he read his way through it. He was permitted to hold prayer meetings in his room in the Ashley mansion. Here he and his young Negro associates would sing and pray and read and write and spell, Andrews being their leader and teacher. It seems that at that time it was either against the law or a violation of accepted custom to teach a slave to read His boldness was probably protected by secrecy or by the influence and broadmindedness of his master.

When Wallace Andrews married, in 1848, the Ashleys provided him a home at what is now Broadway and Tenth Streets. His wife's master was not the same as his own, and the couple were able to live apart here only by her "buying her time," as it was called, from her master. Always deeply religious, Andrews called his new home Mt.

Warren Chapel and held Sunday School and other religious meetings there. Finally, in 1854, the year Charlotte was born, the Ashleys gave the Negroes a parcel of land near Broadway and Eighth on which to build a church. Both at his home and at the new church, Andrews got in as much reading, writing, and spelling as he could, along with his religious leadership. His daughter says that many of the Negroes who were able to participate in public affairs immediately upon Emancipation used to bless "Brother Wallace Andrews" for having taught them to read and write, even at the risk of punishment of himself and his pupils if the laws had been enforced against them.

776

When Little Rock was captured by Union troops in September, 1863, Andrews immediately opened a private school in his church house, assisted by a Negro man named Gray who had come in the wake of the army. Charlotte was one of her father's pupils. After a few months, when missionaries from the Friend's Society (Quakers) came from the north to set up schools for the Negroes, Andrews surrendered his school into their more capable hands and went to Missouri, where he got himself ordained as a minister. He returned to Arkansas and began organizing church societies up and down the river. He died in 1866, while still engaged in this work, and a few weeks later his son died, leaving only Charlotte and her mother in the family. Charlotte was twelve years old at this time.

Already, Charlotte had chosen her life's work. She says, "At the age of nine, I was so happily impressed with the instruction and helpful work of the missionary teachers who had come from the north to help a newly emancipated race that I resolved even then to some day be a teacher, like my beloved Mrs. Allen. . ." The girl continued in the Quaker schools until 1868, when Little Rock organized its own public school system, for both whites and colored. It bought the Quakers' Negro school building and continued the Negro school, with white teachers. It was well along in this first year of free public schools in Little Rock that Charlotte, now fifteen, was appointed to fill out the term. At the close of the school year 1868-1869, Charlotte and three other colored teachers were

elected for the ensuing year. She and these three became
the first colored teachers in the school system, but Charlotte was the very first, by virtue of having taught part
of the preceding year.

The three score and ten years that Charlotte Stephens
was to teach are usually thought of as constituting the
life span of man, not the number of his productive years,
as in her case.

III

Charlotte Andrews did not enter her teaching career
lightly. The fervor for learning and for public service
which had possessed her father and her missionary teachers was also hers. And young as she was, she had witnessed events which must have moved her profoundly.

Her father was appointed a "Commissioner for the
Freedmen" for a certain district, and as such was able to
do much good for his people, who were crowding into
the town from the farms and surrounding country, without means of support or the necessary knowledge and
skills to make a living. She must have been at least partially aware of these things which meant much to her
father.

Part of the solution of these freedmen's problems was
to provide them with living quarters. It was the block by
her father's church, only two blocks from her home, in
the area bounded now by Broadway, Eighth, Shrine, and
Seventeenth Streets, that timber was felled and log cabins
were erected, after the manner of plantation quarters," in
long rows, with passageways in between the rows. She
could not have missed knowing something of the life there.

This particular settlement was called "Lick Skillet,"
the name supposedly being given it by a Union soldier who
once saw a child eating from a skillet there. Another settlement, in another part of town, was called "Hard Scrab-
ble." The conditions that existed among these uprooted
but freed people can only be imagined.

It was on January 1, 1864, that the Negroes in Little
Rock first celebrated Emancipation. Mrs. Stephens has
described the activities of that day in an article published in
a Negro newspaper more than twenty years ago.

777

First, she said, religious services were held that morning at the two Negro churches, her father's and that of Father Brown. As a child of nine, she sat in her father's church and heard her people sing.

"Free! Free! In the day of Jubilee!
Thank God Almighty, we are free at last!"

After services, processions formed at the two churches and met by prearrangement to form one big parade and march through the principal streets of the town. They were led by the music of fife and drum furnished by some of the army musicians. In the parade, too, were companies of local Negro men and boys, parading for the first time in the bright blue uniform of Uncle Sam, part of the Black Regiments. Detachments of the army of occupation, with some of the officers, also took part in the parade and in the addresses which followed at the barbecue held across the river, on one of the large farms lying where North Little Rock now stands.

Mrs. Stephens writes, "We cannot recall the speeches of this occasion. Indeed we were too young to take in much of their deep significance. But we can still feel the deep impression made upon our young mind by the shouts and tears and glad hand-clappings of rejoicing accompanying prayers, speeches, and songs. We can still feel the thrill of those stirring war songs,

"We'll rally 'round the flag, boys,
Rally once again,
Shouting the battle cry of freedom!"
and
"We are coming, Father Abraham,
One hundred thousand strong!"

Six years after this experience, Lottie Andrews began teaching school. When she had taught one full school year, she took her savings and went up to Oberlin College to obtain more knowledge and understanding.

IV

Her trip to Oberlin marked an epoch in transportation in Arkansas, in a way. As far as Memphis, she traveled with a Mrs. Cox and her little daughter, Mrs. Cox being the wife of the secretary of the school board. They were told that they were the first women ever to make the trip from Little Rock to Memphis entirely by train. It would appear that entirely is too strong a word, however, even then. Mrs. Stephens remembers that they traveled from Little Rock to DeValls Bluff by train, from DeValls Bluff to Clarendon by boat, from Clarendon to Brinkley by stage, and from Brinkley to Hopefield (now West Memphis) by train again. Then they crossed the Mississippi River on the ferry, as they had crossed the Arkansas at Little Rock. From Memphis, Charlotte made the rest of her way to Oberlin by train, alone.

779

Almost immediately upon arriving at Oberlin, Lottie Andrews began distinguishing herself, in a small way. At the Ladies' Hall, where she lived with the white girls and a handful of other Negro girls, a spelling match was held one night as an entertainment feature on a recreation program. There were two long lines of people extending through the recreation hall, and Charlotte spelled them all down, seniors, theologues, and all. She chuckles today when she recalls it.

The minor intellectual victory was only in fun. But when she tells us that Oberlin was like Heaven to her, we are aware that she means more than the privilege of living in the same hall with white girls. Here was learning to be had, and here were great teachers to introduce it to her. Her bright mind reached out for it, hungrily. Latin, Biblical Antiquities, Geometry, History of Rome, Music, English—she threw herself heartily into their study. For the first year, while on official leave of absence from teaching in Little Rock, she was in the preparatory department of the college. Then she returned for parts of two more years, pursuing the Literary Course and also enrolling in the Conservatory for Instruction in Music. In History she made a straight 6.0 point average, or a perfect grade. In Geometry she made 5.9. In Biblical Antiquities, 5.7. Even in Latin she made well above a B average.

Among her teachers were Max Eastman's father, Samuel Eastman, and also David Flett and Almond Whitney Burr. Little wonder that her love of learning flourished.

At one time during her stay at Oberlin, there were six or eight colored young women there, some of them as she remembers, strikingly attractive in beauty, manners, and dress. At no time were there more than five colored girls in the Ladies' Hall at one time. Once there were two sisters from Brooklyn, one girl from Helena, Arkansas, one from South Carolina, and herself. She modestly disclaims any social standing at the time, however, even though some of the Negro girls, particularly some of those from the town, were popular. "You know how class-conscious and clannish college students are," she says. "And I was an obscure green, Southern little 'first year' at first, without even a nod-and-speaking acquaintance with the upper class students."

But they are all gone, now—those upper class students—Oberlin reports as far as it knows, Charlotte Stephens is its oldest living former student. Death is a great leveler, and, in one sense, the least among them has become the greatest.

Oberlin was like Heaven to her, yes. But it was an intermittent heaven, and one that must sometime end. She was paying her own way, and she had to return to Little Rock between times and earn expense money. Moreover, the Ohio winters were too rigorous for her health. At length, in 1873, she gave up her college career and returned home to settle down to steady teaching.

V

In 1877 she married John Herbert Stephens, a young carpenter. To them were born eight children, six of whom lived to adulthood. Mrs. Stephens bore all of these children while teaching in elementary school, and never did she miss more than a few weeks, in early fall or late spring, at the coming of any one of them. She smiles today at the memory. The school board was good and kind, she says, and the superintendent "noble." Her mother, who lived with her, took over the rearing of the children. Names of the six who lived are William Asa, John Herbert Jr., Lottie

780

Elizabeth, Franklin Sherman, Elbert Lawrence, and Caroline Rebecca.

Her children were all above the average in brightness, supervisors report. Though my information on them is incomplete, a few facts are available. One son is an attorney in Oklahoma. The widower of one daughter is Dr. J. G. Thornton, who is considered dean of Negro physicians in Little Rock. She has six grandchildren and one great-grandchild. One granddaughter is a teacher of nurses in a large New York hospital. One granddaughter is a school teacher of considerable rank in Oklahoma. A grandson is studying law in Seattle. Another granddaughter has just graduated from A. M. and N. College. And so on. All seem to be bright and worthy.

Mrs. Stephens and a daughter live together today, in a brown cottage at 1522 Bishop Street, in Little Rock. Across the street from her home is the Arkansas Baptist College a Negro institution. Only a block away is one of the city's fine modern functional brick school buildings for Negroes. Her own "name" school, as she calls it, modern and beautiful in every way, is nearing completion in another part of town. At Dunbar High School, where she taught for many years, a fine new gymnasium is under construction. Dunbar High School building itself is still beautiful enough to produce pride. Mrs. Stephens is not sorry that she spent her life working in the public schools of her people, instead of accepting some of the offers made her to teach in academies or even in a college.

She says, "I am thankful to the Heavenly Father for permitting me to work for years in the field of public education for a race so needy and so hungry for knowledge."

Mrs. Stephens has written a history of the Negro schools of Little Rock. It is an interesting paper, sure to be of historical value to future generation as well as the present one. She hopes some day to have this published. She also wrote a series of articles several years ago about the early days in Little Rock, which were published in a Negro paper here, on which her daughter was then editor of the women's page. These articles are valuable as source material for historical research in their field. No one else knows and remembers so much authentic information as she about early Little Rock and early Negro schools. She has also written articles for her church and school publications. Much of the information for this paper has been obtained from her newspaper articles, which she furnished.

VI

Mrs. Stephens' report is a bit obscure as to the salaries she was paid while teaching. All teachers' salaries in Arkansas were low, then, she reminds one. The highest she ever drew was $160.00 a month, and that was then considered princely. She is happy that the salaries of all teachers, both colored and white, are as good as they are today. Records show, however, that her salary was consistently lower than that of white teachers, as was the custom for many years. This inequality has been partially atoned for, however, in the circumstances of her retirement benefits.

She was the fifth teacher to retire in the state under Arkansas's then new Teacher Retirement System. She contributed $48.30, the amount specified under the terms of the System in her case. She was entitled to retire immediately, being then eighty-five years old. At that time, maximum benefits which a retired teacher could draw were $65.00 a month, and minimum benefits were one dollar a month for each year of teaching service. Because she had taught for seventy years, she would, by electing to take the "minimum," draw $70.00 a month, whereas if she elected to take the maximum she would draw only $65.00. Upon the advice of the Director of Teacher Retirement, Charles F. Allen, who knew of her excellence as a teacher, she chose the minimum, because it was more than the maximum. "She is one of those statistical exceptions which drive statisticians crazy," one statistician declared. In the succeeding ten years, she drew benefits in the amount of $6629.30 from the Retirement System. "I have told her story to many Rotary Clubs and other assemblies," said Mr. Allen, "and not one person has ever said she has drawn too much. They all say she deserved it."

On Christmas morning, Mr. Allen delivered her December retirement check in person, and with it a bouquet of red roses, with the compliments of his office. It was a gesture of appreciation and recognition which all of Little Rock—all of the south—indeed, may appreciate, because of the quality and quantity of service rendered by the venerable Charlotte Stephens who, born of slave parents, has lived and influenced others for ninety-six years, to the end that she can now say with some reason, "The Lord hath done great things for us, whereof we are glad."

Beginnings of the Afro-American Family

Alan Kulikoff

Sometime in 1728, Harry, a recently imported African, escaped from his master in southern Prince George's County, Maryland, and joined a small black community among the Indians beyond the area of white settlement. The following year, Harry returned to Prince George's to urge his former shipmates, the only sort of kinfolk he had, to return there with him. More than forty years later, another Harry, who belonged to John Jenkins of Prince George's, ran away. The Annapolis newspaper reported that "he has been seen about the Negro Quarters in *Patuxent*, but is supposed to have removed among his Acquaintances on Potomack; he is also well acquainted with the Negroes at Clement Wheeler's Quarter on Zekiah, and a Negro Wench of Mr. Wall's named Rachael; a few miles from that Quarter is his Aunt, and he may possibly be harboured thereabouts."[1]

785

These two incidents, separated by two generations, are suggestive. African Harry ran away *from* slavery to the frontier; Afro-American Harry ran *to* his friends and kinfolk spread over a wide territory. The Afro-American runaway could call on many others to hide him, but the African had few friends and, seemingly, no wife. These contrasts raise many questions. How readily did African immigrants begin families once they reached the Chesapeake colonies? How did Afro-Americans organize their families, and what role did these families serve in sustaining slave communities and culture? Who lived in slave households? What was the impact of arbitrary sale and transfer of slaves upon family life? How did an Afro-American's household and family relations change through the life cycle? This chapter attempts to answer these questions.[2]

Almost all blacks who lived in Virginia and Maryland before 1780 were slaves. Because their status precluded them from enjoying a legally secure

1. Prince George's County Court Record, O, 414, Maryland Hall of Records, Annapolis (MHR); *Maryland Gazette*, Mar. 12, 1772.
2. Pioneering essays by Russell R. Menard, "The Maryland Slave Population, 1658–1730: A Demographic Profile of Blacks in Four Counties," *William and Mary Quarterly*, 3d Ser., XXXII (1975), 29–54; Peter Wood, *Black Majority: Negroes in Colonial South Carolina, from 1670 through the Stono Rebellion* (New York, 1974), chap. 5; and Mary Beth Norton et al., "The Afro-American Family in the Age of Revolution," in Ira Berlin and Ronald Hoffman, eds., *Slavery and Freedom in the Age of the American Revolution* (Charlottesville, Va., 1983), 175–191, suggest some characteristics of colonial black families. Herbert G. Gutman, *The Black Family in Slavery and Freedom: 1750–1925* (New York, 1976), is the standard work on slave families in the 19th century.

352

Originally published in his *Tobacco and Slaves: The Development of Southern Cultures in the Chesapeake, 1680-1800* (Chapel Hill: University of North Carolina Press, 1986).

family life, slave households often excluded important family members. Households, domestic groups, and families must therefore be clearly distinguished. A *household*, as used here, is a coresidence group that includes all who shared a "proximity of sleeping arrangements" or lived under the same roof. *Domestic groups* include kin and nonkin, living in the same or separate households, who share cooking, eating, child rearing, working, and other daily activities. *Families* are composed of people related by blood or marriage. Several distinctions are useful in defining the members of families. The *immediate family* includes husband and wife or parents and children. *Near kin* includes the immediate family and all other kin, such as adult brothers and sisters or cousins who share the same house or domestic tasks with the immediate family. Other kinfolk who do not function as family members on a regular basis are considered *distant kin*.[3]

786

The process of slave family formation can perhaps best be understood as an adaptive process, based upon relations between masters and slaves and among black kinfolk themselves. Slaves structured their expectations about family security around what they knew the master would permit. No slaves enjoyed the security of legal marriage, but had to accept whatever protection individual masters were willing to provide for their sexual unions. (These unions will be called "marriages" in this chapter, even though they lacked legal status.) Although masters sometimes sanctioned slave marriages and encouraged slave family formation, they could withdraw those privileges whenever they desired and separate slave family members through sales, bequests, or gifts. Masters determined the outward bounds of slave family life, but Africans, and especially their descendants, gave meaning to the relations between members of slave families. In particular, slaves tried to mitigate the insecurity of family life by giving kindred outside the immediate family responsibilities in child rearing and by devising extensive kinship networks.[4]

African Slaves and Their Families

Africans who were forced to come to the Chesapeake region in the late seventeenth and early eighteenth centuries struggled to create viable fami-

3. I have borrowed my definitions of household and domestic group from Donald R. Bender, "A Refinement of the Concept of Household: Families, Co-residence, and Domestic Functions," *American Anthropologist*, LXIX (1967), 493–504 (quote on 498). The use of *immediate family*, *near kin*, and *distant kin* was suggested to me by Herbert Gutman.
4. Sidney W. Mintz and Richard Price, *An Anthropological Approach to the Afro-American Past: A Caribbean Perspective*, Institute for the Study of Human Issues, Occasional Papers in Social Change, No. 2 (Philadelphia, 1976).

lies and households, but often failed. They suffered a great loss when they were herded into slave ships. Their family and friends, who had given meaning to their lives and structured their place in society, were left behind, and they found themselves among strangers. They could neither recreate their families nor devise a West African kinship system in the Chesapeake. The differences between African communities were too great. Some Africans lived in clans and lineages; others did not. Some traced their descent from women, but others traced descent from men. Mothers, fathers, and other kin played somewhat different roles in each community. Initiation ceremonies and puberty rites, forbidden marriages, marriage customs, and household structures all varied from place to place.[5]

787

Though African immigrants did not bring a unified West African culture with them to the Chesapeake colonies, they did share important beliefs about the nature of kinship. Africans modified these beliefs in America to legitimate the families they eventually formed. They saw kinship as the principal way of ordering relations between individuals. Each person in the tribe was related to most others in the tribe. The male was father, son, and uncle; the female was mother, daughter, and aunt to many others. Because their kinship system was so extensive, West Africans included kinfolk outside the immediate family in their daily activities. For example, adult brothers or sisters of the father and mother played an important role in child rearing and domestic activities in many African societies.[6]

Second, but far less certainly, African immigrants may have adopted some practices associated with polygyny, a common African marital custom. A few men on the Eastern Shore of Maryland in the 1740s, and perhaps a few others scattered elsewhere, lived with several women. However, far too few African women (in relation to the number of men) arrived in the Chesapeake to make polygynous marriages common. Only one of the 249 men on Robert "King" Carter's many quarters in 1733, for instance, had more than one wife living with him. Despite the absence of polygyny, the close psychological relations between mothers and children found in African polygynous societies might have been repeated in the Chesapeake colonies. In any event, African slave mothers played a more important role than fathers in teaching children about Africa and about how to get along in the

5. The following works suggest variations in African kinship systems: A. R. Radcliffe-Brown, "Introduction," in Radcliffe-Brown and Daryll Forde, eds., *African Systems of Kinship and Marriage* (London, 1950), 1–85; Meyer Fortes, "Kinship and Marriage among the Ashanti," *ibid.*, 252–284; Jack Goody, *Comparative Studies in Kinship* (Stanford, Calif., 1959), chap. 3; Robert Bain, *Bangwa Kinship and Marriage* (Cambridge, 1972); William J. Goode, *World Revolution and Family Patterns* (New York, 1963), 167–200.

6. Mintz and Price, *Anthropological Approach*, 22–26, 32–43 (esp. 34–35); John S. Mbiti, *African Religions and Philosophy* (New York, 1970), 104–109.

slave system. Both African custom and the physical separation of wives and husbands and fathers from their children played a role in this development.[7]

African forced migrants faced a demographic environment hostile to most forms of family life. At first, older slaves could have become uncles to younger Africans, and Africans of the same age could have acted as brothers, but African men had to find wives in order to begin a Chesapeake genealogy. That task was difficult: most blacks lived on small farms of fewer than eleven slaves, the small black population was spread thinly over a vast territory, and the ratio of men to women was high (and especially high on large plantations where Africans were likely to live).[8]

Africans had competition for the available black women. By the 1690s, some black women were natives, and they may have preferred Afro-American men, who were healthy, spoke English, and knew how to act in a white world, to unhealthy or unseasoned Africans. White men were also competitors. Indeed, during the seventeenth and early eighteenth centuries, white adult sex ratios were as high as, or higher than, black adult sex ratios. At any period whites possessed a monopoly of power, and some of them probably took slave women as their common-law wives.[9] African men competed for the remaining black women, who were mostly recently arrived Africans. These immigrant women often waited two or three years before marrying. Since the number of women available to African men was so small and immigrant men died frequently soon after arrival, many probably died before they could find a wife.

Foreign-born male slaves in Virginia and Maryland probably lived in a succession of different kinds of households. Newly imported Africans had no black kin in the Chesapeake. Since sex ratios were high, most of these men probably lived with other, unrelated men. African men may have substituted friends for kin. Newly enslaved Africans made friends with their nearest shipmates during the middle passage, and after their arrival in the

7. "Eighteenth-Century Maryland as Portrayed in the 'Itinerant Observations' of Edward Kimber," *Maryland Historical Magazine*, LI (1956), 327; Robert Carter Inventory, Carter Papers, Virginia Historical Society, Richmond (VHS); Goode, *World Revolution*, 167–168, 196; Mbiti, *African Religions*, 142–145. Women in polygynous societies nursed infants for three to four years and abstained from intercourse during part of that period. If this pattern was repeated in the Chesapeake, it was partially responsible for the low birthrate among Africans discussed in chap. 2. See Mbiti, *African Religions*, 111.

8. See above, chaps. 1, 8, for data on black demography, plantation size, and other associated issues.

9. P.M.G. Harris, "The Spread of Slavery in the Colonial Chesapeake, 1630–1775" (paper presented at the Third Hall of Records Conference on Maryland History, "Maryland, A Product of Two Worlds," May 1984), 14–15, presents demographic evidence for possible miscegenation.

Chesapeake, some of them lived near these men. New Negroes could live with other recent immigrants because migration from Africa occurred in short spurts from the 1670s to the late 1730s. The high sex ratios of large plantations indicate that wealthy men bought many of these Africans. Even if his shipmates lived far away, the new immigrant could share the experiences of others who had recently endured the middle passage.[10]

Despite difficulties, most Africans who survived a few years eventually found a wife. In societies with a high sex ratio, women tend to marry young, but men tend to postpone marriage. This shortage of women prevented most recently arrived African men from finding a wife on the plantation. For them the opportunity to live with a wife and children was rare. Nonetheless, high sex ratios probably increased the opportunity of older, more established African men to marry younger women. (The sexual imbalance is reduced; that is, there are as many younger women as older men.) By the 1690s, large numbers of Afro-American slave women entered their mid-teens and married. Because plantation sizes were small and individual farm sex ratios were likely to be uneven, the wives and children of married African men very often lived on other plantations. These men still lived mainly with other unrelated men, but at least they had begun to develop kin ties. Though few African men lived with their wives and children, the longer an African lived in the Chesapeake, the more likely he was to live with his immediate family.[11]

Robert "King" Carter, the largest slaveholder in the Chesapeake colonies in the 1720s and 1730s, purchased many Africans in the years before he died. The scale of his operations and the large size of his quarters presented enslaved African men with more opportunities to begin families than most of their fellows. Even though Carter apparently encouraged marriage and family life among his slaves, many of his men probably had no kindred on their quarters when he died in 1732. Over half the men and a similar proportion of boys age ten to fourteen lived with unrelated men. These men were probably recently arrived Africans unable to find wives because of the high sex ratios on Carter's holdings. If a man survived a few years on a Carter plantation, he probably married. About a tenth of Carter's adult male slaves had recently married women who resided on or moved to

789

10. Mintz and Price, *Anthropological Approach*, 22–23; Prince George's Inventories, 1730–1769, MHR. Large plantations were those with 11 or more adult slaves.
11. Prince George's Wills, 1730–1749, MHR, and Inventory of the plantation of Daniel Carroll of Duddington, Charles Carroll of Annapolis Account Book, Maryland Historical Society, Baltimore (MHS). The inventory was taken in 1735 (but never probated), a time of high slave imports, but Carroll sold rather than bought slaves. There were only 2 men between 15 and 29 years of age (but 12 women) on his plantations, and 7 above 60; 2 of the 4 men in their 40s, 2 of the 3 in their 50s, and 6 of 7 who were 60 or older lived with wives and children.

their quarters, but did not yet have children in 1733. Older slave men, whether immigrants or creoles, often lived with their wives and children, and more than a quarter of Carter's men were in this group (see table 39).[12]

A greater proportion of African women than African men lived with kindred, especially on large plantations. There was such a surplus of men on these units that African women who lived on them could choose husbands from among several African or Afro-American slave men; women who found husbands on nearby plantations soon had children living with them. On Robert Carter's plantations, for instance, more than half of the men but only a quarter of the women lived in households that contained no kindred. About three-fifths of the women but only two-fifths of the men lived with their spouses. Proportionately, a third more of Carter's women than his men lived with both children and spouse, and women lived in mother-children households five times more frequently than men lived in father-children units.

Even on small plantations, African women commonly lived with their children. Some African women may have been so alienated that they refused to have children, but the rest raised several offspring, protected by the master's reluctance to separate very young children from their mothers. Since the children were reared by their mothers and eventually joined them in the tobacco fields, these households were domestic groups although incomplete as families.

Because spouses of African-born slaves were usually separated, African mothers reared their Afro-American children with little help from their husbands. Even when the father was present as on large plantations like those of Robert Carter's, the extended kin so important in the life of African children was missing. Mothers probably taught them the broad values that they brought from Africa and related the family's history in Africa and the Chesapeake. When the children began working in the fields, they learned from their mothers how to survive a day's work and how to get along with master and overseer.

Each group of Africans repeated the experiences of previous arrivals. The social position of Africans may have slowly improved, however. As the African slave trade peaked and then declined, adult sex ratios also decreased: the sex ratio on large plantations in Prince George's County, Mary-

790

---

12. Robert Carter Inventory, VHS, shows an adult slave sex ratio of 153 (excluding old people) and a sex ratio among youths 10–14 of 150. Although 51% of the boys lived in households without kindred, only 19% of the girls similarly lacked kin. One can identify those who had been in the country a number of years by the age of their children. The new Negro status of couples without children (30 in total, 3 formed by old people) was inferred from the high fertility of slave couples and the absence of such households on large plantations later in the century.

Table 39. *Slave Household Structure on Robert "King" Carter's Quarters, 1733*

Household Type	Percentage Occupying, by Age				
	Males, 15+ (*N*=249)	Females, 15+ (*N*=175)	Children, 0–9 (*N*=212)	Children, 10–14 (*N*=91)	Overall (*N*=733)
Husband-wife	12	18			8
Husband-wife-children	28	39	57	33	40
Mother-children	a	21	31	23	17
Father-children	4	0	6	3	4
Extended	1	2	1	1	1
No family present[b]	54	20	5	39	30
Total	99	100	100	99	100

Source: Robert Carter Inventory, Robert Carter Papers, VHS.

Notes: [a]Less than .5%. [b]Slaves apparently living alone or in barracks, with no other kindred found in household.

791

land, declined from 249 (men per 100 women) during the years of heavy immigration of the 1730s to 142 in the 1740s after immigration decreased. More new Negroes could therefore take wives after 1740 than in previous decades.[13]

Afro-American Slave Households and Families

Afro-American slaves had a more stable family life than their imported African parents. As children they almost always lived with their mothers and siblings and sometimes with their fathers. When the black population began to grow through a surplus of births over deaths in the 1720s and 1730s, the proportion of native-born adults among slaves rose, and slave family life changed remarkably.

The changing composition of the slave population combined with other changes to restructure Afro-American slave households and families. Alterations in the adult sex ratio, the size of plantations, and slave population density provided slaves with opportunities to enjoy a more satisfying family life. The way masters transferred slaves from place to place limited the size and composition of black households, but slave family members

13. Prince George's Inventories, 1730–1744.

separated by masters managed to establish complex kinship networks over many plantations. Afro-American slaves used these opportunities to create a kind of family life that differed from African and Anglo-American practices.

Demographic changes permitted slaves to create more complex households and families. As the number of adult Africans in the population decreased, the sex ratio declined to between 100 and 110 by the 1750s. This decline gave most men an opportunity to marry by about age thirty. The number of slaves who lived on plantations with more than twenty blacks increased, and the density of the black population and the proportion of blacks in the entire population both rose. The number of friends and kinfolk whom typical Afro-American slaves saw every day or visited with regularity increased, while their contact with whites declined because extensive areas of the Chesapeake became largely black counties.

How frequently masters sold or bequeathed their Afro-American slaves and where they sent them affected black household composition. Three points seem clear. First, planters kept women and their small children together but did not keep husbands and teenage children with their immediate family. Slaveowner after slaveowner bequeathed women and their increase to sons or daughters. However, children of Chesapeake slaveowners tended to live near their parents. Thus, even when members of slave families were so separated, they remained in the same neighborhood.[14] Second, slaves who lived on small farms were separated from their families more frequently than those on large plantations. At their death small slaveowners typically willed a slave or two to the widow and to each child. They also frequently mortgaged or sold slaves to gain capital. If a slaveowner died with many unpaid debts, his slaves had to be sold.[15] Finally, relatively few slaves were forced to move long distances. More slaves were affected by migration from the Chesapeake region to the new Southwest in the nineteenth century than by long-distance movement in the region before the Revolution. These points should not be misunderstood. Most slaves who lived in Maryland or Virginia during the eighteenth century experienced forced separation from members of their immediate family sometime in their lives, and about twenty-six thousand tidewater slaves (a quarter of all the region's slaves) were forced to move to piedmont or to the valley of Virginia between 1755 and 1782, usually over such long distances that they could no longer see their kindred. More than two-thirds of all of

14. These statements are based upon Prince George's Wills, 1730–1769, and court cases discussed below.
15. Prince George's Wills, 1730–1769; mortgages in Prince George's Land Records, libri T, Y, PP. Estate sales were sometimes advertised in the *Md. Gaz.* Slaves could not be sold from an estate until all other movable property had been used to pay debts. Elie Valette, *The Deputy Commissarry's Guide within the Province of Maryland* (Annapolis, 1774), 91, 134–135.

tidewater's slaves, however, probably lived close enough to visit most family members.[16]

These changes led to a new social reality for most slaves born in the 1750s, 1760s, and 1770s. If unrelated people and their progeny stay in a limited geographic area for several generations, the descendants of the original residents must develop kin ties with many other people who live nearby. Once the proportion of adult Africans among slaves declined, this process began. African slave women married and had children; the children matured and married. If most of them remained near their birthplace, each was bound to have siblings, children, spouses, uncles, aunts, and cousins living in the neighborhood. How these various kinspeople were organized into households, families, and domestic groups depended not only upon the whims of masters but also upon the meaning placed on kinship by the slaves themselves.

793

The process of household and family formation and dissolution was begun by each immigrant black woman who lived long enough to have children. The story of Ann Joice, a black woman who was born in Barbados, taken to England as a servant, and then falsely sold into slavery in Maryland in the 1670s, may have been similar to that of African women once they became slaves. The Darnall family of Prince George's owned Ann Joice. She had seven children with several white men in the 1670s and 1680s; all remained slaves the rest of their life. Three of her children stayed on the Darnall home plantation until their death. One was sold as a child to a planter who lived a few miles away; another was eventually sold to William Digges, who lived about five miles from the Darnall plantation. Both the spatial spread and the local concentration of kinfolk continued in the next generation. Peter Harbard, born between 1715 and 1720, was the son of Francis Harbard, who was Ann Joice's child. Peter grew up on the Darnall farm, but in 1737 he was sold to George Gordon, who lived across the road from Darnall. As a child, Peter lived with or very near his grandmother Ann Joice, his father, and several paternal uncles and aunts. He probably knew his seven cousins (father's sister's children), children of his aunt Susan Harbard, who lived on the William Digges plantation. Other kinfolk lived in Annapolis but were too far away to visit easily.[17]

16. Migrations of slaves in the 18th century are discussed above, chaps. 4 and 8, and by Philip Morgan, "Slave Life in the Virginia Piedmont: A Demographic Report" (paper presented at conference, "The Colonial Experience: The Eighteenth-Century Chesapeake," Baltimore, Sept. 1984), 3–4, and table 3. Slave movement in the 19th century is analyzed in Allan Kulikoff, "Uprooted Peoples: Black Migrants in the Age of the American Revolution, 1790–1820," in Berlin and Hoffman, eds., *Slavery and Freedom*, 143–171.

17. Court of Appeals of the Western Shore, BW#10 (1800–1801), 456–483, esp. 459–460, MHR.

As Afro-American slaves were born and died and as masters sold or bequeathed their slaves, slave households were formed and reformed, broken and created. Four detailed examples illustrate this process. Daphne, the daughter of Nan, was born about 1736 on a large plantation in Prince George's owned by Robert Tyler, Sr. Until she was two, she lived with her mother, two brothers, and two sisters. In 1738, Tyler died and left his slaves to his wife, children, and grandchildren. All lived on or near Tyler's farms. Three of Daphne's siblings were bequeathed to granddaughter Ruth Tyler, who later married Mordecai Jacob, her grandfather's next-door neighbor. Daphne continued to live on the Tyler plantation. From 1736 to 1787, she had six different masters, but she still lived where she was born. Daphne had lived with her mother until her mother died, and with her ten children until 1779. Children were eventually born to Daphne's daughters; these infants lived with their mothers and near their maternal grandmother. When Robert Tyler III (the grandson of Robert Tyler, Sr.), Daphne's fifth master, died in 1779, his will divided Daphne's children and grandchildren between a son and a daughter. Daphne was thus separated from her younger children, born between 1760 and 1772. They were given to Millicent Beanes (the daughter of Robert III), who lived several miles away. Daphne continued to live on the same plantation as her four older children and several grandchildren. An intricate extended family of aunts, uncles, nieces, nephews, and cousins resided in several households on the Tyler plantation in 1778, and other, more remote kinfolk could be found on the neighboring Jacob farm.[18]

Family separations might be more frequent on smaller plantations. Rachael was born in the late 1730s and bore ten children between 1758 and 1784. As a child she lived on the plantation of Alexander Magruder, a large slaveowner in Prince George's. Before 1746, Alexander gave her to his son Hezekiah, who lived on an adjoining plantation. Hezekiah never owned more than ten slaves, and when he died in 1769, he owned only two, including one willed to his wife by her brother. Between 1755 and 1757, he mortgaged nine slaves, including Rachael, to two merchants. In 1757, Samuel Roundall (who lived about five miles from the Magruders) seized Rachael and six other slaves mortgaged to him. In 1760 Roundall sold Rachael and her eldest daughter to Samuel Lovejoy, who lived about nine miles from Roundall. At the same time, four other former Magruder slaves were sold: two to planters in Lovejoy's neighborhood, one to a Roundall neighbor, and one to a planter living at least fifteen miles away in Charles County.

18. Chancery Papers no. 5241 (1788); Prince George's Wills, I, 280–285; Prince George's Original Wills, box 7, folder 66, box 13, folder 51; Prince George's Inventories, DD#1, 22–24, DD#2, 379–386, GS#1, 246–248, ST#1, 96–100, all at MHR.

Rachael's separation from friends and family members continued. In 1761, Lovejoy sold Rachael's eldest child, age three, to his neighbor George Stamp. By the time Samuel Lovejoy died in 1762, Rachael had two other children. She and her youngest child went to live with John Lovejoy, Samuel's nephew and near neighbor, but her second child, age two, stayed with Lovejoy's widow. Her third child was sold at age six, but Rachael and her next seven children lived with John Lovejoy until at least 1787 (see map 18).[19]

Hundreds of large and middling slaveholders living in older tidewater counties established plantations in piedmont areas for their children or themselves in the 1750s, 1760s, and 1770s. Perhaps a third of the adult slaves in tidewater Virginia (and a fifth in southern Maryland) were forced to migrate to piedmont to operate these distant quarters. Since masters required some (but rarely all) of their slaves to leave, Afro-American slaves were inevitably separated from kindred. These separations were permanent, for their new homes were at least fifty and often several hundred miles away from their former quarters.[20]

795

In the late 1750s or early 1760s, Peyton Randolph, a member of the Virginia House of Burgesses (and eventually its speaker), organized a plantation in Charlotte County, deep in the southside frontier, located about 150 miles from his homes in Williamsburg and James City County. At first, he transferred a number of youths in their late teens and early twenties to the new quarter. By 1764, sixteen adult slaves and an overseer lived on the thirty-four-hundred-acre tract in Charlotte. Nearly a generation passed before Randolph's slaves rebuilt the kinship networks they had left behind. The young migrants married and had children, and by the 1780s *their* children had matured and begun to marry. There were thirty-two adult slaves on the plantation in 1784, perhaps twenty of them children of the original migrants. Sarah's experience illustrates the process of family destruction and rebuilding. At age twenty she was forced to leave her kindred in James City for Charlotte. Though her three children came with her, her husband was left behind. After she arrived in Charlotte, she remarried and had three more children. In 1784 Sarah lived in Charlotte surrounded by her six children and two grandchildren. Two daughters had married slaves who lived on the Charlotte quarter, and each new family included an infant.[21]

19. Chancery Records, XVI, 298–304; Prince George's Land Records, PP (2d part), 4, NN, 407; Prince George's Original Wills, box 7, folder 3, box 9, folder 52; Prince George's Inventories, DD#1, 438–441, GS#2, 111–112, all MHR.
20. Jackson Turner Main, "The One Hundred," *WMQ*, 3d Ser., XI (1954), 355–384; migration data reported in chap. 8, above.
21. Data on Randolph taken from Randolph Papers (film at Colonial Williamsburg Research

Map 18. *Sale and Later Transfer of Hezekiah Magruder's Slaves, 1755–1780*

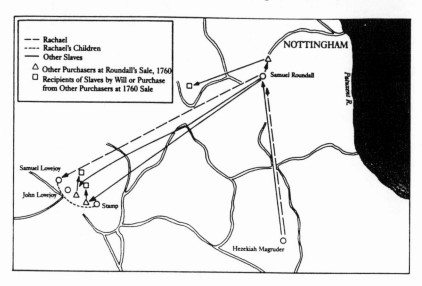

796

These four examples suggest how Afro-American slave households and families developed in the eighteenth century. Three demographic processes combined to create and destroy complex households and families. Husbands and wives, and parents and children were frequently separated by the master's transfers of family members. A young man tended to receive slaves from his parents or purchase them on the open market, thereby separating family members. If economic disaster did not intervene, his slaveholdings grew through natural increase, slave families were reestablished, and extended family networks developed. When the master died, the family's slaves were divided among heirs, and the process began again. Only during the second stage were slave families even relatively secure. At the same time, as generation followed generation, households, or adjacent huts, became increasingly complex and sometimes included grandparents, uncles, aunts, or cousins as well as the immediate family. Since other kin lived on nearby plantations, geographically dispersed kinship networks that connected numbers of quarters emerged during the pre-Revolutionary era.

Department [CW]), as reported in Eileen Starr, "Slaves Belonging to Peyton Randolph" (undergraduate paper, College of William and Mary, 1976); and Landon C. Bell, ed., *Sunlight on the Southside: Lists of Tithes, Lunenburg County, Virginia, 1748–1783* (Philadelphia, 1931), 223. The date of settlement inferred from the ages of Randolph's slaves in 1784 and the appearance of Randolph in the 1764 tax list (but not on the 1753 list).

This second process of building kinship networks had to be started all over again when slaves were forced to migrate to frontier regions.[22]

How typical were the experiences suggested by these examples? How were families organized into households and domestic groups on large and small quarters? Data from the records of four large planters taken between 1759 and 1775 and a census of Prince George's slaves taken in 1776 permit a test of these hypotheses concerning changes in household structure, differences between large and small units, and the spread of kinfolk across space. The data cover both large quarters and small farms and provide a good test of these ideas because by the 1770s most Afro-American slaves could trace a Chesapeake genealogy back to immigrant grandparents or great-grandparents.

797

Kinfolk (immediate families and near kin) on large plantations were organized into three kinds of residence groups. Most of the slaves of large quarters were related by blood or marriage. Domestic groups included kinfolk who lived on opposite sides of duplex slave huts and who shared a common yard and eating and cooking arrangements. Finally, most households included members of an immediate family.

The kinship structures of slaves on large plantations are illustrated by a household inventory taken in 1773–1774 of 385 slaves owned by Charles Carroll of Carrollton on thirteen different quarters in Anne Arundel County. Because Carroll insisted that the inventory be "taken in Familys with their Ages," the document permits a detailed reconstruction of kinship networks.[23] Though the complexity and size of kinship groups on Carroll's quarters were probably greater than on other large plantations, the general pattern could easily have been repeated elsewhere.[24]

The ten men and three women who headed each list were probably leaders of their quarters. Five of the quarters were named for these individuals. They tended to be old slaves who had been with the Carroll family

22. See Gutman, *Black Family in Slavery and Freedom*, 137–139, for a brilliant exposition of much of this model.

23. "A List of Negroes on Doohoregan Manor Taken in Familys with Their Ages Decr. 1, 1773," and other lists of slaves at Popular Island, Annapolis Quarter, and Annapolis taken in Febr. and July 1774, Carroll Account Book, Maryland Historical Society, Baltimore (MHS). I am greatly indebted to Edward Papenfuse for calling this list to my attention. For another, and compatible, analysis of Carroll's slaves, see Norton *et al.*, "Afro-American Family," in Berlin and Hoffman, eds., *Slavery and Freedom*, 177–180.

24. Only a handful of people in the Chesapeake colonies owned as many slaves as Carroll. He could therefore afford to keep his slave families together, an option not open to most slaveholders. Nonetheless, two-thirds of Carroll's slaves lived on units with fewer than 40 people, and 57% of them on quarters with fewer than 30. Only the 130 slaves who lived at Riggs (the main plantation at Doohoregan) developed more extensive kinship networks than was possible for slaves of other large planters.

for many years. While the mean age of all adults was thirty-seven years, the mean age of the leaders was forty-nine, and six of the thirteen were over fifty-five.[25] The leader often lived with many kinfolk and was closely related to 36–38 percent of all the other slaves on the quarter. For example, Fanny, sixty-nine years of age, was surrounded by at least forty near kinfolk on the main plantation at Doohoregan, and Mayara James, sixty-five years of age, lived with twenty-three relatives on his quarter.

Slave genealogies at Annapolis Quarter and at Doohoregan Manor provide detailed examples of the kinds of kinship networks that could develop on quarters after several generations of relative geographic stability (figs. 27, 28). Because most slave quarters had between fifteen and thirty slaves, the network included only two or three households. The kin group at Annapolis Quarter may have been typical. Thirteen of the seventeen slaves who lived there in 1774 were descendants of Ironworks Lucy, ten of them children and grandchildren of Lucy's daughter Sall. One of Sall's sons-in-law and his brother also lived there. Peter and Charles, other descendants of Lucy, lived on the quarter but had families elsewhere.

Nearly half the slaves who resided on Riggs Quarter, Carroll's main plantation, were kinfolk (63 of 130). A slave kinship network of this size could develop only on the home plantations of the largest Chesapeake planters.[26] Each of the members of the group was either a direct descendant or an affine (in-law) of old Fanny. She was surrounded on her quarter by five children, nineteen grandchildren, nine great-grandchildren, four children-in-law, and three grandchildren's spouses. The network grew through the marriage of Fanny's children and grandchildren to children of other residents of the quarter. For example, Cooper Joe, his wife, and thirteen children and grandchildren were closely related to Fanny's family. By the early 1750s Cooper Joe had married Nanny of Kate, and about 1761 Fanny's son Bob married Frances Mitchell of Kate. Joe and Nanny's children were first cousins of the children of Bob and Frances and thereby more remotely connected to all the rest of Fanny's descendants. The alliance of the two families was cemented in 1772, when Dinah, the daughter of Kate of Fanny, married Joe, the son of Cooper Joe.[27]

798

25. There were 139 married adults (all ages) and single people over 21 in the group. Although 46% of the leaders were over 55, only 11% of all adults had reached that age.
26. For example, only a maximum of 6% of slaves in Prince George's, Anne Arundel, Charles, and St. Mary's counties, Md., lived on units of more than 100 in 1790. The 6% is a maximum number because the census taken sometimes combined several of the master's quarters. See U.S., Bureau of the Census, *Heads of Families at the First Census . . . , Maryland* (Washington, D.C., 1907), 9–16, 47–55, 92–98, 104–109. The growth of large units (more than 40 slaves) in Prince George's, 1776–1810, is documented by Richard S. Dunn, "Black Society in the Chesapeake, 1776–1810," in Berlin and Hoffman, eds., *Slavery and Freedom*, 68–70.
27. Joe married his mother's sister's husband's mother's grandchild.

Fig. 27. *Kinship Ties among Charles Carroll's Slaves at Annapolis Quarter,*
1774

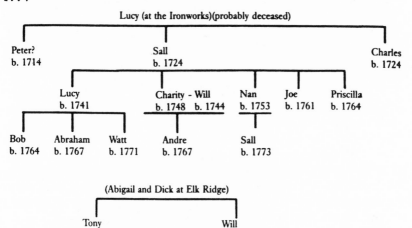

Source: Charles Carroll Account Book, Carroll Papers, MHS.

Note: Will (Charity's Husband), son of Abigail and Dick, appears twice. Peter may not be
Lucy's son, but probably is. Mark (b. 1758) and Jem (b. 1754) apparently were not related to
others on the quarter but had relatives elsewhere on Carroll's plantations.

The intraquarter kinship network was also a work group. Fanny's and
Lucy's adult and teenage kinfolk worked together in the fields. Masters
separated their slaves by sex, age, and strength and determined what each
would do, but blacks judged each other in part by the reciprocal kinship
obligation that bound them. Afro-American slaves worked at their own pace
and frequently thwarted their masters' desires for increased productivity.
Part of this conflict can be explained by the desires of kinfolk to help and
protect each other from the master's lash, the humid climate, and the ma-
larial environment.[28]

Landon Carter's attitude toward his old slave Jack Lubbar suggests the
dimensions of kinship solidarity in the fields. Lubbar had been a foreman
over many groups of slaves and often directed his kindred in their work.
Lubbar alternately protected and pushed those who labored under him. He
was "blessed with his children's company," perhaps because he drove his
charges lightly. In 1766 Carter complained, "Old Jack is both too easy with
those people and too deceitfull and careless himself." When Lubbar died
in 1774, Carter remembered only his loyalty. In Jack's old age, he wrote,

28. See below, chap. 10, for work and work discipline.

Fig. 28. *Fanny and Some of Her Kinfolk on Doohoregan Manor, 1773*

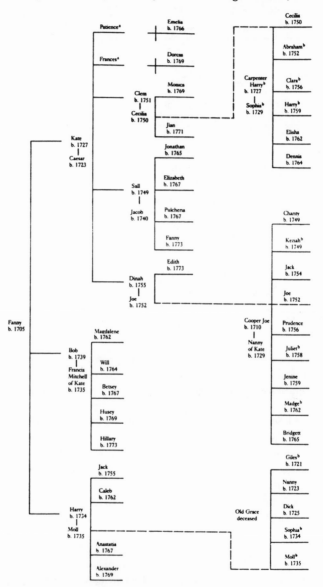

800

Source: Charles Carroll Account Book, Carroll Papers, MHS.

Notes: [a]Those without a birthdate not resident on any Carroll farm. [b]Did not live at Rigg's Quarter (Fanny's Quarter). [c]This family lived at the sawmill at the main quarter of Doohoregan Manor. Frances Mitchell was a sister of Nanny, who was the wife of Cooper Joe.

Lubbar worked at the Fork quarter "with 5 hands and myself; in which service he so gratefully discharged his duty as to make me by his care alone larger crops of Corn, tobacco, and Pease twice over than ever I have had made by anyone." Other slaves did not share Lubbar's occasional desire to produce a large crop for Carter. "At this Plantation," Carter wrote, "he continued till his age almost deprived him of eyesight which made him desire to be removed because those under him, mostly his greatgrandchildren, by the baseness of their Parents abused him much." Lubbar's grandchildren and great-grandchildren were related in intricate ways: parents and children, maternal and paternal cousins, uncles and aunts, and brothers and sisters. They united against Lubbar to slow the work pace and conserve their energy.[29]

801

When Afro-Americans came home each night from the fields, they broke into smaller domestic groups. Their habitat set the scene for social intercourse. On large plantations "a Negro Quarter, is a Number of Huts or Hovels, built at some Distance from the Mansion-House; where the Ne--os reside with their Wives and Families, and cultivate at vacant Times, the little Spots allow'd them."[30] Slaves lived in two kinds of housing. Four early nineteenth-century slave houses still standing in southern Maryland, as well as three homes at Doohoregan Manor, Charles Carroll's home plantation, were duplexes. Each of the southern Maryland houses included two rooms, of about sixteen by sixteen feet, separated by a thin wall. In three of the surviving houses, the two huts shared the same roof but had separate doorways. Two had separate fireplaces, the residents of one duplex shared a fireplace, and one quarter (which was over a kitchen) did not have a fireplace. Neither family had much privacy, and communication must have been commonplace. Most slaves, however, apparently wanted more privacy and built single-family cabins. Slave houses in St. Mary's County at the end of the eighteenth century, for instance, were single-family structures that averaged sixteen by sixteen feet; similarly, sixteen slave houses on Doohoregan Manor were slightly larger, averaging twenty by fifteen feet. Even when slave families lived in separate houses, they were built very close together and surrounded a common yard, where residents could talk, eat, or celebrate.[31]

29. Jack P. Greene, ed., *The Diary of Colonel Landon Carter of Sabine Hall, 1752–1778*, 2 vols. (Charlottesville, Va., 1965), I, 301, 303, 575, II, 836, 840.
30. Kimber, "'Itinerant Observations' of Kimber," *MHM*, LI (1956), 327; references cited in chap. 8, n. 47, above.
31. The best analysis of slave housing (mostly in the antebellum period) will be found in George W. McDaniel, *Hearth and Home: Preserving a People's Culture* (Philadelphia, 1982), chap. 2. I examined the four structures, three in St. Mary's County and the other in Prince George's County. I am indebted to Cary Carson for his data on the St. Mary's buildings and to

On the quarters the smallest local residence unit to contain kinfolk was the household. Household members were not isolated from other kinfolk. They worked with their relatives in the fields, associated with neighbors in the common yard, and cooked meals or slept near those who lived in neighboring huts. Even youths who lived in barracks with other unrelated youths were never far from kindred.[32] Nevertheless, kinfolk who lived in the same household were spatially closer when at home than any other group of kin. Who lived in typical households on slave quarters? How many husbands lived with their wives and children? How many children were separated from their parents? Did kin other than the immediate family live in many households?

Nearly half of all the Afro-Americans owned by four large planters resided in households that included both parents and at least some of their children. More than half of the young children on all four plantations lived with both parents, but a far higher proportion of adults and children ten to fourteen years of age lived in two-parent households on the Carroll quarters than on the other three groups of quarters. About half of the men, women, and youths ten to fourteen lived in two-parent households on Carroll's plantations, but only a third of the women, a quarter of the men, and two-fifths of the youths could be found in two-parent homes on the other farms. Almost all the other children lived with one parent, usually the mother; but more than a quarter of those ten to fourteen years of age lived with siblings or with apparently unrelated people (see table 40).[33]

The differences between Carroll and the other three large slaveowners is striking. Carroll, unlike all but a few other Chesapeake gentlemen, was able to provide his people with spouses from his own plantations and chose to keep adolescent children with their parents. More than half the men (56 percent) and a quarter of the women on Addison's, Wardrop's, and Jerdone's plantations were either unmarried or lived away from spouses and children. On Carroll's quarters only 27 percent of the men and 12 percent of the women were similarly separated from wives and children.

Many slaves on the Carroll, Addison, and Wardrop quarters lived with or near kin other than parents or children. Carroll's and Addison's slaves

---

Margaret Cook for her help with the Prince George's site. For Carroll, see Federal Direct Tax of 1798, Elkridge Hundred, Anne Arundel County, 5–8, MHR. I am indebted to Alexander O. Boulton for calling the Carroll materials to my attention. For St. Mary's, see Bayly Ellen Marks, "Economics and Society in a Staple Plantation System: St. Mary's County, Maryland, 1790–1840" (Ph.D. diss., University of Maryland, 1979), 52–53.

32. Almost all of the boys and men on Charles Carroll's quarters in 1774 had kin on the same or a nearby quarter.

33. Proportions in two-parent households: 49% (Carroll) and 33% (other farms) of women; 51% and 26% of men; 52% and 40% of those aged 10–14.

Table 40. *Afro-American Slave Household Structure on Four Large Plantations in the Chesapeake, 1759–1775*

Household Type	Percentage Occupying, by Age				
	Males, 15+ ($N=189$)	Females, 15+ ($N=158$)	Children, 0–9 ($N=224$)	Children, 10–14 ($N=99$)	Overall ($N=670$)
Husband-wife	3	4			2
Husband-wife-children	37	42	53	46	45
Mother-children	2	19	25	10	15
Father-children	7	0	7	6	5
Siblings	5	3	5	9	5
Mother–children–other kin	3	11	6	10	7
Other extended[a]	3	4	2	5	4
No family in household[b]	40	18	2	15	18
Total	100	101	100	101	100

803

Sources: Prince George's Inventories, GS#1, 73 (James Wardrop's, 32 slaves); and GS#2, 334–336 (Addison's 3 plantations, 109 slaves); Charles Carroll Account Book, MHS (385 slaves); Philip David Morgan, "The Development of Slave Culture in Eighteenth Century Plantation America" (Ph.D. diss., University College, London, 1977), 326 (Francis Jerdone's plantations in piedmont Virginia, rest of slaves).

Notes: [a]Half the slaves lived in two-parent households with other kin; half lived in three-generation households that included grandparents and grandchildren but not the generation in between. [b]Includes some slaves with kinfolk on the plantation, but in other households.

had been with the families for several generations, and extended households thus formed. About 7 percent of these slaves were in the household of a brother or sister, and more than a tenth (13 percent) of parents and children shared their home with another kinsperson. There were several types of these extended households: seven included parents, children, and siblings of the mother; two included a grandmother living with her children and grandchildren; in one household grandparents took care of two young grandchildren; and in one hut, an adult brother and sister lived with her children and one grandchild.

Slave family life on the plantations Francis Jerdone established in piedmont Virginia in the 1740s or 1750s was somewhat less settled than on those in tidewater Maryland. By 1770, when he took a census of his slaves, insufficient time had elapsed to allow the creation of *any* households with extended kindred. Men found marriage on the plantation more difficult than in Maryland: although the sex ratio among black adults was only 110 on the Maryland quarters, it reached 162 on Jerdone's plantations.[34]

Far less can be learned about families on small plantations. On these farms, the slave quarter could be in an outbuilding or in a small hut. All the slaves, whether kin or not, lived together, cooked together, reared their children together, and slept in the same hut. Only 18 percent of the blacks on small units in Prince George's County in 1776 lived in two-parent households. About a third resided in mother-child households, including over half the young children and three-tenths of those ten to fourteen years of age. Nearly three-quarters of the men and two-fifths of the women— some unmarried—lived with neither spouse nor children. More than two-fifths of the youths ten to fourteen years of age lived away from parents and siblings. These differences in the composition of slave households on large and small plantations influenced child-rearing patterns. Although slave fathers played a major role in rearing their children on large units, they were rarely present on smaller farms. On these small units, mothers had to cope with child rearing alone or, perhaps, with the help of an unrelated adult (see table 41).

804

The Life Cycle of Afro-American Slaves

By the 1750s, a peculiarly Afro-American life cycle had developed. Afro-Americans lived in a succession of different kinds of households. Children under ten years almost always lived with their mothers, and more than half on large plantations lived with both parents. Between ten and fourteen years of age, large numbers of children left their parents' homes. Some stayed with siblings and their families, others were sold, and the rest lived with other kin or unrelated people. Women married in their late teens, had children, and established households with their own children. More than two-fifths of the women on large plantations and a fifth on small farms lived with husbands as well as children. The same proportion of men as women lived in nuclear households, but because children of separated spouses usually lived with their mothers, large numbers of men, even on big plantations, lived only with other men.

These life-cycle changes can perhaps best be approached through a study of the critical events in the lives of Afro-Americans. Those events probably included the following: infancy, leaving the matricentral cell, be-

34. Philip David Morgan, "The Development of Slave Culture in Eighteenth Century Plantation America" (Ph.D. diss., University College, London, 1977), 325–327.

Table 41. *Afro-American Slave Household Structure on Small Plantations in Prince George's County, 1776*

Household Type	Percentage Occupying, by Age				
	Males, 15+ (N=275)	Females, 15+ (N=276)	Children, 0–9 (N=325)	Children, 10–14 (N=162)	Overall (N=1,038)
Husband-wife-children	17	18	22	10	18
Mother-children	2	35	56	29	32
Father-children	2	a	4	1	2
Siblings	7	5	6	17	8
No family	72	42	12	43	41
Total	100	100	100	100	101

Source: Gaius Marcus Brumbaugh, ed., *Maryland Records: Colonial, Revolutionary, County, and Church, from Original Sources*, I (Baltimore, 1915), 1–88.

Notes: The household types were inferred from black age structures on individual farms, and the statistics that result are thus conjectural. ªLess than .5%.

ginning to work in the tobacco fields, leaving home, courtship and marriage, child rearing, and old age.

For the first few months of life, a newborn infant stayed in the matri-central cell, that is, received his identity and subsistence from his mother.[35] A mother would take her new infant to the fields with her "and lay it uncovered on the ground ... while she hoed her corn-row down and up. She would then suckle it a few minutes, and return to her labor, leaving the child in the same exposure." Eventually, the child left its mother's lap and explored the world of the hut and quarter. In the evenings, he ate with his family and learned to love his parents, siblings, and other kinfolk. During the day the young child lived in an age-segregated world. While parents, other adults, and older siblings worked, children were "left, during a great portion of the day, on the ground at the doors of their huts, to their own struggles and efforts."[36] They played with age-mates or were left at home with other children and perhaps an aged grandparent. Siblings and age-mates commonly lived together or in nearby houses. In Prince George's

35. For the matricentral cell, see Meyer Fortes, "Introduction," in Jack Goody, ed., *The Developmental Cycle in Domestic Groups*, Cambridge Papers in Social Anthropology, No. 1 (Cambridge, 1958), 1–14, esp. 9; and Sidney W. Mintz, "A Final Note," *Social and Economic Studies*, X (1961), 532–533.
36. Samuel Stanhope Smith, *An Essay on the Causes of the Variety of Complexion and Figure in the Human Species* (1787), ed. Winthrop D. Jordan (Cambridge, Mass., 1965 [orig. publ. New Brunswick, N.J., 1810]), 35, 61–62, 156–157.

County in 1776, 86 percent of those from zero to four years of age and 82 percent of those from five to nine years of age lived on plantations with at least one other child near their own age. Many children lived in little communities of five or more children their own age. Children five to nine years old, too young to work full time, may have cared for younger siblings; in Prince George's in 1776, 83 percent of all children under five years of age lived on a plantation with at least one child five to nine years of age.[37]

Black children began to work in the tobacco fields between seven and ten years of age. For the first time they joined fully in the daytime activities of adults.[38] Those still living at home labored beside parents, brothers and sisters, cousins, uncles, aunts, and other kinfolk. (Even on smaller plantations, they worked with their mothers.) Most were trained to be field hands by white masters or overseers and by their parents. Though these young hands were forced to work for the master, they quickly learned from their kinfolk to work at the pace that black adults set and to practice the skills necessary to "put massa on."

At about the same age, some privileged boys began to learn a craft from whites or (on the larger plantations) from their skilled kinfolk. Charles Carroll's plantations provide an example of how skills were passed from one generation of Afro-Americans to the next. Six of the eighteen artisans on his plantations under twenty-five years of age in 1773 probably learned their trade from fathers and another four from other kinfolk skilled in that occupation. For example, Joe, twenty-one, and Jack, nineteen, were both coopers and both sons of Cooper Joe, sixty-three. Joe also learned to be a wheelwright and, in turn, probably helped train his brothers-in-law, Elisha, eleven, and Dennis, nine, as wheelwrights.[39]

Beginning to work coincided with the departure of many children from their parents, siblings, and friends. The fact that about 54 percent of all slaves in single-slave households in Prince George's in 1776 were between seven and fifteen years of age suggests that children of those ages were typically forced to leave home. Young blacks were most frequently forced from large plantations to smaller farms.[40] The parents' authority was elimi-

806

37. Gaius Marcus Brumbaugh, *Maryland Records: Colonial, Revolutionary, County, and Church, from Original Sources*, I (Baltimore, 1915), 1–88.
38. See below, chap. 10.
39. Carroll Account Book. Elisha and Dennis were sons of Carpenter Harry and Sophia. Joe married Dinah of Kate and Caesar; her brother married Cecilia of Harry and Sophia. Elisha and Dennis were therefore Joe's wife's brother's wife's brothers.
40. Only the children of slaveowners or those who had just bought their first slave were likely to have only one slave, so this data is a useful indicator of the age at which children were first sold. The transfers from large to small plantations can also be seen by comparing the small group (12%) of slaves 10–14 on large plantations who lived away from kin with the large proportion (43%) on small farms (see tables 40, 41).

nated, and the child left the only community he had known. Tension and unhappiness often resulted. For example, Hagar, age fourteen, ran away from her master in Baltimore in 1766. "She is supposed to be harbor'd in some Negro Quarter," he claimed, "as her Father and Mother Encourages her in Elopements, under a Pretense she is ill used at home."[41]

Courtship and marriage (defined here as a stable sexual union) led to substantial but differential changes for slave women and men. The process began earlier for women: men probably married in their middle to late twenties, women in their late teens.[42] Men, who initiated the courtship, typically searched for wives by visiting a number of neighboring plantations and often found a wife near home, though not on the same quarter. Some evidence for this custom, suggestive but hardly conclusive, can be seen in the sex and age of runaway slaves. Only 9 percent of all southern Maryland runaways, 1745–1779, and 12 percent of all Virginia runaways, 1730–1787, were women. Few men (relative to the total population) ran away in their late teens, but numbers rose in the early twenties when the search for wives began and crested between twenty-five and thirty-four, when most men married and began families (see fig. 29). Courtship on occasion ended in a marriage ceremony, sometimes performed by a clergyman, sometimes celebrated by the slaves themselves.[43]

Slave men had to search their neighborhood to find a compatible spouse because even the largest quarter contained few eligible women. Some of the potential mates were sisters or cousins, groups blacks refused to marry.[44] When they were excluded, few choices remained on the quarter, and youths looked elsewhere. Charles Carroll united slave couples once they married, but that usually required either bride or groom to move. Only a fifth of the forty-seven identifiable couples on his plantations in 1773 had lived on the same quarter before they married. Either husband or wife, and sometimes both of them, moved in three-fifths of the cases. The other fifth of the couples remained on different quarters in 1773.[45] Yet most planters

807

41. *Md. Gaz.*, Oct. 1, 1766.
42. See chap. 1 for slave ages at first conception. Age at marriage cannot be determined with precision but can be approximated from the age differences of husbands and wives. On the Carroll, Addison, and Wardrop plantations, 47 husbands were 6.8 (mean) years older than their wives. Carroll Account Book; Prince George's Inventories, GS#1, 73, GS#2, 334–336.
43. Thomas Hughes, *History of the Society of Jesus in North America, Colonial and Federal* (London, 1908–1917), Text, II, *From 1645 till 1773*, 560–561; William Stevens Perry, ed., *Historical Collections Relating to the American Colonial Church* (Davenport, Iowa, 1870), IV, 306–307; Thomas Bacon, *Four Sermons, upon the Great and Indispensible Duty of All Christian Masters and Mistresses to Bring up Their Negro Slaves in the Knowledge and Fear of God* (London, 1750), v–vii.
44. Gutman, *Black Family in Slavery and Freedom*, 88–89; the current research of Gutman and Mary Beth Norton shows few cousin marriages on large plantations in the 18th century.
45. Carroll Account Book. If the previous residence of only one spouse could be determined, I

owned too few slaves, on too few quarters, to permit a wide choice of spouses within their plantations; furthermore, they could not afford to purchase the husband or wife. Inevitably, a majority of slave couples remained separated for much of their married life.

Marriage was far less important for slave women than for white women; slave women, unlike their white counterparts, neither shared property with their husbands nor received subsistence from them. After the relationship was consummated, the woman probably stayed with her family (parents and siblings) until a child was born, unless she could form a household with her new husband.[46] Childbearing, and the child rearing that followed, however, were highly important rites of passage for most slave women. Once she had a child, she moved from her mother's or parents' home to her own hut. The bonding between the slave mother and her child may have been far more important than her relationship with her husband, especially if he lived on another plantation. Motherhood, moreover, gave women a few valued privileges. Masters sometimes treated pregnant women and their newborn children with greater than usual solicitude. For example, Richard Corbin, a Virginia planter, insisted in 1759 that his steward be "Kind and Indulgent to pregnant women and not force them when with Child upon any service or hardship that will be injurious to them." Children were "to be well looked after."[47]

Marriage and parenthood brought less change in the lives of most men. Many continued to live with other men. Able to visit his family only at night or on holidays, the nonresident husband could play only a small role in child rearing. If husband and wife lived together, however, they established a household. The resident father helped raise his children, taught them skills, and tried to protect them from the master. Landon Carter

808

assumed that there was no change if the known spouse lived on the same quarter after marriage, but that there was a change if the known spouse lived on a different quarter. There were 5 unknowns in the 47 cases.

46. Of all marriages of slave women, 1720–1759, in Prince George's, 70% married before age 20 (see chap. 2). Many of these teenage girls should have been pregnant with their first children between 16 and 19. If they were living with their husbands, then their households would include only a husband and wife. On the three Maryland plantations analyzed in table 40, there were only three husband-wife households, and the women in them were 19, 27, and 56 years old. Of the women age 16–19, about a third were married: about one-half with children lived with sisters; the others about equally lived with husband, with husband and children, or without children separated from husband. Most unmarried lived with parents.

47. Deborah G. White, "Female Slaves: Sex Roles and Status in the Antebellum Plantation South," *Journal of Family History*, VIII (1983), 254–258, argues for the primacy of the mother-child bond over that of husbands and wives; the quoted passage is from William K. Scarborough, *The Overseer: Plantation Management in the Old South* (Baton Rouge, La., 1966), 183–184.

Fig. 29. *Age of Runaway Men in Maryland and Virginia.* Data centered at midpoint.

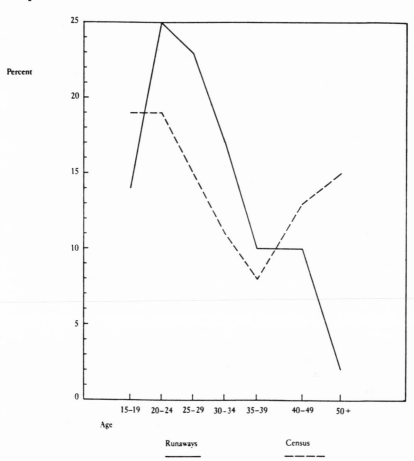

809

Sources: All runaway slave ads published in the *Maryland Gazette*, 1745–1779, and Dunlap's *Maryland Gazette*, 1775–1779 from Prince George's, Charles, Calvert, Frederick (south of Monocacy River), and Anne Arundel (south of Severn River, excluding Annapolis) counties, and any slave born in or traveling to those areas ($N = 72$); all runaway ads (men and women, but few women of reported age) from Virginia newspapers, 1730–1787, reported in Lathan Algerna Windley, "A Profile of Runaway Slaves in Virginia and South Carolina from 1730 through 1787" (Ph.D. diss., University of Iowa, 1974), 80; census for Prince George's County from Gaius Marcus Brumbaugh, ed., *Maryland Records: Colonial, Revolutionary, County, and Church, from Original Sources*, I (Baltimore, 1915), 1–88.

reacted violently when Manuel tried to help his daughter. "Manuel's Sarah, who pretended to be sick a week ago, and because I found nothing ailed her and would not let her lie up she run away above a week and was catched the night before last and locked up; but somebody broke open the door for her. It could be none but her father Manuel, and he I had whipped."[48]

On large plantations, mothers could call upon a wide variety of kin to help them raise their children: husbands, siblings, cousins, uncles, or aunts might be living in nearby huts. Peter Harbard learned from his grandmother, father, and paternal uncles how his grandmother's indentures were burned by Henry Darnall, a large planter in Prince George's County, and how she was forced into bondage. He "frequently heard his grandmother Ann Joice say that if she had her *just right that she ought to be free and all her children. He hath also heard his Uncles David Jones, John Wood, Thomas Crane,* and also his father Francis Harbard declare as much." Peter's desire for freedom, learned from his kinfolk, never left him. In 1748, he ran away twice toward Philadelphia and freedom. He was recaptured but later purchased his freedom.[49]

As Afro-Americans grew older, illness and lack of stamina cut into their productivity, and their kinfolk or masters had to provide for them. On rare occasions, masters granted special privileges to favored slaves. Landon Carter permitted Jack Lubbar and his wife "to live quite retired only under my constant kindness" during the last three years of his life, and after over half a century of service. When Thomas Clark died in 1766, he gave his son Charles "my faithful old Negro man Jack whom I desire may be used tenderly in his old age." Charles Ball's grandfather lived as an old man by himself away from the other slaves he disliked. Similarly, John Wood, Peter Harbard's uncle, was given his own cabin in his old age.[50]

Many old slaves progressed through several stages of downward mobility. Artisans and other skilled workers became common field hands. Although 10 percent of the men between forty and fifty-nine years of age were craftsmen in Prince George's, only 3 percent of men above sixty years of age held similar positions. Mulatto Ned, owned by Gabriel Parker of Calvert County, was a carpenter and cooper most of his life, but he had lost that job by 1750 when he was sixty-five. Abraham's status at Snowden's ironworks in Anne Arundel County changed from master founder to la-

810

48. Greene, ed., *Diary of Carter*, II, 777.
49. Court of Appeals of the Western Shore, BW#10 (1800–1801), 459–460; *Md. Gaz.*, Nov. 2, 1748.
50. Greene, ed., *Diary of Carter*, II, 840; Prince George's Original Wills, box 10, folder 35; Charles Ball, *Fifty Years in Chains*, ed. Philip S. Foner (New York, 1970 [orig. publ. as *Slavery in the United States: A Narrative of the Life and Adventures . . .* (New York, 1837)]), 21–22; Court of Appeals of the Western Shore, BW#10, 549 (1802).

borer when he could not work full time. As slaves became feeble, some masters refused to maintain them adequately or sold them to unwary buyers. An act passed by the Maryland assembly in 1752 complained that "sundry Persons in this Province have set disabled and superannuated Slaves free who have either perished through want or otherwise become a Burthen to others." The legislators uncovered a problem: in 1755, 20 percent of all the free Negroes in Maryland were "past labour or cripples," while only 2 percent of white men were in this category. To remedy the abuse, the assembly forbade manumission of slaves by will and insisted that masters feed and clothe their old and ill slaves. If slaveholders failed to comply, they could be fined four pounds for each offense.[51]   811

As Afro-American slaves moved from plantation to plantation through the life cycle, they left behind many friends and kinfolk and established relations with slaves on other plantations. And when young blacks married off their quarter, they gained kinfolk on other plantations. Both of these patterns can be illustrated from the Carroll plantations. Sam and Sue, who ived on Sam's quarter at Doohoregan Manor, had seven children between 1729 and 1751. In 1774, six of them were spread over four different quarters at Doohoregan: one son lived with his father (his mother had died); a daughter lived with her family in a hut near her father's; a son and daughter lived at Frost's; one son headed Moses' quarter; and a son lived at Riggs. Marriages increased the size and geographic spread of Fanny's relations (fig. 28). A third of the slaves who lived away from Riggs Quarter (the main plantation) were kin to Fanny or her descendants. Two of Kate's children married into Fanny's family; Kate and one son lived at Frost's, and another son lived at Jacob's. Cecilia, the daughter of Carpenter Harry and Sophia, married one of Fanny's grandchildren. Harry and Sophia lived with three of their children at Frost's, and two of their sons lived at Riggs, where they were learning to be wheelwrights with kinsperson Joe, son of Cooper Joe.[52]

Since husbands and wives, fathers and children, and friends and kinfolk were often physically separated, they had to devise ways of maintaining their close ties. At night and on Sundays and holidays, fathers and other kinfolk visited those family members who lived on other plantations. Fathers on occasion had regular visiting rights. Landon Carter's Guy, for instance, visited his wife (who lived on another quarter) every Monday eve-

---

51. Prince George's Inventories, 1730–1760 (age-skill data); Snowden Account Book, Private Accounts; Inventories, XLIII, 320; and Chancery Records, VII, 2–12, 25–34, 50–52, all at MHR; "Number of Inhabitants in Maryland," *Gentleman's Magazine, and Historical Chronicle,* XXXIV (1764), 261. For two examples of ill slaves sold from master to master, see *Maryland Journal, and the Baltimore Advertiser,* Sept. 28, 1779; and Chancery Records, XVI, 469–478 (1789).

52. Carroll Account Book.

ning.[53] These visits symbolized the solidarity of slave families and permitted kinfolk to renew their friendships but did not allow nonresident fathers to participate in the daily rearing of their children.

Even though this forced separation of husbands from wives and children from parents tore slave families apart, slaves managed to create kinship networks from this destruction. Slave society was characterized by hundreds of connected and interlocking kinship networks that stretched across many plantations. A slave who wanted to run away would find kinfolk, friends of kinfolk, or kinfolk of friends along his route willing to harbor him for a while. As kinship networks among Afro-American slaves grew ever larger, the proportion of runaways who were harbored for significant periods of time on slave quarters seems to have increased in both Maryland and Virginia.[54]

There were three different reasons for slaves to use this underground. Some blacks, like Harry—who left his master in 1779, stayed in the neighborhood for a few weeks, and then took off for Philadelphia—used their friends' and kinfolk's hospitality to reach freedom.[55] Others wanted to visit. About 27 percent of all runaways from southern Maryland mentioned in newspaper advertisements from 1745 to 1779 (and 54 percent of all those whose destinations were described by masters) ran away to visit. For example, Page traveled back and forth between Piscataway and South River in 1749, a distance of about forty miles, and was not caught. He must have received help from many quarters along his route. And in 1756, Kate, thirty years old, ran away from her master, who lived near Georgetown on the Potomac. She went to South River (about thirty miles distant), where she had formerly lived. Friends concealed her there. Her master feared that since "she had been a great Rambler, and is well known in *Calvert* and *Anne-Arundel* Counties, besides other Parts of the Country," Kate would "indulge herself a little in visiting her old Acquaintance," but spend most of time with her husband at West River.[56]

Indeed, 9 percent of the southern Maryland runaways left masters to

53. Greene, *Diary of Carter*, I, 329, 348, II, 648, 845, 1109–1110; *Md. Gaz.*, July 11, 1771.
54. Gerald W. Mullin, *Flight and Rebellion: Slave Resistance in Eighteenth-Century Virginia* (New York, 1972), 129 (*cf.* above, table 38), shows that the proportion of visitors increased from 29% before 1775 to 38% of all Virginia runaways whose destinations can be determined from 1776 to 1800. The major problem with the data is the large proportion of unknowns (52% in Maryland and 40% in Virginia).
55. *Md. Gaz.*, July 6, 1779. Other examples of slaves' using the underground to escape slavery are found there, Apr. 28, 1757, July 11, 1771. From 1745 to 1779, 9% of all Maryland runaways (32% of visitors) ran away to visit spouses; 4% (14%) visited other kinfolk; and 15% (54%) visited friends. Total number of visitors was 63 (of 233).
56. *Ibid.*, Oct. 4, 1749, Nov. 11, 1756; for other extensive kinship networks, see Aug. 11, 1751, Mar. 12, 1772, Jan. 30, May 22, 1777.

join their spouses. Sue and her child Jem, eighteen months old, went from Allen's Freshes to Port Tobacco, Charles County, a distance of about ten miles, "to go and see her Husband." Sam, age thirty, lived about thirty miles from his wife in Bryantown, Charles County, when he visited her in 1755. Will had to go more than a hundred miles, from Charles to Frederick County, to visit his wife, because her master had taken her from Will's neighborhood to a distant quarter.[57]

Slave families in the eighteenth-century Chesapeake were often unstable, but Afro-Americans learned to cope with displacement and separation from kindred with some success. Slaves created flexible kinship networks that permitted slaves to adjust to separation. Most slaves were either members of a kin-based household or could call upon kindred on their own or nearby quarters for aid and encouragement. A girl who grew up in a two-parent household on a large plantation, for instance, might be sold in her teens to a small planter, marry a slave from a neighboring farm, and raise her children with minimal help from her husband. She would have learned about alternative child-rearing methods from playmates whose fathers lived elsewhere and would have been familiar with the nocturnal movement of men to visit their families. Her husband's kindred could provide some help and friendship if they lived nearby. If she longed for her old home, she could run away and visit, knowing that kindred and friends would hide her from the whites.

813

In sum, slave kinship networks provided Afro-Americans with an alternative system of status and authority and thereby set outside limits to exploitation by the master. A slave had not only a place in the plantation work hierarchy, mostly determined by the master, but a position within his kin group. Slave culture and religion developed within this system: blacks participated as kindred at work and in song, dance, celebrations, prayer, and revivals at home.

57. *Ibid.*, Mar. 9, 1758, Feb. 6, 1755, Aug. 12, 1773; John Woolman claimed that husbands and wives were often separated. *The Journal of John Woolman* (1774; 1871 ed.) *and a Plea for the Poor* (1793; orig. publ. as *A Word of Caution and Remembrance to the Rich*), Corinth Books ed. (New York, 1961), 59.

Sarah Woodson Early:
19th Century Black Nationalist "Sister"

Ellen N. Lawson

The growing interest in Black history and Women's history in the 1970s has led some scholars to fuse these two fields to research a hitherto forgotten figure in American history—the black woman. A decade ago the *Journal of Civil War History* published an article on Lewis Woodson, "Father of Black Nationalism." Now his youngest sister, Sarah Jane Woodson, also a leader in this movement, merits scholarly attention.[1] One of the first black women college graduates, she was for many years an educator in black schools in antebellum Ohio, in Reconstruction North Carolina, and postwar Tennessee. Like most 19th century Americans, she was deeply religious and as the wife of a pioneer leader in the African Methodist Episcopal Church she actively worked for this first black church and insisted women's efforts be recognized within it. As Superintendent of the Colored Division of the Women's Christian Temperance Movement in the 1880s and 90s, she encouraged moral reform for blacks while helping to politicize black women.

Her life illustrates historian Leonard Sweet's observation, "Afro-American history in the 19th century is the struggle for integration into American life, not separation from it," where "black institutional separation was justified basically as a means to the end of integration."[2] Mrs. Early lived in black communities, worshipped in a black church, taught in a segregated school system, and organized black temperance unions but her ultimate goal was integration through black self-help and improvement of the social condition which (it was believed) would bring an end to white prejudice.

*   *   *   *

Sarah Jane Woodson was born November 15, 1825, in Chillicothe, Ohio, the youngest of the eleven children of Thomas and Jemimma (Riddle) Woodson who had emigrated from Greenbriar County, Virginia in 1820 in a wagon train which also included the Woodson family, the Leaches, and their kin. The Leaches and Woodsons were the only free black families in the county, according to the 1820 census, and this may have been a major reason for their emigration.[3]

Thomas Woodson was the son of a female slave and a white master. Woodson reportedly purchased his own and his family's freedom for $900 and was therefore penniless when they moved into Ohio.[4] They and their children are listed as mulattos on Virginia and Ohio censuses. Oral tradition within the Woodson family traces descent, through this Thomas Woodson, from Thomas Jefferson, third President of the United States, author of the Declaration of Independence, Virginia gentleman, and slaveowner, and from "the slave girl who was half-sister to Jefferson's dead wife."[5] Scholar Fawn Brodie contends Jefferson had a long-standing relationship with Sally Hemmings, slave and half-sister to his wife, following the death of his wife in the early 1780s. Hemmings was pregnant with a child while living with Jefferson when he was Minister to France in 1789 and a son, Thomas, was born in 1790, the same year as Thomas Woodson. (Brodie thinks it likely Woodson is this same child but she has not found conclusive documentation. If this oral history is true, then Sarah Woodson was the grandaughter of Jefferson and Hemmings.)

The Woodsons were very religious and immediately joined the Methodist Church in Chillicothe after they arrived in Ohio. But they and the other black families in the church objected to being seated separately in the Northern gallery apart from white members and to taking communion after the whites. As they saw it, "notwithstanding they contributed their share in supporting the ministers and defraying the contingent expenses of the church," they did not have equal rights.[6] In 1821, not long after their arrival, these black families organized their own black Methodist church, the first such church west of the Allegheny Mountains which later proved pivotal in the growth of the African Methodist Episcopal (A.M.E.) Church in the Midwest.

Three Woodsons (Lewis, Thomas, and John P.) were licensed ministers in the new A.M.E. Church in the 1820s and 1830s when Sarah was still a young child. Given the family's strong religious background and her own precocious nature, she could sing all the hymns in the Methodist hymnal at the age of three and could recite portions of the Bible from memory at five. The black Methodists of Chillicothe believed firmly in temperance, hard work, education, and plain dressing. The women wore no fancy jewels or dresses and the men were simply dressed, and these values were passed on to Sarah. Older brother Lewis began an African Education and Benefit Society in Chillicothe in 1827 when Sarah was two, which provided schooling for black children then excluded from the new public schools. Lewis soon married and moved to Pittsburgh and began a similar educational society there among the free black community where he taught in an early black school in which Martin Delaney was his pupil.

817

When Sarah Jane was five, her parents and a few other families separated themselves completely from white society by establishing an all-black farming community in Berlin Crossroads, Milton Township, Jackson County, Ohio where they had their own day school, Sunday school, and church, and where they helped each other become independent farmers. The community had twenty-three families by 1840, a decade after it was founded, and patriarch Thomas Woodson owned 400 acres and was worth several thousand dollars in real estate. (The settlement reached its zenith in 1860 and slowly died as the first generation of settlers died off or moved away.) In this black community, Sarah Jane Woodson grew up amidst self-sufficient black farmers who owned their own land, harvested their crops, helped each other build their homes, worshipped in their own church, and sent their children to school. A Cincinnati newspaper in 1842 observed how this community thrived and a neighboring white farmer was quoted as feeling these new black citizens cared more about schooling than local whites in the county. Lewis Woodson said the citizens of Berlin Crossroads were given great respect when they did business away from the town, greater than that accorded other free blacks. But *The Philanthropist* reporter noted they still "sometimes were treated with great injustice by whites."[7]

Lewis Woodson carried the belief in black separatism and self-help beyond the confines of this rural community into the urban moral reform community of antebellum Pittsburgh, describing this black town in Ohio as a place where blacks established an egalitarian society and could "thus free themselves from their traditional dependence on whites."[8] An integrated American Moral Reform Society was organized in the 1830s but Woodson was the first black member to urge a separate Moral Reform movement under black clergy in the A.M.E. Church.

Sarah Woodson absorbed these ideas of black nationalism and self-help from her parents and from her oldest brother. Her conversion and membership in the A.M.E. Church when she was 14 in 1839

was a significant event in a life marked by deep religious conviction. Jemimma Woodson was active in the church and Sarah later
listed her mother as an important church pioneer. Sarah observed
first-hand how women assisted at the large Methodist camp-
meetings which were essential to the religious revival in the 1830s.
She said women's practical work of feeding the hordes who came to
the campmeeting made it possible for these communicants then to
feed their souls "With the bread of eternal life from the sacred
altar."[9] And she never forgot Jerrina Lee, an effective A.M.E.
woman preacher who travelled through Pennsylvania, Ohio, and Indiana in Sarah's youth. One can speculate that the Woodson family
closely followed the debate over licensing women as ministers in
the A.M.E. Church at its General Conference in 1848. There were
"spirited discussions" where conservatives defended the exclusion
of women from the ministry asking "Shall the labors of a Paul, a
Silas, a Peter, a Luther, a Calvin, a Wesley, be trusted to the weaker
sex?"[10] Sarah Woodson's own study of the Bible taught her to revere
Lydia as a heroine who "prayed long" to be permitted to take an active role working for God.[11] Women lost this debate but with three
brothers in the ministry and models like Lydia, Jerrina Lee, and her
mother, it would be surprising if the thought of being a minister did
not once cross Sarah Woodson's youthful mind.

Speculations aside, the A.M.E. Church was important to the
Woodsons for non-religious reasons too. Lewis Woodson argued
that "prejudice against color" in white churches, many of which
supported slavery, dictated the need for a black church and clergy
"identified with ourselves."[12] Sarah Woodson also believed in the
political importance of the black Church too and praised it for doing "more to convince the world that colored men possessed in a
high degree the power of self-government, and that their hearts
swelled with the same love of liberty which animated the hearts of
the most noble of earth's sons."[13]

She left home in 1850 to study at the Albany Manual Labor
Academy in Southern Ohio as the A.M.E. Church had not yet
established an academy or college of its own but its leaders encouraged youth seeking education to consider Albany as it was an
integrated school in an integrated environment with "a social and
civil atmosphere in which the colored man can breathe equality
with others."[14] For advanced education, the few colleges congenial
to blacks were recommended by A.M.E. clergy and this included
Oberlin in northern Ohio. Sarah Woodson, accompanied by her
older sister Hannah, journeyed to Oberlin in 1852 to enroll in the
collegiate program while Hannah, despite a small seniority in age,
entered the Preparatory department at the college. Perhaps Sarah
brought along her older sister for emotional support. Albany
Academy may not have been advanced enough for Sarah although

818

it was probably sufficient as a preparatory school. The free black community in Pittsburgh sent several black men and women to Oberlin in the 1840s and the Woodson sisters may have heard of Oberlin through their brother Lewis in Pittsburgh. Many white Oberlin students taught in black and a few integrated private schools in southern Ohio during college vacations and perhaps they were the link which brought Sarah to college.

Oberlin College, like Albany Academy, was a congenial place for Sarah and Hannah Woodson as there was no discrimination by race in classrooms or boarding halls or in the single Congregational church in the town. But in a ten percent black town with a black student population of two to four percent, they were in the minority for the *first* time in their lives. The prevailing tone of Oberlin was one of evangelical moral reform and this was a climate they were familiar with from Berlin Crossroads. In this antebellum atmosphere of abolitionism, temperance, piety, and education, they probably felt quite at home.

Hannah stayed for only a year or two but Sarah remained four years and graduated in 1856. No records exist to indicate why she desired a degree in a time when few white males, not to mention women or Afro-Americans, desired a college education. As a naturally gifted person, she may simply have been thirsty for knowledge. Yet she did not leave home for college until she was 25, which suggests either that it took time to convince herself college was a viable goal or that she encountered family opposition as no one in her family had ever attended college. Her father, worth $15,000 according to the census, could have assisted her with tuition bills: his will shows he loaned her $100 in the 1850s on her inheritance which she may have borrowed for her education.[15] Sarah Woodson earned money teaching during vacations in black schools in Circleville and Portsmouth, Ohio, and this helped meet her college costs.

The year she graduated (1856) Lewis Woodson was named one of four black trustees (out of a total of 24 trustees) of the new black university established by Methodists in Xenia, Ohio, called Wilberforce after the famous English abolitionist.[16] In his church committee report that year, Lewis Woodson explained, "Advantages are opening for educational purposes among us, but we must prepare our minds to avail ourselves of these advantages; and if we cannot adorn our children's bodies with costly attire, let us provide to adorn their minds with that jewel that will elevate, ennoble, and rescue the bodies of our long injured race from the shackles of bondage, and their minds from the trammels of ignorance and vice."[17] Over the next decade (1856-66) his sister did her best to fulfill those educational aspirations stated by her brother by teaching in schools in black Ohio communities on the A.M.E. Circuits of Chillicothe, Gallipolis, Zanesville, Hillsboro, and Hamilton,

819

and occasionally returning to live with her aging parents and to teach in Berlin Crossroads.

In 1866, Woodson was appointed "Preceptress of English and Latin and Lady Principal and Matron" at Wilberforce University, which came under direct control of the A.M.E. Church in 1863 and gradually established itself as a college after beginning mainly at the secondary level. She could claim to be the *first* Afro-American woman to be on a college faculty. This was more than a decade after William Allen became first black male faculty member at short-lived McGrawville College in New York state, and it came a century before Woodson's alma mater (Oberlin) hired a black woman as a professor. It is significant in light of Woodson's black nationalism that this "first" for black women came at a coeducational black college (W.E.B. DuBois, as late as 1910, observed that only 20% of black college graduates were teaching at the college level and few of these were at white colleges or at black colleges controlled by white missionary societies like Fisk, etc.)[18] Although Sarah Woodson was not called "Professor" at Wilberforce this appears to be due to a lack of precedent for calling women by this title and does not reflect on her teaching level. A.M.E. records on Wilberforce's early years refer to the hiring of "competent professors" and then lists in order two male professors and "Miss Sarah J. Woodson." And one scholar later described her status at Wilberforce as a "Professorship."[19]

Woodson left Wilberforce after two years in 1868 to teach in a girls' school in Hillsboro, North Carolina financed by the Freedman's Bureau. Her white female predecessor at Wilberforce, another Oberlin graduate, had suffered a nervous breakdown after an incendiary burned college buildings in 1862 but this had not prevented Sarah Woodson from accepting the same post in 1866 nor did fears of danger now keep her from going south to help in Reconstruction. This work in North Carolina was "attended with danger and difficulty" yet her school was described in an official report as being "well classified, thoroughly disciplined, and the children making rapid progress in their studies and all that pertains to a well-ordered school life."[20]

This teaching career was interrupted in September 1868 when Woodson married Jordan Winston Early, a widower with several young children. She was then 43 and he, a decade older, was at the height of his career as a minister in the growing A.M.E. church-movement in the midwest and south. Born a slave in 1814, Early became free around 1826 when his family migrated from Virginia to St. Louis, Missouri where he became a Methodist at the age of twelve and joined the A.M.E. Church ten years later. Unlike his wife Sarah, Early was illiterate until he was 18 at which time he paid a Presbyterian minister from his earnings on a riverboat to teach him to read and paid a mate to teach him to write. He did not further his education beyond this. Licensed as a preacher in St. Louis in 1836, he began an A.M.E. Church there and started one in New Orleans at the mouth of the Mississippi in the deep south after that. He proceeded with caution because Nat Turner's Rebellion made it difficult for free blacks to be mobile or to organize a new black church which whites feared would be a breeding ground for similar rebellions. The A.M.E. Church paid tribute to work like Early's promoting the church in the slave south, saying, "These were perilous times, and none but men and women of brave hearts, true courage, and daring, were able to brook the terrible pressures of the law and public sentiment."[21]

821

During the first eighteen years of her marriage to Rev. Early, (lasting until his death in 1903), Mrs. Early continued to teach in black schools in Tennessee where her husband's churches were located: in Memphis (1869-72); Nashville (1872-75); Edgefield (1875-79); Nashville again (1880-84); Columbia (1884-85); and Nashville where they lived thereafter. By the time her husband retired in 1888, she had taught for several decades and was credited with instructing 6000 black children and with being principal of large black schools in four major cities. Marriage did not end her teaching career because she was dedicated to the profession, believing her principles of black self-help required her to give her first allegiance to black school children. She also married too late to have children of her own whose demands might have interrupted this career.

Although she was a dedicated educator, she also served ably as a minister's wife being familiar with the expectations for this role, having three brothers as ministers and her mother's churchwork in Berlin Crossroads as a model. Mrs. Early later described this role in the third person telling how she entered "fully into the work of the Gospel with him, assisting in all of his most arduous duties, and sharing most cheerfully with him all his hardships, deprivations, and toils." She always "assisted in superintending the Sabbath-schools when near enough to reach them; always attending and often leading the prayer meetings; and she took an active part in visiting the sick and administering to the wants of the poor and needy, and in raising money to defray the expenses of the Church, and served most heartily in its most laborious duties, and engaged extensively in its educational work."[22] She felt herself part of a strong tradition in the Church of active black women, saying in one speech: "In the early days of the Church, when its ministers were illiterate and humble, and her struggles with poverty and proscription were long and severe, it required perseverance and patience, and fortitude, and foresight, and labor, the women were ready, with their time, their talent, their influence, and their money, to dedicate all to the upbuilding of the church. No class of persons did more to solicit and bring in the people than they."[23]

While promoting her sex's emancipation, she would not detract from the accomplishments of pioneering black ministers like her husband. She observed, "It is certain that we have on record no class of men since the days of the Apostle, who having had no intellectual advantages or moral training, who have accomplished such notable work in the enlightenment and elevation and Christianizing of the people."[24] This is why she wrote and published a laudatory biography of her husband in 1894. Bishop Henry Turner of the A.M.E. Church and Rev. Early, who knew her, once observed how men active in the church, such as Rev. Early and Bishop Coppin, owed much of their success to having married highly educated women (Frances Jackson [Coppin] was an 1865 graduate of Oberlin).[25]

Sarah Woodson Early emerged from her role as local educator and minister's wife to assume a more public stance as a leader in the late 19th century temperance movement. She succeeded F.E.W. Harper as Superintendent of the Colored Division of the Women's Christian Temperance Union in 1888 and served until 1892. She was also spokesperson for the Prohibition Party in Tennessee. At the Chicago World's Fair in 1893 she was named Representative Woman of the World and was featured in two books published that year. Teaching and her church work had prepared her for this public career. She compared her religious efforts to "an open door by which to enter the arena of public action," observing how black women like herself had long "waited for moral and intellectual recognition from the world."[26]

Temperance was a natural place for her to direct her energies as it drew on her antebellum interest in Moral Reform (her brother Lewis was also active organizing blacks in their own moral reform groups).

The postbellum W.C.T.U. movement which began after the Civil War reflected both the growing importance of women in public life and a widespread concern for social control, through temperance, over the social disorder perceived by many to exist in the new large cities among new immigrants whose cultures included liquor and among the newly enfranchised southern freedman. As a southerner, Sarah Woodson Early was concerned with temperance among the freedmen but unlike white southerners her main interest was not social control but self-help, for she had long believed moral reform to be essential to the elevation of the race. In her report to the national W.C.T.U. in 1889, she listed extensive individual efforts to make black men and women in the south appreciate her temperance message. She visited 75 churches, 12 colleges, and 5 prisons, travelled in five southern states, covered 6000 miles, gave

130 lectures, talked privately with over 300 ministers and educators, wrote hundreds of pages on the subject, and spoke at two national church conferences. Temperance was essential, she said, "for the enlightenment of the masses and the education of the young," and "the good women of the W.C.T.U. have done much to bring the subject before the people, and in most instances our [black] women have laid hold and done all that their limited time and straightened circumstances would admit of."[27]

The W.C.T.U. was influential in the passage of the Prohibition Amendment in 1919 and in the politicization of conservative American women who came to see women's suffrage as essential to obtain their goal of temperance. Mrs. Early was not on record as part of the woman suffrage movement but she believed women ought to take a more public role and saw encouraging examples of this trend among black women. She said "Women of all lands should simultaneously see the necessity of taking a more exalted position, and assuming the more responsible duties of life with their favored brothers."[28] She credited black women as well as black men with being instrumental in organizing thousands of mutual aid societies to help the poor, the widowed, and orphans. "Our people have shown a self-confidence scarcely equalled by any other people; a refined sensibility in denying themselves the necessities of life to save thousands of children from want and adults from public charity in screening them from the stinging arrows of the tongue of slander and the carping criticism of a relentless foe," she said.[29] Black women's work in the Civil War assisting the wounded, while not publicized, led Early to point out how many joined the new Women's Relief Corps, auxiliary to the Grand Army of the Republic, the postwar veterans' lobby, working to assist children and wives of black veterans, decorating soldiers' graves on Memorial Day, and introducing the flag into black schools. Through their work in the W.C.T.U., black women like their white counterparts expanded their field of activity to include reform of hospitals and prisons and a movement for "social purity," meaning working against prostitution. The new organizational spirit among black women, she believed, had been good; by meeting, discussing public issues, and making decisions in their clubs and benefit societies, black women were "given hope for a better future by revealing to the colored women their own executive ability."[30]

Sarah Woodson Early's belief in the importance of black women organizing was shared by others and was reflected on the national level in the formation of the National Association of Colored Women in 1895. She was too old to assume a prominent role in this national society but her earlier work supporting Southern black women's local organizations helped sow the seeds for it. Black women formed their own national organization because they were

823

824

excluded from the new white women's club movement and from the woman suffrage movement in the late 19th century as white southern women exerted an increased influence within both movements. Mrs. Early's work within the predominantly white W.C.T.U. in this period is of interest as an effort to bridge the gap between the races within a third women's movement — not suffrage or clubs but for temperance. All her life she lived in black communities yet she had been educated in a white college with the same temperance environment she found in the W.C.T.U. So she was not unfamiliar with this milieu and her past experience may have given her confidence in her role as representative of black women in this largely white W.C.T.U. It is hard to know how she was received socially at the national conventions she attended since none of her private correspondence survives but it is clear from official records that she represented a separate division and was not listed as a delegate from Nashville, which had several white representatives, but was listed solely as Superintendent of Colored Work. Indicative of prejudice she may have encountered as a black woman in this organization is the reception given the single black woman member of a local W.C.T.U. in San Jose, California whose white chairman was sympathetic to her but could not refrain, in her report to the national convention in 1880 from admitting to a "nausea of the flesh, the baleful consciousness of the negro skin."[31]

Mrs. Early died in 1907 at the age of 83. Black contemporaries recognized her in several works written at this time including *Noted Negro Women* (1893), *Women of Distinction* (1893), and *Progression of the Race* (1907), but she nevertheless soon became a "forgotten" woman. Although she was an educator and principal of black schools in postwar Tennessee, a recent scholarly article on black education in that state contains no reference to her or to any black woman. Black history texts frequently mention the earliest black male faculty member, William Allen, whose career was recently featured in a journal article, but no mention is made of her role as the first black woman faculty member. Much attention has been paid to the W.C.T.U. movement and to its feminist head Frances Willard in Women's History but nothing has been said about Mrs. Early's work among black W.C.T.U. organizations and her claim, along with Frances Ellen Watkins Harper, to being the "Frances Willard" of the black women's temperance movement. Her career is a testimonial to her allegiance to racial self-help through the 19th century causes of education, religion, and moral reform. Like most black activists in that century, she believed that *condition* not *color* created prejudice: black separatism and self-help were seen as the best means to improve the condition of Afro-Americans, making integration into American life more likely in the future. Except for her college years and her work for temperance at the national level where she moved among like-minded white reformers, Early lived and worked within the black 19th century reform community by choice and conviction, part of a family heritage from the Woodsons of Berlin Crossroads. But sex made her experiences within this black reform community different from those of male leaders and the lessons she learned reflected this difference. Bishop Daniel Payne of the A.M.E. Church credited this church with proving "black manhood" but Early not only rejoiced in this fact but recounted women's role in the church and said this showed religious black women too could be "as strong as giants."[32] Male leaders in 1890 urged "young men of our race" to stay in high school and go to college and at the same time Early expressed in public her satisfaction that thousands of young black women were also studying in school and college.[33]

Sarah Woodson Early was a black feminist as well as a black nationalist but she was a feminist with a different agenda than contemporary white feminists like Susan Anthony or Lucy Stone. Early's concern was less with political rights than with elevating the black woman to the status of a "lady." In her talk on women's condition in the south in the 1890s, she said, "Hark! I hear the tramp of a million feet, and the sound of a million voices answer, we are coming to the front ranks of civilization and refinement."[34] Scholar Barbara Welters has described the 19th century ideal of the lady as including qualities of piety, purity, submissiveness, and domesticity. White feminists accepted the first two qualities but urged women to repudiate submissiveness and domesticity while remaining "ladies." Nineteenth century black women were perceived by whites, and often by black leaders as well, as immoral because slavery had debased them and supposedly left them impious, impure, overly assertive within the black family, and not domestic. Thus, the condition of slavery left black women lacking two essential qualities to be considered ladies while white feminists took this status for granted for themselves and sought a more assertive image in working for their rights. By her own example and her work within the black church and for temperance, Sarah Woodson Early helped elevate her sex to a pedestal that white feminists had abandoned. Yet by being quietly assertive and public in her role, Early showed she believed black women could be *both* ladies and feminists, but the first goal was the more important because it would lead to her long sought dream of ending prejudice by improving the condition of black women and, hence, of the race. Early was a black nationalist in leading and working with *black* Americans for self-improvement in the 19th century. But she was also a woman, a lady, whose work for the black woman gave her a feminist consciousness and made her a pioneering black "lady" *and* "sister."

FOOTNOTES

[1]Floyd Miller, "Father of Black Nationalism," *Civil War History* (December 1971).

[2]Leonard I. Sweet, *Black Images of America: 1784-1870* (New York: 1976), p. 5.

[3]We are indebted to Minnie Woodson of Washington, D.C. for providing genealogy information on the Woodson family in an unpublished manuscript "Woodson Source Book" (1975).

[4]*N.Y. Colored American,* 31 October 1840.

[5]See Fawn Brodie, "Thomas Jefferson's Unknown Grandchildren," *American Heritage,* 27 (October, 1976), p. 98.

[6]*History of Ross County,* p. 334, quoted in Woodson Source Book.

[7][Cincinnati] *Philanthropist,* 29 June 1842.

[8]Miller, op. cit., p. 315.

[9]S J.W. Early, "The Great Part Taken by Women of our West in our Development of the A.M.E. Church." in Scruggs, *Women of Distinction* (1893), p. 151.

[10]*History of Our A.M.E. Church,* pp. 300-301.

[11]Early, "Part Taken By Women," p. 152.

[12]Miller, op. cit., p. 313.

[13]S.J.W. Early, *Life & Labors of Rev. Early,* (1894), pp. 5-6.

[14]*History of A.M.E. Church,* p. 330.

[15]See 1860 Census for Berlin Crossroads and Woodson's will, written in 1859, in the "Woodson Source Book."

[16]Lewis Woodson donated $100 to the endowment of Wilberforce and perhaps Sarah Woodson borrowed on her inheritance in this amount to do likewise?

[17]*History of A.M.E. Church,* p. 404.

[18]Cynthia Griggs Flemming, "Plight of Black Education in Postwar Tennessee 1865-1920," *Journal of Negro History* (Fall 1979), p. 360.

[19]*History of A.M.E. Church,* p. 430 and Scruggs, *Women of Distinction,* p. 73.

[20]Scruggs, op. cit., p. 73, *Report of General Superintendent of Freedman's Bureau,* January 1, 1868, p. 25.

[21]*History of A.M.E. Church,* p. 34.

[22]Early, *Life & Labors of Rev. Early,* p. 161.

[23]Early, "Part Taken by Women" Scruggs, *Women of Distinction,* p. 150.

[24]. Early, *Life & Labors,* p. 6.

[25]We are grateful to Dr. Linda Perkins of the Bunting Institute for this reference in *The Christian Recorder,* 29 November 1888.

[26]Early, "Part Taken by Women," in Scruggs, op. cit., p. 149. We are indebted to Dr. Marcus Boulware for access to his unpublished Ms. chapters on two black temperance leaders, Early and Lucy Stanton Day Sessions.

[27]Early, *1894 report,* cited by Boulware in unpublished chapter on S.J.W. Early.

[28]*Ibid.*

[29]*Ibid.*

[30]*Ibid.*

[31]*Annual Report of W.C.T.U.,* 1880.

[32]Sweet, *Black Images,* 134 and Early, "Part Taken by Women," in Scruggs, op. cit.

[33]Flemming, op. cit., p. 359 and Early, 1894 report, op. cit.

[34]Report in Boulware's unpublished manuscript, op. cit.

Antebellum Black Coeds
at Oberlin College

ELLEN N. LAWSON
and MARLENE MERRILL

In January 1978, we began collecting information on the first black women students at Oberlin College from 1835 through 1865. The impetus for this project came from Professor Gerda Lerner who, on a visit to Oberlin, remarked that she suspected there was considerable material in the Oberlin College archives that could tell us a great deal about women who have been overlooked or ignored. We decided to do the work as a team. One of us had had some on-the-job archival training; and the other, a recent Ph.D. in 19th century American history, had taught women's history courses.

We began our work unprepared—we now realize in retrospect—for what was to happen as we began uncovering pieces of the individual lives of these early black women students and for what is still happening. We have begun to see Oberlin history in an entirely new way. Black women were an important part of Oberlin College more than a century ago, not merely peripheral additions to the established institution. These women were part of a dramatic period in Oberlin College history. Through this research we found we more fully understood this town, this college and American history.

The first black women at Oberlin College embraced opportunities there that were offered nowhere else. In doing so, they demonstrated special

Originally published in the *Oberlin Alumni Magazine*, Jan.-Feb. 1980, pages 18-21.

courage, conviction and faith—as did their families in supporting them, and the college in educating them. A common belief of the 19th century was that both Negroes and women had inferior intellects. For black women pioneering as college students, both sex and race worked against them. It seems likely that these early women pioneers would have agreed with later black women studying at Oberlin who said the difficulties they encountered as female members of a recently freed race only made their triumphs more sweet.[1]

828

Shortly after Oberlin's founding in 1833, trustees of the Oberlin Collegiate Institute agreed (1835) that "the education of people of color is a matter of great interest and should be encouraged & sustained in the Institution." There had been isolated instances of a few black men enrolling earlier at colleges like Bowdoin and Dartmouth; Oberlin was distinctive for stating its policy frankly. Despite the fact that black students constituted less than five percent of the student body, Carter Woodson, scholar of Afro-American history, wrote that Oberlin College "did so much for the education of Negroes before the Civil War that it was often spoken of as an institution for the education of people of color."[2]

Among Oberlin's early black students during the period 1835-1865 were at least 140 women. Most of them were students in the preparatory department, but 56 were enrolled either in the ladies' (literary) course or in the four-year bachelor of arts program occasionally referred to as "the gentleman's course."[3] Twelve black women completed the literary degree by 1865; three received the A.B. One black woman historian writes: "The first Negro women who entered college were venturesome indeed, considering the fact that their race was still enslaved and that they had no assurances about the future."[4]

The backgrounds of these early black female students appear to be quite different from those of their white sisters at Oberlin. Most of the latter came from the North—first from New England and New York, then from Ohio; black female students were as likely to come from the South as the North, and only a few came from the Northeast. (Oberlin's abolitionist network of friends often provided the contact between black students and the college; this was how they first heard of Oberlin.) Most white female students had rural backgrounds, while a large proportion of the black female students came from Cincinnati, Washington, D.C., Pittsburgh, or other cities. Finally, most white female students at Oberlin were far from wealthy; they found the learning and labor feature of their Oberlin education very welcome as a way

2

of meeting college costs. Several of the black female students, particularly those with white fathers or with fathers who were skilled craftsmen, came from wealthier families and perhaps had less need to work while at Oberlin than their white sisters did. The community of white women students at Oberlin before the Civil War may well have been more homogeneous than the community of black women students, who were diverse in origin, in status at birth (free or slave), and in degree of color (from light mulatto to African).[5]

One of the best-known black women Oberlin graduates was Frances Jackson (Coppin) who graduated in 1965. Her maternal grandfather, half-white, purchased his freedom and that of all his children except for Miss Jackson's mother (for some inexplicable reason). When Miss Jackson was born, therefore, she was a slave because her mother was a slave. Her Aunt Sarah Clark then purchased her freedom for $125 out of a monthly wage of six dollars. Miss Jackson later lived as a servant in the home of a wealthy New England family, where she was permitted to study one hour every other afternoon. Here she sufficiently prepared herself to enter Oberlin in 1860. Her aunt again came to her aid, this time with scholarship money to attend Oberlin.[6]

Her college years were busy ones: she studied Latin, Greek and higher mathematics; took private lessons in French; kept up on the piano and guitar; taught evening classes for freedmen who flocked to Oberlin during the war, and became the first black student to teach a class of preparatory students, both black and white, at Oberlin. Miss Jackson was enough of a rarity to feel, when she rose to recite in her Oberlin classes, that she had, as she put it, "the honor of the whole African race upon my shoulders. I felt that should I fail, it would be ascribed to the fact that I was colored." Occasionally in Oberlin she forgot about color, but her return to the East after graduation sharply brought home the fact that she belonged to a stigmatized race: a streetcar conductor refused her permission to ride in Philadelphia. Returning to Oberlin for a visit soon after this experience, she met Charles G. Finney, the evangelical leader of Oberlin, who asked her how she was growing in grace. She replied that she was growing, "as fast as the American people would let me."[7]

Miss Jackson claimed she had always, from childhood, wanted "to get an eduction and to teach my people." After graduation she worked in Philadelphia at a school which later became the Cheyney Training School for Teachers and is today called Cheyney State College.[8]

829

3

Also in Miss Jackson's class was Frances Jennie Norris who, like Miss Jackson, was born into slavery. Miss Norris' father was a white slaveholder in Rome, Ga., who never married. He saw to it that his daughter received adequate eduction to enter Oberlin in 1860. When he died, he left his fortune to her and this allowed her to develop a career as a businesswoman in Atlanta, specializing in both real estate and catering. Miss Norris was very light-skinned—so light that a friend once noted she could easily have "passed for white." She chose to return South after the Civil War and live her life among others of her race in Atlanta. There is no record that she ever married.[9]

830

It is unlikely that there were many pure African women in our sample. The only examples we definitely know of are Ann Hazle of North Carolina, who appears in a photograph of the class of 1855, and Sarah Kinson, whose African name was Margru and who was stolen from Mendi, Africa, and sold into slavery in Cuba in 1839. She was part of a shipload of slaves being transported from Havana to the other side of Cuba on a Spanish schooner, the *Amistad*, when the slaves on board rebelled and seized control of the ship. Two white navigators not killed in the uprising guided the ship into American waters instead of sailing it back to Africa as the rebels had demanded. The U. S. Navy seized the *Amistad* and imprisoned the rebels pending the outcome of a trial demanded by Spain, which claimed possession of the slaves. Abolitionists like Arthur and Lewis Tappan, funded the slaves' defense during the trial. Former President John Quincy Adams headed this defense. After 18 months the Supreme Court declared the Mendians free, and they sailed back to Africa, Miss Kinson among them.[10]

She returned to America in 1847 to be educated as a missionary. At Oberlin, she lived with a white family and did well in her studies. A fellow student remarked that Miss Kinson was "as black as black can be, and she is dignified, respected and loved. He hair is wool, and she is proud of Africa and is going back to it as soon as possible." She returned to Mendi in 1849.[11]

Unlike our first three examples, most Oberlin black coeds were freeborn. Among them was Mary Jane Patterson, the first black woman in the U. S. to receive the A. B.—in 1862, twenty years after the first white women had earned the A. B. (also at Oberlin) and 40 years after the first black man had earned the degree (at Bowdoin).

Miss Patterson, born in 1840 in North Carolina to Henry and Emeline Patterson, free Negroes, came to Oberlin as a child when her parents

4

migrated northward in the 1850's. Mr Patterson, a skilled mason, possessed $1,500 in real estate and $200 in property when he lived in Oberlin, according to the 1860 census. The oldest son, Henry, became a mason, too, but four of the Patterson children, including Mary Jane, graduated from Oberlin College in the 1860's and early 1870's. None of these remarkable Pattersons educated at Oberlin ever married. After leaving Oberlin, Mary Jane Patterson and her two sisters taught school in Washington, D.C., for children of their race. In 1870, Mary Jane Patterson was named principal of the first preparatory high school for colored youth in Washington, the predecessor of the famous Dunbar High School which has produced so many Negroes of educational achievement in its long history. Miss Patterson remained in charge of this high school "until the school increased numerically to such an extent that it was deemed advisable to place a male in charge."[12] Even then, she continued to teach there.

831

The four women mentioned thus far were either Southern-born or African-born. Blanche V. Harris was typical of Northern-born black coeds. One of five children, she spent her early years in Monroe, Mich., where her father was a carpenter. Since racial prejudice prevented her from entering a young ladies' seminary there, the entire family moved to Oberlin, where she entered the preparatory department and her younger siblings attended the Oberlin public schools. Three of the Harris children graduated from Oberlin: Blanche in 1860, Thomas in 1865 and Frankie (a sister) in 1870.[13]

During and after the Civil War, Miss Harris taught newly freed slaves in Mississippi, North Carolina and Kentucky in schools for freedmen run by the American Missionary Association.[14] In the 1870's, she returned to Oberlin as the wife of a black Oberlin graduate from the class of 1859. As it turned out, she was the first of several generations of black women in her family to attend Oberlin. Her daughter was one of the first women to graduate from the Conservatory in the 1890's and her granddaughter graduated from the college in 1926 and was one of the first Negro women to receive the Ph.D. Other early Oberlin black women also had children and grandchildren who attended Oberlin; this is a subject of research we have only just begun to explore.

The account of Blanche Harris' life reveals some important patterns that hold for many early black women at Oberlin. Both the town and the college provided unique opportunities for black families, especially those with daughters. By the mid-1850's, a growing and substantial black community existed in the town, with many families headed by skilled craftsmen—

carpenters, masons, harnessmakers, etc. The Oberlin census statistics for 1850 and 1860 indicate that these families provided homes not only for kin but for other black students attending the preparatory school and the college.

Oberlin's preparatory department, which Miss Harris attended, enrolled the largest number of students at any given time in these years. Of the 140 black women studying at Oberlin through 1865, 80 percent at some time were enrolled in the prep school. The department seems particularly important for black students and women students, who had fewer opportunities to obtain secondary eduction elsewhere—this would hold true in particular for black women students.[15]

832   Like Miss Harris, Marion Isabel Lewis, class of 1865, was also an eldest daughter—in this case, of a well-to-do blacksmith named William Lewis of Chattanooga, Tenn. Both she and her first husband, John Cook, Oberlin College '64, later taught at Howard University where he was dean of the law school. In trying to locate her papers, we contacted an 81-year-old nephew in Philadelphia who sent us reams of material and photographs of the Lewis family and added, "I hope this will help you in the Colored history of this country which very few know."[16]

A central theme of our research was the importance of the black family. A portrait of Belle Lewis's family, for example, taken in 1878, shows her mother, Jane, who was part Cherokee Indian, and her father, William, son of a white plantation owner. In tracing the family backgrounds of at least 20 of the 56 black coeds enrolled in this period, we found that half of them were from families like the Lewises: with both a mother and father, with the father working as a skilled tradesman. It is interesting to note, in the case of the Lewises, that the family chose to educate its daughters, sending three of them North to school, while the sons followed the father's trade and became blacksmiths and did not attend college. Further research is needed into the family backgrounds of other black coeds to see if there was more family support for education for the oldest daughter than for the oldest son. One explanation would be that education was preparation for the only respectable vocation open to both black and white women in the 19th century—teaching; sons could earn decent livings as skilled tradesmen following their fathers' trades.

We wonder if these families, by virtue of their histories, did not also simply value women more. In the Lewis family, it is worth noting that Mr. Lewis reputedly purchased his wife's freedom before his own! This meant that his children were born free and he did not have to buy the freedom of each in turn. The status of the wife, then, in this family, was important. Perhaps some of this appreciation carried over into the next generation of daughters and affected decisions and aspirations regarding higher education.[17]

Briefly, then, what can we say about early black women at Oberlin College? Although we are still in the midst of our research, we feel the few portraits presented suggest patterns that may persist as we collect more data. First, contrary to a commonly held stereotype, these black coeds were neither all runaway slaves funded by white abolitionists nor all illegitimate daughters of indulgent white slaveowners—although there were some of the latter in our sample. Second, nearly half of these coeds were from nuclear families that had sufficient income and status to afford and desire a college education for its daughters. Third, most of the students were light-skinned, which may have affected their reception at a predominantly white college.

833

No doubt these women were a special group—their experiences *not* typical of most black women in the South or in the North before the Civil War. On the other hand, because they were members of an oppressed race as well as an oppressed sex, their history is significant. It is the history of triumph over sexual and racial barriers—individual triumphs that, collectively, become part of the history of Oberlin College and this country. These early black women who left Oberlin as future mothers and teachers must have had a profound effect on the communities in which they later lived. The values they learned from their families and the college probably influenced the educational aspirations of their children and the larger number of black students so many of them taught. As new scholarship becomes available in black history and women's history, we hope to understand better the part these women played on a larger historical canvas—a canvas that will more fully reveal our collective past.

NOTES

1. Discussion of Mary Church Terrell, Dr. Anna J. Cooper and Mrs. Muflin Gibbs, *Washington Post*, 4 April 1952.
2. Carter Woodson, *Education of the Negro* (New York, 1915), p. 276.
3. The "ladies " degree was a four-year college course that did not require the study of ancient languages and higher mathematics.
4. Jeanne L. Noble, *Negro Women's College Education*, (New York, 1956), p. 20. Official college records did not identify students by race, but Rev. Henry Cowles, editor of the *Oberlin Evangelist*, in 1862 made a list of black students who had studied at the institution (in the preparatory school or college or

both) from memory. Although this list is incomplete, it numbers more than 200.

5. Robert S. Fletcher, *A History of Oberlin College* (Indianapolis, 1943), II, 508-510 has information on the geographical origin of all students at Oberlin in 1836, 1840, and 1860.

6. F.J. Coppin, *Reminiscences* (Philadelphia, 1913) and communication of Linda Perkins to Marlene Merrill, 21 Nov. 1978. Ms. Perkins' doctoral thesis (1978) is "Fanny Jackson Coppin and the Institute for Colored Youth: A Model of Nineteenth-Century Female Education and Community Leadership, 1857-1902."

7. Coppin, *Reminiscences*, p. 14.

8. *Ibid.*, p. 17.

9. E.H. Webster to Donald Love, 19 Nov. 1940, and M.B. Lukens to Oberlin College, 15 Oct. 1912, in Norris file, Alumni Records, Oberlin College.

10. Benjamin Quarles, *Black Abolitionists* (New York, 1969), pp. 76-78, and Fletcher, *Oberlin*, I, 260 have descriptions of the *Amistad* and "Margru."

11. Mattie Parmalee Rose, news clipping, 3 Jan. 1896, Archives, Oberlin College.

12. [Washington, D.C.] *Evening Sun*, 1894 (?), Patterson File, Alumni Records, Oberlin College.

13. For a description of the Harris sisters, see Majors, *Noted Negro Women* (1893), pp. 30-32 and 71-74.

14. Other Oberlin black coeds who taught the freedmen through the A.M.A. were Louisa Alexander, Sarah Stanley, Clara Duncan, Emma Brown and Mary J. Patterson.

15. Oberlin College maintains records, albeit incomplete, on preparatory students as well as college students.

16. William Lewis to Ellen Lawson, 13 Oct. 1978.

17. *Chattanooga Times*, 3 Sept. 1896.

834

BLACK WOMEN STUDENTS AT OBERLIN TO 1865
(Not including Preparatory Dept.)

A.B. Recipients or candidates

Evans, Elizabeth, 1862-64, North Carolina

Jackson, Frances M. (Coppin), A.B. 1865, Washington, D.C.

Mitchem, Georgina (Adams), 1856-58, Peoria, Ill.

Norris, Frances J., A.B. 1865, Rome, Ga.

Patterson, Mary Jane, A.B. 1862, North Carolina

Literary Degree Recipients

Alexander, Louise, Lit. '56, Mayslick, Ky.

Gloucester, Emma (White), '56, New York City

Harris, Blanche (Brooks/Jones), '60, Monroe, Mich.

Hazle, Ann, '55, New Berne, N.C.

Lewis, Marion I. (Cook/Howard), '65, Chattanooga, Tenn.

McFarland, Mary (Hayes), '64, Natchez, Miss.

Reid, Susan (Foster/Oliver), '60, Port Gibson, Miss.

Stanton, Lucy (Day/Sessions), '50, Cleveland, Ohio

Wall, Sarah K. (Fidler), '56, Richmond Co., N.C.

Waring, Maria (Baker/Williamson), '61, Pennsylvania

Williams, Frances (Clark), '53, Cincinnati

Woodson, Sarah J. (Early), '56, Chillicothe

Literary Degree Candidates

Alexander, Rachel

Alexander, Maria (Gibbs), Kentucky

Allen, Sarah, Chillicothe

Alston, Elizabeth, Raleigh, N.C.

Banks, Ellen, Detroit

Boyd, Maria, Cincinnati

Brown, Emma, Washington, D.C.

Chancellor, Ann, Chillicothe

Coburn, Jennie, Mississippi

Copeland, Laura (Avit), North Carolina

Darnes, Mary Ann and Josephine, Cincinnati

Davidson, Chorilla (Alston), Oberlin

Elliott, Rebecca, Cincinnati

Ferguson, Maria and Parthena, Cincinnati

Freeman, Amelia F., Pittsburgh

Freeman, Ada E., Brooklyn, N.Y.

Gilliam, Georgina, Sharpsburg, Pa.

Hazel, Elizabeth, New Berne, N.C.

Henderson, Eleanor, Zanesville, Ohio

Holman, Louisa, Louisville, Ky.

Huffman, Lucinda, Louisville, Ky.

Hunter, Harriet E., Indiana

Iredell, Sarah, Philadelphia

Jones, Matilda, Washington, D.C.

Kinson, Sarah ("Margru") (Green), Sierre Leone, Africa

Lewis, Mary Edmonia, New York

McGuire, Mahala (Gray), Oberlin??

Morgan, Rebecca (Cady), Illinois

Nesbit, Ophelia, Cincinnati

Peck, Louisa E., Pittsburgh

Randolph, Americus, Oberlin??

Sedden, Mary C., Cincinnati

Stanley, Sarah (Woodward), New Berne, N.C.

Thomas, Amanda (Wall), Oberlin??

Tilley, Virginia, Louisville, Ky.

Tinsely, Ann (Baltimore), Cincinnati

Tucker, Georgina, Brooklyn, N.Y.

Wall, Caroline (Langston), Richmond Co., N.C.

835

By BOGART R. LEASHORE

Black Female Workers: Live-in Domestics in Detroit, Michigan, 1860-1880

T HE PARTICIPATION of women in the labor force has attracted increasing attention from social scientists in recent years.[1] Attention to contemporary working women has resulted in efforts on the part of some historians, sociologists, and others to investigate and document the occupational history of women.[2] These historical studies not only afford recognition to the role(s) of working women, but also serve as a means for integrating the labor force participation of women into social history, which is ultimately made more complete.

The history of the labor force participation of women in the United States would be greatly lacking if research did not include investigations of black women as workers since historically they have participated in the labor force in large numbers. Illustrations of their participation can be cited throughout their history in America — from slavery to the present. For example, national data for the year 1890 show that the percentage of black women who were gainfully employed was more than twice that of white women. Furthermore, prior to 1940, black women were much more likely to be gainfully employed than white women.[3]

Although black and white women have made significant occupational gains over the last several decades, black women historically have been discriminated against in the labor force due to race and sex. For example, in 1910 and 1920, 32 percent and 40 percent respectively of the total number of women 16 years of age and over who were employed as domestic servants were black.[4] It seems clear that, at least from an historical perspective, domestic service for black women was rooted in racism, as well as in sexism.

837

---

[1] Works which address the labor force participation of women include Louise Howe, *Pink Collar Workers* (New York, 1976); James Sweet, *Women in the Labor Force* (New York, 1973); Ann Seidman (ed.), *Working Women: A Study of Women in Paid Jobs* (Boulder, Colorado, 1978); Walter Allen, "Family Roles, Occupational Statuses, and Achievement Orientations Among Black Women in the United States," *Signs: Journal of Women in Culture and Society* 4 (1979): 670-86; Valerie Oppenheimer, *The Female Labor Force in the United States: Demographic and Economic Factors Governing Its Growth and Changing Composition* (Berkeley, 1970).

[2] Claudia Goldin, "Female Labor Force Participation — The Origin of Black and White Differences, 1870 and 1880," *Journal of Economic History* 37 (March 1977): 87-108; Elizabeth Pleck, "A Mother's Wages: Income Earnings Among Married Italian and Black Women, 1896-1911," in Michael Gordon (ed), *The American Family in Social-Historical Perspective* (2nd ed., New York, 1978), pp. 490-510; Virginia Yans-McLaughlin, "A Flexible Tradition: South Italian Immigrants Confront a New York Experience," *Journal of Social History* 7 (Summer 1974): 442-45; Barbara Klaczynska, "Why Women Work: A Comparison of Unions Groups — Philadelphia, 1910-1930," *Labor History* 17 (Winter 1976): 73-87; Louise Tilly, "Urban Growth, Industrialization, and Women's Employment in Milan, Italy, 1881-1911," *Journal of Urban History* 3 (August 1977): 467-84. Bonnie Thornton Dill, " 'The Means to Put my children Through': Child-Rearing Goals and Strategies Among Black Female Domestic Servants," in La Frances Rodgers — Rose (ed.), *The Black Woman* (Beverly Hills: Sage Publications, 1980).

[3] Specifically, census data for 1890 show that 36 percent of black and 14 percent of white women 10 years old and over were gainfully employed (see U.S. Bureau of the Census, *The Social and Economic Status of the Black Population in the United States; An Historical View, 1790-1978* (Washington, D.C., 1979), Tables 43 and 44, pp. 66-67.

[4] Joseph Hill, *Women in Gainful Occupations 1870 to 1920* (U.S. Bureau of the Census, 1929), Table 83, p. 114.

Originally published in *Phylon*, Vol. XLV, No. 2 (June 1984).

However, the social science literature includes few studies of these women.[5] Furthermore, live-in domestic service, as distinct from live-out, has received little attention by social scientists.

Study Purpose and Data Source

This study focuses on black females who were live-in-domestic servants in white households in late nineteenth century Detroit, Michigan. It seeks to develop a socio-demographic profile of who these women were, as well as a profile of the white households in which they lived and worked.

Data used for this study were extracted from the United States decennial manuscript census for Detroit, Michigan in the years 1860, 1870, and 1880. The data were systematically collected for all members of any white household in which a black person resided. In determining who were the members of each household, census enumerators were instructed to include all persons who were considered members by the head of households, who usually slept in the house, and who considered it their home or usual place of residence whether present or temporarily absent. There were special instructions for enumerating students in schools away from home, men at sea, and men engaged in internal transportation occupations such as canal men and railroad men.[6] Only those blacks who were enumerated as members of white households and whose occupation was domestic service were extracted for the purposes of this study. Information was collected about all persons listed in each household, including name, race or color, sex, age, and place of birth.[7]

It should be noted that census items varied for each decennial census used in this study. For example, the census of 1860 and 1870, but not that of 1880, inquired as to value of real estate and personal assets. On the other hand, only the 1880 census inquired as to marital status and relationship to the head of household. Although each census included information about individual occupations, the 1870 and 1880 instructions for enumerators considered occupation as one of the most important items. For both of these censuses, enumerators were cautioned to avoid terms which were too general to indicate a definite occupation, e.g., *agent, collector, contractor, apprentice,* and *clerk.* They were urged to be as specific as possible, e.g., *bank clerk, apprenticed to carpenter,* and so forth.[8] With specific reference to domestic service, the instructions stated that:

838

---

[5] See Isabel Eaton's "Special Report on Negro Domestic Service," in W.E.B. Dubois, *The Philadelphia Negro* (New York, 1899); David Katzman, *Seven Days A Week: Women and Domestic Service in Industrializing America* (New York, 1978); Elizabeth Haynes, "Negroes in Domestic Service in the United States," *Journal of Negro History* 8 (October 1923): 384-442. Harriet E. Wilson (2nd ed., with Introduction and Notes by Henry Louis Gates, Jr.), *Our Nig; or, Sketches from the Life of a Free Black* (New York, 1983).
[6] Carrol Wright and William Hunt, *The History and Growth of the United States Census* (Washington, D.C., 1900), p. 151.
[7] Data for this study were extracted from a larger data set which consisted of all blacks enumerated in Detroit, Michigan for the decennial censuses of 1850, 1860, 1870, 1880. The author extends sincere appreciation to Dr. Richard A. English, University of Michigan at Ann Arbor, for the use of these data and to Mrs. Annette Alleyne-Dawson for assistance in preparing this manuscript.
[8] Wright and Hunt, op. cit., p. 92.

... The organization of domestic service has not proceeded so far in this country as to render it worth while to make distinction in the character of work. Report all as "domestic servants."[9]

The number of black male and female domestic servants who were enumerated in white households was as follows: seventy-four (74) in 1860, one hundred and sixteen (116) in 1870, and one hundred and sixty-nine (169) in 1880. During each of the three years studied, the majority of black live-in domestics was female. Table 1 indicates that in 1860, 82 percent of the black domestics living in white households were female, with 18 percent being male. In 1870 and 1880, 72 percent and 74 percent respectively were female, while 28 percent and 26 percent respectively were male.

TABLE 1   839

SEX OF BLACK DOMESTICS LIVING IN WHITE
HOUSEHOLDS: 1860-1880

Sex	1860		1870		1880	
	N	%	N	%	N	%
Female	61	82	83	72	123	74
Male	13	18	33	28	46	26
Total	74	100	116	100	169	100

As the data are limited to Detroit, findings cannot be generalized to other cities; however, comparative considerations will be made with related studies. It is also recognized that there are many inherent problems and limitations in the use of census data, e.g., inaccurate reporting and recording of information.[10] Nevertheless, such data can be an important source of information for research projects, especially those of a descriptive nature such as the present study. The section which follows is an overview of the social, political, and economic climate of Detroit during the late nineteenth century, particularly from a black/white perspective.

Late Nineteenth Century Detroit, Michigan

Prior to 1850, Americans emigrated to Detroit primarily from New York and New England. This was followed by a gradual influx of a variety of foreign-born ethnic groups, especially German and Irish.[11] As a relatively small town prior to the mid 1800s, the City of Detroit underwent a period of rapid growth between 1860 and 1880. Although the city's black population gradually increased during this period, it represented a very small proportion of the total population. Table 2 provides data regarding the black, white and total population of Detroit during the period 1850-1880.

The city's waterfront geography and railway transportation greatly facilitated Detroit's economic development as an important commercial, as well as manufacturing center. Prior to the emancipation of blacks, Detroit's geo-

[9] Ibid., pp. 159, 172.
[10] Henry Shryrock and Jacob Siegel, *The Methods and Materials of Demography*, Vol. I (Washington, D.C., 1973).
[11] Silas Farmer, *The History of Detroit and Michigan* (Detroit, 1884).

geographic proximity to the Canadian border made it an important station of
the "Underground Railroad," and runaway slaves were constantly routed
through the city. In addition, the Refuge Aid Society was organized in Detroit
to provide assistance to runaway slaves; the society operated from 1854 to
1872.[12]

Although residents of Detroit fought in the Civil War, the order for military
drafting was met with some disloyalty and intensified dislike for blacks, who
were the presumed cause of the War.[13] After the War, Michigan ratified the
13th, 14th, and 15th Amendments of the Constitution.[14] However, despite the
15th Amendment's provision recognizing the right of blacks to vote, they did
not do so with ease. Efforts to prevent blacks from voting were so great that in
1884 intervention was required from the federal government.[15]

840

TABLE 2

BLACK, WHITE, AND TOTAL POPULATION OF DETROIT 1850-1880

Year	White		Black		Total	
	N	%	N	%	N	%
1850	20,432	97	587	3	21,019	100
1860	44,216	97	1,403	3	45,619	100
1870	77,338	97	2,231	3	79,577	100
1880	113,475	98	2,821	2	116,340	100

Sources: *Seventh Census,* 1850, p. 896; *Eighth Census,* 1860, p. 246; *Ninth Census Compendium,* 1870, p. 229;
Tenth Census Compendium, 1880, p. 390.

Residentially, blacks were confined largely to the city's east side between
1860 and 1880. Throughout this period, at least 83 percent of all the blacks
lived on the east side.[16] Further, because a large number of blacks who had
been born in Kentucky lived on the east side, on and near Kentucky Street,
the area was commonly known as the Kentucky District.[17]

Economically, most blacks in late nineteenth century Detroit held low-
paying, unstable, and unskilled jobs. Professionally trained blacks experienced difficulty securing jobs comparable to their education or skills. It was
not until the turn of the century and the subsequent emergence of black
community development that the number of black white-collar workers
increased. It was not until World War I that blacks were employed by the
factories in Detroit. Between the Civil War and World War I, Detroit's largest
proportion of blacks was engaged in personal and domestic service.[18]

The economic, social, and political climate of nineteenth century Detroit
has been described as one embedded in prejudice and discrimination against
blacks. The caste-like structure of black-white relations was basically the

---

[12] Ibid.
[13] George Catlin, *The Story of Detroit* (Detroit, 1923).
[14] John Dancy, "The Negro People in Michigan," *Michigan History Magazine* 24 (Spring 1940): 221-40.
[15] David Katzman, *Before the Ghetto: Black Detroit in the Nineteenth Century* (Urbana, 1973), p. 102.
[16] Ibid., p. 67.
[17] Donald Deskins, *Residential Mobility of Negroes in Detroit, 1837-1965* (Ann Arbor, 1972), p. 103.
[18] Katzman, op. cit., pp. 106-07.

same as it had been prior to the Civil War. Other ethnic groups enjoyed the prosperity of an increasingly industrialized city while blacks on the whole were barred from sharing the same.[19]

Socio-Demographic Profile of Black
Domestics Living in White Households

As was indicated previously, in 1860-1880, the majority of blacks living in Detroit's white households as domestics was female. Analyses of age and sex showed that for each of the three years studied, the largest single age category for black female and male live-in domestics in white households was 15 to 19 years. Specifically, during each year, the percentages in this age category ranged from 26 percent to 40 percent. Further, in 1860, 56 percent of the black   841 female and 54 percent of the black male domestics living in white households were under 25 years old. In 1870, 65 percent of the black female and 55 percent of the black male domestics were under 25 years old; similarly, in 1880, 64 percent of the black females were in this age group while the black male percentage dropped to 43 percent. The age and sex distribution of black domestics living in white households are presented in Table 3, which follows.

TABLE 3

AGE BY SEX OF BLACK DOMESTICS LIVING IN
WHITE HOUSEHOLDS IN 1860-1880 DETROIT

Age	Sex and Census Year											
	1860				1870				1880			
	Female		Male		Female		Male		Female		Male	
	N	%	N	%	N	%	N	%	N	%	N	%
14 years and under ...	6	10	3	24	4	4	2	6	5	4	0	0
15-19	16	26	4	30	26	31	13	40	40	32	14	30
20-24	12	20	0	0	24	30	3	9	34	28	6	13
25-29	10	16	0	0	10	12	6	18	12	10	6	13
30-34	6	10	1	8	5	6	1	3	12	10	4	9
35-39	3	5	1	8	4	5	1	3	5	4	5	11
40 and over	8	13	4	30	10	12	7	21	15	12	11	24
Total	61	100	13	100	83	100	33	100	123	100	46	100

Analysis of data regarding the place of birth of black females living in white households as domestics indicated that in 1860 nearly two-thirds (n=61) were born in Kentucky (30%), Canada (16%), or Virginia (15%), with the remaining one-third born, for the most part, in Michigan, Ohio, New York, or Pennsylvania. In 1870, approximately two-thirds (n=83) were born in Canada (23%), Kentucky (17%), Virginia (15%), or Michigan (12%); the remaining one-third were from several states, including Ohio, Pennsylvania, Maryland and Missouri. By 1880, there were fewer Southern-born black females living as domestics in white households; i.e., nearly two-thirds (n=123) were born in Canada (37%), Michigan (18%), and Ohio (8%). Only 10

---

[19] Ibid., p. 211.

percent were born in Kentucky or Virginia. The remaining were born in several other states.

The Pre-Civil War census of 1860 enumerated most of the black live-in domestic servants as *servant;* the 1870 census enumerated most of them as *domestic*, while the 1880 census saw the return to the occupational title of *servant*. Examination of the total number of black females living as domestic servants in white households from 1860 to 1880 (n=267) revealed only 24 instances when the terms *domestic* or *servant* were not listed as the occupation. These 24 instances included: two cases where the term *housemaid* was used, one case of a *child's nurse*, four cases of the use of *house servant*, eight cases of the use of *hired servant*, and nine cases which used the term *cook*. It should be noted that the same occupational terms, i.e., *servant* or *domestic*, were used for most of the black male domestic servants enumerated in white households during 1860-1880.

842

The marital status of black females living in white households was analyzed for 1880 only because the 1860 and 1870 census did not include this as an item of inquiry. Data for 1880 indicated that the majority (78%) were single, 10 percent were married, nine percent were widowed; no marital status was reported for 3 percent of the women, and none was reported as divorced. Age-specific data revealed that the majority (56%) of the single females were between 18 and 25 years old, while 25 percent were 17 years of age or younger, and 19 percent were 26 years old or older. Most of the women who were widowed were 36 years of age or older, while the married were nearly equally distributed between the age ranges of 18 to 25 years and 26 to 35 years old.

Socio-Demographic Profile of White
Households with Live-in Black Domestics

The description of the white households in which blacks lived as domestic servants is based on the total number of these households enumerated, with no differentiation as to the sex of the black domestics. This has been done in view of the fact that most of the domestics were women, and some of the households had both a female and a male servant present.

These white households were located in nearly all of Detroit's municipal wards. However, the majority was located on the east side of the city in wards which had the heaviest concentration of blacks, i.e., wards 3,4,6, and 7. Specifically, in 1860, 51 percent (N=59) of the white households with black live-in domestics were located on the east side; in 1870, 54 percent (N=95), and in 1880, 56 percent (N=138) of these households were located on the east side of Detroit.

The mean size of the white households increased from 7.6 persons (SD=4.0168) in 1860 to 8.2 persons (SD=5.0459) in 1870. In 1880, the mean household size was 7.3 persons (SD=3.9304), the smallest size during the period studied. Although most of the households were headed by males, there was a continuous decrease in the proportion of these households. For example, in 1860, 92 percent were male-headed, while in 1870, 87 percent and in 1880,

79 percent were male-headed households. During each of the census years, approximately three-fourths of the white heads of households were 35 years of age or older.

In 1860, nearly half (47%) of the white heads of households were born in the State of New York, 24 percent were foreign-born, and the remaining 29 percent were born in other states. In 1870, 26 percent of the white heads of households were born in New York, 35 percent were foreign-born, 18 percent born in either Michigan or Ohio, and the remaining 21 percent in other states. By 1880, 37 percent of the heads of households were foreign-born, 23 percent was born in New York, 19 percent in Michigan, and the remaining 21 percent in other states.

The marital status of the white heads of households in 1880 indicated that 98 percent (n=109) of the male heads were married, while only 17 percent (n=29) of the female heads were married; 48 percent were widowed, 20 percent were single, and 14 percent were divorced. The majority of white male heads of households were engaged in trade, professional, and manufacturing/mechanical occupations. For the most part, the white female heads of households were not in the labor force, except for a few who themselves were in domestic or personal service.

843

In 1860, the majority (54%) (N=59) of the white heads of households did not report owning real estate. Among those heads who reported owning real estate (n=27) in this same year, the majority (60%) valued it as not more than $13,000, while 40 percent valued it as $20,000 or more. In 1870, approximately one-third (N=95) of the heads of households did not report owning real estate; among those who did, the majority (65%) owned real estate valued up to $19,000, while 35 percent owned real estate valued at $20,000 or more.

A much larger percentage (88%) (N=59) of the white heads of households reported owning personal property as compared with real estate in 1860. Of those who reported personal property, 67 percent valued this property at less than $4,000 but not greater than $15,000; 29 percent valued their property as more than $4,000 but not greater than $15,000, while the remaining 4 percent valued their personal property at $20,000 or more. Similarly, in 1870, 86 percent (N=95) of the white heads of households reported owning personal property. Of this group, 65 percent valued their property at less than $4,000, while 22 percent valued it as more than $4,000 but not greater than $15,000; 13 percent valued their personal property at $20,000 or more.

The 1860 census reported none of the white heads of households as unable to read and write. In 1870 only one of these heads was reported as unable to read and write, while in 1880 only one was reported as unable to write.

Discussion

Analyses of data regarding black domestic servants who lived in white households in Detroit in 1860-1880 revealed that the majority was young and single, as opposed to married females. When compared with the findings of other studies, black female live-in domestics in 1860-1880 Detroit were somewhat younger.[20] The preference for young single females as live-in domestic servants was indicated in a study which included information from employment agents in several cities throughout the United States, including Detroit, in the early 1900s. It was found that the agents objected to hiring married females because they took food from their employers to help feed their own families; their responsibilities to their own families frequently made them physically and mentally exhausted; and it was generally more problematic for them to live in the homes of their employers. The agents felt that the most desirable domestics were females between the ages of 20 and 25 years.[21]

In 1860 and 1870 Detroit, significant proportions of the black female live-in domestics were born in Kentucky and Virginia. It seems likely that many of these women had migrated to Detroit from the South in order to escape oppressive conditions encountered by blacks, particularly before the abolition of slavery. Furthermore, since significant proportions were born in Canada, it was likely that they were the children of blacks who had found their way to Canada in search of freedom. The decline in the number born in the South as reported by the 1880 census lends additional support to the idea of migration to the North to escape racial oppression in the South.

Although the majority of black domestics, both male and female, who lived in white households in 1860, 1870, and 1880 could read and write, there was a sharp decline for both groups in 1870. This post-Civil War decline may have been due to earlier migration from the South of blacks who had limited opportunities for learning to read and write during slavery.

Despite findings that the majority of black domestics could read and write in 1860-1880 Detroit, domestic service during the nineteenth century has been characterized as a verbal work agreement which generally specified wages, time off, and the areas of work to be done. Living conditions and other specifics were generally worked out on the job.[22] The lack of a more formalized agreement, as well as other factors such as race, sex, age, and the need to work doubtlessly contributed to the economic exploitation of many live-in domestic servants.

The white households in which black domestics resided in 1860-1880 Detroit were typically headed by white, married males who were generally 35 years of age or older. The majority of these heads of households were engaged in occupations which enhanced their ability to afford the services of a live-in domestic, i.e., trades, manufacturing/mechanical industries, and professional. The financial assets of these heads as reported by each census further suggested their ability to afford a live-in servant(s).

During each of the three years studied, the majority of the heads of households was born in New York or was foreign-born, despite a decline in the

844

---

[20] An exact comparison cannot be made with other studies because they include live-out domestics, who were generally older women; these studies also involve later time periods than the present study. See Dubois, op. cit., p. 438; Haynes, op. cit.
[21] Haynes, op. cit.
[22] Katzman, op. cit.

number born in New York over the period studied, and an increase in the number of foreign-born heads during the same period. Thus, the status and conditions of live-in domestic service as an occupation for black females during the period studied were maintained by non-Southern white males.

The continuous growth in the number of black female live-in domestic servants in late nineteenth century Detroit indicates active labor force participation by a group of relatively young females who were obviously willing to work. The limited opportunities for other types of work based on their race and sex seemingly left few occupational choices from which they could elect to work. Any appeal of live-in domestic service work was probably associated with the provision of housing accommodations, as well as wages. Furthermore, given their relative youth and migration from other areas, especially the South, live-in domestic service was perhaps a first major attempt at independence for many of these black women. Simultaneously, it served as a means for some not only to support themselves, but other family members as well. In addition, the experience of living with and providing services for white families probably made many aware of racial differences in the quality of life enjoyed by white families as compared to their own family of origin and other black families. Moreover, for some the exposure to and interactions with whites served as another vehicle for adjusting to and coping with economic, political, and social environments beyond the household which generally manifested negative attitudes and behaviors toward blacks in general. Indeed, the experience of being a live-in domestic servant may have fostered the ability of these women to adequately socialize their own children in later years for living in a society which would exemplify much hostility toward them based on race.

Conclusion

Although the limitations of the data used for this study preclude the emergence of extensive socio-demographic profiles of either black live-in domestic servants or the white households in which they lived and worked, several factors were discernible. Specifically, it was found that in 1860-1880 Detroit, the majority of black live-in domestic servants were young females who were not married. Further, it was found that in 1860 and 1870 a significant proportion of these women had migrated from Canada or Southern states, especially Kentucky and Virginia. However, in 1880 while there was also a sizeable number who had migrated from Canada, there were fewer, as compared with 1860 and 1870, who had migrated from the South. These changes may have been a consequence of the abolition of slavery.

During the census years studied, enumerators made few distinctions within the domestic service occupation among black live-in domestic servants; typically the occupation listed was either *domestic* or *servant*. Although the majority of black live-in domestics in 1860-1880 was reported as able to read and write, there was a significant drop in the proportion reported by the census of 1870. This decline in literacy may have been due to migration of Southern blacks with limited education. In the three years studied, black live-in domestic servants, for the most part, were reported as not owning real estate or personal property.

The majority of the white households in which black live-in domestics lived and worked in 1860-1880 Detroit was located on the east side of the city in wards which had the heaviest concentration of blacks. Thus, black live-in domestics were found in white households that were closest to the black community.

The average white household with a live-in black domestic servant consisted of at least seven persons in 1860-1880 Detroit. These households tended to be headed by white married males who were at least thirty-five years of age or older. During each of the years studied the majority of these heads of households were either born in New York or was foreign-born and was engaged in trade, manufacturing/mechanical, and professional occupations. Although the majority of the heads of households in 1860 did not report owning real estate, the majority did report owning personal property. In 1870, the majority reported owning both real estate and personal property. None of the heads was reported as unable to read or write in 1860, and only one in 1870 and 1880 was reported as unable to read and/or write.

The findings of this study do not provide a comprehensive picture of the black live-in domestic servants nor of the white households in which they resided. Further, these findings are limited to Detroit and the late nineteenth century, and therefore cannot be generalized to other times and places. Consequently, there remains a need for research on live-in, as well as live-out, domestic service in the United States. This research should include a host of cities, different time periods, and other ethnic groups. It should include attention to social forces which may have impacted on domestic service as an occupation, and on those who engaged in it.

846

FREE BLACK WOMEN AND THE QUESTION OF MATRIARCHY: PETERSBURG, VIRGINIA, 1784-1820

SUZANNE LEBSOCK

In 1853, Eliza Gallie, a middle-aged, free black woman of Petersburg, Virginia, was arrested and charged with stealing cabbages from the patch of Alexander Stevens, a white man. She was tried in Mayor's Court and sentenced to thirty-nine lashes. There was nothing unusual in this; free black women were frequently accused of petty crimes, and for free blacks, as for slaves, whipping was the punishment prescribed by law. What made the case a minor spectacle was that Eliza Gallie had resources, and she fought back. She filed an appeal immediately, and two weeks later she hired three of Petersburg's most eminent attorneys and one from Richmond as well. "If the Commonwealth, God bless her, has not met her match in Miss Liza," a local newspaper commented, "it won't be for lack of lawyers." The case came up in Hustings Court in March 1854. Gallie's lawyers argued first of all that her ancestors were of white and Indian blood and that she should therefore be tried as a white person. The court was unconvinced. On the trial's second day, her counsel argued that she was innocent of the theft. The court was again unconvinced. Gallie was pronounced guilty and sentenced to "twenty lashes on her bare back at the public whipping post . . . ." At first she set another appeal in motion, but deciding that the case was hopeless, Eliza Gallie dismissed her lawyers and took her punishment.[1]

Gallie's case was in many ways an unusual one, and yet her story cuts straight to the central contradiction in our common image of the historic black woman. Eliza Gallie was, relatively speaking, a powerful woman, propertied, autonomous (divorced, actually), and assertive. But she was helpless in the end, the victim of the kind of deliberate humiliation that for most of us is past im-

Feminist Studies 8, no. 2 (Summer 1982). © 1982 by Feminist Studies, Inc.

agining. So it is with our perception of the history of black women as a group. On the one hand, we have been told that black women, in slavery and afterward, were formidable people, "matriarchs" in fact. On the other hand, we know that all along, black women were dreadfully exploited. Rarely has so much power been attributed to so vulnerable a group.

The contradiction can be ironed out, with sufficient attention to definition and evidence. All the evidence used here comes from Petersburg, Virginia, and it comes mainly from the Petersburg of Eliza Gallie's youth, when the first generation out of slavery, the women emancipated in the wake of the American Revolution, established a pattern of female responsibility radically different from that prevailing among whites. Petersburg had fewer than seven thousand residents in 1820, but for its time and region, it was a city of some consequence. Flour milling, tobacco manufacture, and the commerce generated by the farmers of Southside Virginia sustained Petersburg's growth, while the horse races and the theater gave it touches of urban glitter. Only two cities in Virginia had larger populations, and no other Virginia town had a higher proportion of free blacks among its people. Before the statute of 1806 brought manumissions to a near standstill, Petersburg's free black population grew at a prodigious pace, its size swelled by a high rate of emancipation in the town itself and by the hundreds of migrants from the countryside who came in search of kin, work, and community. By 1810, there were over one thousand free blacks in Petersburg; nearly one-third of Petersburg's free people (31.2 percent) were black.[2]

Some definitions are called for. The term "matriarch" has been used in so many different ways that it has become almost useless as a descriptive term. But it should be understood that the word "matriarch" would never have been applied to black women in the first place were it not for our culture's touchiness over reduced male authority within the family. It is a telling fact that "matriarchy" has most often been used as a relative term. That is, women are called matriarchs when the power they exercise relative to men of their own group is in some respect greater than that defined as appropriate by the dominant culture. Given this standard, women need not be the equals of men, much less men's superiors, in order to qualify as matriarchs. The acquisition by women of just one commonly masculine prerogative will do, and hence it becomes possible to attribute matriarchal power to some of society's most disadvantaged people. The woman who had no

848

vote, no money, and no protection under the law was nonetheless a "matriarch," so long as she also had no husband present to compete with her for authority over her children.

Concern over the reduction of male authority has also been the touchstone of scholarship on black family life (relatively little has been written on the history of black women per se). For all the disagreements among scholars on the character of the historic black family, it has been assumed on almost all sides that female-headed families are, and were, pathological. There were two key assertions in the classic thesis advanced by E. Franklin Frazier four decades ago and revived in 1965 in the Moynihan Report. First, as a result of slavery and continued discrimination, an alarming proportion of black families were "matriarchal," that is, the husband/father was either absent or (Frazier added) he was present, but of negligible influence. Second, the woman-dominant family was unstable and disorganized, at once the symptom and cause of severe social pathology among black people.[3] The Frazier-Moynihan thesis came under heavy fire in the 1970s when scholars began to check the matriarchy image for historical accuracy. And yet the historians, too, reinforced the prevailing prejudice against female-headed households. Working for the most part with census data from the second half of the nineteenth century, several historians found that female-headed households were outnumbered by two-parent households. This, along with additional evidence of the statistical insignificance of the woman-headed household, was offered in defense of the Afro-American family: Black families were not generally matriarchal/matrifocal/female-headed (the term varies), therefore they were not disorganized, unstable, or otherwise pathological after all.[4]

This is a dangerous line of defense, and its problems are highlighted when we encounter evidence like that for early Petersburg. Here was a town in which well over half of the free black households were headed by women. Shall we therefore label it a nest of social sickness? It would make better sense to disentangle our evidence from conventional, androcentric value judgments on what is healthy and what is not.

For the time being, it would seem wise to set aside the issue of the integrity of black family life (by what standard, after all, are we to judge it?) and to concentrate instead on the impact of racial oppression on the status of women and on the distribution of power between the sexes. When we do this for Petersburg, we are confronted once again with the dual image of strength and ex-

849

ploitation. Women were prominent among Petersburg's free blacks. They outnumbered the men three to two, they headed more than half of the town's free black households, and they constituted a large segment of the paid labor force of free blacks. Yet this was for the most part the product of wretched poverty and persistent discrimination. The "matriarch" and the victim, it turns out, were usually the same woman.

Still, the fact remains that among free blacks there was less inequality between the sexes than there was among whites; when black women of the present say they have always been liberated, they have a point. Among those free blacks who managed to accumulate property in early Petersburg, a high proportion — about 40 percent — were women. And because they were more likely than their white counterparts to refrain from legal marriage, free black women were more likely to retain legal control over whatever property they did acquire. It may well have been that free black women valued their relative equality and did their best to maintain it.

How all this came to be is not entirely clear, for census data are sketchy, measures of wealth are crude, evidence on the occupational structure is thin, and vital records do not exist. It seems likely, however, that the preponderance of women in the free black population began with the cumulative decisions of emancipators: Women slaves stood the better chance. Before the Virginia legislature tied the hands of would-be emancipators in 1806, 173 slaves were manumitted in Petersburg.[5] Ninety-four of them (54.3 percent) were female. Of the manumitted adults, meanwhile, 59.3 percent (54 of 91) were female. Sexual intimacy, antislavery principle, and economic calculation could all have been responsible for women's easier access to emancipation.

That a number of manumissions resulted from sexual unions would seem to be a good bet for a town full of well-to-do bachelors, many of whom were a long way from home. Documentable cases, however, are few. Only one white emancipator was known to have acknowledged his kinship with his former slaves, and in only two instances is there strong circumstantial evidence of a sexual connection. In 1814, Mary Moore, a "great, large, fat, bouncing-looking" Irish woman, manumitted Sylvia Jeffers, as she was authorized to do by the will of her late brother John Jeffers. Sylvia was apparently John's daughter; in any case, in 1853 she talked the local court into escorting her across the color line, claiming descent from Indians and whites only.[6] Betsy Atkinson, too, won the special affection of her owner. A week after James Gibbon freed her, he wrote his last will. To Atkinson, he left a slave and furniture already in her possession, some livestock, and three hundred dollars.[7]

Anti-slavery principle may also have accounted for the women's edge in emancipation. Under Virginia law, the child inherited the status of the mother. To free a man, therefore, was to guarantee the freedom of but one person. The emancipation of a woman in her childbearing years might secure the freedom of generations.[8]

In the short run, meanwhile, the emancipation of a woman   851
meant a lesser loss of income for the owner. Women suffered a distinct disadvantage in earning power, a disadvantage that began in slavery and that showed in the inability of slave women to purchase themselves. Hiring oneself out was illegal, but both women and men did it, and most of them got away with it.[9] The women who hired themselves out did not, however, command wages equivalent to those of men, or so it appears from the incidence of self-purchase. Self-purchase was uncommon in this period; from 1784 to 1820, just nine of the two hundred slaves emancipated bought themselves. Amy Jackson, who paid her master $410 in 1819, was the sole woman among them.[10]

The same disparity in earning power limited the numbers of slaves whom emancipated women managed to free in turn. Altogether, free blacks themselves were responsible for thirty-three manumissions (one-sixth of the total to 1820), and although about one-half of the black emancipators were women (7 of 15), no woman was able to liberate more than one slave. Graham Bell showed what could be done with a remunerative skill (shoemaking), hard work, and business sense. In 1792, Bell set free his wife, or possibly his daughter, and five sons. From 1801 to 1805, he emancipated his brother, two women, one of whom he had purchased "for the express purpose of manumitting or emancipating her," and a child.[11] No one else came near Bell's record, but four of the other men did manumit at least two slaves. In the years after 1820, several women would join the ranks of the multiple emancipators. Meantime, one apiece was the best they could do.[12]

Emancipation was itself a step up on the economic ladder; the woman at last owned her person and her labor. In Petersburg, she was not likely to own anything else, not in the beginning anyhow. White emancipators expected their former slaves to fend for themselves. James Campbell made it explicit in 1802 when he freed forty-two-year-old Sally, "whom I have reason to believe is an honest woman, and one that will earn by her labour a proper support for herself."[13] A few emancipators may have granted their former slaves some kind of economic assistance, but in only one deed was something promised in writing. Persons manumitted by will did not fare much better. Of the twenty-seven slaves whose freedom was directed by will, only four were staked by their masters, and three of the four were men.[14]

The emancipators no doubt believed they were giving their former slaves an even chance. Given the circumstances under which many of the women were freed, however, making a living would be an uphill struggle. Some emancipators freed the children with the mother, and while this spared the women from trying to save to buy their children (and from the pain of being unable to save enough), it did mean extra mouths to be fed. Most of these women had one child or two, but three or four or five was not unusual.[15] Age was important as well. The emancipators who stipulated the ages of the persons they freed were too few to provide a reliable sample, but the ages that were recorded suggest that relative to the men, the women were disproportionately middle-aged. A large proportion of the women set free were, or would soon be, past their best wage-earning years.

TABLE 1.   AGE AT EMANCIPATION

Age	Women	Men
18-30	9	4
31-40	1	4
41-50	8	2
51 and up	0	1

The most significant handicap, however, was the near absence of occupational options. The vast majority of free black women engaged in domestic employment of one kind or another. This was not a matter of choice, and it was more a matter of sex than of race. Nothing made the women's occupational bind plainer than the apprenticeship orders issued by the court for free black children. Among the masters who took on free black boys as apprentices were a carpenter, a cabinetmaker, a painter, a cooper, a barber, a blacksmith, a hatter, a boatman, and a baker. So limited were the girls' options that the clerk hardly ever wasted ink on

specifying the trade. The few specific orders contained no sur-
prises. In 1801, Lucy Cook was ordered bound "to learn the
business of a Seamstress & Washer." On the same day Polly Flood
was "bound to Abby Cook, to learn to Sew & Wash &c untill of
lawful age — being now about 9 years of age." Polly was bound
to a second master "to learn Household business" five years later.
And Polly White, an orphan just five years old, was apprenticed
"to Mrs. Brewer to learn the duties of a House Servant."[16]

There were some women who broke the mold and engaged, at
least part time, in more specialized occupations. Betty Morris and
Aggy Jackson were nurses, Judy Denby and Judy Darvels were
midwives. A few engaged in legitimate commerce. Amelia Gallé
ran a bath house, Lurany Butler operated a dray, Nelly White was
a baker, and Elizabeth Allerque and Sarah Elliott were licensed
storekeepers.[17] As with white women, just as many pursued illegitimate commerce. At least five black women were nabbed by
the Petersburg Grand Jury for keeping a "tippling house" or for
selling liquor without a license.[18] The fact that specific occupations can be identified for only a dozen black women is testimony
to the predominance of domestics among them. Cooks, cleaning
women, washerwomen, seamstresses, and child-nurturers did not
advertise, nor were they likely to surface in any of the public
records.[19]

If the gentlemen of the Grand Jury had been asked, they would
probably have identified prostitution as a major enterprise of free
black women. In 1804, the Grand Jury registered a grievance
against the invasion of free black "strangers," many of whom
"come only for the purpose of Prostitution . . . ."[20] There is no
telling whether or how often free black women in fact resorted to
prostitution, but the Grand Jury was right about the invasion.
Dismal as economic opportunities were in Petersburg, they were
apparently worse in the countryside, particularly for women.
Black migration from the country was thus spearheaded by
women. By 1820, the sex ratio among free blacks aged fourteen
and above was 85.0 (males per 100 females) for eastern Virginia as
a whole. In Petersburg it was 64.5.[21]

Petersburg was, relatively speaking, a land of opportunity, and
a few of the women emancipated there did register gains. Betty
Call was freed on Independence Day, 1786, and within four years
she managed to buy her grown son, London, from an Amelia
County owner. After ten years, she set him free. Betty Call never
did own any real estate, but she was taxed on a female slave

853

(evidently hired) for years, and when she died in 1815, the sale of her household goods netted just over seventy dollars.[22] Emancipated on the same day as her mother, Teresa Call saved for nine years. In 1795, she purchased a small lot and continued to live there for decades.[23] Dolly Clark acquired a female slave five years after her manumission. On the other hand, women like Nancy Hall and Sally Steward accumulated no traceable property. Emancipated in 1799 and 1805, respectively, their continued residence in Petersburg was confirmed by entries in various public record books, but neither of them owned the land or slaves or horses or carriages that would have resulted in their appearance on the tax lists.[24]

New arrivals fared worse than the natives. Only nine free black women were among the town's taxpayers in 1810, and most of them were old-timers. All but one had lived in Petersburg as free women for at least six years. Betty and Teresa Call had both been free for twenty-four years, while Sarah Vaughan held the record for longevity on the tax lists. Vaughan owned real estate when Petersburg's first land tax book was assembled in 1788, and thirty years later she still held, and presumably rented out, her "4 small tenements."[25] On the average, the nine women had been paying taxes for almost nine years, and they held on to what they had. In the decade after 1810 three of them died, but the remaining six, all landowners, were still paying real estate taxes in 1820.

By that time they had more company. In 1820, there were thirty-eight free black women among the taxpayers. However one chooses to measure it, this was an impressive relative increase. In 1810, black women constituted but 2.2 percent of (9 of 413) of the town's taxpayers. In 1820, their proportion was 5.5 percent (38 of 687). The increase is not attributable to any relative growth in the free black female population. A count of the percentage of taxpayers among heads of families does help control for possible population shifts; similarly, it indicates a doubling of property holding among free black women. In 1810, 5.1 percent (7 of 138) of the black women designated as heads of families in the census schedules were also listed in the tax books; by 1820, the proportion had risen to 10.1 percent (17 of 168). All in all, blacks were gaining on whites, women were gaining on men, and black women were gaining on black men.[26]

At least three developments accounted for the sudden economic ascent of a portion of the free black female population. With the deaths of propertied men, a few black women claimed

854

their inheritances. More important were the hard-won savings of the women themselves. And third, it looks very much as though the Panic of 1819 forced slaveholders to put their slaves on the market at prices more women could afford.

Among the black female taxpayers of 1810, only Molly James had acquired her property by inheritance. James was the heir to the house and lot her husband had owned at his death in 1804. By 1820, two more legacies marked the passing of the first generation of prosperous black men. Graham Bell in 1817 left to his wife, Mary, a life estate in one of his town lots, while Elizabeth Graves was daughter and one of two surviving heirs of Richmond Graves, a livery stable operator.[27] Mary Ann Vizonneau and Amelia Gallé, meanwhile, were heirs of white merchants. Vizonneau's Scottish father, John Stewart, had threatened to disown her when she married Andre Thomas Vizonneau. But moments before his death in 1813, Stewart relented and directed that Mary Ann be given "all the money he then had in the Bank and the house & Lot he then lived on," on the condition "that her husband . . . might have no manner of Controul over, or right, to the same." This was a considerable bequest, worth over eighteen thousand dollars, and it made Mary Ann Vizonneau one of the wealthiest women in Petersburg.[28]

855

Amelia Gallé was also the heir of a white merchant. She had earned her inheritance. Amelia Gallé was still a slave when she first arrived in Petersburg, and she was known by a slave name, Milly Cassurier. In 1800, French merchant Jean Gallé bought her for eighty pounds, and he emancipated her four years later, after she had borne him a son. Jean Gallé died in 1819, and while in his will he termed Milly "my housekeeper," it was clear from the provisions of the will that she had been his wife in every sense but the legal one. He acknowledged her son Joseph as his natural son. He left to the two of them the greater part of his estate. And he enjoined Milly to act as mother to his "mulatto Girl slave" Catherine Gregory, charging her "to support the said Catherine and bring her up to lead a moral and religious life.[29]

Jean Gallé also left to Milly Cassurier his bathhouse, a business she had apparently been running for years. When she assumed sole management of the bathhouse in the spring of 1820, she became the first black businesswoman in Petersburg to exploit the full possibilities of newspaper advertising. At first she settled for a two-sentence announcement that the bathing season had arrived. By midsummer, however, her appeal was more effusive.

The character of this bath, is so well known that it needs no comment. The subscriber is resolved if possible to improve it, by consulting the comfort and convenience of the visitants — and to enable her to do so more effectually, she humbly solicits a continuation of that patronage which has so liberally supported the institution till this time. Having had several years experience in this business, the subscriber believes she will generally succeed in pleasing — and therefore, with stronger confidence humbly solicits a portion of the public support . . . .

For several years thereafter, she opened the season with just a brief announcement. Two or three months later, as the heat of the Virginia summer grew tediously oppressive, she would follow with greater fanfare. "She has the pleasure of tendering to her patrons," came the notice of May 1823, "her most grateful thanks for their former encouragement, and begs a continuance of the same." August brought the harder sell.

856

HEALTH
Purchased Cheap!

In consequence of *Small Change* being scarce, and wishing to contribute towards the health of the ladies and gentlemen, the subscriber has the pleasure to inform her patrons and the public, that she has reduced the price of her baths to 25 CENTS for a single one. She will make no comments on the necessity of Bathing in warm weather: — suffice it to say, that with Mr. Rambaut's FAMILY MEDICINES, and some Cold or Warm BATHS, the health of her friends will keep at a proper degree of the thermometer, without the aid of Calomel or any other mineral Medicines.[30]

These advertisements were not just a means of drumming up business. They were also the means by which a free black claimed for herself the respect due a propertied widow. In her first advertisement, she signed herself "Milly Cassurier." In the second, she was "Milly Galle." She signed the third "Amelia Galle." In the fourth, she was "Amelia Galle, widow." How far others accorded her the respect she asked for is an open question. She made some progress with the census taker, who listed her as "Milly Gallie," but to the tax collector she was still Cassurier, "col[d] at Galle's."[31]

Amelia Galle, Mary Ann Vizonneau, Elizabeth Graves, and Mary Bell were the only black female taxpayers of 1820 whose property was (documentably) acquired by inheritance. More significant was the economic maturation of the women themselves, and here the foremost success story belonged to Elizabeth Allerque. "Madame Betsy," she was called, "a French colored woman" who was probably a refugee from St. Dominigue She was, in any case, well connected with Petersburg's French immigrant community, and the connections in combination with her commercial talent spelled steady financial progress. Allerque first opened a store in 1801. At some point she added a partnership with French merchant André Vizonneau (Mary Ann Vizonneau's father-in-law), who in 1809 made sure that Allerque would be paid her full share of the proceeds when the firm was dissolved by his death: "I declare that the partnership which I had entered into with Elizabeth Alergues was joint and equal both as to capital and profit . . . ." Five years later, French physician L. J. Hoisnard wrote his will, charging Allerque with the care and legal guardianship of his daughter. Moreover, "in consideration of her good attention to me during the latter part of my life," Hoisnard left to Allerque and her two children a legacy of a thousand dollars.[32] Even without this bequest, Elizabeth Allerque would have done well for herself. She first invested in real estate in 1806 and improved it several times thereafter. In 1806, too, she became a slaveholder for the first time. Allerque was one of Petersburg's few black commercial slaveholders; in 1806 she advertised in the Richmond and Norfolk newspapers for the return of her runaway woman Charlotte. Madame Betsy died in 1824, free of debt and the owner of land and six slaves.[33]

Most free black women had neither the skills nor the connections of an Elizabeth Allerque, but a few had enough savings to take advantage of the Panic of 1819. While the general economic dislocation that surrounded the Panic must have caused great suffering among many black women, it also afforded the better-placed the opportunity to hire or purchase slaves for the first time. (The tax lists, unhappily, do not indicate whether the taxpayer owned or hired the slave.)[34] As more and more whites scrambled to find the money to pay their debts, more and more slaves were put up for hire or sale, and probably at bargain prices. There is no estimating just how many slaves changed hands during the Panic years. In 1819 and 1820 alone, however, Petersburg owners mortgaged over 240 slaves; these slaves would be sold at auction for whatever they would bring if the owners failed to pay their creditors on schedule.[35]

For the master class the time was unnerving, for the slaves it was potentially disastrous, but for the free black woman with some savings, here was a rare opportunity, a chance to acquire a loved one or a laborer. Three-quarters of the black women taxed

857

in 1820 (27 of 38) made their debuts on the tax lists in 1819 or
1820. And all but two of the newcomers were taxed on one or
more slaves.

It was in slaveholding that black women registered their
greatest gains by 1820 and in slaveholding that they came closest
to economic parity with black men. In 1820, forty-six slaves were
held by black men, forty-five by the women. Women were farther from equality in other measures of the black sex ratio of
wealth, but they were gaining on the men. Two-fifths (13 of 32)
of the black landowners of 1820 were women, a somewhat larger
fraction than in 1810.[36] Two-fifths of the black taxpayers of 1820
were women, up from one-fourth in 1810. And two-fifths of the
tax collected from free blacks in 1820 was collected from
women, again, up from one-fourth in 1810.

Measured against comparable figures for whites, these were
stunning proportions. In 1820 women were but 12.8 percent of
the white taxpayers (76 of 593), and they accounted for only 3.5
percent of the tax money collected from whites.

This glaring disparity in the status of black and white women
relative to men of the same race fades somewhat when sex ratios
are taken into consideration. It should also be said that free black
women were more likely than were white women to maintain
their legal eligibility to control property. Virginia was a common-
law state, and the common law made razor-sharp distinctions between single and married women. Single women and widows had
the same property rights and obligations as men. But the instant a
woman married, she surrendered both her rights and her obligations to her husband; if she had owned taxable property, the sur-
render was manifested in her summary disappearance from the
tax lists.[37]

It is impossible to estimate how many of Petersburg's free black
women shunned lawful matrimony, but the qualitative evidence
suggests that the proportion was high, higher than among whites.
The sex ratio, the law, poverty, and preference conspired to keep
a great many free black women single, and to the extent that
women remained single, they remained free agents in the
economic realm.

The sex ratio and the law together dictated the single life for
one-third of Petersburg's free black women. Because blacks were
not permitted to marry whites, and slaves were not permitted to
marry anyone, the pool of marriageable men was restricted to free
blacks, and there were simply not enough of them to go around.

A few black women did take up with whites, and more, apparently, were coupled with slaves. These matches yielded some interesting economic arrangements. Milly Cassurier, when she was
still known by that name, acquired property in her own right
while she was living with Jean Gallé, something she could not
have done had the two of them been married.[38] When a free
woman cohabited with a slave, meanwhile, here were the legal
materials for a complete sex-role reversal, for the woman assumed all legal rights and responsibilities for the pair. In 1800, a slave
named David White was jailed for going at large and trading as a
free person. The fine for White's misdeeds fell on his wife, Polly   859
Spruce, a free woman who had hired White for the year and who
was therefore legally answerable for his behavior. Nearing her
death years later, Jane Cook found it necessary to make special
provision for her slave husband, Peter Matthews. Cook had purchased two small boats, "the Democrat and the experiment," as
her husband's agent and with his money. These she bequeathed
to Matthews, appointing a free black man to act as his agent and
to stand guardian to her daughter, to whom she left her own property.[39]

The women whose mates were white or enslaved had no
choice but to remain technically single, but it is by no means certain that all of them would have married had they been given the
chance. When free black women entered into partnerships with
men who were also black and free, legal wedlock was not the inevitable result. For one thing, marrying did cost money. Ministers
were authorized to charge one dollar for their services, and the
clerk's fee was a quarter. If a poor couple found that amount an
obstacle, they likely found it well-nigh impossible to locate a third
party willing to post the $150 bond required to obtain the
license.[40]

Nonmarriage among free blacks, however, was evidently as
much a matter of ethics as of expenses, for even the propertied
showed no consistent tendency to make their conjugal ties legal
ties. Christian Scott was hardly well-to-do, but he did own some
animals and a goodly stock of household furniture; "having for
some time past lived with Charlotte Cook by whom I have a son
called Jesse Mitchell . . . ," Scott explained, "And being desirous
from the friendship & Regard I bear to the said Charlotte Cook &
affection to my said Son, to convey the property aforesaid to
them," Scott deeded them the property, dividing it exactly as it
would have been divided had Scott married Cook and then died

intestate (without a will). James Vaughan was far wealthier than Scott. He was also in trouble. In 1806 Vaughan was tried for the murder of "his supposed wife," Milly Johnston. After his conviction, a contrite Vaughan was permitted to write a will to direct the distribution of an estate that included cash and bonds worth over two thousand dollars, a town lot, three horses, and four slaves. Vaughan gave half of his estate to Sarah Vaughan, his daughter by Polly Hull. The other half went to John Vaughan, his son by Ann Stephens. Whether James Vaughan's relationships with Johnston, Hull, and Stephens were simultaneous or sequential is both unclear and beside the point. The point is that he did not marry any of them.[41]

860

So much the better for the women's control over their property and wages. Polly Hull, for example, bought a town lot a few months before James Vaughan wrote his will and was taxed on it for more than a decade thereafter.[42] There were other free black women in roughly similar circumstances. Charlotte Rollins was part of an uneasy triangle that included a free black named Captain Billy Ash and a slave named Julius. Ash was tried for "shooting and wounding" Julius in 1802, and Rollins's sister and brother-in-law were examined in the case: "On their being asked if Charlotte was wife of the prisoner, it was answered, that they both, the prisoner & Julius, resorted where she was." It is unclear what became of Billy Ash, but Charlotte Rollins never married him or anyone else. In 1810, she was listed as the head of a three-person family, and in 1817, she disposed of her household furniture and kitchen utensils by deed of gift, a probable substitute for the writing of a will. [43] Nelly White, unhappily, was unable to enjoy the property she had acquired in her baking business. In 1811, White was examined on suspicion of knifing a free man named Tom, and a witness described their relationship. "Tom & the Prisoner had lived in the same House, in different apartments — and been considered as man & wife but lived badly together after wrangling." White was convicted in District Court and sent to the penitentiary. She left behind "some property & Estate," and the town sergeant was ordered to look after it while she served her sentence.[44]

A member of one of Petersburg's most prominent free black families, Molly Brander married once, but opted for cohabitation the second time around. The first time, she married Nathan James. After his death in 1804, Molly began a new family, taking James Butler "as her husband tho not lawfully married," and adopting her orphaned niece. Because she did not marry Butler, Molly James retained her rights to the house and lot she had inherited from her first husband, and when she died intestate in 1812, her mother and brothers inherited the property in turn. Before her death, however, Molly James had told her family that she wanted the lot to pass to James Butler and her adoptive daughter; the family complied in 1815 by means of a deed of gift.[45]

Just how commonly black women acquired some kind of property and retained legal control over it by not marrying the men in their lives is a mystery, for evidence surfaces only sporadically in trial reports (hence the prevalence of violent crime in the preceding paragraphs) and in a very occasional deed. Moreover, these few documents give no clues as to whether the women deliberately refused marriage for the sake of maintaining their property rights. The legacy and continued presence of slavery no doubt provided cause enough. Slave marriages were necessarily based on mutual consent; for a good many black couples, consent was sufficient in freedom as well, an attitude that the black churches would combat with mixed success in the decades that followed.[46] Still, it may have been that women so recently emancipated, and women accustomed to providing for themselves, did not give up their legal autonomy lightly.[47] Certainly free black women had unique incentive for staying single. For the woman who hoped to buy an enslaved relative, legal wedlock meant that her plan could be sabotaged at any time by her husband or by her husband's impatient creditors. The common-law disabilities of married women added an ironic twist to chattel slavery's strange fusion of persons and property: Matrimony could pose a threat to the integrity of the free black woman's family.

Whether by necessity, deliberation, or default, sufficient numbers of free black women avoided legal marriage to constitute a major departure from the white norm. The contrast with the experience of white women was sharper still in the extent to which black women shouldered the burden of supporting their families. If most of the women listed by the census taker as "heads of families" were primary breadwinners, then the magnitude of economic responsibility borne by free black women was truly staggering. In 1810, 56.3 percent (138 of 245) of the free black households of Petersburg were headed by women. For 1820, the figure was 58.1 percent (168 of 289). In 1820, these female-headed households sheltered over one-half (52.3 percent) of all free black persons living in black households and an even larger proportion (57.3 percent) of free black children under fourteen.

So uninformative are these early census returns, and so suspect the given numbers, that no satisfactory reconstruction of household composition is possible.[48] From the unembellished hashmarks that made up the 1820 schedules, the one safe conclusion is that there was no typical free black household structure. The most commonplace household type (87 of 289) was, it appears, the female-headed family containing one woman and her (?) children. Further guesswork suggests that the second most frequent arrangement was the male-headed household containing an adult couple and their children (51 of 289).[49] Thirty-seven households were composed of but one person, twenty-nine of them female, and there were apparently twenty-four childless couples. The remaining households, about one-third of the total, contained persons of ages and sexes that defy categorization. Worth noting, however, is the incidence of extended or augmented families. One-fifth of all free black households contained at least one "surplus" person over the age of twenty-five.[50]

It should be emphasized that there was no typical household structure among whites either.[51] The difference was that Petersburg's multiform white households were overwhelmingly male-headed. The proportion of white households headed by women was 15.7 percent in 1810 and 17.0 percent ten years after. In addition, a disproportionately small number of whites lived in these female-headed households. The census taker of 1820 found only 13.3 percent of white children under sixteen resident in female-headed households, while 12.8 percent of all white persons lived in households headed by women.[52]

Nineteenth-century census data usually raise more questions than they answer, and this is particularly true of the early returns. It is impossible to discern the precise family structure within households, much less assess the meaning of familial roles played by neighbors and nonresident kin. This last blind spot is especially troublesome given the probability that for numerous free blacks, spouses and close kin remained the slaves of white owners. Least of all does the census tell us anything about love, commitment, giving children a chance in life — those qualities that despite our disclaimers usually lurk behind our reading of the numbers.

These problems only begin the list of the source limitations that frustrate any attempts to recapture the experience of the mass of free black women. We do know that there was a flourishing free black Baptist church in Petersburg before 1820 and that in 1820 a Sunday school run by free blacks had girls as well as boys among its two hundred students.[53] But there are no records for the church in this period and none at all for the Sunday school. Newspapers reported next to no local news. The whites whose correspondence is preserved wrote of their own kind; only rarely did they discuss their slaves, and free blacks were never mentioned. While the local public records are surprisingly rich, they are decidedly slanted toward the property owners. The majority of free black women thus appear to us only as names — or worse, as numbers — on the census schedules.

863

The conclusion nevertheless stands. In a slave society of the early nineteenth century, there developed among free blacks a relatively high degree of equality between the sexes. There is not much material here for romanticizing. For free black women, the high rate of gainful employment and the high incidence of female-headed households were symptoms of oppression. Neither was chosen from a position of strength; both were products of a shortage of men and of chronic economic deprivation. The high incidence of female property holding, meanwhile, was largely the consequence of a system that limited the achievement of black men.

Yet there was autonomy of a kind, and the fact that its origins lay in racial subordination should not detract from its significance. The autonomy experienced by the free black women of Petersburg was relative freedom from day-to-day domination by black men. We cannot say for certain how free black people looked on this. The fact that so many couples refrained from legal marriage, however, at least suggests that the women valued their autonomy and that one way or another the men learned to live with it. The tragedy for the nineteenth century — or one of many tragedies — was that white people were unable to use the free black example to call their own gender arrangements into question, that no one outside the free black community took anything positive from the free black experience. Perhaps we can do better.

NOTES

The author wishes to thank the Colonial Williamsburg Foundation and the Woodrow Wilson National Fellowship Foundation Program in Women's Studies for their support of the research on which this article is based. She would also like to thank Sharon Harley for her comments on an earlier version of the article.

864

¹*South-Side Democrat,* 29 November, 12 December 1853 (first quotation), 17 March, 18 March, 20 March 1854; Minutes, 15 December 1853, 16 March, 17 March 1854 (second quotation).

All references to minutes, deeds, wills, accounts, and marriages are to the records of the Petersburg Hustings Court, on microfilm in the Virginia State Library, Richmond, Va. References to land books, personal property books, and legislative petitions are to the original manuscripts in the Virginia State Library.

²Calculated from *Aggregate Amount of Persons Within the United States in the Year 1810* (Washington, 1811), p. 55a. According to this census, Petersburg contained 1,089 free blacks, 2,173 slaves, and 2,404 whites. The town's free black population grew to only 1,165 by 1820. In reading these figures, allowance should be made for probable undercounting.

³E. Franklin Frazier, *The Negro Family in the United States* (Chicago: University of Chicago Press, 1939); U.S. Department of Labor, Office of Policy Planning and Research, *The Negro Family: The Case for National Action* by Daniel P. Moynihan (Washington, D.C.: U.S. Government Printing Office, 1965.) More detailed summaries of these works may be found in the articles by Gutman, Lammermeier, and Shifflett, cited in note 4.

⁴John W. Blassingame, *Black New Orleans 1860-1880* (Chicago and London: University of Chicago Press, 1973), pp. 79-105; Frank F. Furstenberg Jr., Theodore Hershberg, and John Modell, "The Origins of the Female-Headed Black Family: The Impact of the Urban Experience," pp. 211-33; Herbert G. Gutman, "Persistent Myths About the Afro-American Family," pp. 181-210; Crandall A. Shifflett, "The Household Composition of Rural Black Families: Louisa County, Virginia, 1880," pp. 235-60, all in *Journal of Interdisciplinary History* 6 (Autumn 1975); Herbert G. Gutman, *The Black Family in Slavery and Freedom, 1750-1925* (New York: Pantheon Books, 1976), pp. 432-60; Paul J. Lammermeier, "The Urban Black Family of the Nineteenth Century: A Study of Black Family Stucture in the Ohio Valley, 1850-1880," *Journal of Marriage and the Family* 35 (August 1973): 440-56; Elizabeth H. Pleck, "The Two-Parent Household: Black Family Structure in Late Nineteenth-Century Boston," *Journal of Social History* 5 (Fall 1971): 3-31. Pleck, however, does point out the value-laden nature of terms like "family disorganization," and in *Black Migration and Poverty: Boston 1865-1900* (New York: Academic Press, 1979), has reevaluated the significance of two-parent households.

⁵This may be a slight overcount; of the two dozen slaves directed freed by will, some may have remained in slavery due to owners' indebtedness or to litigation. The law of 1806 discouraged manumission by requiring all newly freed persons to leave the state within one year of emancipation, and for a time it was extremely effective. There were no emancipations in Petersburg from 1807 to 1810. Emancipations began again in 1811, but from 1811 to 1820 were granted at less than half their pre-1807 rate, even though a new statute of 1816 made it easier for the manumitted to obtain permission to remain in Virginia.

The female advantage in emancipation seems to have been more than a reflection of the sex ratio among slaves; calculations from the Personal Property Book for 1790 show that females constituted only a 51.5 percent majority of slave adults.

[6]Mary Cumming to Margaret Craig, December 1811, Margaret and Mary Craig Letters, Virginia Colonial Records Project, Alderman Library, University of Virginia, Charlottesville, Virginia (quotation); Wills I, 238 (1796); Deeds IV, 304 (1815); Luther P. Jackson, "Manumission in Certain Virginia Cities," *Journal of Negro History* 15 (July 1930): 310. John Jeffers's will also authorized the emancipation of Sylvia's mother.

[7]Deeds V, 324 (1818); Wills II, 163 (1819).

[8]Luther P. Jackson counted the deeds of emancipation recorded in Petersburg and Richmond from 1784 to 1806 and found more in Petersburg, even though it was the smaller city. This he attributed to the early presence in Petersburg of antislavery Methodists. See Jackson, "Manumission," pp. 281-82. By my count, six Methodists accounted for almost one-fifth of Petersburg emancipations to 1806.

[9]Six women were apprehended and jailed for hiring themselves out. The court had the choice of selling them or fining their masters; two of the six were ordered sold. Minutes, 5 April 1802, 5 September 1803, 2 January, 9 February, 4 April 1809, 6 May 1811. See William Waller Hening, *The New Virginia Justice, Comprising the Office and Authority of a Justice of the Peace in the Commonwealth of Virginia . . .* 2nd. ed. (Richmond: Johnson & Warner, 1810), p. 549.

865

[10]Deeds VI, 51 (1819).

[11]Deeds II, 157 (1792), III, 58 (quotation), 74 (1802), 236 (1805).

[12]Two of the women freed their sons; no relationship was stated by the others. Deeds II, 174 (1792), 581 (1799), 701 (1800), 737 (1801), Deeds III, 75 (1802), 116 (1803), Deeds V, 325 (1818).

[13]Deeds III, 78 (1802).

[14]Deeds III, 267 (1805); Wills II, 69 (1812), 114 (1815), 139 (1817), 161 (1819).

[15]At least sixteen women were manumitted with their children (this does not include those freed by husbands or other kin from whom they could expect financial assistance). Six had a single child, five had two children, and five had three or more.

[16]Minutes, 1 June 1801, 6 January 1806, 7 August 1809.

[17]Accounts I, 31, 55 (1808), 37 (1809), Accounts II, 189 (1821); Luther Porter Jackson, *Free Negro Labor and Property Holding in Virginia, 1830-1860* (New York and London: D. Appleton-Century Co., 1942), p. 221; Personal Property Books, 1801-1820.

[18]Minutes, 2 November 1790, 5 August 1799, 2 March 1812.

[19]There were probably more gainfully employed women among free blacks than among whites, but because the whites were more likely to escape (paid) domestic service, they are far more visible; specific occupations can be identified for more than 150 white women. These women, with a few exceptions, were milliners, dressmakers, midwives, teachers, and keepers of taverns, boardinghouses, and stores. Meanwhile, the only female occupations in which no free black women were found were teaching and millinery.

[20]Minutes, 4 November 1804.

[21]Calculated from the United States *Census for 1820* (Washington, D.C.: Gales and Seaton, 1821). The imbalance may also have been due to a higher rate of male migration to the free states. It does not appear to have been due to higher mortality rates among men, because the sex ratio was higher (71.3) among free blacks aged forty-five and above.

[22]Deeds I, 270 (1786), Deeds II, 116 (1800); Personal Property Books, 1795-1804; Accounts I, 75 (1817).

[23]Deeds I, 303 (1787), Deeds II, 379 (1795); Land Books, 1795-1820.

[24]Deeds II, 205 (1792), 593 (1799), Deeds III, 237 (1805); Personal Property Books, 1797-1802; Wills II, 69 (1812); Minutes, 5 October 1812, 8 August 1815, 5 March 1816, 17 July, 16 October 1818.

Few of the persons emancipated in Petersburg can be traced. Emancipators stated last names for fewer than one-third of the slaves freed (black emancipators were more prone than whites to state surnames), and because ex-slaves hardly ever took the name of the last owner, inference is of little help.

[25]Land Book, 1820.

[26]Taxable property consisted of land (taxed according to its annual rental value), slaves over twelve years of age (taxed by the head), horses, carriages, and exports from the tobacco warehouses. My calculations include all taxes paid by living individuals, except those paid on tobacco exports, there being no comparable taxes on other businesses.

It should be emphasized that all along, white men controlled the lion's share of the taxable wealth, ranging from 85 percent in 1790, when town matriarch Mary Marshall Bolling was in her heyday, to 94 percent in 1820. The best way to characterize the trend for the decade after 1810 is that more white women and blacks of both sexes were acquiring small pieces of an expanding pie. The following table shows the proportion, in percent, of the persons listed in the census schedules as heads of families who also paid taxes:

	1810	1820
White men	60.1	61.8
Black men	21.5	24.8
White women	14.8	30.3
Black women	5.1	10.1

[27]Deeds III, 300 (1806), Deeds IV, 351 (1815); Wills II, 141 (1817).

[28]Legislative Petitions, 23 December 1839; Wills II, 94 (1814).

[29]Deeds III, 156 (1804); Wills II, 161 (1819). Amelia Gallé's son Joseph later on became the husband of Eliza Gallie.

[30]Petersburg *Republican,* 18 April, 7 July 1820, 23 May, 22 August 1823.

[31]United States Manuscript Census Schedule, 1820; Personal Property Books, 1819, 1820.

[32]Accounts I, 91 (1814) (first quotation); Deeds IV, 332 (1815) (second quotation); Wills II, 40 (1809) (third quotation), 95 (1814) (fourth quotation).

[33]Accounts II, 68 (1824-1826); Deeds III, 279 (1806); Land Books, 1806-1820; Personal Property Books, 1801-1820; *Republican,* 29 October 1816.

[34]Slave sales were not usually publicly recorded, and this adds to the difficulty of determining the extent of slave ownership.

[35]The number of slaves mortgaged was calculated from the deed books. During the same two years, Petersburg newspapers advertised the sale of about eighty slaves "according to a deed of trust," in other words, for owners' indebtedness. Both figures given here are lower than the actual totals, because the advertisements and deeds of trust did not always stipulate the precise numbers of slaves involved. Anyone prone to discount the significance of the threat of forced sale would do well to sample some deed books. In 1819 and 1820 alone, at least one-tenth of Petersburg's slaves were put up as collateral for owners' debts.

[36]In 1810, eight of twenty-three black landowners were women.

[37]By using the legal loopholes provided by the equity tradition of jurisprudence, a few married women were able to exempt their property from the control of husbands and husbands' creditors. Mary Ann Vizonneau provides one example. Her father's

stipulation that her inheritance was not to be controlled by her husband set up a "separate estate," which was formalized in 1818 by a separation agreement executed by Vizonneau and her estranged husband. Deeds V, 284 (1818). In this period, however, separate estates were still very rare.

[38]In his will, Jean Gallé apprised his executors that the woman slave Faith and all but two of the beds in his house belonged to Cassurier and not to his estate. Wills II, 161 (1819).

[39]Minutes, 3 September 1800; Wills II, 192 (1822).

[40]Joseph Tate, *A Digest of the Laws of Virginia, which are of a Permanent Character and General Operation; Illustrated by Judicial Decisions: To which is Added, An Index of the Names of Cases in the Virginia Reporters* (Richmond: Shepherd and Pollard, 1823), pp. 415-18, secs. 1, 11, 13. Because the Marriage Register did not stipulate race, not even a rough estimate of black marriage rates can be made.

[41]Deeds V, 124 (1817); Minutes, 21 November 1806; Wills II, 182 (1821). Vaughan was born free and the son of the Sarah Vaughan who appeared year after year on the tax lists.

[42]Deeds III, 376 (1807); Land Books, 1809-1820.

[43]Minutes, 27 January 1802: Deeds V, 197 (1817).

[44]Minutes, 6 April 1811 (first quotation), 6 May 1812 (second quotation).

[45]Land Books, 1806-1812; Deeds IV, 330 (1815) (quotation).

[46]Records of the Gillfield Baptist Church suggest that as late as 1860, there was still ambivalence on the marriage issue. An entry of 29 January 1860, for example, reads: "It was moved & 2nd that the Past Action of the church be reconsidered of mutual concent being considered Man & Wife Carried — non considered Man & Wife But those joined together By Matrimony." Gillfield Baptist Church Record Book, Alderman Library.

[47]Two cases suggest that some free black women were aware of the law and concerned about its consequences. Two days before she married Jacob Brander, Nancy Curtis deeded her furniture and livestock to her teenaged children, a clear attempt to protect the rights of her own heirs. Lydia Thomas maintained her property rights in a slave and some furniture, despite her marriage to John Stewart, by entering into a prenuptial contract with him. This gave her a separate estate, much like that of Mary Ann Vizonneau. Deeds IV, 335 (1815), Deeds V, 288 (1818); Marriages, 1814, 1817.

[48]The 1810 census listed the names of free black heads of households, but the only further information given was the total number of free blacks (with a separate total for slaves) living in each household. The census for 1820 is somewhat more informative, supplying the number of persons of each sex in each of four age categories (under fourteen, fourteen to twenty-five, twenty-six to forty-four, and forty-five and above).

[49]The first figure is the total of all households in which one female from fourteen to twenty-five was listed along with one or more children under age fourteen, and in which one female of twenty-six or above was listed along with one or more persons under age twenty-six. The same age categories were used for the second figure.

[50]For female-headed households, surplus adult is defined as anyone over twenty-five listed in addition to the head. For male-headed households, surplus adults are those listed in addition to one man and one woman. There were twenty-one surplus women and six men in male-headed households, thirty surplus women and twenty-three men in female-headed households.

[51]Even counting resident slaves and free blacks out of the analysis, fewer than one-third of the households headed by whites can be reasonably classified as nuclear, that is, as being composed of an adult couple or an adult couple with their children with no surplus persons.

One-tenth of Petersburg's free blacks were listed as residing in households headed by whites. Three-fifths of these free blacks were males, and they outnumbered females resident in white households in every age group except the over-forty-four category.

[52] The incidence of female-headedness among poorer white households was considerably higher, as might be expected. In 1820, 27.1 percent of the households of nontaxpaying whites were female headed. Comparison of white and black households is complicated by the fact that different age categories were used for the two groups.

[53] Luther P. Jackson, *A Short History of the Gillfield Baptist Church of Petersburg, Virginia* (Petersburg: Virginia Printing Co., 1937); *Republican*, 17 October 1820.

868

Sojourner Truth, Bold Prophet:
Why Did She Never Learn to Read?

By CARLETON MABEE

An analysis of Sojourner Truth's illiteracy combines views of the black experience in nineteenth-century America with present-day knowledge of the learning experience. Carleton Mabee is Professor Emeritus of History at the State University of New York, College at New Paltz.

869

SOJOURNER TRUTH EMERGED from the miasma of slavery in New York State to become, with her tall, bony figure and queenly walk, a national figure in the movements to advance the rights of women and blacks. Amazingly, she accomplished this without ever learning to read and write.

Her illiteracy has long been well known, but the question of why such an able and purposeful woman remained illiterate has usually been only casually considered, if at all.[1] The question is difficult to answer because the original sources available on Sojourner are thin. Also, much of the writing about her, in her time and ours, has been bent more toward making her into a myth for inspiration rather than toward documenting the reality of her life; and Sojourner herself sometimes contributed to the mythmaking.[2] However, the increasing awareness in our time that illiteracy is disturbingly widespread in America, and especially so among blacks, makes the question of why she remained illiterate more poignant.[3]

The U.S. Post Office officially issued a Sojourner Truth stamp at a ceremony held Feb. 4, 1986, in New Paltz, N.Y., where she had long lived as a slave. It was issued there in the State University College's library, which with magnificent irony has been named, since 1971, the Sojourner Truth Library after a woman who could not even read. The issuance of the stamp stimulated the college to hold on March 11, 1986, a seminar on Sojourner at which this paper, in its original form, was given. I

The common explanation for Sojourner's not learning to read and write, usually casually given or merely implied, is that she was brought up a slave and thus was denied the opportunity to learn.[4] It is a natural explanation to give especially because Sojourner, as an antislavery speaker, was often presented as having felt in her own person the wrongs that slavery could inflict, and these wrongs were commonly understood to include denying slaves an education.

Sojourner's friends sometimes claimed, if indirectly, that slavery had prevented her from being educated. The abolitionist Sallie Holley, while speaking with Sojourner in Ohio in 1851, wrote privately that Sojourner "shows what a great intellect slavery has crushed." The novelist Harriet Beecher Stowe, writing an article on Sojourner in the *Atlantic* in 1863 —an article that did much to make Sojourner well known— mourned that Sojourner, like other noble blacks, had come out of bondage cramped and scarred, and Stowe longed to

870

---

am grateful to the library staff for their help, especially in locating sources, and to my daughter, Susan Mabee Newhouse, psychotherapist, for her help, especially in interpreting Sojourner.

1. In the period 1850-1858, when Sojourner was becoming well known, of 30 descriptions of her, published in periodicals and examined for this purpose, 56 percent mentioned her illiteracy or quote her as mentioning it. Of 32 obituaries of her published in periodicals in Nov. or Dec., 1883, 50 percent mention her illiteracy. From 1885 to the present, of 231 descriptions of Sojourner in periodicals, encyclopedias, collected biographies, or the like, 63 percent mention her illiteracy. No books or articles that I know of deal systematically with why Sojourner did not learn to read or write.

2. There are two indispensable books on Sojourner, both of which mention her illiteracy. One is Gilbert Vale, *Fanaticism: Its Source and Influence, Illustrated by the Simple Narrative of Isabella, in the Case of Matthias* (New York: 1835) (hereafter cited as Vale). Vale was a white N.Y.C. teacher and editor, and he wrote with care for evidence. The other is *Narrative of Sojourner Truth* (Boston, 1875). Hereafter cited as *Narrative*. It was first published in Boston and New York in 1850, and written anonymously by Olive Gilbert, a self-effacing New England abolitionist friend. It was expanded in two later editions, the first published in 1875, and the last and fullest published in 1884. These last two editions were written anonymously by Frances W. Titus, a white Quaker of Battle Creek, Michigan, who in Sojourner's later years managed her affairs. Gilbert and Titus were partisans of Sojourner and the causes she espoused, were gullible, and particularly Titus was not careful in handling documents, often not citing them so that a scholar can verify them, and sometimes altering them without acknowledgment.

There is no comprehensive, scholarly biography of Sojourner. Popular biographies, somewhat fictionalized, which contain invented situations and conversations and hence are likely to contribute to myths about Sojourner, include: Arthur Huff Fauset, *Sojourner Truth: God's Faithful Pilgrim* (Chapel Hill: Univ. of North Carolina, 1938); Hertha Pauli, *Her Name was Sojourner Truth* (New York: Avon,

know what Sojourner would have been like if she had been allowed to unfold under the kindly influences of education.[5]

Sojourner herself sometimes directly claimed that slavery had prevented her from learning to read and write. In more than one speech she said slavery had "robbed" her of an education. In another speech, she recalled that her slave masters had not even allowed her "to hear the Bible or any other books read." In a newspaper interview, Sojourner explained that while she was a slave, "There was nobody to tell me anything; I was just like a heathen." My slave masters "were very close and ignorant, and so, naturally, to this day I can neither read nor write."[6] How justified are these claims?

871

While Sojourner Truth respected truth telling, as her choice of her own name suggests, she sometimes seemed to lend herself to creating myths about the story of her life, myths that might make slavery seem more terrible, or herself seem more colorful. For instance, while she made it clear that

1962); Jacqueline Bernard, *Journey Toward Freedom: The Story of Sojourner Truth* (New York: Norton, 1967); Aletha Jane Lindstrom, *Sojourner Truth, Slave, Abolitionist, Fighter for Women's Rights* (New York: Messner, 1980). All four of these books mention Sojourner's illiteracy, and all lack reference notes. Bernard and Lindstrom are intended for school children.

To offset the usual inadequacy in documenting the story of Sojourner's life, I have tried to cite sources precisely, and to cite the earliest, most reliable sources I can.

3. New York *Times*, April 21, May 7, July 22, Sept. 16, 25, 26, Oct. 30, 1986, June 2, July 16, 1987; *Time*, May 5, 1986; Carman St. John Hunter, et al., *Adult Illiteracy in the United States: A Report to the Ford Foundation* (New York: McGraw-Hill, 1979); Jonathan Kozol, *Illiterate America* (Garden City, N.Y.: Anchor, 1985). While the present article concerns Sojourner's basic illiteracy, that is, her inability to read and write at all, current interest is usually in what is often called functional illiteracy, that is, the inability to read and write well enough to function adequately in our increasingly complex society.

4. *Liberator*, Sept. 15, 1854; *Narrative*, 1853, v, vii; New York *Daily Tribune*, Sept. 7, 1853, Nov. 27, 1883; Orange, N.J., *Journal*, July 29, 1876; New York *Evening Post*, Nov. 27, 1883; Harriet Carter, "Sojourner Truth," *Chautauquan* 7 (May, 1887), 478; J.H. Brown, "Sojourner Truth," Battle Creek *Moon-Journal*, April 26, 1929; Janey Weinhold Montgomery, *A Comprehensive Analysis of the Rhetoric of Two Negro Women Orators—Sojourner Truth and Frances E. Watkins Harper* (Hays, Kan.: Fort Hays Kansas State College, 1968), 40; Bruce Bliven, *A Mirror for Greatness: Six Americans* (New York: McGraw-Hill, 1975), 138.

5. John White Chadwick, *A Life for Liberty: Antislavery and Other Letters of Sallie Holley* (1899, reprinted New York: Negro Universities Press, 1969), 80; Harriet Beecher Stowe "Sojourner Truth, the Libyan Sibyl," *Atlantic* 11 (April, 1863), 480.

6. New York *Daily Tribune*, Sept. 7, 16, 1853 (this latter article is misidentified in *Narrative*, 208-209, as from a Williamsburgh, L.I., paper of about 1871); Chicago *Daily Inter-Ocean*, Aug. 13, 1879; New York *Evening Telegram*, Nov. 26, 1883.

one of her children was sold away from her, as is believed to be true, she seemed to hint that others might have been also.[7] In her old age, she often incorrectly claimed that she was over one hundred years old, and she relished making such outrageous remarks as that she did not know if she ever had been born, and that she had decided not to die until American women could vote.[8] Thus it would scarcely be surprising if she lent herself to mythmaking about why she didn't learn to read and write.

872

Sojourner was born a slave in Ulster County, New York, near the Hudson River, about 1797. As a small child Sojourner—then known as Isabella—heard her parents grieving over her older brothers and sisters having been sold away from them. When Sojourner was nine, she herself was sold away from her parents, which must have been traumatic for her. She never lived with her parents again. By the time she was thirteen, she had been sold twice more.[9]

According to her recollections, as told to a white friend who wrote them down in the *Narrative* of her life, Sojourner was brought up by her slave parents and the earliest of her slave masters—all of whom lived in Ulster County—to speak only Dutch, the language of many of the early settlers of the region. When she was sold away from her parents, however, it was to a family who could speak only English, and this led to her misunderstanding their orders to her, for which they whipped her cruelly, doubtless contributing to the scars which remained all her life on her back and mind.[10] According to the recollections of a family that bought her two or

7. Her own story as reported in *Narrative*, 44-54, directly reports only her son Peter as having been sold away from her (and she afterwards recovered him). But two other passages, both p. 194, could be interpreted to mean that others of her children had also been sold away. Frances D. Gage, "Sojourner Truth," *National Anti-Slavery Standard*, May 2, 1863, reported her as saying almost all her children had been sold away. The New York *Daily Tribune*, Sept. 7, 1853, reported her as saying slavery had robbed her "of her children." J.A. Dugdale, in *National Anti-Slavery Standard*, July 4, 1863, quoted her as saying, "My children was sold from me."

8. New York *Herald*, Dec. 16, 1878; Detroit *Post* in *Women's Journal*, Aug. 10, 1878, 255; New York *Sun*, Nov. 24, 1878; Chicago *Daily Inter-Ocean*, Aug. 13, 1879; New York *Times*, Dec. 4, 1880.

9. *Narrative*, 15-18, 26-29.

10. *Narrative*, 26-27; Elizabeth Cady Stanton, et al., *History of Women Suffrage*, I (1887), reprinted New York: Source Book, 1970), 115; Springfield (Mass.) *Daily Republican*, Nov. 27, 1883.

three years later, she still seemed to be learning English "with much difficulty."[11]

While some of her early owners seemed narrow and cruel, the family that bought her at this time, the English-speaking John J. Dumont and his family, seemed different. The Dumonts, whom she served as a slave from about the age of thirteen to thirty, lived in what was then part of New Paltz, but now is West Park, overlooking the Hudson River. They were educated people, with connections to prominent families. For the most part they were not cruel to Sojourner, according to the standards of the time. After Sojourner was freed from slavery, she often spoke well of the Dumonts and visited them. While Mrs. Dumont was not fond of Sojourner, Mr. Dumont was, and he was protective of Sojourner's children. Mr. Dumont valued her for her refusing to lie and steal. He also praised her for her physical strength and willingness to work; and in response she worked so hard that Dumont boasted, to Sojourner's delight, that she did as much work in the fields as his best man, and Sojourner became known among Dumont's other slaves as a "white folks' nigger."[12] When Sojourner was doing domestic work for this family, as she often did, it would be hard to believe that she would not be exposed to school books, newspapers, the Bible, almanacs, or the like, and would not have heard them read aloud. However, long afterwards two of the Dumont children—who were only a little younger than Sojourner, and one of them, Gertrude, very supportive of her—recalled that "it seemed almost impossible to teach her anything."[13] This suggests the possibility that by this time there were important factors within Sojourner herself which contributed to her not learning to read and write.

In New York State from early colonial times there had been a thread of concern to Christianize the slaves, which often included teaching them to read the Bible. In the early 1800s, when the push to end slavery in the state was far advanced, many whites were becoming convinced that blacks, since they

873

11. H. Hendricks, "Sojourner Truth: Her Early History in Slavery," *National Magazine* 16 (1891), 671.
12. *Narrative*, 29-38, 124; Vale I, 11, 17.
13. Hendricks, "Sojourner Truth," 669.

were to be free, would look after themselves more responsibly if they were Christianized and taught to read. Churches in the region where Sojourner lived often admitted blacks, including slaves, to membership.[14]

It is true that during slavery in New York State, up to about 1827 when it was abolished, most blacks, like Sojourner, were illiterate. But educating slaves in New York State was never prohibited, as it was in many Southern states. And in 1810, about when Sojourner was sold to Dumont, the state, as part of its plan to abolish slavery by gradual steps, adopted a law providing that slave masters must have their slave children taught to read the scriptures.[15]

From soon afterwards, a considerable number of schools in the state were open to slaves and other blacks. Particularly from about 1815, before public schools were yet common in the state, there was a strong movement for the establishment of Sunday schools, which were often intended to teach not only religion but also reading and writing to those who had no opportunity to study them otherwise. These Sunday schools, which were sometimes church-affiliated, often welcomed slaves and other blacks; and blacks, including adults, attended them in numbers greater than their proportion in the population. We know that there were separate Sunday schools for blacks in Ulster County, one in Kingston by 1817, one in Stone Ridge by 1818.[16] There were probably other Sunday schools in the county open to blacks, and certainly other kinds of schools as well. Why didn't Sojourner, bright and aggressive as she was, seek them out? She lived at the time about nine miles from Kingston, farther from Stone Ridge; and she recalled later that as a slave she had never been allowed to go anywhere.[17] She also often said that though her mother taught her at a very early age to talk to God, and doing so became a great outlet for her resentments against the cruelties of her situation, while she remained a

874

14. In the period 1803-1806, the New Paltz Reformed Church admitted six blacks to membership, at least three of whom were slaves. William Heidgerd, *Black History of New Paltz* (New Paltz, N.Y.: Elting Memorial Library, 1986), 48.

15. Carleton Mabee, *Black Education in New York State: From Colonial to Modern Times* (Syracuse: Syracuse University, 1979), chs. 1-2.

16. Mabee, *Black Education*, ch. 3 and p. 287.

17. New York *Daily Tribune*, Sept. 7, 1853.

slave she never attended church.[18] More significantly, however, Sojourner was probably not ready, whatever the reasons, to learn to read and write.

Like Sojourner herself, Sojourner's first child, Diana, born about 1816 as a slave of the Dumonts, never learned to read and write. While Diana was still living with her mother at the Dumonts', as Diana recalled afterward, Diana was sent to school for just one week, "but had no idea what the school was for, or why she was sent there. The school teacher never spoke to her while she was at school."[19] Diana's story indicates that Sojourner did not prepare her daughter significantly for attending school. Her story also suggests, contrary to what the Dumont children implied, that the Dumonts did not significantly encourage the education of their blacks. Perhaps the Dumonts' sending Diana to school was merely their grudging response to the law requiring masters to have their slave children taught to read. Diana's story also suggests, however, that the Dumonts would not have prevented their slaves, including Sojourner and Diana, from attaining a basic education if they had pursued it actively.

875

Compare Sojourner Truth with another bright slave child, Frederick Douglass. Douglass grew up as a slave in Maryland where there were more slaves in the population proportionately than in New York, and thus more reason for whites to be anxious to keep slaves under control by not educating them. Douglass' master and mistress, after some wavering, tried to prevent Douglass from learning to read and write. But Douglass learned anyway. One way he did so was by cajoling the white children he met on the streets of Baltimore, where he lived, to teach him—he cajoled them by giving them bits of food they wanted, or by making a game out of who could best write something on the pavement.

If Douglass could learn to read and write in Maryland, why couldn't Sojourner do so, at about the same time in more liberal New York State, even if her master did not encourage

18. New York *Daily Tribune*, Sept. 16, 1853; Stowe, "Sojourner Truth," 476; *Narrative*, 1884, "A Memorial Chapter," 6.

19. Obituary of Diana Corbin, Battle Creek *Daily Journal*, Oct. 25, 1904. A predisposition to reading disability may be genetic. See Stanley S. Lamm, *Learning Disabilities Explained* (Garden City, N.Y.: Doubleday, 1982), 36.

it? Douglass had the advantage of living much of the time in a city, where he was considerably free to mix with white children in the street, and do what his master did not know about, while Sojourner, living in a rural area, may have had less freedom of that kind. Probably more important, Douglass, for whatever reason, had a burning drive to learn. For him it was associated with his desire to be free. He insisted on learning to write, for example, so that he would be able to write a pass for himself, a pass such as slaves were obliged to carry, which he would need for his plan to escape from slavery.[20] But Sojourner seems to have had no association in her mind of learning and freedom. In fact, during much of the approximately eighteen years that she lived with the Dumonts, if the *Narrative* of her life as she told it to a friend can be believed, she did not wish to be free. She believed slavery was right, and idolized her master Dumont.[21] Also, I cannot find evidence in her *Narrative* or elsewhere that while she was a slave she desired to learn to read or write at all.[22] She was probably, like most slaves, so weighed down by the experiences of slavery, so conditioned to the usual expectation that slaves would not learn to read or write, so lost in ignorance (she recalled that slaves were so ignorant that their thoughts were no longer than their fingers), so lacking in role models of slaves who had attained any meaningful education, that she had no significant desire to learn.[23] If she had had the burning desire to learn that Douglass had, it seems possible that Sojourner, bright as she was, would have found a way.

After Sojourner legally acquired her freedom from slavery in about 1827, when all the remaining slaves in the state were being freed, did she use her freedom to push to learn how to read and write?

At about this time, Sojourner discovered that her son had been sold illegally into slavery in the South; becoming out-

20. *Narrative of the Life of Frederick Douglass* (1845, reprinted New York: Signet, 1968), 52-58.

21. *Narrative*, 33-34, 37.

22. *Narrative*, 29, says that while Sojourner was living with her master Scriver, she was devoid of desire to improve herself. I cannot find evidence to support the claim of Carter, "Sojourner Truth," 478, that "Surrounded by circumstances tending to keep her in dense ignorance, her singularly alert mind had ever reached out to grasp every shred of knowledge which accidentally came in her way."

23. *Narrative*, 24.

raged, she took a very bold course for an illiterate black: she brought suit in a Kingston court to recover him. With the help of Quakers and other whites, she succeeded. In this process she was beginning to emancipate herself; as she later recalled, she gained confidence in God's justice, and learned to feel "so tall within."[24] At about this time, according to her narrative, she was suddenly converted by an inward experience to faith in Jesus, and began to attend church for the first time in her life; she chose a Methodist church in Kingston.[25] Methodists, like Sojourner, emphasized personal faith, talked in the vernacular, and liked to sing.

877

Soon afterward, with the help of a white teacher, Sojourner moved to New York City to seek greater opportunity. In New York, where she remained about fourteen years, she struggled to support herself and her youngest children. She usually worked as a domestic in the homes of substantial, educated whites, some of whom took considerable interest in her because she seemed unusually honest and industrious. She attended Methodist churches, one a predominantly white church, another a black one. It was clear that she was circulating among people who could open the way for her to pursue an education—Quakers, Methodists, whites and blacks, a benevolent teacher, benevolent employers—if she asked them to. Sojourner recalled afterwards that, at this time, "despised" as she was as an "ignorant" black who could not even "speak English very well,"she was determined to "go among the white people and learn all she could."[26]

New York City in this period, just after the last blacks were freed from slavery in the state, was an exciting place for alert, ambitious blacks. New York blacks started a newspaper of their own for the first time. They organized black churches and black self-help societies. They worked with whites in abolitionist societies and in the Underground Railroad. They supported existing schools for blacks and helped to organize more such schools, public and private. They pushed for more black teachers for the black schools in the state, and by the 1840s probably most of the teachers were blacks, and about

24. *Narrative*, 45.
25. *Narrative*, 67-69, 79; *Narrative* (1884), "A Memorial Chapter," 6.
26. New York *Daily Tribune*, Sept. 7, 1853.

half of them were women, women who were setting new standards for other black women to emulate.[27]

Though exposed to this new black activism, and to the example of both black and white women teachers, Sojourner is not known to have responded significantly to them. Sojourner had been legally emancipated, and had begun her inward emancipation, but as yet was scarcely open to the progressive reform movements of the time. What Sojourner meant by learning all she could seems to have been primarily about Jesus, which did not seem to include learning to read the Bible, even though she believed that knowing the Bible was important. She put much of her abundant surplus energy into becoming an evangelist, putting a high value on her own inner experience of Jesus. She vigorously prayed, preached, and sang, often in association with whites, at prayer meetings, at camp meetings, at meetings to evangelize prostitutes.[28]

Certainly during this period Sojourner was handicapped by not knowing how to read and write. She could not guide her rascal son Peter in his school work: He was supposed to be attending a New York City navigation school, but she did not know for a long time that he was only pretending to attend. She had a bank account, but could not read the bank records. She was placed in awkward situations by her lack of understanding of vocabulary. As she herself enjoyed telling it, once when she was looking in a court house for a grand jury, she went up to a man who looked grand to her, and asked him if he was the grand jury.[29] Her lack of education helped to make her so naive that she allowed herself to be gulled into living for a time in a crackpot, woman-degrading community, led by a bearded charlatan who claimed to be a reincarnation of God the Father, a community that shared its wealth (including Sojourner's—she lost all her savings to it), shared some of its women (not including Sojourner), and finally blew up in scandal (including the false charge that Sojourner had assisted in murdering one of its members).[30] Thereafter,

27. Mabee, *Black Education*, ch. 4 and p. 293.
28. *Narrative*, 86-87; Vale, I, 18-19; New York *Daily Tribune*, Sept. 7, 1853.
29. *Narrative*, 47, 74-75; Vale, I, 53-54.
30. Vale; *Narrative*, 87-98; William L. Stone, *Matthias and His Impostures* (New York, 1835).

though Sojourner became more hard-headed, she still scarcely put forth any discernible effort to learn to read and write, even to help protect herself from entanglement in such embarrassing scandal.

The only available evidence for this period that associates her with an attempt to learn to read is this: According to a newspaper report of a speech she gave in her old age, she recalled that, "when liberated, and an attempt was made to educate her . . . she could never get beyond her a, b, abs [*sic*]."[31] It may be significant that her recollection is expressed as someone else trying to teach her, not as her initiating an attempt to learn.

Compare James W.C. Pennington's effort to obtain an education with Sojourner's. Pennington, born a slave in Maryland, came to believe that slavery had robbed him of an education, much as Sojourner claimed that slavery had robbed her. But while still in slavery, Pennington struggled to learn to write letters, as we have no evidence that Sojourner did. Pennington did so by writing with the quills of feathers he picked up from the ground, with ink that he made from berries. As soon as Pennington ran away from slavery to the North, which was at about the same time that Sojourner was freed from slavery, Pennington began to learn to read. Pennington studied first with the Pennsylvania Quaker family who sheltered him on his escape, as Sojourner probably also could have studied with the Quakers who assisted her at about the time she was freed. Later in Brooklyn, Pennington attended Sunday and evening schools, and sought out tutors, as Sojourner could also have done in Manhattan. Soon Pennington was himself teaching at a black public school in Queens. Within a few years, he was also promoting the founding of more black schools, writing for black newspapers, pastoring black churches, and leading in the Colored National Convention movement.[32]

The period when Sojourner became a national public figure opened for her in 1843, when, disillusioned with her

31. A supposed Philadelphia paper, ca. 1871, in *Narrative*, 222. The Detroit *Post and Tribune*, Nov. 28, 1883, claimed that Sojourner when freed "was too old and too much occupied by other matters to set about learning to read."

32. James C.W. Pennington, *The Fugitive Blacksmith* (London, 1849); Mabee, *Black Education*, 37, 45, 57, 85, 123-125.

879

life as it was, she felt called by God to leave New York City, carrying with her a change of clothing in a pillow case, to walk from town to town, preaching the "truth." In accordance with this new role in her life, she gave up her slave name and adopted the new one which she believed God had given her, "Sojourner Truth."

After a few months of walking and preaching, Sojourner came across a religiously tolerant, well educated, predominantly white, utopian socialist community in Northampton, Massachusetts, and settled there for several years. It was especially through this community that Sojourner learned to combine her evangelism with advocating black and women's rights; it was here that she came to know such leading white abolitionists as editor William Lloyd Garrison who encouraged her to become an abolitionist speaker. From this time, her closest associates were usually white reformers who were often very literate and very well aware that she was not.

She became close to such leading white reformers as abolitionist editor Marius Robinson, who publicized her speechmaking and helped her find more opportunities to speak; journalist Frances D. Gage, who recalled that when many women feared the effects of allowing an uncouth black woman to speak to a woman's rights convention, she nevertheless insisted on allowing Sojourner to do so; and abolitionist lecturer Lucy Colman, who took her to the White House to visit President Lincoln. These three, as well as others of her white associates, at one time taught schools for blacks, and would be likely to be open to teaching Sojourner.[33] For her part, Sojourner, in a discussion with the white abolitionist Henry C. Wright on the proper role of abolitionists in reaching down to the uneducated, seemed at least tentatively open to having abolitionists teach her. "Suppose I want to learn to read," she asked, who will "learn me? Will friend Wright come down to teach me?"[34]

33. Russell B. Nye, "Marius Robinson, A Forgotten Abolitionist Leader," *Ohio State Archaeological and Historical Quarterly* 55 (April-June, 1946), 143-144; "Gage, Frances Dana," *Appleton's Cyclopaedia of American Biography* II (1887); Lucy N. Colman, *Reminiscences* (Buffalo, 1891), 16, 63. Other white reformer associates of Sojourner who also taught blacks included Laura Haviland, Josephine Griffing, and Lucy Stone.
34. *Anti-Slavery Bugle*, Nov. 8, 1856.

In fact, according to a story of uncertain origin, in Ohio in the early 1850s editor Robinson tried to teach Sojourner to read, but she failed to learn. She was probably about fifty-five years old at the time, but, according to this story, she told Robinson: "My brains is too stiff now."[35] While certainly childhood is the most natural time to learn to read, few educators today would say that being fifty-five years old is in itself a reason why a person could not learn to read.

Long afterward, an abolitionist pastor reported that Sojourner had tried to learn to read once when she was said to be too old. This might refer to Robinson's attempt to teach her or to another such attempt. This report, written by the pastor after he had talked with her while she was speaking in Kansas in 1879, quoted her as saying, in explanation for her failing to learn: "The letters all got mixed up and I couldn't straighten them out."[36]

881

In 1880, three years before she died, Sojourner apparently tried to sign her name, in capital letters, in an autograph book which has been preserved in a museum in Battle Creek, Michigan, where she lived in her last years. The museum calls this effort her "only known signature."[37] The first two letters are recognizable as S and O. The third could be an upside-down J. The last three could be S O J in reverse. Two years before she died, when she made out her will, she still was

---

35. Saunders Redding, *The Lonesome Road: The Story of the Negro's Part in America* (Garden City, N.Y.: Doubleday, 1958), 78; Pauli, *Her Name Was Sojourner Truth*, 181. Neither Redding nor Pauli documents this story. When I wrote Redding asking if he could cite a source for this story, he replied (May 16, 1986) that though he checked his notes, he could not. The Curator of Manuscripts, Western Reserve Historical Society, Cleveland, which has Marius Robinson papers, reports (to CM, June 4, 1986) that it has found no reference to Sojourner in those papers, and has no other suggestions as to the source of the story. Robinson was the editor of the *Anti-Slavery Bugle*, Salem, O., 1851-1859. By May, 1851, Sojourner was speaking in Ohio (*Bugle*, June 7, 1851). On Aug. 28, 1851, Sojourner wrote William L. Garrison (Boston Public Library), giving her address as care of Robinson, Salem, O. (Of course all of Sojourner's letters were written for her by someone else.) She was still speaking in Ohio according to the Windsor (Canada West) *Voice of the Fugitive*, Oct. 21, 1852.

36. Richard Cordley, "Sojourner Truth," *Congregationalist*, March 3, 1880, 65. Pauli, *Her Name Was Sojourner Truth*, 146, may be referring to this same effort to teach Sojourner, when she reports adults tried to teach Sojourner to read, but "the letters blurred before her eyes." Pauli, who as usual provides no sources, associates this experience with Sojourner's stay at the Northampton utopian community, but I know of no evidence for this.

reported to be unable to sign her own name.[38] After Sojourner died in 1883, her obituary in a magazine edited by her physician, director John Harvey Kellogg of the Battle Creek

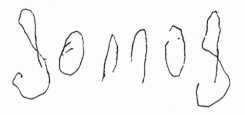

882

Sojourner's signature. Courtesy of Historical Society of Battle Creek.

Sanitarium (Kellogg was later to become well known as the originator of flaked breakfast cereals), reported that in her "last years" she "began to learn to read," but since, according to the same obituary, she nevertheless remained "unlettered and untaught," whatever progress she made in learning must have been insignificant.[39] Her Battle Creek friend and manager, Mrs. Titus, in her account of Sojourner's last years and death, reported assertions that Sojourner remained illiterate, and did not contradict them.[40]

Since Sojourner found that she could not learn to read or write letters, and that they seemed to become jumbled before her eyes, is it possible—a possibility that has not, to my knowledge, been directly proposed in previous studies—that Sojourner had a learning disability of some kind, which at the time might not have been understood? Perhaps it was a physiological disability, or perhaps a psychological one, or a combination of the two. For instance, perhaps she had a

37. Kimball House Museum to Carleton Mabee July 14, 1986, with photocopy of the signature.

38. Chicago *Tribune*, Dec. 22, 1881. Sojourner regularly signed with her "mark" (*Narrative*, 282).

39. *Good Health*, Dec., 1883, 382.

40. *Narrative*, 1884, "A Memorial Chapter," 13, 15, 22.

883

Sojourner Truth. Courtesy of the State University of New York, College at New Paltz.

visual perception problem, more of a problem than her glasses could correct.[41] Or perhaps the whippings she received as a Dutch-speaking child for not understanding her new owner's English could have set up psychological blocks about language which interfered with her learning to read.[42] Today experts believe that perhaps 5 to 20 percent of Americans have reading disabilities, but they also believe that with strong determination and appropriate guidance, these disabled can usually learn to read.[43]

41. For some years Sojourner at times wore glasses when speaking (New York *World*, May 11, 1867); when she had her picture taken (as in the picture of her in *Frank Leslie's Illustrated Newspaper*, Dec. 25, 1869, 245, and in the frontispiece of her *Narrative*, 1875); and, she said, when ironing (Chicago *Daily Inter-Ocean*, Aug.

In the middle and late years of her life, Sojourner clearly respected certain kinds of education. During the Civil War when she called on President Lincoln, and he proudly showed her a Bible given him by blacks, she told him that she grieved that slaves had been prevented from learning to read the Bible.[44] Soon afterward she herself was teaching ragged refugee Southern blacks, recently freed from slavery, how to keep themselves clean, to sew, to make effective use of the small assistance payments the government gave them, to insist on their rights, and to send their children to school.[45] After the war, when Sojourner came to believe that government welfare was degrading the freedmen, she campaigned for Congress to give them free public land in the West, so they could establish farm colonies where they could be taught, she said, to read and support themselves and "be somebody." She also became an advocate, like Booker T. Washington, of industrial schools for blacks.[46]

However, while she had come to see basic education as useful, she continued to display signs of negative attitudes toward more intellectual education. Speaking in a church, she ridiculed "Greek-crammed" preachers who focused on the remote past instead of on the teeming present. Speaking at a

884

13, 1879). In 1877, after she had recovered from a long illness, she discovered that she no longer needed glasses, and stopped wearing them, blessing God for "putting new glass in the windows" of her "soul" (Chicago *Daily Inter-Ocean*, Aug. 13, 1879). About that time she seems to have said that she had worn glasses for, variously, 50 years (in Blue Rapids, Kan., *Times*, July 18, 1878, and New York *World*, Dec. 7, 1878); and 60 or 70 years (in Chicago *Daily Inter-Ocean*, Aug. 13, 1879; but Mrs. Titus, in *Narrative*, 1884, "A Memorial Chapter," 30, in quoting the *Inter-Ocean*, evidently altered this passage, without acknowledging that she was doing so, to 30 or 40 years, because she thought this more reasonable). In these references by Sojourner to her wearing glasses to correct her eyesight, she does not make any connection between her eyesight and her failure to learn to read and write.

42. Difficulties with speech can set up blocks in learning to read. R.M.N. Crosby, *The Waysiders: Reading and the Dyslexic Child* (New York: Day, 1976), 210.

43. *Time*, April 21, 1986, 70; New York *Times*, May 7, 1986; Jan. 13, Dec. 8, 1987; Stanley S. Lamm, *Learning Disabilities*. I am particularly indebted to my colleague Prof. Donald Roper for pressing me to consider that Sojourner might have had a reading disability.

44. Sojourner Truth to Rowland Johnson, *National Anti-Slavery Standard*, Dec. 17, 1864.

45. Capt. G.B. Carse in *National Anti-Slavery Standard*, Dec. 17, 1864; *Narrative*, 181-195; Fred Tomkins, *Jewels in Ebony* (London, 1866?), 3-4; Colman, *Reminiscences*, 65.

46. Boston *Post*, Jan. 2, 1871; *Narrative*, 195, 197-200, 226-227; *Zion's Herald*, Feb. 23, 1871, 92.

college, she ridiculed the students for writing down notes on what she said, advising them instead to take notes as she did in her head.[47]

Sojourner herself, instead of pursuing literacy, learned to use her illiteracy to her advantage. To avoid clashing with someone over religious doctrines, she would say that if she could read the Bible she might see the matter differently. As a speaker, she would play provocatively with her illiteracy, as in this one-liner which won her applause: "I tell you I can't read a book, but I can read de people."[48] Or like this: "You read books; God Himself talks to me." Remarkably, she seemed to be able to use her illiteracy to lift herself up into a high pulpit from which she then could more effectively scold an audience, as she did once thus: "With all your opportunities for readin' and writin', you don't take hold and do anything."[49]

885

For many of Sojourner's listeners, her lack of literacy and culture contributed to her charm as a speaker, and of course, shrewd as she was, she knew it. She towered about six feet tall, and was exceedingly black—the blackest woman I ever saw, recalled one of her friends; "hideously black," said a New York newspaper report which Sojourner said she especially liked.[50] Unlike Douglass, she was usually believed to be of unmixed black ancestry, so that her white listeners could not conveniently attribute her brilliance to the white share of her ancestry. Her speech—delivered in a robust voice, so deep that some of her enemies suspected that she was a man—evidently consisted of a unique combination of elements, including, as different observers understood it, a guttural Dutch accent from her early childhood, the broken English of white illiterates, and black (but not, she insisted, Southern black) dialect.[51] In her early years as an agitator for reform, the New York *Tribune* said her English was

47. New York *Daily Tribune*, Nov. 8, 1853; Carter, "Sojourner Truth," 479.
48. *Narrative*, 110; Boston *Post*, Jan 2, 1871.
49. New York *Evening Telegram*, Nov. 27, 1883; Springfield *Daily Republican*, Feb. 24, 1871.
50. Colman, *Reminiscences, 66; New York World*, May 11, 1867; Elizabeth Cady Stanton, letter to editor, New York *World*, May 13, 1867.
51. *Liberator*, Oct. 15, 1858; Blue Rapids (Kan.) *Times*, July 18, 1878; Chicago *Daily Inter-Ocean*, Aug. 13, 1879; New York *Herald*, Dec. 16, 1878; Hendricks, "Sojourner Truth," 671; Cordley, "Sojourner Truth," 65; New York *World*, May 10, 1867; New York *Herald*, Dec. 16, 1878; Chicago? *Daily Telegraph*, clipping,

"tolerably correct," but her "homely" expressions "enhanced" her style. A British journalist who met her in Washington during the Civil War claimed that she was "able to speak in correct and beautiful English" when she chose.[52] As the years advanced, despite her association with many cultured people, she did not usually seem to choose to use more correct English. If anything, she seemed to make her speech less grammatical, more folksy, more in black dialect because she found her audiences liked it that way; it made her more picturesque to them, more bewitching, more memorable. As the perceptive Frederick Douglass recalled, "She seemed to please herself and others best when she put her ideas in the oddest forms." In 1867 Sojourner complained to a New York newspaperman that he wasn't reporting her words accurately, but she also admitted "good naturedly," he said, that her speech was difficult to record because she was speaking in "an unknown tongue." In the 1870s, when she spoke in Boston, the Boston *Post* reported that although her pronunciation was so outlandish that she pronounced her own name as "Sojoum' Trute," nevertheless her "inimitable patois" enhanced the "piquancy of her remarks."[53]

Sojourner spoke largely from her own experience, but what she said reflected an awareness of current clashes of thought, and she was sometimes able to cut through them with startling flashes of insight of her own. She spoke extemporaneously, not knowing what the Lord would put into her mouth, she said, explaining, "I go to hear myself as much as anyone else comes to hear me."[54] She spoke some phrases deliberately, emphasizing them, but raced through others, and often interrupted herself with droll asides. As she recalled, she did not always have natural pauses in her flow of speech.[55] Her foes could call her "crazy, ignorant,

Aug. 1879?, in Berenice Lowe, ed., "Sojourner Truth: Data Collected," 1964, Michigan Historical Collections, University of Michigan, microfilm, Section IX.

52. New York *Daily Tribune*, Sept. 7, 1853; Tomkins, *Jewels in Ebony*, 6.

53. Frederick Douglass, "What I Found at the Northampton Association," Charles A. Sheffield, ed., *The History of Florence, Massachusetts*, (Florence, 1895), 132; New York *World*, May 11, 1867; Boston *Post*, Jan. 2, 1871. Mrs. Titus, in reprinting this *Post* story in *Narrative*, 213, evidently found the story's report of Sojourner's pronunciation of her name extreme, and without acknowledgment changed it to "Sojourn' Truth."

54. New York *Sun*, Nov. 24, 1878.

repelling,'' but a group of Oberlin College students found themselves "vastly entertained" by watching her demolish a clergyman who opposed her views.[56] According to the *National Antislavery Standard*, she was majestic and inspiring. According to a Detroit newspaper, she had both "a heart of love" and "a tongue of fire." According to women's advocate Lucy Stone, she spoke "with direct and terrible force, moving friend and foe alike."[57]

As much as Sojourner turned her illiteracy to her advantage in her speaking, her inability to read and write continued to handicap her in many ways. Her participation in the movements she supported was often marginal, doubtless in part because of her independent nature, but also in part because of her illiteracy. While during the time she was a slave most blacks in New York State were illiterate, the same as she was, already by 1850 about 50 percent of blacks in the state had become literate, and by 1880 about 80 percent, and similarly in the North at large. Under these circumstances, of course, her opportunities for leadership among blacks as well as whites were likely to be limited. She never became a regular lecturer for antislavery societies, as Douglass did. She never became a member of the decision-making inner councils of the abolitionists, or of the Colored Convention movement, or of the women's suffrage movement, all of which Douglass did. She was also often poor, doubtless in part because of her illiteracy. She once warned friends that while she wanted them to come to visit her, she could not afford to provide food for them, and asked them to bring food along. When she was on speaking trips, to reduce expenses she often depended on friends for a place to stay. Whether on speaking trips or at home, to support herself and her children and grandchildren who sometimes lived with her, she often sold copies of her *Narrative* and copies of photographs of herself, and when at home she sometimes worked as a domestic or sold berries door to door.[58] In addition, especially during fre-

887

55. New York *World*, May 11, 1867; New York *Herald*, Dec. 16, 1878.
56. A New Jersey paper, 1870?, in *Narrative*, 204; Chadwick, *A Life for Liberty*, 57.
57. *National Anti-Slavery Standard*, July 4, 1863; Detroit *Advertiser and Tribune*, Nov. 23, 1863; Lucy Stone, "Sojourner Truth," *Woman's Journal*, Aug. 5, 1876, 252.

quent periods of illness in her later years, she and her friends were often obliged to appeal for charitable contributions for her support.[59]

Occasionally Sojourner could express frustration that she could not read or write. Once she conceded that it was "hard work" to get as many letters written for her as she wanted written. In another instance, thanking a correspondent for her "kind words," Sojourner replied, as a friend wrote it down for her, "Oh, if I could but write and answer them myself!"[60] But more characteristic of her tone was her jaunty comment, as recorded by the woman suffragist Elizabeth Cady Stanton: "I know and do what is right better than many big men who read." According to Lucy Stone, Sojourner often even said that she "was glad she never knew how to read," for "all the great trouble of the world came from those who could read, and not from those who could not."[61] In fact, to the distress of Frederick Douglass, she seemed to revel in being uncultured. She "seemed to feel it her duty," Douglass recalled," to ridicule my efforts to speak and act like a person of cultivation and refinement . . . . She was a genuine specimen of the uncultured negro. She cared very little for elegance of speech or refinement of manners." Uncultured as she was, she seemed to carry herself without fear or

888

58. Sojourner Truth to Amy Post, Nov. 4, 1867, Amy Post papers, University of Rochester; Berenice Lowe, "Michigan Days of Sojourner Truth," *New York Folklore Quarterly* 12 (Summer, 1956), 128.

59. For example, Sojourner or her friends appealed in the Detroit *Advertiser and Tribune*, Nov. 25, 1863, for contributions to render her "comfortable"; in *Frank Leslie's Illustrated Newspaper*, Dec. 25, 1869, 247, to help pay off the mortgage on the barn she converted into a dwelling; in Sojourner Truth to Amy Post, Aug. 26, 1873, Post papers, for a loan. Sojourner Truth to William Still, Jan. 4, 1876, William Still papers, Historical Society of Pa., reports her house had been mortgaged again in part because of her paying for burying her grandson Samuel who otherwise would have been buried by the town. Titus wrote, in Boston *Journal?*, Dec., 1879? clipping, Sojourner Truth papers, Library of Congress, that she had "taken upon myself the whole responsibility" for Sojourner's "support, else she would have been a public charge for the past five years."

60. Sojourner Truth to Amy Post, Aug. 25, 1867, Post papers; Sojourner to Mary K. Gale, Feb. 25, 1864, Sojourner Truth papers.

61. Stanton, letter to editor, New York *World*, May 13, 1867; Stone, "Sojourner Truth," 252. This latter quotation suggests that Sojourner was like the many learning-disabled children who, instead of admitting they can't learn, say they don't want to learn. (Sally L. Smith, *No Easy Answers: Teaching the Learning Disabled Child*, Cambridge, Mass: Winthrop, 1979, 63.) This quotation also seems to cast doubt on the claim of Rose Lindley Kent, "Isabella: The Story of Sojourner Truth," *Negro Digest* 11 (Oct., 1962), 20, that Sojourner "keenly lamented her lack of schooling."

shame. According to Harriet Beecher Stowe, she conveyed "almost an unconscious superiority." When Garrison was helping Sojourner by arranging the printing and distribution of copies of her *Narrative*, she gave him directions about how to do it as if he were her secretary.[62]

Several conclusions lead from this analysis of Sojourner Truth's illiteracy. First, it was misleading for Sojourner to say, in her old age, that she "never had an opportunity" to learn to read.[63] Both in slavery and afterwards, she had opportunities to learn, but she did not seize such opportunities, while other blacks, like Douglass and Pennington, did seize them. She did not seize them because she was not ready to seize them, as many inner city youths today have not been ready to seize opportunities to learn.

889

Also, for Sojourner and others to say that slavery prevented her from learning to read and write was too simple and lent itself to mythmaking. From the limited information available, it is more accurate to say that she failed to learn because of a complex interaction among the effects of slavery, the impact of a probable learning disability, and her own character.

Sold away from her parents, cruelly whipped for not understanding English, not significantly encouraged to learn to read and write by her masters, lacking in role models among other blacks, Sojourner experienced much in slavery to scar not only her body but also her mind and emotions. Moreover, she probably had a learning disability which made it difficult, though not impossible, for her to learn to read. In addition, she reacted to her early experiences by developing personality traits which could interfere with her learning. She struggled to preserve her independence by developing a stubborn willfulness which helped her to resist guidance. She struggled to maintain her individuality by withdrawing into her own inner experience, including listening to God's voice within her, instead of striving to master knowledge about the objective world. She struggled to offset the degradation of

62. Douglass, "What I Found at the Northampton Association," 131-132; Stowe, "Sojourner Truth," 473-474; Sojourner Truth to William L. Garrison, Aug. 28, 1851.
63. Chicago *Daily Inter-Ocean*, Aug. 13, 1879.

slavery by developing personal qualities of which she could be proud, such as her honesty, physical strength, and industry. With the help of such compensations, Sojourner, unlike Douglass, often reined in her rebellion against slavery, and for much of her early adulthood accepted her status as a slave, and with it evidently accepted the idea that slaves were not expected to learn to read or write.

Was rebellion against whites a factor in Sojourner's failure to learn to read, as it has often been said in our time to be a factor in black youths remaining functional illiterates? Jonathan Kozol, in his book *Illiterate America* (1985), cited Sojourner's provocative statement that she could not read books but could read people, and then Kozol proceeded to use her statement in a way that I believe Sojourner herself would not use it. Kozol used it to compare Sojourner to poor blacks today who cannot read books but who can read the style of middle class white workers who come to recruit them for literacy programs, and read it as indicating that these workers are so different in background from themselves that they are turned off by them.[64] Certainly Sojourner's personal style, emerging out of her early experiences, was significantly different from the style of educated whites, but Sojourner was not usually turned off by educated whites, and in fact during much of her life chose to associate closely with them. So rebellion against whites per se seems misleading as an explanation of Sojourner's failure to learn.

After she was freed, her personal religious experience reinforced her inwardness, and lent itself to fostering in her a touch of contempt for intellectual learning and refinement. From the time she left New York City, her overwhelming faith that God had called her to a special mission to the world, helped to give her such confidence that at least outwardly she scarcely would admit a need for learning. On another level, we can say that she gradually developed her youthful stubbornness into a bravado that helped her to spin myths about herself, cover up her inferiority feelings, and play on her illiteracy to her advantage.

Even without conventional education, she was quick and

64. Kozol, *Illiterate America*, 103-105.

890

wily enough to find a role of significant, though circumscribed, leadership in the turbulent life of her time, as an uncultured Mother in the Israel of Reform.[65] It was a role which
she found satisfying enough to take the force out of any impulses to seek learning that she may have had. We have no
clear evidence that at any time in her life Sojourner herself initiated an attempt to learn to read and write.

In our time, the myth-enshrouded life of Sojourner Truth
has often been used to inspire both blacks and whites, young
and old, with faith, courage, and the will to struggle against
the folly and injustice of the world. With a bit of the myth
peeled away, Sojourner's life, particularly as it relates to her
illiteracy, remains startling, contradictory, and provocative.
She can be seen as disquieting for advocating basic education,
and yet not only failing to achieve it for herself, but sometimes even glorying in her lack of it. She can also be seen as
an example of how illiteracy may limit even a brilliant
person's leadership, and contribute to that person's poverty
and dependence on others. Sojourner can also be seen, however, as inspiring for rising above her extremely adverse circumstances as a slave, a black, a woman, and an illiterate. In
particular, she can be seen as inspiring for transforming her
illiteracy from a handicap into an advantage that helped to
give her a strong, intuitive, original, constructive voice in the
long, on-going struggle for human rights.

891

65. The Washington, D.C. *New Era*, April 21, 1870, called Sojourner a "worthy
mother in the Israel of reform."

Black Women in the 'White City'

by ANN MASSA
University of Leeds

I

The scope of the Chicago World's Fair of 1893, which celebrated, albeit a year late, the four hundredth anniversary of Columbus's discovery of America, ranged over many centuries, numerous nations and almost every type of human achievement. The 27 million people who came to the five months long Fair were able to see Grace Darling's boat or Spanish galleons of Columbus's time; they could follow the history of transport from coracles to cars; they could see the latest in Krupp's cannon and Bell's telephone in a classically styled Machinery Hall six times the size of the Coliseum. With the exception of Louis Sullivan's golden Transportation Pavilion, the buildings which housed the Fair, covered uniformly with staff, composed a classical ' White City ', grouped round a complex of lagoons and fountains on Chicago's Lake Front.

In this ' White City ', nations, arts and occupations vied with each other in pavilions and conferences to demonstrate the latest thinking in religion or the most efficient techniques of ship-building; and in the U.S. especially, each state and every section of the host nation did its self-conscious best to boom and boost itself. Elliot M. Rudwick and August Meier, in their article ' Black Man in the " White City " : Negroes and the Columbian Exposition, 1893 ',[1] demonstrate the problems of participation and exhibition confronting one disadvantaged and sectionalized section of American society. Should black men work for a separate exhibit or an integrated one? Should they ask for or accept special (or discriminatory) help in collecting such an exhibit? Should they work for the appointment of a black collector or co-operate with a white one, if white co-operation were forthcoming? Precisely the same problems were involved in the impressive series of collective and individual attempts which both obscure and well-known black women made to secure an effective display of black women's achievement at the Fair. Moreover, the unceasing, embattled flow of ideas and activities from these women made as effective a display of race pride and talent as any static exhibit in the Fair's pavilions might have provided.

[1] *Phylon*, **26** (Winter 1965), 354–61.

Originally published in *Journal of American Studies*, Vol. 8, No. 3 (December 1974).

Since the World's Columbian Commission had given the Board of Lady Managers plenary power as ' the channel of communication through which all women or organizations of women may be brought into relation with the Exposition, and through which all applications for space for the use of women or their exhibits in the buildings shall be made ',[2] the black women focused on the Board. On 16 November 1890, three days before the Board's first meeting, the *Chicago Tribune* announced: ' There will be a Ladies' mass-meeting at Bethesda Baptist Chapel . . . next Monday evening [November 24] at eight o'clock relative to the position in which colored ladies' exhibits shall be placed in the National Columbian Exposition.'[3] The organizers were apparently in touch with Mary S. Logan,[4] the formidable, reputedly liberal widow of one of Illinois' emancipating triumvirs, Lincoln, Lovejoy and John A. Logan; she was in Chicago as Lady Manager for Washington, D.C. On 25 November she presented the Board ' a communication from the colored women of Chicago ':

WHEREAS no provisions have, as yet, been made by the World's Columbian Exposition Commission for securing exhibits from the colored women of this country, or the giving of representation to them in such Fair, and WHEREAS under the present arrangement and classification of exhibits, it would be impossible for visitors to the Exposition to know and distinguish the exhibits and handwork of the colored women from those of the Anglo-Saxons, and because of this the honor, fame and credit for all meritorious exhibits, though made by some of our race, would not be duly given us, therefore be it

RESOLVED, that for the purpose of demonstrating the progress of the colored women since emancipation and of showing to those who are yet doubters, and there are many, that the colored women have [made] and are making rapid strides in art, science, and manufacturing, and of furnishing to all information as to the educational and industrial advancement made by the race, and what the race has done, is doing, and might do, in every department of life, that we, the colored women of Chicago request the World's Columbian Commission to establish an office for a colored woman whose duty it shall be to collect exhibits from the colored women of America . . .[5]

Mrs Logan's motion that the resolution be referred to the Executive Committee of the World's Columbian Commission was carried; but the petitioners suspected, rightly, that the Commission would take no action. The following

894

---

2 *Report of Mrs Potter Palmer, President, to the Board of Lady Managers, September 2, 1891* (Chicago, 1891), pp. 7–8.   3 *Chicago Tribune*, 16 November, 1890.
4 Biographies and bibliographies for Mary Logan and the following women mentioned in this article can be found in Edward James (ed.): *Notable American Women, 1607–1950* (Cambridge, Mass.: The Belknap Press, 1971); Hallie Brown, Matilda Carse, Fanny Coppin, Phoebe Couzins, Frances Harper, Isabella Hooker, Bertha Palmer, Ida Wells-Barnett, Fannie Williams.
5 *Approved official minutes of the Board of Lady Managers of the World's Columbian Commission*, 19–26 November (Chicago, 1891), p. 79.

morning the Board received two pressing communications from the women, and agreed to hear their spokeswoman, Mrs Lettie A. Trent. She reiterated their ' wishes and claims ' with a slight shift of emphasis: she ' asked to have a colored woman designated by the Commission and legally authorized to be placed in charge of the exhibit of the colored people ',[6] underlining that it was an executive post, not a fieldworker, that the women had in mind. The President of the Board, Mrs Bertha Honoré Palmer, wife of Chicago property tycoon, Potter Palmer, suggested a committee of three to confer with the delegation over lunch: Mrs Logan, Mrs Helen Brayton [7] of South Carolina, a philanthropist involved in helping the dependants of lynch-law victims, and Mrs Mary Cecil Cantrill, wife of Representative James Cantrill of the Kentucky legislature, who ' expressed her deep interest in the race and her desire to use all her powers in their elevation and advancement, and seemed to feel that her long and intimate acquaintance with them gave her peculiar opportunities for helpfulness '.[8]

895

The report submitted in the afternoon differed significantly from Mrs Trent's request in that it did not specify a ' colored woman ' as organizer.

The committee . . . has the honor to report that the colored people request that the Lady Managers recommend to the Columbian Commission that in designating persons to solicit exhibits, that they recognize them in securing exhibits by their race, and that the President of the Lady Managers, in appointing the Executive Committee of the Ladies' Board, be respectfully requested to appoint some Lady Manager on that Committee to represent the interest of the colored people.[9]

The report bears several interpretations. The committee, speaking for rather than to the Board, might be stating that the Board would not appoint or co-operate with a black woman organizer, but was not opposed to a black women's exhibit. Alternatively, the intention might be to indicate that the Board would co-operate with a black male organizer. In all probability the committee had framed a resolution which, without committing the Board to any specific action, would convince the petitioners that some progress was being made.

From 26 November 1890, when the first meeting of the Board ended, the

6 *Ibid.*, pp. 91–2.

7 Brayton to Albion W. Tourgée, 13 April, 1892, in the Albion W. Tourgée Papers, Chautauqua County Historical Society, Westfield, N.Y.; hereafter cited as *TP*. Tourgée, radical-liberal judge, journalist and author, was the adviser and confidante of black and white liberals; and as ' Bystander ' of the *Chicago Inter-Ocean*, had a special interest in the city. Dean H. Keller, ' An Index to the Albion W. Tourgée Papers ', *Kent State University Bulletin* (May, 1964), numbers the items in the Brayton-Tourgée correspondence, 4361, 4717, 4789, 6181.

8 Susan G. Cooke. ' To all interested in the colored people ', 3 pp. carbon typescript, Logan Family Papers, Library of Congress, Washington, D.C.; hereafter cited as *LP*.

9 *Approved official minutes . . . November 19–26*, p. 92.

Lady Managers and the lobbyists did their best to determine who Mrs Palmer would appoint to her twenty-five member executive committee, which, since Congress seemed certain to refuse to fund frequent meetings of the unwieldy and expensive 115 member Board, would become the *de facto* female power centre.[10] Would it be more southern than northern, since Mrs Palmer was originally from Kentucky? Mrs Trent, now President of the Woman's Columbian Association, badgered the Board as appointment day drew near. She wrote Mrs Logan:

As Mrs. Potter Palmer is about to appoint the executive board of Lady Managers, our Association sent a petition to her asking that in the interest of the colored women of this country that she appoint Ladies whose names would be inspiring to them, that they might feel assured of having friends on the board of Managers. We . . . request that your name should head the list. Knowing how thoroughly your name is known among our people it would certainly make them feel more at liberty to send their exhibits.[11]

But there were black women in Chicago who did not agree with Mrs Trent's plan to stage a separate exhibit, her attempt to work through white women, and her apparent willingness to be represented by white women. On 27 February 1890, a rival organization, the Women's Columbian Auxiliary Association came into being, registered as a corporation under the State of Illinois, with an all-female board of seven women directors and seven women officers, President, Mrs R. D. Boone. A seven-man advisory panel included Frederick L. Barnett, a Chicago lawyer who in 1895 married Ida B. Wells, and Dr Daniel Hale Williams, founder of Provident Hospital, whose all-black governors and staff admitted black and white patients equally. The W.C.C.A., quickly claiming a hundred committed members, had organizational strengths and race ambitions lacking in the W.C.A. In the first stages of its existence the W.C.C.A. was only secondarily concerned with women at the Fair. Its first care was that this ' best opportunity . . . to give evidence to the world of the capability of the race . . . just what it has accomplished since Emancipation ' should not be passed up; and that opportunity had to be seized independently.

We cannot expect for the American people to expend their energy and tax their best efforts to help any one class of American citizens. Still less can this be expected when we consider that toward the colored race there exists a well defined prejudice which in almost every avenue of action tends to work against us.

The W.C.C.A.'s members opted for an integrated exhibit.[12] They did not

---

[10] *Congressional Record*, 51:2, 24 February 1891, pp. 3196–7.

[11] Trent to Logan, 25 March 1891, LP.

[12] The Board had faced ' the burning question . . . whether the work of women at the Fair should be shown separately or in conjunction with the work of men ' and had decided to integrate. *Mrs Palmer's Address to the Fortnightly Club of Chicago* (Chicago, 1891), p. 4.

896

want to be set apart, for ' we are American citizens and desire to draw no line that would tend to make us strangers in the land of our birth '. They appealed, then, to blacks for information, volunteers and money, and outlined eight areas where they expected to demonstrate black achievement: music, art, church work, education, agriculture, mining, skilled work and woman's work. In the last area, the W.C.C.A. would act as ' a supplement to the labors of the Lady Board of Managers '.[13]

II

Like the officers of the Board, only one of whom, Mrs Charles Price of South Carolina, was a Southerner, the Executive Committee, appointed in late March, had few Southern members. Lady Manager Mrs R. A. Felton of Georgia complained to Mrs Logan, who was appointed: ' From Washington city to the Mississippi river, the six states of Virginia, South and North Carolina, Georgia, Alabama and Mississippi – not a single lady.' [14] When the Committee met in April, in accordance with the Board's minutes, and as a filial, compensatory gesture by Mrs Palmer to her home state, the South, and the lady who had nominated her for President, Mrs Cantrill of Kentucky was appointed to represent the coloured people. The appointment was a *faux pas*. Mrs Cantrill was so soaked in Southern paternalism that she was incapable of recognizing her own discriminatory practices.[15] Mrs Trent protested the appointment, though, since she was still prepared to work through, with and under white women, she based her protest on a claim that the Board's minutes and the subsequent Executive Committee procedure was incorrect. ' In the conference we had at the Palmer House it was settled to have three ladies to look after the interest of our women although the minutes read one lady.' Mrs Boone protested the Booker T. Washington-style approach of Mrs Trent.[16]

It is not specifically known how Mrs Cantrill construed or fulfilled her office, with one exception; she did refer all representations from black women

897

13 Women's Columbian Association, *Aim and Plan of Action. Constitution and Bylaws* (Chicago, February 1891); 10 pp. carbon typescript, TP. Keller, *loc. cit.*, items 5384A, 6148. Apart from Mrs Boone, *infra*, only one of the fourteen ladies has been identified as subsequently active: Mrs Lloyd [Connie E.] Curl, who became President of the Women's Civic League of Illinois, 1896–8, and Recording Secretary of the National Association of Colored Women, 1899–1900. See [Elizabeth Lindsay Davis], *The Story of the Illinois Federation of Colored Women's Clubs, 1900–22* [n.p., n.d.], pp. 50–1, 98.

14 Felton to Logan, 30 March 1891, LP. Presumably southern representation was slight because Mrs Palmer expected to find most evidence of women's progress in the North.

15 Logan to Palmer, 16 October 1891, LP.

16 Trent to Logan, 25 March, 4 April 1891, LP.

in Illinois [17] to the State Woman's Exposition Board, and this may have been her regular procedure. Events in September and October, 1891, showed that the black women's organizations, whose numbers had grown from two to four, and even some members of the Board, were discontented with Mrs Cantrill. Between April and September, 1891, when the Board held its second meeting, the black women canvassed the Lady Managers, especially three professional women who coveted Mrs Palmer's post and resented the authority of a society woman: lawyer Phoebe Couzins of St Louis, journalist Mary Lockwood of Washington, D.C., and suffragist-politician Isabella Beecher Hooker of Connecticut. Mrs Trent found that only these women, Mrs Logan, Mrs Brayton and a few others were 'in favour of doing justice and right by the colored women' [18]. Mrs Boone claimed that only three of the responses she received were favourable; the majority of the Board

898

ignored the letters of inquiry entirely, while some were frank enough to speak their pronounced opposition to any plan which would bring them in contact with a colored representative, and to emphasize the opposition by a declaration that they would resign in case [of] such an appointment.[19]

When the Board met in September, 1891, members interested in the black women's cause had difficulty in bringing Mrs Cantrill to the bar. In the morning of the sixth day, 8 September, she still 'required further time'; in the afternoon 'on the motion of Mrs [Matilda B.] Carse [the egalitarian business manager of the W.C.T.U.] Mrs Cantrill's report on the work among the colored people was made the special order of business for the following morning'. The only point of information in her vague report was that 'many of the questions referred for decision and action did not properly belong to our Committee [Mrs Cantrill: a Committee of one] and we have not jeopardized the interest of a state of our great Exposition, but gladly and appropriately lay before the proper authorities these questions'.[20] The sense of the meeting defined itself: a minority 'felt that the colored women should

[17] Frances B. Philips, ' To all interested in the colored women ' (Office of the Illinois Women's Exposition Board, 1 October 1891); 1 p. carbon typescript, LP.

[18] See *An Official Statement of the Act of the Executive Committee of the Board of Lady Managers in removing from office Miss Phoebe Couzins* (Chicago, 1891); *infra*, note 25; Hooker to Palmer, 8 May, 17 June 1891, Palmer to Hooker, 4 June 1891, in Correspondence of Mrs. Bertha Honoré Palmer, President, Board of Lady Managers of the World's Columbian Commission, Chicago Historical Society; hereafter cited as PP.

[19] ' The Appeal to the representative negro women of the United States ', *Boston Courant*, 24 October 1891; issued ' a few weeks ago ', *ibid*. Ida B. Wells (ed.), *The Reason Why the Colored American is not in the World's Columbian Exposition* [Chicago, 1893], p. 71. Cooke, *loc. cit.*, ' The Appeal . . . , loc. cit.*, and Palmer to Mrs Russell Harrison, 3 November 1891, PP, all mention four organizations.

[20] *Official Manual of the Board of Lady Managers of the World's Columbian Commission, November 10, 1890–September 9, 1891* (Chicago, 1891), pp. 264, 282, 299.

be treated separately, and their exhibit placed by itself ', and a majority ' were in favor of no unjust discrimination in color but favored placing the colored women on the same footing with white women, giving them the same latitude and opportunity . . . ' [21] The summary resolution of Mrs Paul of Virginia was adopted :

That the work of arousing interest in each of the several States and Territories, and the District of Columbia, among the colored people, and the best methods to be adopted and pursued therein, be and the same are expressly referred to the Lady Managers . . . in each State and Territory, and the District of Columbia.[22]

On paper justice had been done, for manageable size and financial reality dictated the state as the effective organizational unit, as Mrs Palmer had told her Executive Committee :

899

We must depend upon State Boards for all statistics as to woman's work . . . [to] ascertain what exhibits the women of their States will make . . . so that we may apply to the Installation Committee for the needed space . . . [to] suggest to us proper members for the juries of award.'[23]

The Board's annual appropriation from Congress of $36,000 barely covered running costs. Most states financed their own World's Fair's Boards, and catered for them by allotting a percentage of the entire appropriation, or a specific sum, or by honouring itemized accounts, *per diem* and travelling expenses. In practice, justice was out of the question, even given the hypothetical goodwill of the Lady Managers. The Southern States were, on the whole, late in setting up Boards (Kentucky, June, 1892; Louisiana, August, 1892); women in Alabama, Mississippi and South Carolina had to raise money by subscription; Kentucky's and Missouri's national Lady Managers had no expense accounts.[24]

III

Specious referral to the states momentarily united Mrs Trent, whose appeal for special help and a separate exhibit had thereby been refused, and Mrs Boone, who took the spirit, if not the letter of the resolution to mean that the Board was ' bitterly opposed to any advancement of the Negro race '. Both women wanted redress for the slanderous, racist remarks and jibes they believed had been made about them at the Board's September meeting.

[21] Cooke, *loc. cit.*

[22] *Ibid.*

[23] *Report of Mrs Potter Palmer, President, to the Board of Lady Managers, September 2, 1891* (Chicago, 1891), p. 29.

[24] ' Report of Amy M. Starkweather, Superintendent, State Work, Chief of Installation and Superintendent of Woman's Building ', Appendices ' A-1 ' through ' A-11 '; carbon typescript, Chicago Historical Society.

Representative from Arkansas: ' I wish to exhibit the work of the poor white cotton pickers.' Representative from Georgia: ' I want to exhibit the work of the cotton pickers – I mean the white cotton pickers.' Democratic representative from Texas: ' The darkies are better off in the white folk's hands. The Negroes in my State do not want representation.' Representative from Washington, D.C., who desired to have a delegation of colored women heard, was told by the President that if she ever brought up the colored question, she would never be forgiven for it. ... This the representative from Washington informs the delegation.[25]

Two of the petitioning organizations, whose splits, according to Mrs Palmer, were related to their affiliation to different brands of Methodism, decided to take their cause to Washington, to appeal to the Ecumenical Methodist Conference opening there on 9 October, and perhaps to Congress, for, they recalled, ' the colored people had friends in Congress in the dark days of slavery, and they have friends today '. In preparation for this visit each group issued a circular. One was from the Women's Independent Organisation, which, led by Mrs J. Roberts and Mrs Mary A. Henderson of Chicago, issued an ' appeal to the representative colored women of the United States ... to resent the insult hurled at the women of our race at the last session of the Board of Lady Managers '.[26] The other circular, which named no organization and no leaders, called on ' the representative Negro Women of the United States, urging them to meet at Washington, D.C., October 21, 1891, to take steps relating to the Negro woman's interest in the world's Columbian exposition ', and ' earnestly solicited ' a number of ' representative colored women to be present and lend their assistance in this great and important movement '. Lettie Trent was the only Chicago woman of the eleven named; the list included the well-known Sarah J. Early of Tennessee, school principal and national superintendent of temperance work among the coloured people; Fanny Jackson Coppin of Philadelphia, Oberlin graduate, missionary and vocational training pioneer; Frances W. E. Harper of Philadelphia, anti-slavery lecturer, poet and suffragist; and others from Kentucky, South Carolina, New Jersey and Massachusetts, Ohio and Texas. The text was apparently kept out of the Chicago papers by Mrs Palmer, and out of the Washington papers by Mrs Logan, but it did appear in the *Boston Courant*, and presumably circulated in the black press.[27] It was an effective piece of rhetorical

[25] ' The Appeal . . .', *loc. cit.* The representative was Mrs Lockwood. See Palmer to Cantrill, 17 October 1891; Palmer to Lockwood, 18 October 1891, PP.

[26] Palmer to Logan, 15 October 1891, LP; *Washington Star*, 7 October 1891. Roberts and Henderson later joined the W.C.A.; they were signatories to the resolution of 16 December 1891, *infra*, p. 328 and note 41.

[27] For Sarah J. Early, see L. A. Scruggs, *Woman of Distinction* (Raleigh, N.C., 1893). No mention of the black women's circulars has been located in the black press, which was as diverse in its concepts of a black exhibit as the rest of the black community – see Rudwick

questioning, punctuated by the refrain ' the Board of Lady Managers, created by an act of Congress, says no '.

Shall the Negro Women of this country have a creditable display of their labor and skill at the World's Columbian Exposition in 1893? . . . Shall five million of Negro women allow a small number of white women to ignore them in this, the grandest opportunity to manifest their talent and ability in this, the greatest expression of the age? . . . Ought not the work of the Negroes and their interest to be placed in the hands of Negro women? It ought or else the work of all the bureaux of white women should be placed in the hands of colored women . . .[28]

But the black women were far from united. Mrs Boone was not a signatory to the circular, for the Illinois Woman's Exposition Board had convincingly welcomed her in her self-styled supplementary function. Mrs Trent had developed strong personal ambitions, and offered to compromise. In return for ' a commission to take care of the interest of the colored people . . . she would go to Washington, address the convention and allay all discontent '. But, as Mrs Palmer discovered, the Board would have to pay the price for the black women's delays and frustrations: ' Mrs Trent's plan, which she read me in full, provided for a President, a Secretary, stenographers and clerks and officers – in fact for a duplicate of our organization for the special benefit of their race.'

901

In spite of her sarcastic comment on Mrs Trent's plan – ' Of course it is very easy to understand from that standpoint why they were dissatisfied with our actions for them '[29] – Mrs Palmer was apparently not trying to kill off a black exhibit. At this time she was weighing the merits of a variety of proposals about the exhibition, including one suggestion made to her by a coloured minister that there should be state-wide conventions of black churchwomen, each of which would elect an organizer and work through her.[30] But Mrs Palmer's interest in black representation was minimal. Above all she cared for the reputation of her Board, which must be without blemish if it were to exemplify woman's superior competence and probity, ' I do not want them to vilify us,' she stated; but ' apart from that I am perfectly willing that they should present all the petitions they choose to Congress.'[31]

and Meier, *loc. cit. The State Capital*, Springfield, Ill., 17 October 1891, published Susan G. Cooke's circular without comment. Mrs Palmer claimed the black press ' more universally than any class of publication demanded pay for the insertion of articles relating to the exhibit, which of course prevented their readers from gaining the information . . . this created the impression among them that their interests are being neglected '. Palmer to Hallie Q. Brown, 4 July 1892, PP.

28 ' The Appeal . . .', *loc. cit.*
29 Palmer to Logan, 3 November 1891, PP; Trent to Logan, 4 November 1891, LP.
30 Palmer to Logan, 15 October 1891, LP.
31 *Ibid.*

For assistance and outlet she turned to Mrs Logan [32] who held a political salon of some importance in Washington. On 11 October 1891, she wrote her: ' I am greatly annoyed by the antagonisms of some of the negro women who have recently issued a circular which . . . is a tissue of lies. . . I beg that you will see Fred Douglass and Bishop Fowler at once.' [33] Again she referred the issue to the states, this time with a public relations flourish. She asked ' all our southern ladies ' to send Mrs Logan ' an expression of their goodwill and wish to help the colored people in their respective states ', and she asked Mrs Logan, ' in case the response is quite general please make use of the fact '. The expression of goodwill took the form of a pledge to sign:

902

As a Lady Manager of the State of —— I shall do all in my power to further the interests of the colored women of my state, and will take pleasure in giving them all the information and assistance possible by sending them the publications issued by the Board . . . and in every other way striving to promote their interest. I shall be glad to co-operate with any person appointed to represent the colored people in the state, in order that the whole exhibition of our State may be brought out. This is entirely in accordance with the feelings of our whole Board.

In addition, the Board and the Illinois Women's Exposition Board issued counter-circulars to the black women's, the first recounting the ' true ' history of negotiations and the second reassuring ' all the women of Illinois . . . that without regard to nationality, or color, and in every respect, their work stands upon the same footing before this Board, believing that to give the colored women this absolute equality is the highest honor the Board can confer upon them '. This resolution met with Mrs Boone's ' hearty approval '.[34]

The Southern ladies rallied to a woman, though any publicity Mrs Logan gave the solidarity was exclusive; Mrs Trent tried in vain to obtain the text of the pledge.[35] Sight of the paternalistic, condescending letters which accompanied the signed pledges would have inflamed the black women. Mrs R. A. Felton of Georgia wrote:

I went to Atlanta and talked with the colored woman at the Passenger Depot who has charge there – and who sees every person passing through and told her I was ready and anxious to do all I could in this line & if it could be so arranged I would like to talk with them about it whenever they wished information.

---

[32] Cantrill was in a sanatorium in Georgetown, Kentucky. In a 28 pp. letter to Palmer, 21 September 1891, PP, she barely mentioned the black women, except to refer to Trent as ' most irritating to my nostrils physical and spiritual '.

[33] Bishop Charles Fowler of Minneapolis had been a pastor in Chicago, and President of Northwestern University. For Douglass's role in the black exhibit controversy, moderate until his speech on 25 August 1893, ' Colored People's Day at the Fair ', see Rudwick and Meier, *loc. cit.*

[34] Palmer to Logan, 11 and 15 October 1891, PP; Philips, *loc. cit.*; ' As a Lady Manager . . .', 1 p. carbon typescript, LP.

[35] Trent to Logan, 1 November 1891, LP.

The circular also gave the Lady Managers a chance to speculate on the situation which had produced the need for them to sign a pledge. Florence Olmstead of Georgia expressed the prevalent Lady Managers' belief that some white woman must be behind such articulate and sustained protests. Mrs Cantrill suggested Mrs Logan; Mrs Palmer suggested Mrs Carse.[36] In fact, there is no evidence to suggest that anyone was behind the black women except the black women. The intermittent co-operation of a Lady Manager was no spur to action; only a voting majority of the Board could have helped them. As it was, the Board was never faced with any real likelihood that Congress or the W.C.C., which were comparably 'colour-proof', would press it to accept a special black representative. It did not even need to join issue with the black women; instead, its members anticipated and prevented potential adverse publicity – 'we do not want to be ridiculed by paragraphs all over the country'[37] – though with a degree of overkill that was a tribute to the tenacious, emotive, cogent power of the black women's organization and presentation. Mrs Palmer believed that 18,000 copies of the circulars had been issued, and suspected a conspiracy:

903

I think their [the black women's] plan is to appear before Congress as soon as it convenes and make a strong protest against our Board, and then Mrs. Hooker and Miss Couzins will enter their complaints, so that we will seem guilty of acts of wrongdoing and Congress may hesitate to give us an appropriation.

She even got Mrs Russell B. Harrison, Lady Manager for Montana, to lobby her father, President Benjamin Harrison.

I am very much obliged to you for your compliance with my request to write to the President about the matter of the colored people. Our aim was to have their meeting amounting to nothing, and I think we have reason to congratulate ourselves on the work we did in advance which produced the desired result.[38]

Although the divisions of the women were not in themselves invidious, the Board made them seem so in such (unverifiable) statements as 'our Board was entirely willing to appoint a national representative from the Negro women, and only refrained from doing so because they were quarrelling so among themselves and could not decide on a leader...'[39] The consequent fear of sympathizers that they might be caught in black crossfire, and on the losing

---

36 Olmstead to Logan, 14 October 1891; Felton to Logan, 17 October 1891, LP; Cantrill to Palmer, 21 September 1891; Palmer to Cantrill, 17 October 1891, PP. There is no evidence that Logan was anything but solid behind state referral. Letters to Palmer, 16 October 1891, and Trent, 10 November 1891, PP, show she disliked Trent. Palmer to Cantrill, 17 October 1891, PP, claimed Mrs Carse tried to have Mrs Paul's resolution voted down.

37 Palmer to Mrs Charles Price of South Carolina, 11 August 1891, PP.

38 Palmer to Logan, 3 November 1891; Palmer to Harrison, 3 November 1891, PP.

39 Palmer to Logan, 11 October 1891; Logan to Trent, 4 November 1891, LP; Cooke, *loc. cit.*

side, must have contributed to the frustration of the Washington lobbyists. Their petition(s) did not get onto the floor of Congress; the Methodist conference refused to hear them; their convention took the form of a private conference where about forty people condemned the conduct of the Board. Mrs Trent claimed that the convention elected her 'Chairman of the National Council of Colored Women', and lobbied Mrs Logan and Mrs Palmer through December.[40] The last known gesture of the W.C.A. was the resolution passed on 16 December 1891, which has formed the chief basis for the charges of pettiness against the women.

904

Whereas we understand that a request has been made by a woman representing no organisation or workers, for two clerkships to satisfy nine millions of citizens, we do emphatically protest against such an action as we already have a very capable young gentleman of our race filling such a position. ... We deem it necessary to present you this protest . . . as we sincerely believe this woman's proposals to be detrimental to our works. . . .[41]

'This woman' was Fannie Barrier Williams, wife of a Chicago lawyer, member of the élite black community and its exclusive, twenty-five-member Prudence Crandall Study Club, whose art and music department she headed. There was clearly resentment that perhaps by virtue of her friendship with leading liberal Chicago whites, Mrs Williams, formerly unconnected with the women's protest activities and in that sense unrepresentative of those who had clamoured for representation, might achieve at a single stroke what numbers of obscure women had laboured for in vain. But, fundamental to the objection, two token clerkships were no approximation of the executive machinery which had become the W.C.A.'s goal.[42]

IV

Organized black protest had peaked and failed; individual action took over, exemplified in the action of Rose E. Lumpkin Brown of Chicago, who called on Mrs Palmer with a delegation from Mrs Trent in late December, 1891, and then wrote to Mrs Palmer of her reaction

[40] Logan to Trent, 4 November 1891, LP.

[41] Women's Columbian Association, 'Whereas we understand that a request has been made . . .', 16 December 1891, PP. The young man was James Johnson (Wells, *The Reason Why* . . . , p. 74); Mrs Johnson was an officer of the W.C.A. (*supra*, note 13).

[42] 'Cultured Negro Ladies', *Chicago Tribune*, 28 October 1888. The W.C.A. may have misunderstood the nature of Mrs Williams's application. According to the *Chicago Tribune*, 16 December 1891, her application was made with black Illinois State Congressman E. H. Morris, and requested that 'a department be created and placed in charge of a colored man or woman to promote the interest of the World's Columbian Exposition throughout the U.S.'; Wells, *The Reason Why* . . . , p. 75, cites a resolution urging 'the expediency of having the department of Publicity and Promotion employ a colored man and a colored woman to promote the interest of the World's Columbian Exposition throughout the U.S.'.

when you remarked that you have not recognized any colored organization, as I have several times been informed that you had recognized the Columbian Association society, Mrs. L. A. Trent, President, as the band of workers. . . . That is the reason I joined with them. . . . But if none of the organizations are recognized by the Lady President, then I don't see any use of them continuing their meetings, paying admission fees, and car fares.

She put forward a scheme for a staff of five: an all-in-one ' Afro-American World's Fair Agent . . . Editor and Business Collector with four salaried clerks. Let one come from the North, South, East and West. Five for eight millions. Business like, earnest, dignified, not ashamed of their race people.' [43]

Of the twenty-three women whose letters suggesting modes of black female representation at the Fair were listed in Mrs Palmer's Employment Application Index (Colored), only one woman's application seems to have been seriously considered on an individual basis; that from Hallie Quinn Brown, teacher, elocutionist and lecturer; dean of Allen University (1885–9), lady principal of Tuskegee Institute (1892–3), and organizer of a black exhibit at the Southern Interstate Exposition, Raleigh, North Carolina, 1891. Hallie Brown had not as much faith in Mrs Palmer as Rose Brown, and she made her approach for the position of ' Solicitor of Exhibits among the Colored People for the Columbian Exposition' through Isabella Beecher Hooker in February, 1892. She rightly considered herself well suited, for through her platform performances she had ' been brought into closest contact with the best element as well as the masses of the colored people in every section of the country . . . nearly every State in the Union.' As one hundred following letters of recommendation from twenty states would show, she was the ' necessary . . . wide-awake person to go among them to arouse an interest.' She had already ' talked Exposition in the strongest and most forcible language I could command . . . I wish I could convey to you, Madam, the enthusiasm that was awakened. . . . Articles of merit and beauty were brought to me – even children caught the inspiration and came with their baby offerings.' [44]

Mrs Hooker replied she had no influence with Mrs Palmer; Miss Brown asked her to send the letter to Mrs Logan, who remitted it to Mrs Palmer. March 1892 found Hallie in Chicago for an interview with Mrs Palmer who aptly summed up Hallie's formidable and admirable persona: ' Intelligent . . . inclined to be very dramatic and make telling statements ' – statements which were some of the most cogent and moving that were made in the cause of a black exhibit.

905

---

[43] Rose Brown to Palmer, 19 December 1891, PP.
[44] Hallie Brown to Hooker, February 1892; Hooker to Logan, 11 April 1892; Brown to Logan, 19 April 1892. LP; Palmer to Cantrill, 30 March 1892, PP. The other twenty-two women came from Col., Fla., Ill., Ind., Mich., Mo., N.J., Ohio, Pa., S.C., Miss. and Wash. D.C.

Are nine million of American Citizens to be humiliated in the eyes of the world by the absence of even one black face in the administrative corpus of the Fair? These questions to me seem far more pertinent than vindictive. I am neither for self-emolument or for personal aggrandisement, but I stand upon the broad platform of justice and equity, leading for the women of my race.

What a grand thing it would be if we were, all over this country, permitted to be and to act as American Citizens; but unfortunately the laws of heredity, in the Negro's case are suspended – he must *now* be all that the modifying environment of centuries have made the Anglo-Saxons. And if he have all this, his color alone directly fixes his station in one half of the United States, and, indirectly, in the other half. My perplexity is, is the same spirit which dominated the legislation of this country for nearly one hundred years yet active and aggressive in its application to World's Fair matters?

906

She not only impressed Mrs Palmer; that lady, who had believed that ' the negro trouble has all subsided . . . we hear nothing more of it '. was worried. Hallie had ' written to the organizations of colored people in most of the States asking what communication they had received from the Lady Managers and what had been done to secure an exhibition of their work, and . . . the answers invariably were, that they had had no communications and no one had approached them in any way.' In other words, Mrs Paul's palliative resolution and the process of State referral had not been implemented. Mrs Palmer's excuses to Hallie Brown virtually admitted the process had been a deliberate sham. Each state had made a more or less mean appropriation, and she ' could not blame our lady managers for not spending money for postage and stationery in order to write appeals in every direction '. Aware that now she really was open to adverse publicity, for the first time Mrs Palmer seriously contemplated the appointment of a black women's black representative. A post in the Department of Publicity and Promotion would be suitable.

She could write for the colored papers, keep in communication with the prominent women of her race; and keep them informed as to what was going on so that they would feel they had ' a friend at court ' and were receiving proper attention. . . . Of course she would be employed by the Exposition authorities . . . but the Board of Lady Managers might find her a little extra pay from time to time for working for them. I would even be willing to do this myself should the occasion demand.[45]

But Hallie was not convinced that she could organize a black exhibit from a glorified secretarial position; and she was not prepared to compromise. On 8 April 1892 she sent the Lady Managers a circular spelling out the injustice of the situation. ' Considering the peculiar relation that the Negro sustains in this country, is it less than fair to request for him a special representation? ' [46] Mrs Logan's bland answer – you already are specially represented, by Mrs

[45] Palmer to Cantrill, 30 March 1892.

[46] Hallie Q. Brown, ' It seems to be a settled conviction . . .', (Chicago, 8 April 1892), 1 p. carbon typescript, LP; Brown to Logan, 19 April 1892, LP.

Cantrill – was probably typical. Undaunted, Hallie went in person to Washington, where, in a speech at the 15th Street Presbyterian church, ' she urged upon Mrs Palmer to yield her claim to membership of the Board, where she could, like Esther of old, make supplication, officially, for the people '.[47] Hallie's variant of the black women's black representative would not only have special powers, and special funds, but would also be a member of the Board of Lady Managers, and by that membership dispel the vestiges of paternalistic discrimination that could cling to the appointment of a mere special representative, however wide her powers. It was not within Mrs Palmer's immediate power to alter the composition of the Board but she kept this legal, delaying trump card in cautious reserve. Instead, she wrote to Hallie:

907

> I could quite understand after learning from you that you were making several thousand dollars a year in comparatively light work employing your own secretary and relieved from the drudgery, with the excitement of a semi-public life, that the only position in our power to offer would seem by comparison an undesirable one to you.
>
> I asked you to name a salary that you would consider the equivalent of your services and as you have not done so, presume you did not find the position one you cared to fill. Lamenting that this is the case, I certainly cannot blame you, and hoping we may yet find the proper person to take the place.[48]

V

Mrs Palmer was still concerned that the black women would ' begin making complaints at the time of the installation of exhibits ', and in January, 1893, put the black Mrs A. M. Curtis, wife of a Chicago physician, in charge of any black exhibits that arrived. Mrs Curtis, apparently unconnected with any organization, and perhaps by that token acceptable, soon resigned; the post was farcical given the few exhibits and the unco-operativeness of the Chief of Installation, Amy M. Starkweather.[49] Mrs Palmer then turned to Fannie

---

47 Elizabeth Lindsay Davis, *Lifting as they climb* [National Association of Colored Women, 1933], p. 20. Davis, the official historian of the N.A.C.W., claimed, *ibid.*, that Miss Brown's oratory, which inspired the women present to form ' The Colored Women's League ', proved that it was due to her ' that the women stepped across the threshold of the home into the wider area of Organized Womanhood '; but the occasion was equally the result of cumulative onslaughts on the black female consciousness.

48 Palmer to Brown, 4 July 1892, PP.

49 Rudwick and Meier, *loc. cit.*; Curtis to Starkweather [1893], PP. *The Reason Why . . .*, p. 74, suggests Mrs Curtis stepped into a post vacated by Mrs Williams, but this has not been substantiated. Mrs N. F. Mossell, *The Work of the Afro-American Woman* (Philadelphia: George S. Ferguson Co., 1894), pp. 21, 84, and John W. Cromwell, *The Negro in American History* (The American Negro Academy, 1914), pp. 10–11, suggest that Mrs Curtis was also on the Illinois State Board of Lady Managers, and that three other women were

Barrier Williams, who after incessant compaigning for a representative appointment, had, late in 1892, finally accepted an ordinary secretarial post in Major Handy's Department of Publicity and Promotion. On the strength of Handy's recommendation – ' excellent character – pleasing address . . . considerable literary ability . . . excellent typewriter ' – Mrs Palmer appointed her to help supervise the installation of all exhibits in the Woman's Building. Fannie was appalled to find herself unsalaried, but, construing the post as ' a gracious recognition of large number of colored women of intelligence in this country who would like to be interested in and inspired by women's work as displayed in your department ', decided to remain.[50] In March, 1893, she was asked to give an address to the 17 May session of the Departmental Congress of the National Association of Loyal Women of American Liberty at the World's Congress of Representative Women, on ' The Progressive and Present Status of the Colored Women of the United States and their progress since Emancipation '. The W.C.A.'s doubt that she could represent anything except an élite was partially confirmed, as Mrs Williams had to apply to Tourgée for help in compiling her speech: ' If there be any literature upon this sex phase of the Negro question that you can refer me to or any accessible data that tell unmistakably of the steady and sure development from a degraded peasantry toward a noble womanhood, I would be duly obligated '.[51]

Whether for lack of information or through recognition of her speciality, Mrs Williams finally spoke on ' The Intellectual Progress and Present Status of the Colored Women of the United States since the Emancipation Proclamation '.[52]

Mrs Williams was by no means the only black woman to take part in the Congress, though perhaps she opened the door for those who participated in integrated sessions. Her own address was followed by a discussion led by Mrs Anna Julia Cooper, school principal in Washington, D.C., and author of *A Voice from the South* (1892). The next day, Sarah J. Early spoke on ' The Organized Efforts of the Colored Women in the South to improve their Condition ', and Hallie Brown led the discussion. At the Suffrage Congress, Frances Harper spoke on ' The Race Line of Suffrage '. Seven women spoke at the conferences of the African Methodist Episcopal Church, and in the

908

---

appointed to State Boards: Florence A. Lewis, World's Fair's correspondent of the *Philadelphia Times* (Pa.); Mrs S. A. Williams, founder of an orphanage in New Orleans (Miss.); and Joan Imogen Howard (New York). For details of Miss Howard's work, *infra*, p. 335.

[50] Williams and Palmer were in correspondence on 15 December 1891; 6 September, 5 October, 28 November 1892; 1, 5 July, 16 August 1893, PP.

[51] Williams to Tourgée, 12 March 1893, TP; Keller, *loc. cit.*, item 6735.

[52] May Wright Sewall (ed.), *The World's Congress of Representative Women* (Chicago: Rand, McNally & Co., 1894), p. 396.

Educational Congress, Session of the Association of the Educators of Colored
Youth, ten women gave addresses.[53] And, though no description of the items
in situ has come to light, a small 'Afro-American exhibit' which included
Edmonia Lewis's statue of Hiawatha, and a statistical compilation about the
black women of the United States, collected by a black woman, was exhibited
at the Fair. The collector was Joan Imogen Howard, graduate of the University of the City of New York, and appointed by the Governor of New York
to the State Board of Lady Managers. A teacher, and one of five members of
the Board's Education Committee, Miss Howard was commissioned to collect
statistics for New York State. At the State Board's suggestion, she made the
scope of her project nationwide, an act which raised Western hackles, for, at
the Board's meeting in May 1893, 'Mrs Roosevelt reported that there were
difficulties in the matter; the colored women at the west [Chicago?] objecting
to its being a national exhibition'. Miss Howard personally visited Philadelphia, Boston and Washington, preceded by a circular letter in newspapers
requesting co-operation, and leaving behind her forms to be filled out and
forwarded. Conscious before she began her survey that black deprivation had
created a cultural lag, Miss Howard was not worried by a collection of un-
startling statistics, which led her to ask the State Board to 'permit me, instead
of marking this compilation of facts " Statistics of the Distinguished Work of
the Colored Women of the United States ", to inscribe on the cover, " Evi-
dences of the Advancement of the Colored Women of the United States ".'

909

Her report was notable for its integrationist assessment of the black women
of the United States:

They feel themselves American, as truly as do those who proudly trace their
ancestry back to the Pilgrim Fathers, the Puritans of England, the broad, liberal-
spirited Hollanders, the cultivated and refined French Huguenots; and as an
element in the progress of this boundless home, we trust, the worthiest representatives of all nations there is implanted in the minds of the best of this struggling
people a determination to rise to a common level with the majority.[54]

Not on official display at the Fair was the militant black symposium *The
Reason Why the Colored American is not in the Columbian Exposition*, the

---

53 *Ibid.*, pp. 711–9; World's Congress of Representative Women, *Suffrage Congress, August
9, 1893*, official programme; World's Congress Auxiliary, *The American Association of the
Educators of Colored Youth, July 25–9, 1893*, official programme; John Henry Barrows
(ed.), *The World's Parliament of Religions* (Chicago: The Parliament Publishing Co.,
1893), vol. 2, 1895. For Anna J. Cooper, see Cromwell, *op. cit.*, p. 11.

54 *Minutes of the meeting[s] of the Board of Women Managers of the State of New York at
the World's Columbian Exposition, June 7, 1892 [–January 17, 1894, n.p., n.d.]*, pp.
22–32, 75, 104; *Report of Miss J. Imogen Howard to the Board of Women Managers of the
Exhibition of the State of New York at the World's Columbian Exposition* [n.p., n.d.], pp.
3–5, 29–30.

brain child of its editor, Ida B. Wells, a truly radical black woman. The editor of her own paper in Memphis, she had been run out of town for her impassioned denunciation of local lynchings. Open denunciation of lynchings became for her the acid test of a human being worthy of the name; and her insistence on discussion and division on the issue made her an embarrassment to blacks and whites who were content to define humanity as non-violence in the immediate community. Early in 1893, Miss Wells returned to Chicago from a European lecture tour and was dismayed to find that black representation at the Fair seemed likely to be limited to the presence of Frederick Douglass, U.S. Ambassador to Haiti, in the Haitian pavilion. Accordingly she resuscitated an idea she had floated before her tour: publishing a record of and appeal against the disadvantages of blacks seeking representation at the Fair.

910

Miss Wells had Chicago's black women organize meetings at their respective churches, and it was the $500 so raised which financed the printing of *The Reason Why....* Her action was timely, coming as it did, when, with the news of Mrs Williams's forthcoming speech, the cause of black representation might have flagged. It was well-publicized, too; in April, 1893, Miss Wells issued a pledge-circular 'To the Friends of Equal Rights':

Whereas, the absence of colored citizens from participation in the Fair ... will be construed to their disadvantage by the representatives of the civilized world ... I the undersigned, recommend ... that a carefully prepared pamphlet setting forth the past and present condition of our people and their relation to the American civilized world, be prepared.[55]

She secured written contributions from Douglass, Frederick L. Barnett of the Afro-American League and from journalist and editor I. Garland Penn; she culled information from Mrs Boone, Hallie Brown and Miss Howard; she pieced together a detailed, impassioned, unique and indispensable account of yet one more post-Emancipation example of discrimination against blacks. The pamphlet substantiated her proud, ironic subtitle: "The Afro-American's Contribution to Columbian Literature'. Thousands of copies were sold, many by Ida B. Wells herself, sitting at a desk in the Haitian pavilion.

In her memoirs, *Crusade for Justice*,[56] Miss Wells tended to play down her pamphlet while giving the accolade for black achievement at the Fair to Frederick Douglass's speech at a Tambo and Bones 'Negro Day', hastily put on by the Fair's authorities under prodding scrutiny from ' the representatives

[55] *The Afro-American*, Baltimore, 29 April 1893, p. 3.

[56] Alfreda M. Duster (ed.), *Crusade for Justice: the Autobiography of Ida B. Wells* (Chicago: University Press, 1970), pp. 115–9.

of the civilized world '. But one may be forgiven for disagreeing with Miss Well's assessment. Douglass's speech was as comprehensive and impressive as ever; but it had neither the rarity nor the climactic, pioneering significance of *The Reason Why* ... : an appropriate highlight to the ultimately irrepressible efforts of black women and their organizations to have fitting representation at the Fair, and a milestone in the burgeoning career of the remarkable Miss Ida B. Wells.

911

By R. LYNN MATSON

Phillis Wheatley — Soul Sister?

Feelin' tomorrow like I feel today,
Feelin' tomorrow like I feel today,
I'll pack my grief and make my getaway.
                              Bessie Smith, "St. Louis Blues."

PHILLIS WHEATLEY has been condemned for more than a century by whites and blacks alike for failing to espouse in any way the plight of her race. No one denies that she was a genius; no one denies her the right to be called a poet; no one denies that she was an extremely clever imitator; but almost all deny that Phillis Wheatley was race con-   913
scious, or what could be called by any stretch of the imagination a protester of slavery. The common view, in effect, is that she was the white man's ideal of a good "nigger"—so good, in fact, that she was almost white.

Vernon Loggins, who has written the most extensive criticism on her poems, says, "She dwelt at length on the common notions of her day regarding liberty, but she neglected almost entirely her own state of slavery and the miserable oppression of thousands of her race."[1] Loggins goes on to say, "Like the rest of neoclassical sentimental verse, her poems offer slight interest to the modern reader."[2] He sums her up as a clever imitator, nothing more.[3]

James Weldon Johnson was also disappointed with Miss Wheatley:

> . . . But one looks in vain for some outburst or even complaint against the bondage of her people, for some agonizing cry about her native land. In two poems she refers definitely to Africa as her home, but in each instance there seems to be under the sentiment of the lines a feeling of almost smug contentment at her own escape therefrom.[4]

The modern anthologizers of black verse seem to follow the same worn path of opinion concerning Phillis Wheatley:

> . . . If this ex-slave had dared to put into her poetry more than just that of Miss Wheatley, if she had had the strength to give all that was really hers, and not that which others had given her, she might have become a really important figure and not, as she is now, a literary curio.[5]

---

[1] Vernon Loggins, The Negro Author (Port Washington, 1964), p. 24.
[2] Ibid., p. 16.
[3] Concerning her imitating of Pope he says: "Her power to attain this place of eminence must be pronounced as due to her instinct for hearing the music of words, an instinct which was possibly racial." Ibid., p. 27.
[4] James Weldon Johnson, The Book of American Negro Poetry (New York, 1922), p. xxvii.
[5] Rosey E. Poole, Beyond the Blues (Lympne Hythe Kent, 1962), p. 14.

Originally published in *Phylon*, Vol. 33, No. 3 (Fall 1972).

> . . . Phillis Wheatley . . . , the first poet of African descent to win
> some measure of recognition, had almost nothing to say about the
> plight of her people. And if she resented her own ambiguous position
> in society, she did not express her resentment.[6]

Even Julian Mason, Jr., who is to be thanked for recently bringing out a
new authoritative edition of Phillis Wheatley's poems and letters, says of
her:

> . . . The neoclassical influence also may have been responsible for
> the fact that there is little about Phillis herself in her poems. She cer-
> tainly leaves the reader of her poems only slightly aware of her being
> a Negro and a slave.[7]

914

One of the most recent, and perhaps most devastating, condemnations
of Phillis Wheatley is shown by her exclusion from the popular anthology of writings by Negroes *Dark Symphony* (MacMillan, 1968). Phillis
has often been the recipient of backhanded compliments, such as the following by Arthur Schomburg (one time secretary of the Negro Society
for Historical Research), "There was no great American poetry in the
eighteenth century, and Phillis Wheatley's poetry was as good as the best
American poetry of her age."[8] But seldom has she been ignored wherever
black writing was discussed. This leads one to surmise that Phillis Wheatley is hardly appreciated among the black intelligentsia in this age of
extreme race consciousness—a miscarriage of justice, because Phillis
Wheatley has much to offer black (and white) readers of today. Not only
is she America's first accomplished black poet (a fact that by itself should
insure her a safe place in our literary history), but her poetry is a record
of a Negro's survival in our white culture. Though Phillis Wheatley may
not have been a black nationalist (and of course such a stand would have
been impossible considering the time and her position), nonetheless she
was very race conscious, very aware of her position as a slave, and not at
all "smug" in this position (as comparatively desirable as it may have
been) in the Wheatley household. In fact, it can be shown that she protested slavery, after her fashion, often implicitly through the use of various escape themes in her poetry.

Before dismissing the critics, however, it must be stated that there was
at least one early Wheatley admirer who saw that Phillis was not color
blind. He is Arthur Schomburg, quoted above:

> . . . Phillis Wheatley is a jewel—priceless to the literature of the
> Negro in America. Her name stands as a beacon light to illuminate
> the path of the young, who will surely pass every year. Let us with
> diligence weave to her memory as affectionate and loving a feeling
> for her sacrifice, *in keeping with the manifested race pride shown in*

---

[6] Robert Hayden, ed., *Kaleidoscope, Poems by American Negro Poets* (New York, 1967), p. xx.
[7] Phillis Wheatley, *The Poems of Phillis Wheatley*, ed. by Julian Mason, Jr. (Chapel Hill, 1966),
p. xxv.
[8] Phillis Wheatley, *Phillis Wheatley, Poems and Letters*, ed. by Charles F. Heartman (New
York, 1915), p. 19.

her poems, that they may stimulate us to nobler deeds and loftier purposes in life.[9]

For a man who has brought out such a careful edition of Phillis Wheatley's work, Mason's comment above—that "there is little about Phillis herself in her poems"—is truly surprising. More than ten years before Mason's edition of Phillis Wheatley's poems, an article appeared in *Phylon* by Arthur Davis entitled "Personal Elements in the Poetry of Phillis Wheatley."[10] Davis does an excellent job of fulfilling the objectives of his title, and there is no need here to rehash his findings. One of his themes, however, may be expanded—the idea of Phillis Wheatley's race consciousness. He mentions the several (and obvious) instances in which Phillis refers to herself as *Afric* or *Ethiop.* She does this in part no doubt to capitalize on her reputation as the famous black poetess of Boston, but it also suggests that she is proud of her blackness.

It is not true that Phillis Wheatley was "smug" and unconcerned about her black brothers and sisters. A look at her letters makes this clear. In a letter dated May 19, 1772, to Obour (or Arbour) Tanner, also a slave girl, we can see Phillis expressing a sort of black unity. (And in the letters to this girl one can imagine that Phillis was most at ease and frank, although she could not let her guard down completely since the letters were usually delivered by white acquaintances.) Phillis is speaking of their fortunate deliverance to a Christian country. She is obviously responding to some news about blacks when she says, "It gives me very great pleasure to hear of so many of *my nation* seeking with eagerness the way of true felicity."[11] "My nation" is Africa. In another more guarded letter to Obour Tanner (October 30, 1773) she writes:

> . . . What you observe of Esau is true of all mankind, who, (left to themselves) would sell their heavenly birth rights for a few moments of sensual pleasure . . . *Dear Obour, let us not sell our birthright for a thousand worlds,* which indeed would be as dust upon the balance.[12]

Ostensibly she is talking about religious matters, but would it be going too far to expect that a person of Phillis Wheatley's intelligence could write intentionally ambiguous passages, and that "birthright" might be a racial allusion? The possibility becomes even more probable when one considers her position—a slave who enjoys all the benefits of a kind and enlightened family, a position to be guarded, and yet an enslaved muse, infinitely more intelligent than many of her white "betters." We must keep this in mind when looking later at what are possible double meanings in her poems. First, however, it is necessary to look at one more letter of Phillis's that shows her special concern for her black race. Having heard of "two Negro men" who were desirous of returning to Africa to

915

---

[9] *Ibid.,* p. 19. (Italics here and elsewhere are mine.)
[10] *Phylon,* XIV (June, 1953), 191-98.
[11] Phillis Wheatley, in Mason, *op. cit.,* pp. 103-04.
[12] *Ibid.,* p. 106.

preach the gospel, she tells the Reverend Samuel Hopkins:

> . . . My heart expands with sympathetic joy to see a distant time the thick cloud of ignorance dispersing from the face of *my benighted country*. Europe and America have long been fed with the heavenly provision, and I fear they loath it, while Africa is perishing with a spiritual Famine. *O that they could partake of the crumbs, the precious crumbs, which fall from the table of these distinguished children of the kingdom.*
> . . . Ethiopia shall soon stretch forth her hands unto God.[13]

916

Phillis Wheatley considered herself extremely fortunate in being brought to America, not because she was well-treated here, not because she was at least physically comfortable in slavery, but because America was where she discovered Jesus Christ. From evidence such as this passionate letter it would seem that she was not smug or self-satisfied but instead deeply concerned for the spiritual welfare of her people.

The overpowering concerns of Phillis Wheatley's life were God and salvation. In understanding her feelings about being black and a slave, it is crucial to examine her view of life in relation to God and salvation. It is important to keep in mind that she was once a pagan. This, in addition to her being a Negro, gives her a decidedly different (non-white) slant on religion.

Concerning Negroes and Christianity, LeRoi Jones has said:

> . . . One of the reasons Christianity proved so popular was that it was the religion, according to older Biblical tradition, of an oppressed people. . . . In the early days of slavery, Christianity's sole purpose was to propose a metaphysical resolution for the slave's natural yearnings for freedom, and as such it literally made life easier for him.[14]

Judging from her poems and what little we know about her life, it appears that Phillis Wheatley's most emotional religious experience came from the preaching of the Reverend George Whitefield. Whitefield was a Boston evangelist, known for his spirited sermons and his concern for orphans and other unfortunates. Although he defended slavery on biblical grounds, he was quite sympathetic to the plight of Negroes. [15] Other than the elegy on Whitefield's death, we have no record of Phillis's writing about him. However, it is probable that her attraction to his type of preaching arises out of a racial predilection for religious emotionalism.

We are fortunate to have an eyewitness account of one of Whitefield's performances from another slave poet, Gustavus Vassa:

> . . . When I got into the church I saw this pious man exhorting the people with the greatest fervor and earnestness, and sweating as much as I ever did while in slavery on Montserrat beach. . . . I was very much struck and impressed with this; I thought it strange that I

13 *Ibid.*, p. 110.
14 LeRoi Jones, *Blues People* (New York, 1963), p. 39.
15 Phillis Wheatley, in Mason, *op. cit.*, p. 67.

had never seen devines exert themselves in this manner before, and
was no longer at a loss to account for the thin congregations they
preached to.[16]

About Whitefield's preaching and Negroes, Loggins says:

> . . . The Christianity which Whitefield and his emotional predeces-
> sors preached in America brought to the Negro a religion which he
> could understand, and which could stir him to self-expression. He re-
> sponded to it with enthusiasm, allowed his imagination to run riot
> with it, loved it with passion. *It afforded him a mental escape from this
> wretchedness of his social position.* . . .[17]

This emotional, participatory reaction to religious preaching was the
same kind of reaction found later at camp meetings, out of which in turn
came the Negro spiritual and a whole progression of black music from
Blues to Soul.

917

The question now facing us is did Phillis Wheatley have what could be
called an escapist view of death and Christianity? Arthur Davis points to
the following passage in the poem "On the Death of the Rev. Mr. George
Whitefield," saying "All through this passage there runs the obvious
theme of escape through leveling which was Christianity's primary appeal to the slave."[18]

> Take him [Christ], ye wretched, for your only good,
> Take him, ye starving sinners, for your food;
> Ye thirsty, come to this life-giving stream;
> Ye preachers, take him, for your joyful theme,
> Take him, my dear Americans, he said,
> Be your complaints on his kind bosom laid;
> Take him, ye Africans, he longs for you;
> Impartial savior is his title due;
> Washed in the fountain of redeeming blood,
> You shall be sons, and kings, and priests to God.[19]

The theme of escape expressed in these last four lines becomes even more
apparent in another version of the same poem (probably published in
England). Here these lines read:

> Take him, ye Africans he longs for you,
> Impartial savior is his title due.
> *If you will walk in Grace's heavenly Road,*
> *He'll make you free, and Kings, and priests to God.*[20]

We can only guess at why the poet changed "He'll make you free" to
"You shall be sons" in the Boston version of the poem. Did she feel that
she was being too obvious, and, in order to protect herself, felt the need
to delete a personal reference and insert an abstraction?

[16] Loggins, *op. cit.*, p. 4.
[17] *Ibid.*
[18] In *Phylon, op. cit.*, 194.
[19] *Ibid.*, 193.
[20] Phillis Wheatley, in Mason, *op. cit.*, p. 70.

Another of Phillis Wheatley's great concerns was death (18 of her 46 poems are elegies). Her elegies are usually dismissed as the mere sentimental effusions of a young black girl. They certainly are sentimental, even bathetic in some cases, but what is overlooked is this same theme of escape, in this case, escape (freedom) through death. In "On the Death of a Young Lady of Five Years of Age" Phillis writes:

> From dark abodes to fair ethereal light
> The' enraptured innocent has wing'd her flight;
> On the kind bosom of eternal love
> She finds unknown beatitude above.
> This know, ye parents, nor her loss deplore,
> She feels the iron hand of pain no more:
>   . . . . . .
> Let then no tears for her henceforward flow,
> No more distress in our dark vale below,
>   . . . . . .
> Freed from a world of sin, and snares, and pains,
> Why would you wish your daughter back again?[21]

918

The poet goes on to tell the parents to endure until "Yourselves, safe are landed on the blissful shore."[22] One must also notice in these poems the metaphors of death as a flight or a voyage over water which later became so popular in Negro spirituals. In "To a Lady on the Death of Three Relations" Phillis Wheatley describes the dead as,

> *From bondage freed,* the exulting spirit flies . . .
>   . . . . . .
> Weep not for them, who with thine happy mind
> To rise with them, and leave the world behind.[23]

While in another elegy, the dead

> Invite you there to share immortal bliss
> Unknown, untasted in a state like this.
> With tow'ring hopes, and growing grace arise,
> And seek beatitude beyond the skies.[24]

Heaven is a place "Where grief subsides, Where changes are no more,/And life's tumultuous billows cease to roar."[25] On the death of the Reverend Dr. Sewell (1769) Phillis writes:

> See Sewell number'd with the happy dead.
> Hail, holy man, arriv'd th' immortal shore,
>   . . . . . .
> Thrice happy saint! to find thy heav'n at last
> What compensation for the evils past.[26]

Some would say that these lines could be dismissed as mere clichés and

[21] Phillis Wheatley, in Heartman, *op. cit.,* pp. 88-89.
[22] *Ibid.*
[23] *Ibid.,* p. 86.
[24] *Ibid.,* pp. 68-69.
[25] *Ibid.,* p. 61.
[26] *Ibid.,* pp. 34-35.

poetic conventions of the day. Indeed they could if they came from the
pen of a white poet, but since they come from the soft-spoken Negro
slave of John Wheatley, and a slave who was probably a genius, perhaps
the lines take on an added significance. Perhaps Phillis Wheatley was
much more shrewd than she is given credit for.

Even Phillis Wheatley's severest critics admit that there are two or
three poems in which she does seem to make some reference to her own
position. One of these much-quoted poems is "To the Right Honorable
William, Earl of Dartmouth . . ." The Earl of Dartmouth had just been
appointed Secretary of State for the Colonies, and Phillis is addressing
him, ostensibly on the subject of America's liberty:

> No more America in mournful strain   919
> Of wrongs, and grievance unredress'd complain,
> No longer shalt thou dread the iron chain,
> Which wanton tyranny with lawless hand
> Had made, and with it meant t' enslave the land.
>   Should you, my Lord, while you peruse my song,
> Wonder from whence my love of Freedom sprung,
> Whence flow these wishes for the common good,
> By feeling hearts alone best understood,
> I, young in life, by seeming cruel fate
> Was snatch'd from Afric's fancy'd happy seat:
> What pangs excruciating must molest,
> What sorrows labour in my parents breast?
> Steel'd was that soul and by no misery mov'd
> That from a father seiz'd his babe belov'd
> Such, such my case. And can I then but pray
> Others may never feel tyrannic sway?[27]

The last stanza above is usually cited as an example of Phillis speaking
out (not too harshly) on slavery, which indeed she is. But what is overlooked, by critics who cite only this stanza, is its relation to the rest of
the poem. Why does she suddenly insert some very personal references to
herself right in the middle of a poem about American freedom? The last
stanza above makes a very curious juxtaposition with the first stanza.
This juxtaposition gives the poem a whole new slant. It suddenly becomes more forceful, even angry. "Wanton tyranny" with its "lawless
hand" in juxtaposition with Phillis's biographical details makes strong
language indeed. But yet, she always keeps her guard up, never leaving
herself unprotected.

This use of possible double meaning and ambiguity becomes more and
more clear to the close reader of Phillis Wheatley's poems. One tip-off to
this deliberate use of ambiguity is in the nature of some of her revisions.
A prime example is in "To the University of Cambridge, in New England
(1767)." This is one of her few peevish poems. Here she is admonishing
the gallant young Harvard men to avoid sin and sloth and to make the

---

[27] Ibid., pp. 73-74.

most of their fortunate positions. The last stanza of the published 1773 version of the poem reads:

> Improve your privileges while they stay,
> Ye pupils, and each hour redeem, that bears
> Or good or bad report of you to heav'n.
> Let sin, that baneful evil to the soul,
> By you be shunned, nor once remit your guard;
> Suppress the deadly serpent in its egg.
> Ye blooming plants of human race devine,
> An Ethiop tells you 'tis your greatest foe;
> Its transient sweetness turns to endless pain,
> And in immense perdition sinks the soul.[28]

920 This is hardly a strong admonition. But after all, how presumptuous could a little slave girl be in addressing the young white aristocracy? However, the manuscript version of this stanza is more illuminating:

> Improve your privileges while they stay:
> Caress, redeem each moment, which with haste
> Bears on its rapid wing Eternal bliss.
> Let hateful vice so baneful to the soul,
> Be still avoided with becoming care;
> *Suppress the sable monster in its growth,*
> Ye blooming plants of human race, divine,
> *An Ethiop tells you tis your greatest foe;*
> Its transient sweetness turns to endless pain,
> And brings eternal ruin on the soul.[29]

The published version has obviously been toned down, made milder. But why did she delete completely the line "Suppress the sable monster in its growth" in favor of "deadly serpent?" Could she have been afraid that "sable monster" might have been interpreted as the enslaved black race?[30] Keep in mind that Phillis at this time would have been approximately the same age as these young dandies, and had an insatiable thirst for knowledge. It does not seem unreasonable that she might have felt strong resentment over this privileged class not taking their opportunities seriously enough, while her own educational and social opportunities were definitely limited. She had much cause to be bitter, yet more cause to hide it.

In his article, Arthur Davis points to Phillis's constant striving for poetic excellence (and lamenting her lack of it) as an example of a personal element in her poetry. We may go a step further and say that this is a continuation of the escapist or flight theme examined earlier. Like Baudelaire's albatross, beautiful and free in flight, but ugly and awkward out of the air, Phillis Wheatley longed to soar to poetic heights. She could be free metaphorically, at least. In "To Maecenas" she envies Virgil, and especially Terence (an African).

---

[28] *Ibid.*, p. 33.
[29] Phillis Wheatley, in Mason, *op. cit.*, pp. 63-64.
[30] In the poem "To Maecenas" Phillis refers to Negroes as "Africa's sable race." Heartman, *op. cit.*, p. 90.

But here I sit and mourn a grov' ling mind,
That fain would mount and ride upon the wind. . .

. . . . . .

But I, less happy, cannot raise the song;
The faltering music dies upon my tongue.[31]

And finally let us look at "To S.M., a young African Painter, on Seeing His Works," a poem in which she swells with pride over this black artist's accomplishments. She is telling him her hope that they can be better artists in the freedom of the next world:

But when these shades of time are chas'd away,
And darkness ends in everlasting days,
On what seraphic pinions shall we move,
And view the landscapes in the realms above?[32]

921

But sadly, she is brought back to her present state, and ends her poem with "Cease, gentle muse! the solemn gloom of night/Now seals the fair creation from my sight."[33] It is obvious that she is talking about poetic inspiration. What is not so obvious, and we should allow Phillis Wheatley this possibility, is that her writing on the figurative level corresponds exactly with her real position in life. It is entirely probable that the slave whom she is addressing in the poem would interpret such phrases as "shades of time" and when "darkness ends" much differently than a white man of the day would.

Phillis Wheatley was not a great poet; but then neither was the American poetry of the eighteenth century a remarkable literature. She can be dismissed as just another mediocre versifier without doing her a great injustice (although some of her poems have real merit, comparatively). But she cannot be dismissed, as she has been, on the grounds that she abandoned her race and completely assimilated into the slave society. If she is not exactly a soul sister, she is certainly a distant relative.

---

[31] *Ibid.*, pp. 89-90.
[32] *Ibid.*, pp. 58-59.
[33] *Ibid.*

RACE, SEX, AND THE DIMENSIONS OF LIBERTY IN ANTEBELLUM AMERICA

Jean Matthews

The world has never had a good definition of the word 'liberty,' "
wrote Abraham Lincoln in 1864, "and the American people . . . are
much in the want of one." In antebellum America the continued prominence of revolutionary traditions together with the existence of slavery
made it tempting to celebrate liberty rather than probe deeply into
its meaning. Yet the meaning of liberty was being explored, deep-
ened, and extended in this period as new groups laid claim to inclusion in the republican heritage. Two kinds of people in particular had
reason to grapple with the nature of liberty: free blacks and white
women. As Jane and William Pease have pointed out, free blacks knew
from often bitter experience that freedom was not synonymous with
the legal status of freedman. From the 1830s onwards spokesmen for
free blacks in the northern states were giving formal articulation to
ideas about what freedom must mean for them, through state and
national conventions, through a black press, and through individual
polemical writings. Similarly, some of the women attached to the abolition movement began to apply antislavery ideas to themselves, scattered groups petitioned for property and political rights, and from 1848
onwards women's rights conventions met to become the focus for a fledgling
feminist movement.[1]

Ms. Matthews is a member of the Department of History at the University of
Western Ontario in London. This essay is a revised version of a paper presented
at the SHEAR conference in Indianapolis in July 1984 and at a meeting of the Pacific
Coast branch of the AHA at Stanford in June 1985.

[1] Quoted in John P. Diggins, *The Lost Soul of American Politics: Virtue, Self-Interest,
and the Foundations of Liberalism* (New York 1984), 313; Jane H. Pease and William
H. Pease, *They Who Would Be Free: Blacks' Search for Freedom, 1830-1861* (New York
1974), 3-5. For the free black demands for equal rights and the black convention

The connection between the two movements lies in a certain overlap of personnel as well as in the structural similarities of racism and sexism. Not all feminists were immune from racism, not all black males avoided sexual chauvinism, but a significant number of *male* feminists were black men and the majority of antebellum women feminists had connections and sympathies with the abolition movement. Though the voices to be discussed here are primarily those of black men and white women, black women were involved in movements for the freedom of their sex as well as for the freedom of their race. It is not necessary to claim that the frustrations felt by white women were in any sense equivalent to the oppression faced by free blacks of both sexes, to note that it was quite natural for participants in both movements and for hostile white men to see certain similarities in their situations. "How did woman first become subject to man as she now is all over the world?" demanded the New York *Herald* in 1852. "By her nature, her sex, just as the negro is and always will be, to the end of time, inferior to the white race, and, therefore, doomed to subjection." There were, of course, many ways in which blacks were deprived of freedom which had no real analogies in the experience of white women. Further, the whole problem of injecting the concept of freedom into the sphere of family relations was a question crucial to women but hardly perceived by black men. However, there were certain things that both groups conceived as vital components of freedom, even if not always in exactly the same ways.[2]

To concentrate on the published words of self-defined radicals means dealing with a few prominent and articulate leaders with a very shadowy

924

---

movement see, besides Pease and Pease, Leon F. Litwack, *North of Slavery: The Negro in the Free States, 1790-1860* (Chicago 1961), and Leonard P. Curry, *The Free Black in Urban America, 1800-1850: The Shadow of the Dream* (Chicago 1981), esp. chs. 12 and 13. For antebellum feminist organizations see Eleanor Flexner, *Century of Struggle: The Woman's Rights Movement in the United States* (rev. ed., Cambridge, Mass. 1975), Ellen C. DuBois, *Feminism and Suffrage: The Emergence of an Independent Women's Movement in America, 1848-1869* (Ithaca 1978), and Elizabeth Cady Stanton et al., *History of Woman Suffrage* (6 vols., New York and Rochester 1881-1922). The use of the term "feminist" is anachronistic for this period, yet it is the most convenient shorthand to designate demands for equality and individual self-expansion, which was one, and arguably the most important one, of the streams that fed into what later became known as the feminist movement.

[2] Quoted in Stanton et al., *History of Woman Suffrage*, I, 854. Such prominent free blacks as Charles Remond, James Forten, and Robert Purvis were all supporters of women's rights, but the most important was Frederick Douglass. See Philip S. Foner, ed., *Frederick Douglass on Women's Rights* (Westport, Conn. 1976), and Waldo E. Martin, Jr., *The Mind of Frederick Douglass* (Chapel Hill 1984), ch. 6.

following. No doubt there were many unknown blacks and white women who read the reports of these conventions and other polemics in silent assent, but it was very difficult actually to mobilize large numbers of either blacks or women behind the rallying cries of liberty and equality. Few things infuriated feminists quite as much as the numerous women who blithely asserted that they had "all the rights they want," and who were often uncomprehending or hostile at any attempt to translate female concerns into the masculine political language of "rights." Frederick Douglass complained bitterly that a national convention of blacks to assert their rights might draw fifty people, while a black Masonic or Odd-fellows celebration could bring out from four to five thousand at a cost that would have supported several newspapers.[3]

925

Why was it so hard for these often highly talented and dynamic individuals to transfer their own passionate concern with liberty to a mass following? Isaiah Berlin has pointed out that "the lack of freedom about which men or groups complain amounts, as often as not, to the lack of proper recognition." And, he added, "the only persons who can so recognize me, and thereby give me the sense of being someone, are the members of the society to which, historically, morally, economically, and perhaps ethnically, I feel that I belong." A key phrase here is "*feel* that I belong"; the community to which in some objective sense one belongs, or to which one is assigned by others, may not necessarily be the group with which the individual identifies himself and from which he seeks recognition. American culture increasingly consigned all blacks to the community of an inferior and proscribed caste, and all women to a separate sphere which was at the same time flattered and divorced from public power. Through custom and public opinion as much as law, it operated very powerfully to prevent any black from ever being *not* a black or any woman not a woman.[4]

Women, at least, could find certain compensations in this. Nineteenth century American culture offered women a range of identities, all with a certain status, which were clearly more enticing and satisfy-

---

[3] Stanton *et al.*, *History of Woman Suffrage*, I, 184; Frederick Douglass in the *North Star*, July 14, 1848, quoted in Howard Brotz, ed., *Negro Social and Political Thought, 1850-1920* (New York 1966), 204. The feminist and temperance advocate, Clarina H. Nichols, recalled that on speaking tours she could often disarm audiences hostile to the idea of woman's rights by smuggling them into the context of woman's "wrongs." Stanton *et al.*, *History of Woman Suffrage*, I, 184.

[4] Isaiah Berlin, "Two Concepts of Liberty," in *Four Essays on Liberty* (Oxford, Eng. 1969), 155-156.

ing to most women, as well as less risky, than that of equal citizen: the "Republican Mother," for example, or the "lady." Moreover, the various levels of "women's culture," which historians have begun to explore so fully, from communities of female kin to various kinds of benevolent and moral reform associations, probably provided a quite satisfactory recognition, by other women, of talents and status. American culture as a whole did not offer similar prestigious identities to free blacks, but the community itself developed hierarchies and organizations that offered status and recognition by other blacks. While in both cases these developments enhanced self-respect and sometimes offered the opportunity to develop organizational skills, they probably served to deflect their participants from examining their situation in terms of the central American language of liberty and equality.[5]

926

The antebellum feminists and the black leaders who boldly organized to demand full civil rights, including the franchise, were those who for one reason or another—education, class, personal experience, or personality—had dislocated themselves psychologically from what others considered their "natural" community of race or sex, and instead sought recognition from and status within the world of white males. This is not to say that they were deferential towards contemporary white men—quite the reverse—but that their reference point was western civilization; their standard of achievement was the highest standard held up to white males. Their exclusion from participating fully in this culture, the disabilities that prevented them from achieving in its terms, was felt acutely and personally as deprivation of freedom and as *humiliation*.

Elizabeth Cady Stanton singled out the experience of humiliation as crucial to the experience of both free blacks and women. She pointed to Robert Purvis, a Philadelphia black man who, wealthy and cultivated, was yet "denied all social communion with his neighbors, equal freedom and opportunity for himself and children, in public amusements, churches, schools, and means of travel because of race." A poor white man, she imagined, might think to himself: "If I were Robert Purvis,

---

[5] For the development of black organizations, see Litwack, *North of Slavery*, and Curry, *The Free Black in Urban America*. On the separation of black leaders from the mass of the black community, see Pease and Pease, *They Who Would Be Free*, 289-293. On women's culture, communities, and organizations, see Nancy F. Cott, *The Bonds of Womanhood: "Woman's Sphere" in New England, 1780-1835* (New Haven 1977); Mary P. Ryan, "The Power of Women's Networks: A Case Study of Female Moral Reform in Antebellum America," *Feminist Studies*, 5 (Spring 1979), 66-85; and Carroll Smith-Rosenberg, "The Female World of Love and Ritual: Relations between Women in Nineteenth-Century America," *Signs*, 1 (Autumn 1975), 1-29.

with a good bank account, and could live in my own house, ride in my own carriage, and have my children well fed and clothed, I should not care if we were all as black as the ace of spades." But, she added, that man had never experienced the "humiliation of color." Similarly, men could not appreciate

the subtle humiliations of women possessed of wealth, education, and genius . . . and yet can any misery be more real than invidious distinctions on the ground of sex in the laws and constitution, in the political, religious, and moral position of those who in nature stand the peers of each other? And not only do such women suffer these ever-recurring indignities in daily life, but the literature of the world proclaims their inferiority and divinely decreed subjection in all history, sacred and profane, in science, philosophy, poetry, and song.[6]

927

In both her examples it is the exceptional person, in terms of wealth, talent, and cultural background, who feels the sting of discrimination because it is felt to be more unnatural and therefore more unjust than the injuries of class. The disabilities of early nineteenth century women and free blacks were felt most acutely by those who knew themselves capable of doing and achieving things which the laws or prejudices, or even the internalized prohibitions, of American society prevented them from doing, or which restrained them from enjoying the influence, status, or comforts to which their talents or wealth entitled them. Caste operated unnaturally to deflect the "normal" operations of class, the accepted sifting mechanisms of free society. Color, complained Charles Remond, protesting the segregated cars on Massachusetts railroads, had the effect of wiping out all distinctions among blacks: "It is said we all look alike. If this is true, it is not true that we all behave alike. There is a marked difference; and we claim a recognition of this difference."[7]

If we accept Stanton's focus on humiliation as central to the subjective experience of these black and feminist leaders, then it is not surprising that they should have conceived of liberty primarily in individualistic terms: as equal access to all aspects of American life and as the career open to talents. It was one of the principal sins of man, according to the Seneca Falls Declaration of 1848, that he had closed against woman "all the avenues to wealth and distinction which he

---

[6] Stanton *et al.*, *History of Woman Suffrage*, II, 266.

[7] Charles Lenox Remond, Address to a Massachusetts Legislative Committee, 1842, in Philip S. Foner, ed., *The Voice of Black America: Major Speeches by Negroes in the United States, 1797-1971* (New York 1972), 73.

considers most honorable to himself." The black doctor, John Rock, lamented, "there is no field" for the young black man of talent. "You can hardly imagine," he continued, "the humiliation and contempt a colored lad must feel by graduating first in his class and then being rejected everywhere else because of his color."[8]

To note their individualism is to acknowledge that these psychologically marginal people were in the intellectual mainstream of American, and indeed nineteenth century western, culture. Historians interested in the development of American individualism have seldom noticed the extent to which both feminist and black claims were part of that swelling tide of individual self-assertion and the separation of self out of the group. Eric Foner has suggested that "only a movement that viewed society as a collection of individuals . . . that believed every individual had the right to seek advancement as a unit in a competitive society" could condemn slavery as completely as the abolitionists did. One might add that it took men and women who had a burning awareness of themselves as individuals unjustly cramped, thwarted, and humiliated because of their membership in a subordinate group to demand that the logic of liberal individualism be applied without consideration of race or sex.[9]

To do so implied that the individual could, in a sense, be abstracted from the accidents of race and sex and be seen as essentially the freehold owner and user of energies and talents. Feminists in particular were drawn to the Romantic versions of individualism which conceived of the individual less as a finished unit than as a bundle of potentialities which required freedom as their essential medium of growth. To deprive the individual of the necessary scope for development was thus the ultimate injustice because it violated the essence of human nature. "The fundamental principle of the Woman's Rights movement," resolved a convention of 1853, "is . . . that every human being, without distinction of sex, has an inviolable right to the full development and

928

---

[8] "Declaration of Sentiments," Seneca Falls, 1848, in Stanton et al., History of Woman Suffrage, I, 71; John S. Rock, 1862, in Foner, ed., Voice of Black America, 258.

[9] Eric Foner, "The Causes of the American Civil War: Recent Interpretations and New Directions," in Politics and Ideology in the Age of the Civil War (New York 1980), 23-24. For the individualism of most feminist thinkers see James L. Cooper and Sheila M. Cooper, eds., The Roots of American Feminist Thought (Boston 1973), introduction; for a critique of that individualism, see Elizabeth H. Wolgast, Equality and the Rights of Women (Ithaca 1980). A recent brief essay on American individualism is J. R. Pole, American Individualism and the Promise of Progress (Oxford, Eng. 1980). The romantic individualism of personal growth is discussed in Yehoshua Arieli, Individualism and Nationalism in American Ideology (Cambridge, Mass. 1964), esp. ch. 12.

free exercise of all energies." Women are human, exclaimed the editor of the feminist paper, *The Una*, "and must have the freedom which an unlimited development demands."[10]

If white women tended to put rather more emphasis on freedom as the medium for individual growth, rather than the access to the economic opportunities and rewards of American life which preoccupied black men, it was partly because they could afford such a luxury. But it was also because freedom for women entailed a domestic dimension absent from the struggles of black men—it meant disentangling oneself from the mesh of domestic relations, being ready to refuse, or at least deal coolly with, the "family claim." "A woman is nobody. A wife is everything," declared a Philadelphia newspaper, horrified at the goings-on at Seneca Falls. That was the problem. The prevailing ideology of true womanhood made self-sacrifice the most womanly of virtues; it was the suppression of her own self in the home which allowed it to be a nurturing place for male selves. Elizabeth Stanton thought that the moral freight attached to female self-sacrifice was one of the hardest things for women to bring themselves to repudiate. "Put it down in capital letters," she told a reporter in later years, "SELF-DEVELOPMENT IS A HIGHER DUTY THAN SELF-SACRIFICE." The yearning for self-development and the doubt that it could be accomplished in the feminine sphere of home was one of the things which drew middle class women to the idea of work. They saw work outside the home as providing a field in which women could realize those latent selves stifled at the domestic hearth. Nothing could supply the place of work to a woman, said the first American woman doctor, Elizabeth Blackwell: "In all human relations, the woman has to yield, to modify her individuality . . . but true work is perfect freedom, and full satisfaction."[11]

929

---

[10] Stanton *et al.*, *History of Woman Suffrage*, I, 855; Paulina Wright Davis, *The Una*, 1 (June 1853), 73. For the idea of "possessive individualism" and its more dynamic nineteenth century developments, see C. B. Macpherson, *Democratic Theory: Essays in Retrieval* (Oxford, Eng. 1973), 199, 32.

[11] Philadelphia *Public Ledger and Daily Transcript*, quoted in Stanton *et al.*, *History of Woman Suffrage*, I, 804. Stanton is quoted in Judith Nies, *Seven Women: Portraits from the American Radical Tradition* (New York 1977), 67, and Blackwell in Lee Virginia Chambers-Schiller, *Liberty, a Better Husband: Single Women in America: The Generation of 1780-1840* (New Haven 1984), 66. Access to greater educational opportunities was an important goal for both feminists and free blacks since education seemed the key to achieving both individual advancement and individual development. It gave the means to develop and extend talents, to move up in the world, and to throw off the shackles of felt inferiority to well educated white men.

Work offered more than self-development, however; it offered in-dependence. Conceiving of freedom in individualist terms led both feminists and black leaders into an instinctive adherence to the tradi-tional republican horror of dependence. Dependence was degrading and essentially antithetical to liberty. But blacks and feminists inter-preted what dependence meant in different ways. To the middle class feminist it meant the inability to be economically self-supporting. The paucity of careers open to women hardly enabled them to live de-cently without being forced to marry for a home or live uneasily in the home of parents or married siblings. Dependence meant financial dependence on a husband. Feminists took as a particular target the common law rules on the property of married women which reduced the wife, in the words of one female petition, to "a mere pensioner on the bounty of her husband." In a culture that elevated the moral value of work, in which even upper class males continually empha-sized the amount of hard work they did, the sensitive woman in a well-to-do household could easily come to feel herself a parasite, en-joying a standard of comfort which she had not "earned." Perhaps most important, feminists came to interpret the status of being "kept" as entailing the same kind of degradation of character which tradi-tional republican theory bestowed upon the dependent male: dependents became servile and underhanded because they had to please a master. " 'Rule by obedience and by submission sway,' or in other words study to be a hypocrite," wrote the abolitionist Sarah Grimké con-temptuously, "pretend to submit, but gain your point"; that "has been the code of household morality which woman has been taught."[12]

Because of their lack of control over economic resources feminists could see *all* women as in a sense "poor" and degraded, not so much by material hardship, but by the lack of independence and thus self-respect that poverty entailed. There were many women, of course, as feminists recognized, who were literally poor and who did not have the choice of dependence, who had to earn their own living and often that of their children. And few of them earned wages sufficient to pro-vide a decently independent life. Feminists interpreted the problem of the working woman, not in terms of the economic system, but of

930

---

[12] "Memorial to the [state] Constitutional Convention adopted by Woman's Rights Convention, Salem, Ohio" (1850), in Gerda Lerner, ed., *The Female Experience* (Indianapolis 1977), 344. Sarah Grimké, *Letters on the Equality of the Sexes, and the Con-dition of Woman* (1838; rep. New York 1970), 17. For the republican horror of dependence see, for example, Jack P. Greene, *All Men Are Created Equal: Some Reflec-tions on the Character of the American Revolution* (Oxford, Eng. 1976), 20-21.

the pernicious workings of caste. Male prejudice restricted the number of jobs open to women; women's own internalization of male opinion of their capacities, social conventions of propriety, and the torpor induced by subordination meant that few took the time and trouble to acquire marketable skills. "I know girls who have mechanical genius sufficient to become Arkwrights and Fultons," said one speaker at a woman's rights convention, "but their mothers would not apprentice them. Which of the women at this Convention have sent their daughters as apprentices to a watchmaker?" The result was that women were crowded into a very few lines of work and so continually drove down each other's wages. The feminist solution for both lady and mill girl was wider economic opportunities and the will to use them. "Poverty is essentially slavery," wrote Paulina Davis in *The Una*, "if not legal, yet actual." Women must understand this and "they must *go to work*":

931

> They must press into every avenue, every open door, that custom and the law leave unguarded, aye, and themselves withdraw the bolts and bars from others still closed against them . . . . They *must* purchase themselves out of bondage . . . . For as long as the world stands, its government will go with its cares, services and responsibilities. Children and women, till they can keep themselves, will be kept in pupilage by the same power which supports them.[13]

Several historians have pointed out that abolitionists had no sympathy with the concept of "wage slavery" and refused to see any analogy between the working class in the developing capitalist economy and the slave on the plantation. For feminists too, "wage slavery" might metaphorically describe wretchedly low wages, but not the structure of the employment relationship itself. Men of the revolutionary generation had considered wage-earning, as opposed to freehold farming or self-employment, as a form of dependence, and many American workingmen were still clinging to that conception. But to feminists, for women to be paid a specific cash wage, in return for specific work

---

[13] J. Elizabeth Jones at the Syracuse National Woman's Rights Convention of 1852, quoted in Stanton *et al.*, *History of Woman Suffrage*, I, 530; Paulina Wright Davis, *The Una*, 1 (Sept. 1853), 138. Jones made her own living as a lecturer on science and insisted that it was within women's own power to apprentice themselves to skilled trades. "There is no law against this!" Lucretia Mott replied, "The Church and public opinion are stronger than law," and Lucy Stone pointed out that when some women in Massachusetts had apprenticed themselves as printers, they "were expelled because men would not set type beside them." Stanton *et al.*, *History of Woman Suffrage*, I, 530-531.

outside the home, was a step upwards and onwards from the multiple dependencies of woman's traditional domestic sphere. The impersonal capitalist marketplace, however harsh, offered an escape from the more galling personal dependence on particular men.[14]

Like women, free black men, when employed at all, were crowded into a very few occupations, most of which were not only low paid but of little prestige in the wider culture. In many ways they shared with women the task of "servicing" white males. Black spokesmen like Frederick Douglass and Martin Delany denounced black men for their "dependency," by which they meant this employment in "servile" tasks. Black men were barbers, shoe blacks, and porters, and their women were domestic servants and washerwomen—servicing whites rather than their own families. This denunciation immediately got Douglass and Delany into hot water with many people in the black community and they had to back off somewhat and protest that they accepted any useful and honest labor as worthy of respect. But they would not give way too far: the association of blacks with "menial" work only served to depress the estimation in which the community was held by the larger society. He knew, wrote Delany, that he would offend many blacks by suggesting that to be a servant was degrading: "It is not necessarily degrading; it would not be, to one or a few people of a kind; but a *whole race of servants* are a degradation to that people." Both urged blacks to abandon the servicing of whites and instead take up land and become farmers and apprentice their children to the skilled trades. These were ideal "republican" occupations in which a man was self-employed and independent. One of the attractions of farming, in particular, was that not only did it seem a traditional road to economic independence but, according to one committee report in the black national convention of 1843, it bestowed respectability and "character" and

> puts the one farmer, be he whom he may, upon the same level with his neighbors . . . ; his neighbors see him now, not as in other situations they may have done as a servant; but as an independent man; . . . farmers, they respect their own calling, feel themselves independent— they must and will respect his, and feel that he is alike independent.

---

[14] For wage earning as dependency and "slavery" see, for example, Foner, *Politics and Ideology in the Age of the Civil War*, 60; for the abolitionist attitude, see *ibid.*, 71, and Jonathan A. Glickstein, " 'Poverty is not Slavery': American Abolitionists and the Competitive Labor Market," in *Antislavery Reconsidered*, ed. Lewis Perry and Michael Fellman (Baton Rouge 1979), 195-218. *The Una* devoted a good deal of space to the problem of women's employment and obviously struck a chord with its readers since there were several readers' letters on the subject.

Frederick Douglass put particular faith in the crafts. He urged blacks to get their sons apprenticed in the "blacksmith's shop, the machine shop, the joiner's shop, the wheelwright's shop . . . ," although he acknowledged elsewhere that white prejudice seemed most solidly entrenched among the craftsmen of the skilled trades and that it was almost impossible to persuade a white craftsman to take a non-white apprentice. Yet the glamour of the independent craftsman in his own shop, though it might be economically obsolescent, was his status as an independent republican citizen.[15]

In asserting the necessity of being independent, blacks and feminists were linking themselves to an established republican tradition, one of the most strongly held values of Jacksonian America. But for them to appropriate this value as a right for themselves was to court considerable risk. Tolerated in menial positions, blacks invoked the fury of whites when they competed with white workers or asserted a claim to equal rights and dignity. Even well disposed whites preferred blacks as objects of benevolence rather than as equal citizens. Though women were not the targets of mob violence like blacks, their assertion of independence was also dangerous, since to most Americans there was an implicit equation of dependence with femininity. As many commentators on womanhood asserted, it was women's dependence which

933

---

[15] Martin Robison Delany, *The Condition, Elevation, Emigration, and Destiny of the Colored People of the United States* (1852, rep. New York 1969), esp. 42-43, 200 (quotation); Report of the Committee upon Agriculture, "Minutes of the National Convention of Colored Citizens: Held at Buffalo . . . 1843," 32, in *Minutes of the Proceedings of the National Negro Conventions, 1830-1864*, ed. Howard Holman Bell (New York 1969); Frederick Douglass, "An Address to the Colored People of the United States," Sept. 29, 1848, in Brotz, ed., *Negro Social and Political Thought*, 211. See also the "Resolves of the National Colored Convention, Cleveland, 1848," 13, in Bell, ed., *Proceedings of the National Negro Conventions*. These views on "servile" occupations obviously had a constituency outside the leadership of the conventions and men like Douglass and Delany. A black in California wrote to the press making the same point. Urging every black to abandon such positions as "boot-blacks, waiters, servants and carriers," he added: "I do not wish to be understood as despising any of the callings I have mentioned above, [but] . . . so long as we follow such pursuits, so long will we be despised. The world may preach the dignity of labor . . . . But however pretty this may be in theory, everyone is aware that it does not exist in reality. The man is judged and courted, not for his inherent qualities, but for his position and wealth." San Francisco *Mirror of the Times*, in Martin E. Dann, ed., *The Black Press, 1827-1890: The Quest for National Identity* (New York 1971), 334. For some of the acrimony over the contemptuous expressions employed by some leaders about service jobs, see "Resolves of the National Colored Convention, Cleveland," 5-6, and Howard Holman Bell, *A Survey of the Negro Convention Movement, 1830-1861* (1953, rep. New York 1969), 102-104.

made men love them, so that to repudiate dependence was to risk not only being unloved but also male retaliation. In several antifeminist polemics there is an only partly veiled assumption that the natural attitude of men towards women is antagonism. Women could deflect this antagonism by deferential and dependent behavior, but if they abandoned that behavior men would turn upon them with the full force of untrammeled aggression and competitiveness. "All the sacred protection of religion, all the generous promptings of chivalry, all the poetry of romantic gallantry, depend upon woman's retaining her place as dependent and defenceless," warned Catherine Beecher. The clergy were particularly quick to warn women that when they assumed "the place and tone of a man" then "we put ourselves in self-defence against her"; if, in a favorite metaphor, the vine sought to emulate the independence of the oak, in the resulting disorganization of society, the vine would be "the first to fall and be trodden under foot."[16]

Their emphasis on individual effort, "elevation," and self-development made the relationship of these black and feminist leaders with the black community and with "womanhood" as a whole deeply ambivalent. On the one hand, feminists and black leaders dissociated themselves from many aspects of the culture of "their" group; yet on the other, their identification with it was so deep that any injury or insult to any black or any woman evoked not merely sympathy, but was felt as a personal insult. Further, the attainment of personal freedom for individual members of an identifiable group of inferior status could not in fact be achieved without the elimination of the legal disabilities and the wall of prejudice that hemmed in the whole group.

There was thus a reciprocal relationship between individual and community: the whole must be freed and to some extent "elevated" before the individual could rise about it, but it was also the success of the talented and exceptional individuals who would help to elevate the group. After chastising a meeting of free blacks in Canada for their shortcomings, Frederick Douglass pointed out they must bear

---

[16] Catharine E. Beecher, *An Essay on Slavery and Abolitionism, with Reference to the Duty of American Females* (Philadelphia 1837), 101-102; pastoral letter from "The General Association of Massachusetts (Orthodox) to the Churches Under Their Care" (1837), in Alice S. Rossi, *The Feminist Papers: From Adams to Beauvoir* (New York 1973), 305; Jonathan F. Stearns, "Discourse on Female Influence" (sermon, 1837), in Aileen S. Kraditor, *Up From the Pedestal: Selected Writings in the History of American Feminism* (Chicago 1968), 47-50. See also Litwack, *North of Slavery*, 103; and Brotz, ed., *Negro Social and Political Thought*, 283.

in mind "that he is closely linked with them; and in proportion as they ascend in the scale of intellectual and moral improvement, so will he; whereas, if they allow themselves to sink into degradation, he also is dragged down along with them." He deplored the jealousy many blacks displayed towards the few who had risen above the general level. "They see colored people occupy a better position, but they say, 'What has Frederick Douglass done for us?' " Douglass did not specify what he and other black leaders whom he named had done for the average black but he implied that they had raised the reputation of the whole race in the eyes of whites and that by their mere existence they ought to raise the self-respect of every black. Some measure of what J.R. Pole has called "equality of esteem" for the whole race or sex had to be wrung out of American society before individual freedom would be truly possible.[17]

It was essentially as a vital symbol of "equality of esteem" that blacks and feminists demanded the vote. Liberty as equal access, self-development, and independence, and liberty as membership in the political body of self-governing citizens are logically distinct, and certainly both blacks and women had reason to doubt any easy equation of freedom with republican institutions, and to ask: "of what advantage is it to us to live in a Republic?" It became a commonplace among feminists that republics were in fact particularly inimical to female self-expression outside the home and that women, as women, had more access to political power and a wider range of personal freedom in aristocratic societies. Blacks who traveled to Europe as feted guests of British abolitionists returned to report that they had been free to travel without segregation or insult, had been easily accepted by white society, and had generally felt themselves to be much freer than in democratic, republican America.[18]

---

[17] Frederick Douglass, "Advice to My Canadian Brothers and Sisters: An Address Delivered in Chatham, Canada West, on 3 August 1854," and "Self-Help: An Address Delivered in New York, on 7 May 1849," in John W. Blassingame et al., *The Frederick Douglass Papers*, Series 1: *Speeches, Debates, and Interviews*, Vol. 2: *1847-1854* (New Haven 1982), 537, 168-169; J. R. Pole, *The Pursuit of Equality in American History* (Berkeley, Calif. 1978), xii-xiii, 150, 302.

[18] Isaiah Berlin, "Two Concepts of Liberty," 131; Mary Mott to the Westchester Woman's Rights Convention, 1852, in Stanton et al., *History of Woman Suffrage*, 1, 829. On blacks' experience of travel abroad see the remarks of Charles Lenox Remond in Foner, ed., *Voice of Black America*, 74-75, and Litwack, *North of Slavery*, 237. The English naturally liked to rub in the deficiencies of republican America: "Tell the Republicans on your side of the line," said the governor of Upper Canada to a delegation of blacks seeking to settle in Canada, "that we royalists do not know men by their color." Quoted in Litwack, *North of Slavery*, 73.

Even so, feminists and black spokesmen insisted on the right of full citizenship in the American republic as the necessary complement of the more private liberty of self-development. While the vote was not the only measure of liberation for antebellum feminists, it was central to them from the beginning. Similarly, every black convention demanded the vote on equal terms with whites. For blacks the issue of the franchise was particularly galling, since in several states after the late 1820s they were in fact disfranchised and deprived of a right that they had once possessed. Yet free blacks were too few to have exercised much real political clout as voters, and while women would certainly have had the power of numbers, much of what feminists wanted, in terms of access and opportunity, could not have been achieved through legislation in the lightly governed America of the early nineteenth century. It was less a question of power, however, than of self-respect. To be excluded from the central ritual of the nation in which they lived was to be deprived of that recognition which was needed to feel oneself a free person.[19]

The demand for inclusion in the political community was the most stoutly resisted of all black and feminist demands. White men, too, seem to have regarded political participation through the rituals of party loyalties and electoral contests less as a means to practical ends, or even as the exercise of power, than as an affirmation of an essential equality as *men*. A republican polity was a fraternal community. Very few white men were prepared to include black men within that fraternity, and even fewer were ready to acknowledge women as brothers.[20] For blacks the symbolic association of suffrage with masculinity made its possession of vital psychological importance. The state of Pennsylvania, claimed a convention of its free black inhabitants, by disfranchising them had "striken a blow at our manhood, and not only ours,

936

---

[19] Pease and Pease, *They Who Would Be Free*, 173-193; Litwack, *North of Slavery*, 75-93; Charles H. Wesley, "Negro Suffrage in the Period of Constitution-Making, 1787-1865," *Journal of Negro History*, 32 (Apr. 1947), 143-168.

[20] John L. Stanley, "Majority Tyranny in Tocqueville's America: The Failure of Negro Suffrage in 1846," *Political Science Quarterly*, 84 (Sept. 1969), 412-435. The most common argument against the enfranchisement of free blacks in the conventions for revising state constitutions in the period was that they were essentially *aliens*, "by the broad distinction of race"; since most white men were unwilling to admit any kind of equality of social intercourse with blacks, this necessarily meant that they could not be admitted to the fraternal bond of political equals. See, for example, the debate on this subject in William G. Bishop and William H. Attree, eds., *Report of the Debates and Proceedings of the Convention for the Revision of the Constitution of the State of New York, 1846* (Albany, N.Y. 1846), 1014-1036, 1045-1048. The quotation is at 1030.

but a majority of those who people this globe." A white writer supporting black claims concurred: the vote was "a public recognition of the manhood of the enfranchised man." If women were to claim the attributes of manhood, free and independent individuality, then they too would have to be included in the formal community of such individuals. "In no other way," said a speaker at an Ohio woman's rights convention in 1853, "can we so surely rouse her to the recognition of her individual worth and responsibility, her independent selfhood, as by securing for her the rights of citizenship, the privileges of free men."[21]

Frederick Douglass in 1865 summed up the reasons why he wanted the vote for black men, in terms with which feminists would have concurred. He wanted it, he said, first because it was a *right*, and men who consented to be deprived of rights were "insulting their own nature." Second, he wanted the vote as a means of educating black people:

937

> Men are so constituted that they derive their conviction of their own possibilities largely from the estimate formed of them by others. . . . By depriving us of suffrage, you affirm our incapacity . . . you declare before the world that we are unfit to exercise the elective franchise, and by this means lead us to undervalue ourselves, to put a low estimate upon ourselves, and to feel that we have no possibilities like other men.

If he lived in a monarchy, he continued, he could accept being without the vote, since it would be no "particular deprivation"; but in a nation with "manhood" suffrage "to rule us out is to make us an exception, to brand us with the stigma of inferiority."[22]

Both feminists and black leaders thus saw the ballot less as an in-

---

[21] "An Appeal to the Colored Citizens of Pennsylvania," in Philip S. Foner and George E. Walker, eds., *Proceedings of the Black State Conventions, 1840-1865* (2 vols., Philadelphia 1979-1980), I, 126; "Extension of the Elective Franchise to the Colored Citizens of the Free States," *The New Englander*, 5 (Oct. 1847), 523; Ohio Woman's Rights Convention, quoted in *The Una*, 1 (July 1853), 86. The Seneca Falls declaration was not the first formal claim for the suffrage for women. The constitutional convention of New York in 1846 received a petition from six women claiming complete civil and political equality with men. *Report of the Proceedings*, 646. For the fraternal and symbolic nature of antebellum politics see the brilliant article by Paula Baker, "The Domestication of Politics: Women and American Political Society, 1780-1920," *American Historical Review*, 89 (June 1984), 620-647.

[22] Brotz, ed., *Negro Social and Political Thought*, 279. Several black and feminist leaders would have been agreeable to accepting a qualified franchise, as long as the qualification was sex and color blind. See, for example, Robert Purvis, in Curry, *The Free Black in Urban America*, 222. For the relation of suffrage to female autonomy see DuBois, *Feminism and Suffrage*, 46-47.

strument for practical ends than as an attribute of individual freedom and self-respect. Its exercise would at the same time affirm personal worth and teach its possessors how to be free. In this way they combined older, classical republican ideas of liberty as a function of the participation of equals in the public realm with newer, liberal ideas of individual freedom as a personal possession.

Finally, both blacks and feminists realized that the removal of external constraints was not sufficient. Freedom, while it was exercised in the society of one's fellow men, began in the head. The worst effect of lack of liberty was that in the long run it unfitted people for the use of freedom. They internalized their oppression, became incapable of even realizing their degraded state, and in the end did, indeed, exhibit the inferiority with which prejudice branded them. Erik Erikson has spoken of that "cold *self*-appraisal in historical terms which no true revolutionary movement can do without." These black and feminist leaders endeavored to force their constituencies into painful self-analysis. Though antebellum feminists did not always escape the alluring notion of female moral superiority, on the whole they had a chastened sense that being oppressed is not particularly good for one's character. They had harsh words for women as they found them: "mawkish, and treacherous, and petulant and meager," and "poor, weak, imbecile, helpless things," most of them as yet scarcely fit to "touch the Chariot of Liberty." Men like Douglass and Martin Delany sometimes feared that the degradation of the slave parent continued to be handed down from father even to free sons, an acquired characteristic of " submission and servitude, menialism and dependence, until it has become almost a physiological function of our system, an actual condition of our nature." They condemned black frivolity, addiction to display, and lack of concern for their own elevation. The black woman lecturer, Maria Stewart, flailed black men for their "want of laudable ambition and requisite courage" which made her "blood to boil."[23]

Liberty, then, required first of all that women and black men acknowledge that they were *not* free. They must cease to shield

938

---

[23] Erik H. Erikson, "Once More the Inner Space," in Jean Strouse, ed., *Women and Analysis* (New York 1974), 334; Elizabeth Oakes Smith, *Woman and Her Needs* (New York 1851), reprinted in *Liberating the Home* (New York 1974), 106; letter from Mrs. Lydia Jane Pierson to Salem, Ohio, Equal Rights Convention, 1850, in *The Lily*, 2 (June 1850), 41; Delany, *The Condition . . . of the Colored People*, 47-48; Maria Stewart, "An Address, Delivered at the African Masonic Hall, Boston, 27 February, 1833," in Bert James Loewenberg and Ruth Bogin, eds., *Black Women in Nineteenth-Century American Life* (University Park, Pa. 1976), 196.

themselves from this insight by self-delusion and the shelter of their separate spheres. "Though we are servants; among ourselves we claim to be *ladies* and *gentlemen* . . . and as the popular expression goes, 'Just as good as anybody,' " wrote Martin Delany contemptuously, but, "we cannot at the same time, be domestic and lady; servant and gentleman. We must be the one or the other." Paulina Davis in *The Una* produced an extended comparison between the situation of women and that of both slaves and free blacks, in the hope that the analogy with "the most hated and despised race of earth, may startle some who sleep . . . and compel them to feel their own false, unnatural, and despicable position . . . . [I]f it rouse[s] one woman to feel her degradation, its suggestions will have accomplished their mission . . . ." Blacks and white women must recognize the myriad ways in which lack of freedom had contorted and vitiated the character and come to terms with the realization that they had to some extent cooperated in their own debasement. This was the crucial act of self-emancipation, and should lead, not to despair, but rather to a new vigor, self-confidence, and readiness for action.[24]

A favorite quotation, which turns up again and again in both free black and feminist discourse, is the line from Byron: "Who would be free, themselves must strike the blow." This had the implication, not merely that white men were likely to be reluctant emancipators and unreliable allies, but that the act of striking was, in a sense, in itself the liberation. Only by coming to feel their invisible chains and by taking some action, however small, to break them, could black men and women of both races begin to make themselves the free and independent individuals whose creation was the ultimate end of modern free society.

939

---

[24] Delany, *The Condition . . . of the Colored People*, 200-201; Paulina Wright Davis, "Pecuniary Independence of Woman," *The Una*, 1 (Dec. 1853), 186.

Coincoin: An Eighteenth-Century "Liberated" Woman

By Gary B. Mills

LEGENDS ARE USUALLY REGARDED AS QUASI-HISTORY, INTERESTING but undocumented accounts of unusual people or events. Passed orally from generation to generation, unfettered by the restrictions placed upon written history, legends are embroidered, romanticized, and popularized until a multiplicity of forms appear. Attempts to document the various versions frequently result in their being discredited.

One such popular narrative in Louisiana is the legend of Coincoin. Through ten generations the story of this exceptional black woman has been passed from father to daughter to grandson, idealized as an example of success in the face of extreme adversity, immortalized as the chronicle of the beginnings of an unusual colony of people. Eventually, the legend of Coincoin spread beyond the colony which perpetuated it and was popularized by a fascinated public.

Like most legends, the legend of Coincoin exists in several versions, most of which have appeared in the past half century. While popular writers have repeated the legend, they have made no serious attempt to document it, but, on the contrary, they have often woven more colorful threads of fancy into the fabric of the legend. Unlike most legends, however, the story of Coincoin can be documented, and its details, for the most part, prove to be valid.

This eighteenth-century "liberated" woman was, unquestionably, a *femme extraordinaire.* For thirty-eight years a slave, Coincoin won her freedom through exceptional faithfulness, love, and devotion, and then set out to purchase her children and grandchildren from the bonds of slavery. For forty-six years a house servant, Coincoin took to the fields when her former master gave her a tract of eighty arpents[1] of unimproved land. With determina-

---

[1] An arpent during this period was equal to slightly less than one acre.

Mr. Mills is a part-time faculty member of Mississippi State University, who is presently preparing a bicentennial history of the U. S. Corps of Engineers of the Vicksburg District.

THE JOURNAL OF SOUTHERN HISTORY
Vol. XLII, No. 2, May 1976

tion and industry, she increased her holdings from this small farm into an estate of over a thousand arpents and at least sixteen slaves. A strong matriarch, a fervent Catholic in spite of trying circumstances, Coincoin produced a family that lived by, and prospered upon, the principles of piety, industry, and mutual assistance, a family which has remained a distinct social group in Louisiana society for almost two centuries. For her role in the development of this society, Coincoin's story has been reverently immortalized.

On August 24, 1742, a black slave infant was baptized at the fledgling outpost of Natchitoches in the French colony of Louisiana. The baptismal registers of the old parish of St. François des Natchitoches identify the child as the property of Louis Juchereau de St. Denis, the intrepid French-Canadian who had founded the Natchitoches post in 1714 and had served since 1721 as its commandant. The child was baptized under the Christian name of Marie Thérèze,[2] but she was named Coincoin by her African parents, and it was this name for which she evidenced a lifelong preference.

Little is known of Coincoin's African heritage. Her parents, François and Marie Françoise, both slaves in the St. Denis household, had been married six years before Coincoin's birth, shortly after François's arrival at the post.[3] In some colonial records of the post, both civil and ecclesiastical, slaves were identified by the African nations from which they came, but no such information was recorded for François or Marie Françoise. The only clues to their tribal origins are provided by the African names they gave to three of their eleven children.[4] Their eldest daughter, Marie Gertrude, was called Dgimby. Their eldest son, François, was given a name variously spelled as Kiokera and Choera. Marie Thérèze, the second daughter, was more commonly known as Coincoin (or its occasional variant spellings Quoinquin, Kuenkuoin, and Cuencuen). This name, according to one authority on African dialects, provides the

---

[2] Registers of the Parish of St. François des Natchitoches (Immaculate Conception Church, Natchitoches, Louisiana), Book 1, unnumbered page. This source is hereinafter cited as Natchitoches Registers.

[3] Ibid., ninth page numbered as 7.

[4] The children of François and Marie Françoise were: (1) Marie Gertrude, called Dgimby, baptized November 18, 1736; (2) François, Jr., called Kiokera or Choera, born about 1738; (3) Jean Baptiste, born about 1740; (4) Marie Thérèze, called Coincoin, baptized August 24, 1742; (5) Barnabé, born September 9, 1744; (6) Marie Jeanne, baptized June 25, 1746; (7) Marie Louise, born about 1748 or 1749; (8) Bonaventure, baptized June 18, 1751; (9) Hyacinthe, baptized September 13, 1753; (10) Marguerite, born 1755 or 1756; and (11) Françoise, baptized April 21, 1758. Natchitoches Registers, Books 1 and 2, unnumbered pages; Succession of St. Denys, Docs. 176–78, September 20, 1756: Succession of Wife of St. Denys, Doc. 203, August 1, 1758; Doc. 204, April 28, 1758; and Doc. 205, April 25, 1758, Natchitoches Parish Records (Office of the Clerk of Court, Natchitoches, Louisiana).

best link between François and Marie Françoise and their African heritage. A phonetic equivalent of Coincoin is Ko Kwî, the name reserved in the Glidzi dialect for second-born daughters of the Ewe tribe which occupied the coastal region of Togo.[5]

Coincoin grew to maturity in a slave household that does not fit the usual stereotyped description of slave society. Her parents were legitimately married, not merely according to "the law of the plantation" but also according to "the law of the church." From the time of their marriage until their concurrent deaths twenty-two years later, they were never separated from each other by sale.[6] This pattern of family stability served as the example for Coincoin and the family that she eventually produced. Moreover, it is apparent that François and Marie Françoise instilled in their children a respect for their African heritage. Not only did their children continue to use their African names in obvious preference to their Christian names, but according to the tradition preserved by the descendants of Coincoin the parents also trained this daughter well in the native use and application of medicinal herbs and roots. Tradition also relates that Coincoin was fluent in an African dialect in addition to the French and Spanish languages that dominated eighteenth-century Louisiana.[7]

St. Denis died in 1744; his widow in 1758. When the St. Denis estate was settled, Coincoin was inherited by a St. Denis son who subsequently passed her to his sister, Marie de Nieges de St. Denis, wife of the colorful defector from the Spanish colonies, Antonio Manuel Bermudez y de Soto.[8] Little is known of Coincoin's life during this period. In fact, the only available information is found in the incomplete and inconsistent registers of the church.

Religious fervor was not strong at the Natchitoches post. For the first twenty years of its existence the post did not have a resident priest, a situation which was to repeat itself a number of times throughout the first century of its settlement. Commandant and Mme. de St. Denis were bulwarks of the local religious congregation during their lives and insisted upon the administration of the Christian sacraments to their slaves and the practice of Christian

[5] Dr. Jan Vansina to author, May 12, 1973.

[6] François and Marie Françoise died in an apparent epidemic at the Natchitoches post and were buried the same day, April 19, 1758, in the parish cemetery. Natchitoches Registers, Book 2, unnumbered page.

[7] Interview with Mrs. Lee Etta Vaccarini Coutii, Isle Brevelle, Louisiana, March 24, 1974. Mrs. Coutii is a fifth-generation descendant, several times over, of Coincoin.

[8] Succession of St. Denys, Doc. 176, September 20, 1756; Succession of Wife of St. Denys, Doc. 203, August 1, 1758; Doc. 204, April 28, 1758; and Doc. 205, April 25, 1758, Natchitoches Parish Records. The document whereby young St. Denis transferred Coincoin to his sister is not extant.

precepts among them.[9] Thus it was that François had been provided with a wife shortly after his arrival at the post. The example set by the St. Denis couple was followed during this period by most area residents, but the practice did not long outlive the commandant and his wife. By the 1760s the registers of the church reflected a much smaller percentage of marriages among slaves, and this number steadily dwindled. Like most Natchitoches slaves who reached maturity after the close of the St. Denis hegemony, Coincoin was not provided with a husband, nor was she encouraged to adhere to the Christian code by her new owners. In fact, her last mistress, Marie de St. Denis de Soto, had herself borne a child out of wedlock prior to marriage.[10]

Economic considerations were in part responsible for the relaxation of religious principles in the slave households of the St. Denis heirs. The youths were not wealthy, and their small slaveholdings at this time contained no males of appropriate age who could be paired with Coincoin except her own brothers. Apparently, too, they could not afford to purchase a husband for her at this point. At the same time, it was a fundamental principle of the institution of slavery in North America that much of a young female slave's value was dependent upon her ability to produce more slaves. Coincoin fulfilled the duty expected of her. The year following her inheritance by the St. Denis son, the seventeen-year-old slave bore her first child. In 1761, 1763, and 1766 the registers of the church again recorded the baptisms of slave infants she produced.[11] No records identify the father or fathers of these children.

The year 1767 marked the turning point in the life of the young slave. It had been more than three decades since her forebears had been taken from the coast of Africa and sold into slavery in the New World. It would be almost a century before the majority of American blacks would know any measure of the freedom their ancestors had enjoyed. But according to tradition Coincoin did not passively accept her lot. Never did she resign herself and the children she had borne to conditions accepted by other slaves in desolation or with

944

[9] Henry F. Beekers, A History of the Immaculate Conception Catholic Church, Natchitoches, Louisiana, 1717–1973 (Natchitoches, 1973), unnumbered pages; Books 1–4, Natchitoches Registers. Immaculate Conception is the present name of the old parish of St. François.

[10] Baptism of Marie Eleonore de St. Denis, November 5, 1750, Natchitoches Registers, Book 1, unnumbered page.

[11] Baptism of Marie Louise. slave of M. de St. Denis, September 8, 1759; baptism of Thérèze, September 24, 1761, Natchitoches Registers, Book 2, unnumbered pages; baptism of Francesca, July 8. 1763; and multiple baptism of Jean Joseph and others, March 29, 1766, ibid., Book 1, unnumbered pages. The last section of Book 1 falls chronologically after Book 2 rather than before it.

indifference. Coincoin and her children would be free within the next three decades.

The means by which Coincoin could have achieved her emancipation were limited. The catchall phrase under which most slaves were manumitted was "good and faithful service." Closer examination of the records reveals three basic reasons for emancipation: (1) the slave bore a blood relationship to the master who freed him; (2) the slave had saved the life of the mistress or a member of the owner-family; or (3) a female slave had served her master "well and faithfully" as his mistress. For Coincoin, who had neither Caucasian blood nor free black relatives, the first method was impossible. No document has been found which indicates that she had the opportunity (or luck) to earn her freedom by the second method. Only the last of these alternatives was available to her.

It was apparently in 1767 that a new immigrant, Claude Thomas Pierre Metoyer, arrived at the Natchitoches post and established himself in trade.[12] In a settlement the size of Natchitoches it was probably not long before Metoyer met the slave of Marie de St. Denis de Soto. No accounts of Coincoin's personal characteristics have been found, but it is obvious that her appearance was comely and her personality appealing. Already twenty-five years of age and the mother of four children, she had probably seen her best years; the bloom of youth did not remain long on the faces of the women who endured the harsh environment of colonial Louisiana. Yet Coincoin was to attract the attention of this sophisticated, city-bred gentleman (who was, in fact, two years her junior) and was to hold his affection until she was well past forty.

Obviously impressed with Coincoin's charms, Metoyer soon persuaded the de Sotos to lease her to him. In exchange for her services, he agreed to provide her with room and board, and Coincoin moved into Metoyer's home.[13]

This arrangement remained in effect for almost two decades, during which time Coincoin and Metoyer became the parents of ten children.[14] All children born to Coincoin during her slavery, of

945

[12] Born in La Rochelle on March 12, 1744, Metoyer apparently came from a family of well-to-do bourgeoisie. Much background material on Metoyer is available in the following records: (1) birth certificate of Claude Thomas Pierre Metoyer, May 14, 1744; (2) marriage of Baptiste Nicolas François Metoyer and Marie Anne Drapron, February 20, 1743; and (3) burial record of B. N. F. Metoyer, May 15, 1766. All are preserved in the Archives of the Department of Charente-Maritime at La Rochelle. Copies in possession of author.

[13] Pierre Metoyer to Athanase de Mézières, *King* v. *de Soto*, Proceedings, Doc. 1227, October 25, 1777, Natchitoches Parish Records.

[14] The children of Coincoin and Metoyer were (1) and (2) Nicolas Augustin and Marie Suzanne, twins, born January 22, 1768; (3) Louis, born about 1770; (4) Pierre, born about 1772; (5) Dominique, born 1774; (6) Marie Eulalie, born January 14, 1776; (7) Antoine

course, were the property of her legal owners, the de Sotos. In 1776 Metoyer purchased from Mme. de Soto the oldest four of the six children that Coincoin had borne him up to that time; apparently, his financial situation precluded the purchase of the others.[15]

It was at this time that a new priest, Father Luis de Quintanilla, arrived at the Natchitoches post to serve the religious congregation that had been for several years without a cleric. Father Quintanilla baptized the sixth child, and, as convention demanded, he wrote in the registers that the father's identity was not known.[16] Within a few months, however, Coincoin was again pregnant, and the priest's conscience would no longer allow him to ignore the situation. Metoyer and Coincoin's concubinage was by no means unique; the baptismal registers of the post contain numerous references to infants of mixed blood. Apparently, however, the other Frenchmen involved in such liaisons exercised a certain amount of discretion, whereas Metoyer and Coincoin had lived together openly for a number of years.

Father Quintanilla first counseled the couple privately, urging them to marry. This advice was obviously impractical since the *Code Noir* demanded the expulsion from the colony of any parties involved in a white-black marriage. Father Quintanilla's alternative suggestion that the couple terminate their romance was likewise ignored. Incensed, the Spanish priest filed charges of public concubinage against them with the commandant and insisted upon official action. Coincoin must be expelled from Metoyer's household, he insisted, and forbidden ever to enter his house again. Moreover, Coincoin's owner, Mme. de Soto, must be commanded to control the behavior of her slave or face the retribution of the church.[17]

The controversy continued for over eight months. The priest succeeded in having Coincoin expelled from Metoyer's household, but the separation was a brief one. Mme. de Soto furiously defended the behavior of her slave, Metoyer, and herself and retaliated with accusations of misconduct against the priest, which she threatened to take as high as necessary in the church hierarchy if the priest did not cease his interference in their lives.[18]

Joseph, born January 28, 1778; (8) Marie Françoise Roselie, born December 9, 1780; (9) Pierre Toussaint, born November 10, 1782; and (10) François, born September 26, 1784. Natchitoches Registers, Book 2, unnumbered pages; Book 4, pp. 312, 330, 345.

[15] Mme. Manuel de Soto to Pierre Metoyer, Sale of Slaves, Doc. 1161, March 31, 1776, Natchitoches Parish Records.

[16] Baptism of Marie Eulalie, January 28, 1776, Natchitoches Registers, Book 2, unnumbered page.

[17] *Code Noir; ou Loi Municipale, Servant de Reglement pour le Gouvernement . . .* (New Orleans, 1778), 2; *King v. de Soto*, Proceedings, Doc. 1227, October 23, 1777, Natchitoches Parish Records.

[18] *King v. de Soto*, Proceedings, October 23, 1777, to June 27, 1778.

The extant records of the post do not reveal the official outcome of the controversy, but it is clear from subsequent events that the priest did not succeed. Commandant Athanase de Mézières was the brother-in-law of the recalcitrant Mme. de Soto and was obviously reluctant to treat her with any severity. Moreover, Coincoin's sister Marie Jeanne was a favored slave in the de Mézières household. To the commandant's credit, it must be pointed out that the political and economic situation existing at the post at that time presented him with many problems more serious than the private conduct of Metoyer and Coincoin. Although the *Code Noir* specifically demanded that free men who fathered children by women slaves should be assessed a heavy fine,[19] de Mézières did not impose a penalty on Metoyer.

In 1778, after Father Quintanilla temporarily succeeded in having Coincoin expelled from Metoyer's household, Metoyer countered by purchasing his concubine and their seventh and youngest child from Mme. de Soto; the mother and the child immediately returned to Metoyer's home.[20] The new situation presented a further difficulty. The terms of the *Code Noir*, had Commandant de Mézières decided to impose them, required that any master who fathered children by his own slave would suffer the loss of the slave and the child; both would be sold for the benefit of the hospital at New Orleans and never be allowed freedom.[21] Metoyer's alliance with Coincoin had already resulted in seven children; future cohabitation would undoubtedly bring more, and it was obviously not his desire to forfeit Coincoin and their next child for the benefit of the hospital. Only one solution to the dilemma remained. Therefore, shortly after the execution of the purchase of 1778, Metoyer called in two friends and neighbors, and in a private document drawn in their presence he declared Coincoin and their infant son to be free.[22]

Liberation initially had little effect upon Coincoin's life-style. At the age of thirty-eight she was still penniless and propertyless. In contrast to many other former slaves whose white benefactors gave them homes or other property, Coincoin received nothing at this time but her freedom. For eight more years she remained with

947

[19] Carter G. Woodson, ed., "The Beginnings of the Miscegenation of the Whites and Blacks," *Journal of Negro History*, III (October 1918), 338.

[20] Marie de St. Denis to Pierre Metoyer, Sale of Slaves, Doc. 1312, July 29, 1778, Natchitoches Parish Records.

[21] *Code Noir*, 3.

[22] The document whereby Metoyer manumitted Coincoin and young Antoine Joseph is not extant. Reference is made to the manumission in the testament of Claude Thomas Pierre Metoyer, February 26, 1783, Acts of Leonardo Mazange, No. 7 (January 2–April 7, 1783), New Orleans Notarial Archives (Civil Courts Building, New Orleans, La.).

Metoyer in much the same status. In 1780 Metoyer purchased his two remaining children still owned by Mme. de Soto.[23] They, like the four he bought in 1776, remained in slavery. Only the infant born in 1778 was officially free, and to this number were added three additional children that Coincoin bore between 1780 and 1784.

Metoyer's business enterprises were rapidly expanding. The Spanish government had granted him a concession of land, and his merchandising activities provided capital for the purchase of additional plantations.[24] Now in his forties, he had no sons to whom he could legally bequeath the considerable fortune he was accumulating. Apparently, too, a deeply ingrained consciousness of his family's social position and the religious code by which he had been raised were also weighing heavily on his mind. Perhaps even more significantly, the captivating woman whose charms had lifted her from the hopeless station of her birth was now a middle-aged matron.

It was apparently in 1786 that Metoyer and Coincoin agreed to end their alliance. In November of that year he gave to her a small tract of eighty arpents cut from the corner of his main plantation. Coincoin promptly petitioned the Spanish government for confirmation of title, and that confirmation was made on January 18, 1787. Metoyer also promised, apparently at this same time, that he would pay to her a lifetime stipend of 120 piasters per year.[25] This land and annuity, he believed, would be sufficient for the basic needs of Coincoin and their children. It was not a generous sum; servants in the employ of the Spanish government drew wages of 180 piasters annually.[26] Having provided sufficiently, according to his own conscience, for the needs of Coincoin and their children, Metoyer took a legal wife of his own race and background.[27]

Coincoin was forty-six years of age. Most of her life, apparently,

[23] Marie de St. Denis to Pierre Metoyer, Doc. 1473, April 7, 1780, Natchitoches Parish Records.

[24] François Ledoux to Pierre Metoyer, Sale of Land, Doc. 1500; Jean Deslouche to Pierre Metoyer, Sale of Land, Doc. 2113; Natchitoches Parish Records. Both documents are listed in the Index to French Archives, Natchitoches Parish Records, but both are now missing. Claims A1684 and A1685, State Land Records (State Land Office, Baton Rouge, La.)

[25] An entry in the Index to French Archives, Natchitoches Parish Records, lists this deed as Doc. 2119. Here again, the actual instrument is missing. In his will of 1801 Metoyer reiterates the terms of the donation. The original of this will is likewise missing, but a photocopy is on file in the Natchitoches Parish Library. Coincoin's title to the tract given her by Metoyer is recorded in Book of Patents, 17–18, and in Claim A1679, State Land Records. The tract was later identified by the American survey system as Sections 18 and 89 of T8N R6W.

[26] A. P. Nasatir, ed., "Government Employees and Salaries in Spanish Louisiana," Louisiana Historical Quarterly, XXIX (October 1946), 924.

[27] On October 10, 1788, Metoyer married Marie Thérèze Buard, the widow of his old friend from La Rochelle, Étienne Pavie. Natchitoches Registers, Book 4, unnumbered page.

had been spent as a house servant. Nineteen years had been dedicated to serving the French gentleman who had found her attractive and who had been willing to shelter her and provide for her needs in return for her service and devotion. Now in the middle of the fifth decade of her life, Coincoin was a free woman, legally and emotionally, dependent for the most part on her own abilities and resources for the present and future welfare of her offspring. Despite her age and apparent inexperience, Coincoin took to the fields.

For the newly freed woman and her children, these years were undoubtedly lean ones. There was an infinite difference between the absolute dependency of a slave and the responsibilities of a free citizen; the chasm could not be bridged in a day or even a year. Although Coincoin had been legally free for eight years, it was not until the dissolution of her alliance with Metoyer that she was forced to accept the responsibilities of her new station. Overnight she was given a small tract of land, and with it the sole responsibility for its success or failure. Such a transition was not an easy one. Numerous slaves in that era were freed and given tracts of land on which they lived and died in drudging poverty. Coincoin, however, was destined to succeed where the others had failed.

949

Coincoin and her free children settled in a small cabin on the land Metoyer gave her and began the cultivation of tobacco. It was a difficult crop which demanded considerable attention to each individual stalk and which was also subject to rigorous governmental regulations.[28] Yet, with experience Coincoin's harvest increased until by 1792 her annual production was of such size that she was sending her own barge to New Orleans loaded with rolls of tobacco for sale in the markets of the provincial capital. One passport for shipment, issued by Commandant Louis Charles De-Blanc to Coincoin on April 20, 1792, is still extant.[29]

In addition to these agricultural endeavors, the legend of Coincoin credits her with various other economic enterprises. For generations her descendants have recounted how their family's matriarch trapped the wild bears in the Natchitoches wilderness and sent their grease to market in large stone jars. Such grease, they were

[28] In 1777 Bernardo de Galvez issued a stringent seventeen-point set of regulations designed to control every aspect of tobacco production and marketing. Lawrence Kinnaird, ed., Spain in the Mississippi Valley, 1765–1794, Pt. 1: The Revolutionary Period, 1765–1781, American Historical Association, Annual Report, 1945, II (Washington, 1949), 237–38. A firsthand description of the mechanics of tobacco production in colonial Louisiana is provided by Antoine-Simon Le Page du Pratz, The History of Louisiana . . . (London, 1774, reprinted at New Orleans, [1947]), 172–73.

[29] Etat de la Cargaison d'un Bateau apartenant à Pierre Metoyer et d'un gabarre à Marie Thérèze, Reel 1, Jack D. L. Holmes Collection (Eugene P. Watson Memorial Library, Northwestern State University, Natchitoches, La.)

told, was a valuable commodity in Europe, needed to keep coaches, wagons, and artillery pieces running smoothly.[30] The passport for the barge sent by Coincoin to New Orleans in 1792 noted that the shipment included grease and hides.[31] Hunting, quite possibly, was a major source of income for her and her family, since the area abounded with wild animals and fowl. Further proof of Coincoin's activity in this economic area is provided by the last will and testament Metoyer drafted in 1801; in this document he noted that he was indebted to Coincoin for turkeys that she had furnished him.[32]

By 1793 Coincoin had succeeded in establishing an efficient plantation operation on her small tract of land, and she desired to extend her holdings. Much unclaimed land still lay within the parish, and the colonial government encouraged its citizens by freely granting lands in reasonable quantities to deserving heads of households. Coincoin petitioned for a grant of land in late 1793, and on May 14, 1794, that petition was answered with the grant of twenty arpents frontage by a depth of forty located on the west bank of the Old River branch of the Red River, several miles from Coincoin's original land.[33]

Grants made in Spanish Louisiana were basically free, but certain regulations, nevertheless, had to be observed by all recipients. A small cash outlay was required in the form of a surveyor's fee, which was based on the actual size of the grant. Within the first three years of possession grantees were required to clear the entire front of their tracts to the depth of two arpents. Every inhabitant was bound to enclose within this same period the front of his land and to reach agreement with his neighbors for the enclosure of the remainder of his property. Grantees were also required to construct roads and bridges where necessary and keep them in good repair. If the lands were used for grazing all cattle had to be branded. The cattle must also be fenced in from the beginning of crop planting until the end of the harvest season (which constituted the largest portion of the year) in order to protect the crops of neighbors. Any cattle found running loose during this period could be killed and consumed by anyone who found them.[34] The obligation which

[30] A Visit to Melrose with François Mignon, recorded interview (produced at Alexandria, Louisiana, 1967), No. B224 (Howard-Tilton Memorial Library, Tulane University, New Orleans, La.).

[31] État de la Cargaison . . . , Holmes Collection.

[32] Metoyer's will of 1801, Natchitoches Parish Library.

[33] Claim B2146, State Land Records. Coincoin's Spanish grant is identified on American survey maps as Section 55, T8N R7W.

[34] "O'Reilly's Ordinance of 1770," Louisiana Historical Quarterly, XI (April 1928), 237–40; James A. Padgett, ed., "A Decree for Louisiana Issued by the Baron of Carondelet, June 1, 1795," ibid., XX (July 1937), 597–600.

Coincoin assumed in accepting her new grant of land was not a small one.

Coincoin's concession did not include high-quality farmland. Recognizing its limitations, she put it to use as a *vacherie*, a grazing range for her herd of cattle. About 1797, after making the improvements required of her in the first three years of possession, Coincoin hired a Spaniard named José Maré to live on the *vacherie*. For ten years Maré oversaw her cattle business and cultivated corn and similar crops on the better portions of the land.[35]

In the early years of her growth in property Coincoin had one overriding goal: the liberation of her still-enslaved children. She had brought fourteen children into the world. Two had died in childhood; two of the twelve living children were free from birth; and a third had been bought and freed in infancy by his father. Five more were still their father's property,[36] but for these there was no immediate concern. As long as Metoyer was alive, their enslavement was little more than a legality. It was her older children, the ones whom she had borne before her alliance with Metoyer, who most concerned her. Of these four children, records can be found of only two. Both were still in bondage.

On September 9, 1786, Coincoin reached an agreement with a planter of the parish, Sieur Pierre Dolet, for the purchase of her oldest daughter, Marie Louise. This daughter was a cripple as the result of a gun accident, so Dolet asked only three hundred piasters for the twenty-seven-year-old slave. Since Coincoin was only beginning her plantation operation and was of limited means, Dolet agreed to accept payment in three annual installments, and Coincoin thereby committed herself to pay Dolet almost all of her annuity from Metoyer for the next three years. Marie Louise was declared to be free. Apparently, some legal technicality or other difficulty subsequently arose, since nine years later Coincoin appeared before the commandant and again declared Marie Louise to be a free woman.[37]

In the years since Mme. de Soto had sold Coincoin to Metoyer, the de Sotos had moved from Natchitoches to the post of Ope-

951

---

[35] Claim B2146, State Land Records.

[36] Marie Françoise Roselie, who was born in 1780, died before her father drafted his will of 1783. In his will of 1801 Metoyer stated that Marie Eulalie had died after 1788. The death record of neither has been found. Pierre Toussaint and François were free from birth; Antoine Joseph was freed the year of his birth. Nicolas Augustin, Marie Suzanne, Louis, Pierre, and Dominique were the five whom their father held in slavery until they reached adulthood.

[37] Pierre Dolet to Marie Thérèze Coincoin, Sale of Slave, Old Natchitoches Data, II, 289, Cammie G. Henry Collection (Eugene P. Watson Memorial Library, Northwestern State University); Marie Thérèze Coincoin to Marie Louise, Doc. 2596, January 29, 1795, Natchitoches Parish Records

lousas. With them they took Thérèze, the second daughter of Coincoin. By 1790 Thérèze was herself almost thirty and the mother of at least one child. There is no evidence that she like her mother had found a French gentleman to provide her with the opportunity for social and economic advancement. Moreover, her mistress, Mme. de Soto, was now an invalid and aging woman. The future which faced young Thérèze was a doubtful one.[38]

After completing payment of the debt she had assumed in the purchase of her first daughter Coincoin began to save for the purchase of her second-born. By the fall of 1790 she had accumulated only fifty dollars, but with the infinite hope that spurs mothers to action she set out for Opelousas, determined to make arrangements with her former mistress for the freedom of her daughter and her grandson. Mme. de Soto, a shrewd, dominant, and hard-bitten matron whom few people ever bested, accepted the small downpayment and agreed to a price of only 700 piasters for the two slaves. The only condition which she placed upon the purchase was that young Thérèze continue to serve her through her illness until her death. She also agreed to permit Thérèze to raise cattle in order to help earn the remaining 650 piasters that were due. No statements were made as to how the young slave would obtain the necessary stock to enter the cattle trade; apparently, it was furnished by her mother. Marie de St. Denis de Soto died in 1797. As promised seven years earlier, Coincoin's daughter and sixteen-year-old-grandson were passed to her for manumission.[39]

Late in 1794 Coincoin executed another slave purchase and manumission. This fourth recipient of her love and generosity was also a grandchild, the daughter of her still enslaved Metoyer son Louis.[40] On August 27, 1794, widow Jean Baptiste LeComte sold to Coincoin for 150 piasters cash "a small mulattress named Catiche, or Catherine, aged five years or about, actually in the possession of the said Coincoin for several years, having been entrusted to her at the age of two." Three days later Coincoin filed a second document by which she freed little Catiche.[41]

[38] Marie de St. Denis to Marie Thérèze Coincoin, Sale of Slaves, Doc. 2804, September 28, 1790, Natchitoches Parish Records.

[39] Ibid., January 13, 1793; December 12, 1796; Burial of Da. Maria Saint Denis, August 10, 1797, Book 1, Registers of the Parish of St. Landry des Opelousas (Church of St. Landry, Opelousas, La.), 33.

[40] Father A. Dupre, Metoyer Family Genealogy (Rectory of the Parish of St. Augustine, Isle Brevelle, La.), unnumbered pages. From 1878 to 1889 Father Dupre was pastor of the Church of St. Augustine, the church founded by the children of Coincoin. His informal genealogy is based partly upon the Natchitoches Registers and partly upon information provided him by the family.

[41] Marguerite LeRoy, Widow LeComte, to Coincoin, Sale of Slave, Doc. 2550; Coincoin to Catiche, Manumission, Doc. 2552, Natchitoches Parish Records.

The first five children whom Coincoin had borne to the Sieur Metoyer remained their father's slaves until all had reached adulthood. On August 1, 1792, Metoyer freed his eldest son, the twenty-four-year-old Nicolas Augustin. On January 15, 1795, he freed his fifth child, the twenty-one-year-old Dominique.[42] It was not until 1802, however, that the remaining three, Louis, Pierre, and Suzanne, received their freedom, and a condition was placed on their manumission. In exchange for their freedom their mother was required to forfeit the annual stipend which Metoyer had promised her for life. After Coincoin agreed to the terms on May 28, 1802, Louis and Pierre were liberated. Suzanne was declared a *statute liberi*; that is, she would become free at the time of her father's death.[43]

953

During the first years of her own freedom Coincoin had labored primarily to earn the sums necessary to purchase her offspring from the bondage of slavery. With this behind her the aging black woman did not lessen her toil. Freedom is one of the most basic requisites of humanity, but the poor free man or woman is still yoked to financial and social servitude. In colonial and antebellum plantation society the passport to real independence was land, slaves, and money. It was for these that Coincoin and her children now labored.

No official records reveal exactly when Coincoin first began to purchase slaves for labor. Her only slave purchases for which records are now extant are those executed for the purchase of her children and grandchildren. It is apparent that Coincoin owned no slaves prior to 1790, since the church tax list compiled that year, placing a poll on every free head of household, every free male over fourteen, and every slave, indicated that she held no bondsmen.[44] Documents executed in 1816, however, named twelve slaves that she owned, and the registers of the church record the identities of four other slaves on her plantation who were still alive at the time of her death.[45] Tradition holds that she owned many more, but numbers are often exaggerated with the passage of time. Tradition also insists that even though she purchased other humans and held

---

[42] Pierre Metoyer to Nicolas Augustin, Manumission, Doc. 2409; Pierre Metoyer to Dominique, Manumission, Doc. 2584, *ibid.*

[43] Pierre Metoyer to Marie Thérèze Coincoin, Donation, Misc. Book 2, pp. 206–207, *ibid.* This document is actually mislabeled. It should read: Marie Thérèze Coincoin to Pierre Metoyer, Annulment of Donation.

[44] Répartition a l'ocasion de 75p. que la Comunote de Mesrs les habitants son Convenu de Payer a Mr J. Bte Maurin fette le 1r Mars 1790, Folder 1, Natchitoches Parish Records Collection (Department of Archives and Manuscripts, Louisiana State University Library, Baton Rouge, La.)

[45] Marie Thérèze Coincoin to [various heirs], Docs. 351–59, March 27, 1816, Conveyance Book 3, pp. 524–38, Natchitoches Parish Records; Books 4-B and 5, Natchitoches Registers, unnumbered pages.

them in bondage, she always treated her slaves with gentleness, never forgetting that she herself had once been a slave. Coincoin, reportedly, administered no corporal punishment; misbehavior on her plantation was corrected with imprisonment in the "jail" which she had erected for that purpose.[46]

In 1807 Coincoin increased her landholdings with the purchase of a third tract of land. On June 7 she and the Sieur Jean LaLande appeared before the local notary to draw up a deed of sale in her favor. For 500 piasters she bought LaLande's plantation on Red River, not far from the original tract which Metoyer had given her.[47] Coincoin did not acquire this land for her own use, however. Now in her mid-sixties, she had already begun to turn over her holdings to her children, helping them to get their starts in life. The LaLande tract was given to her thirteenth child, the twenty-five-year-old bachelor Pierre Toussaint. Apparently, no rent was requested, and young Pierre Toussaint was allowed seven years to build his estate before repaying his mother for the property.[48]

One tradition, which can neither be proved nor disproved, holds that Coincoin was the recipient of another grant of land, as large as all of her other holdings combined. This tract of 912 acres, located several miles down Red River from her central farm, was given to her second son, Louis, according to the tradition. The earliest record of the tract, dated 1806, indicates that it was acquired by Coincoin or her family ten years earlier; her son Louis at that time claimed to be the original owner. However, since Louis was still a slave at the time of the grant, and remained in slavery for several years following, it would not have been legally possible for a concession to have been made in his name.[49]

The plantation which Coincoin or her son Louis developed from this grant distinguished itself for several decades as one of the most prosperous cotton plantations in the region. It is still intact today, and several colonial and antebellum buildings remain on the

954

---

[46] Interview with Mrs. Coutii, March 24, 1974.

[47] Copie de Vente de Terre, Conveyance Book 42 (original instruments), Doc. 501, Natchitoches Parish Records.

[48] No rent contract or deed of donation was executed when Coincoin turned over this property to her son. Three years after its purchase a neighboring tract of land exchanged hands; in the deed of conveyance, like most such documents executed in that period, holders of adjoining tracts were named. The proprietor of the tract which Coincoin purchased from LaLande was therein identified as "Pierre Metoyer, free mulatto." On September 14, 1814, the aged mother executed the official deed of sale to her son Pierre Toussaint. Louis Verchere to Dominique Rachal, Sale of Land, February 12, 1810, Doc. 3768; Marie Thérèze Coincoin to Toussaint Metoyer, Sale of Land, Conveyance Book 3, pp. 308–309, Natchitoches Parish Records.

[49] Claim B1953. State Land Records; Memorial of Louis Metoyer to Board of Land Commissioners, folder dated May 1796, Opelousas Notarial Records Collection (Louisiana Archives and Records Service, Baton Rouge, La.)

estate grounds, including two which tradition claims were built by Coincoin. Known as Melrose Plantation, it has recently been declared a National Historical Landmark in recognition of the unique character of the family which developed it.[50]

Despite the fact that Coincoin's citizenship was at best only second-class, she readily assumed her share of responsibility for the welfare of the community in which she lived. When the church congregation was faced in 1790 with the necessity of hiring a carpenter to make repairs and enlargements, Coincoin was taxed one real; she paid two.[51] In 1793 and 1794 another list was drawn up of all area inhabitants who had made a contribution of their labor for the benefit of the parish. Among those who had volunteered to maintain the parish cemetery was Coincoin, despite the fact that she lived more than a dozen miles from the village.[52]

The exact date of Coincoin's death is not known. The last records which exist for her are dated 1816. On April 20 of that year Coincoin presented nine documents to the parish judge at Natchitoches for filing, by the terms of which she transferred to her children and grandchildren twelve of the slaves which she owned, having a total value of $5,250.[53] On December 31, 1817, Coincoin's son Pierre filed a contract of marriage with his second wife at Natchitoches, in which he identified himself as the son of the *deceased* free woman of color, Marie Thérèze *dit* Coincoin.[54] The death of the old matriarch, therefore, occurred between April 1816, when she filed her last document, and December 1817, when Pierre filed his marriage contract. No record of her death can be found in the incomplete registers of the church maintained during those two years.

Tradition holds that prior to her death the elderly matriarch also divided the land granted to her in 1794 among the children whom she left behind. Many later documents which related to her grant show that the land was divided into ten strips, each with two arpents of frontage on the river and a depth of forty arpents. This tradition is further supported by the deed of sale from her son Pierre Toussaint to his nephew Auguste, dated March 20, 1830, in which Pierre Toussaint stated that he had acquired the land "by

---

[50] For a general study of this noted plantation see Gary B. and Elizabeth S. Mills, *Melrose* (Natchitoches, 1973).

[51] Répartition a l'ocasion . . . , Natchitoches Parish Records Collection of Louisiana State University.

[52] Role de Corvées et Contributions public, Folder 1, *ibid.*

[53] Marie Thérèze Coincoin to [various heirs], Docs. 351–59, actually drawn March 27, 1816, filed the following month in Conveyance Book 3, pp. 524–38, Natchitoches Parish Records.

[54] Pierre Metoyer and Marie Henriette, Marriage Contract, Books 2 and 3, Marriages and Miscellaneous, 1816–1819 (bound together in one volume), unnumbered page, *ibid.*

partition made by his mother Coincoin between her children."[55]

Tradition offers one further detail relevant to the death of Coincoin. Although she was some seventy-four years of age at the time of her death, she still insisted upon maintaining her independence and lived alone. When she became ill shortly before her death, her eldest Metoyer son, Augustin, took her to his home, and it was there she died. She was buried in the cemetery at Natchitoches in which her parents, Pierre Metoyer, and at least two of her children were also interred. Tradition insists that the burial was a fine one.[56]

The estate which Coincoin accumulated amounted to approximately one thousand arpents of land (exclusive of the Melrose tract) and at least sixteen slaves. If landownership maps of this period may be used as an acceptable guide, her holdings compared well with those of the white inhabitants of the parish and certainly exceeded those of the other propertied free people of color, most of whom were her offspring. Moreover, the 1810 census of the parish, the last one taken before her death, shows that only 13 percent of the households had as many or more slaves than the dozen which Coincoin then owned. Three of the householders who matched or exceeded that number were her children.[57]

Building upon the estate left them by their mother, the Metoyer children of Coincoin developed a vast and exceedingly prosperous plantation empire. The Metoyer domain in its peak period of affluence encompassed some 15,000 acres of what was described by contemporaries as "the most productive cotton growing land in the State" and "the richest cotton growing portion of the South."[58] In 1830 the children and grandchildren of Coincoin and Metoyer, whose slaveholdings then numbered 282, were apparently the largest slaveowning family of color in the nation.[59] By 1850 the

956

[55] Toussaint Metoyer to Auguste Metoyer, Sale of Land and Slaves, Misc. Book 20, pp. 334–35, *ibid.*

[56] Interview with Mrs. Coutii, April 26, 1974.

[57] See Manuscript Census Returns, Third Census of the United States, 1810, Natchitoches Parish, Territory of Orleans, National Archives Microfilm Series No. M-252, Roll 10. This census does not enumerate Coincoin. Either she was overlooked by the enumerator in his search for households in the rural areas of the parish, or else she was included as a member of the household of one of her sons who were enumerated with sizable slaveholdings.

[58] Orton S. Clark, *The One Hundred and Sixteenth Regiment of New York State Volunteers* (Buffalo, 1868), 150; Harris H. Beecher, *Record of the 114th Regiment, N.Y.S.V.* (Norwich, N.Y., 1866), 304. The extent of the holdings accumulated by the Metoyers is figured from a study of all conveyance records dealing with this community that are available for the parish for this period, both those in public collections and those in private ones.

[59] See Manuscript Census Returns, Fifth Census of the United States, 1830, Natchitoches Parish, Louisiana, National Archives Microfilm Series No. M-19, Roll 44; Carter G. Woodson, "Free Negro Owners of Slaves in the United States in 1830," *Journal of Negro History*, IX (January 1924), 41–85, especially 50. Of the 282 slaves owned by Coincoin's descendants, 230 were held by individuals bearing the surname of Metoyer (variously spelled). Woodson's tabulation of slaveowners of color in 1830 lists no other single family name with holdings anywhere near large as those of Metoyers. Other members of the Metoyer clan (with a

number of their bondsmen had swelled to 436.[60]

Large and stately homes, appointed with simple but elegant furnishings, graced the Metoyer plantations. Sterling silver, organs, pianos, racehorses, and other such symbols of the southern planter's wealth were all included among the Metoyer property inventories of this period. Private tutors and Continental education were provided for their offspring. Coincoin's oldest Metoyer son, Augustin, established a Roman Catholic church in the midst of their colony in a period when even the wealthy white planters of the area did not have a church to serve them. The whites accepted the Metoyer invitation to worship with them and graciously took a back seat to Augustin and his family.[61]

Although the family's prosperity was destroyed by the upheaval of Civil War and Reconstruction, the colony has continued to be recognized as a distinct ethnic group within Louisiana society. Throughout their period of affluence, their decline, and their more recent social and economic resurgence, the Metoyer colony of Isle Brevelle has reverently perpetuated the memory of their family's matriarch.

Although strict moralists have criticized the manner in which Coincoin accomplished her goals, no one can deny that there was almost no other course of action by which she could have achieved them. The idealistic guidelines by which man strives to live are often negated by reality. The society into which Coincoin was born laid down the rules by which she had to abide. She was a slave and had no privileges, no opportunities, no hope, unless her master

957

---

different surname) listed by Woodson included Augustin Cloutier, Pier Rachal, Louis Balthasar, John Bt. Rachal, Naciest Metgier [Narcisse Metoyer], Manieuel Laricce [Manuel Llorens], Sarahan Rock [Nerestan Rock or Rocques], Jerom Samper [Sarpy]. Ameal Dupas [Emile Dupart], and Florentine Corner [Florentin Conant]. They held 52 slaves.

It should be noted that Woodson made one error in his tabulation of slaveowners of color in Natchitoches Parish. Mary R. Metyier, a free woman of color, was enumerated on the manuscript census of 1830 as a head of household with five children of color, one white male, and fifteen slaves. Woodson omitted this household from his tabulation; apparently, he assumed that the white male was actually the head of household who shared his home with a free woman of color and their children. This assumption is not correct. Mary R. Metyier was, more correctly, Marie Rose Metoyer, a widow of comfortable means, while the white male in her household was an impecunious migrant from North Carolina whom Marie Rose "housed and fed" for several years. See *Adams v. Hurst*, 9 La. 243 (1836); James Hurst to [unknown], January 1843, Natchitoches Parish Records Collection, Box 4, Folder 62 (Louisiana State University Archives); *Guillaume Coindet et alii v. Marie Rose Metoyer, Tutrix*, Suit No. 942 (1829), Natchitoches Parish Records, Marie Rose Metoyer to Louis Baltazar, August 21, 1829, Book A, 34, *ibid*.

[60] See Manuscript Census Returns, Seventh Census of the United States, 1850, Natchitoches Parish, Louisiana, Schedule II, Slave Population, National Archives Microfilm Series No. M-432, Roll 244.

[61] For a detailed study of the Metoyer colony on Isle Brevelle see Gary B. Mills, "The Forgotten People: Cane River's Creoles of Color," (unpublished Ph.D. dissertation, Mississippi State University, 1974).

chose to give them to her. Only by seeking a generous master and earning his affections could she improve her base existence.

Although she was forced by the laws of society to defy one of the Christian precepts, tradition still insists that Coincoin was a religious woman. Through the generations her descendants have maintained that their family's matriarch died as a devout Catholic. According to the legend, she personally taught her children the Rosary, and upon the occasion of their First Communions she gave to each of them a chain of Rosary beads which she had carved herself. At least one of these was preserved until well into the twentieth century.[62]

958

Some versions of the legend describe the "fabulous" heritage that Coincoin left her children and attempt to explain it in material terms, crediting to her all the accomplishments of her children. But it was not a fully developed estate of thousands of acres that she left them, an estate whose proceeds would allow them to spend their lives in the idle pursuit of luxuries and pleasures. At least a thousand arpents of land and sixteen slaves was a sizable estate in her society, but even estates of this extent are suddenly rendered small when divided among ten heirs.

It appears that the greatest legacy which Coincoin left to her children was the example of determination, loyalty, industry, frugality, mutual assistance, and the ability to work with the dominant race rather than against it in order to achieve one's goals. It was these qualities, enhanced by native shrewdness, which enabled her sons and daughters to expand the property that she left them into the vast, rich plantation system which they owned in central Louisiana.

---

[62] E. J. Metoyer to François Mignon, September 3, 1972, copy in possession of author. The Rosary which Coincoin supposedly carved for her youngest son, François, is the one that older family members recall. Its last known owner was his great-grandson Herman ("Garçon") Metoyer of New Orleans. After Herman's death there a number of years ago the family lost track of the Rosary. Mrs. Coutii to author, June 27, 1974.

Wilson Jeremiah Moses
Southern Methodist University

959

Domestic Feminism Conservatism, Sex Roles, and Black Women's Clubs 1893-1896

ABSTRACT. Black women living in an age of Victorian sexual morality were confronted by a special set of problems. As John Blassingame puts it. "More than one hundred years of slavery and oppression left Negroes. . .with. . .a heavy burden of sexual immorality, ignorance, broken families, fear and improvidence." This was in contrast to the genteel standards of courtship and family life as portrayed in Currier and Ives prints and popular magazine fiction. The black women's club movement saw its primary work as encouraging the masses of peasant poor to adopt the Victorian morality of the middle classes. They hoped that a dramatic change in the sexual behavior of the masses would make them more acceptable to the white-American mainstream and would ease interracial tensions.

The National black women's club movement began when a number of local clubs—some of them tracing their origins to the early 1800's—finally came together as a national organization during the 1890's. In order to grasp the functions of the national black women's club movement, it is necessary to understand something of the backgrounds against which they worked. The black women's clubs came into existence, not only because black women were barred from participation in white women's clubs, but because black women felt they had a special work to do. The movement was no mere imitation of parallel white institutions. Even before emancipation, free black women in the Northern States began to organize themselves in small local groups for social, intellectual and political purposes. Not all black women

Originally published in *Journal of Social and Behavioral Sciences*, Vol. 24, No. 4 (Fall 1987).

were slaves, of course, and free black women, no less than free black men, felt the need for independent organization. By the 1830's a number of black women's club existed in such states as Pennsylvania, New York and Massachussets. These "literary clubs", as they were called, typically concerned themselves with the "diffusion of knowledge, the suppression of vice and immorality, and. . .cherishing such virtues as will render us happy and useful to society." They also had typical benevolent society, mutual aid obligations. If, f example, any member in good standing of the Afric-American Female Intelligence Society of Boston were taken ill, she received "one dollar per week out of the funds of the Society as long as consistent with the means of the institution." In addition to mutual aid and literary programs, the clubs seem to have had an interest in abolitionism. Membership overlapped with that of anti-slavery societies, and activities of the clubs were reported in the abolitionist press. Naturally, only a minute fraction of black women participated in such activites, since the majority of them were slaves in the South, where independent institutions were ruthlessly suppressed, if not successfully stifled.[1]

960

Sexual Mores and the Heritage of Slavery

Typically, the lives of Afro-American women before the Civil War were hard. The recent studies of Engerman and Fogel have attempted to show that the average slave woman was a prim and proper puritan, materially happy but inclined towards spinsterism. They described the marriages of slave women as stable and secure and usually occuring the their early twenties.[2] This departs considerably from the bulk of prior scholarship, from the eyewitness accounts of contemporaries, from the evidence of the slave narratives, and from the oral tradition. E. Franklin Frazier portrayed the life of black women under slavery in less positive terms. The black woman was an exploited worker. The conditions of her family life were deplorable. Frazier felt that instances of the brutalization of black woman to the point of obliterating maternal feeling were common enough to deserve comment. He wrote:

> Even under the more normal conditions of slavery, childbirth could not have had the same significance for the slave mother as for the African mother. In Africa tribal customs and toboos tended to fix the mother's attitude toward her child before it was born. In America this traditional element in the shaping of maternal feeling was absent. . . .[3]

Calling upon evidence from two typical slave narratives and the journal of Frances Kemble, Frazier went on to describe how slave mothers were deprived of contact with their children by the rigors of the plantation system. He then proceeded to the startling conclusion that "where such limitations were placed upon the mother's spontaneous emotional responses to the needs of her children and where even her suckling and fondling of them were restricted, it was not unnatural that she often showed little attachment to her offspring." Still Fràzier emphasized the point that "slave mothers developed a deep and permanent love for their children, which often caused them to defy masters and to undergo suffering to prevent separation from their young."[4]

Frazier argued that the slave family was not stable, and that "the duration of marriage as well as its inception was subjust to the will of the masters." Slave families were, according to Frazier commonly broken up at the auction block, and there were other factors leading to instability. Slave marriages were often mere fortuitous connections, entered upon with little expectation of permanent committment. Promiscusity was encouraged among the slaves; systematic slave breeding was common. Frazier supported these arguments with ample evidence from the slave narratives; recent studies of slave narratives have tended to confirm his findings.[5]

Frazier's discussion of the black woman of the South was consistent with the findings of Alexander Crummell, a black social thinker born in 1819, who had written half a century before Frazier:

> From the childhood [the slave woman] was the doomed victim of the grossest passions. All the virtues of her sex were utterly ignored. If the instinct of chastity asserted itself, then she had to fight like a tigress for the ownership and possession of her own person. . . . *This* year she had one husband; and next year, through some auction sale, she might be separated from him and mated to another. There was no sanctity of family, no binding tie of marriage, none of the fine felicities and the endearing affections of home. None of these things were the lot of Southern black women. Instead thereof a gross barbarism which tended to blunt the tender sensibilities, to obliterate feminine delicacy and womanly shame, came down as her heritage from generation to generation; and it seems a miracle of providence and grace that, notwithstanding these terrible circumstances, so much struggling virtue lingered amid these rude cabins, that so much womanly worth and sweetness abided in their bosoms, as slaveholders themselves have borne witness to.[6]

W.E.B. Du Bois once quoted from this same essay of Crummell's when writing on "The Damnation of Women". In his study of 1909, *The Negro*

American Family, Du Bois viewed slavery as disruptive of family life and sexual mores. Du Bois listed the "essential features of Negro slavery in America" as: "No legal marriage, No legal family, No legal control over children. . .The great body of field hands were raped of their own [African] sex customs and provided with no binding new ones." Du Bois felt that in the area of sexual morals the behavior of black Americans was "furthest behind modern civilization." This was the result of slavery, he said, which had disintegrated the ancient Negro home and put nothing in its place. The curse of American slavery was that "The morals of black men and white women are found to be ruined."[7] The heritage of slavery had left lasting scars on the morality of the black community, according to Du Bois, Crummell, and Frazier. This was a source of bitter torment to all of them. It was one of the areas of greatest sensitivity to the black middle class and a matter of deep concern to the black women's club movement during the 1890's.

The sexual morality of the black peasant masses of the South was, as Du Bois observed, markedly different from the Victorian ethic of the urban upper middle classes, white and black. But it was certainly not inferior, nor was it nonfunctional to the situation in which it had evolved. The sexual attitudes of the black rural southerner in the late nineteenth and and early twentieth centuries were influenced by traditions established during slavery, as Charles S. Johnson argued. Certain aspects of the plantation culture persisted after the emancipation, due to the isolation of black agricultural workers from outside social influences. In some communities, Johnson observed, "There is no such thing as illegitimacy." Premarital sex was generally accepted in practice, although not openly advocated as an ideal form of behavior. Although there were, of course many families that were stable and that conformed to "conventional" sexual mores, Johnson was able to note the occurence of certain common features of rural black life that were not conventional. These were: "the unevenness of life, the amount of sexual freedom, the frequency of separation and realignment of families, the number of children born out of wedlock." But it would be wrong to say that these people lived without morality, or that they had no concept of respectability, or that they had no "codes or conventions consistent with the essential routine of their lives." Johnson felt that the sexual morality of the black peasant had persisted because of the presistence of the plantation economy and that positive changes could not occur without economic changes in the South resulting from intelligent and "comprehensive planning, which affects not merely the South but the nation."[8]

In her description of black rural sexual mores, Hortense Powdermaker made many of the same observations that others had made. She cited legal cases to demonstrate that slaves were denied normal marital security, as Du

Bois had done earlier. She too felt that the comparatively loose and per-
missive sexual ethic of the black rural South could be explained as the
heritage of slavery.

> The congestion of living quarters, in itself a hindrance to familial pri-
> vacy, probably tended against observance by the slaves of a strict
> sexual morality according to the tenets of the white code. More sig-
> nificant was the fact that white men had the right of access to any
> Negro woman, and frequently exercized it. The constant invasion
> of the Negro home, against which there was no means of protest in
> act or word, was assuredly not conducive to the development of
> firmly integrated family units. Nor was it calculated to make the
> Negro feel as vital and binding the injuctions to chastity and conti-
> nence which he was receiving as part of the white man's religion.[9]   *963*

Hortense Powdermaker's assessment represents what is still the most accepted view on the nature of black family existence under slavery. Recent
tendencies to accentuate the positive in the history of black Americans, and
recent tendencies to de-emphasize the cruelties of the slavery system have
attacked this view. Nonetheless this is the view of the black family under
slavery, accepted by most people who lived through it. This was the view
impressed upon those early students of the black family who worked
among former slaves and their children. Most importantly, this was the view
of the black family and of the condition of slave women that was accepted
by the founders of the National Association of Colored Women.

The Negro Improvement Tradition

From Booker T. Washington to Marcus Garvey, the proponents of "Negro
Improvement" argued that the proper way for black people to secure their
fortune was by changing themselves rather than by attempting to change
their environment. Under s)avery, the Negro Improvement tradition had not
addressed itself directly to the cause of immediate abolitionism. Rather it
sought to demonstrate the Afro-American's fitness for emancipation by
proving the fitness of black people of freedom. Schemes for black uplift
were associated with the tradeschool movement in the Northern states, and
with the back to Africa movement. The Negro Improvement advocates
believed that if black culture could be developed both at home and in
Africa, whites would be inclined to believe in the black man's worthiness for
inclusion in American life. There was only one thing wrong with such programs. They did not take into account that prejudice is irrational. No matter
how much the Afro-American people achieved, they would still be victims of

prejudice. Racism is blind to achievement. Furthermore, social values change. What was to guarantee that when black people had accomplished certain achievements, the achievements would still be considered important? If black people were to achieve a genteel standard of victorian sexual conduct, for example, could it be guaranteed that Victorian morality would always be important to Americans? There was no way, of course, for black Americans to predict in 1895 that Victorian sexual codes would diminish in importance. And so it was that the work of Afro-American woman, during the 1890's, was closely tied to the promotion of the bourgeois feminine values of the mauve decade. Foremost among these was the promotion of a genteel code of sexual conduct.[10]

Origins and Purposes of the NACW

No black woman in America was better suited to the task of promoting genteel conduct and "civilization" of the masses than Josephine St. Pierre Ruffin of Boston. She was a woman of mixed ancestry, her mother having been English and her father of African and American Indian descent. In appearance she was definitely identifiable as an Afro-American, but she belonged to that class of black Bostonians who enjoyed comparative social equality because of their fair complexions and relative wealth. Mrs. Ruffin was born in 1843 and in 1859 married George L. Ruffin, later a Judge in Charlestown, Massachussetts. She became active in women's clubs in Massachussetts, apparently finding a reasonable degree of acceptance from white women who were inclined towards feminism, intellectualism and reform movements. She founded the first magazine in America to be published exclusively by black women. This magazine, *The Woman's Era* was an advocate of genteel domestic feminism, and featured articles on the women's movement and on current racial issues. Mrs. Ruffin's social contacts with white women of a radical and liberal bent made it possible for her to serve as an advocate for black interests in upper-class Boston social circles. Her afternoon tea parties provided a means of contact between Boston young people of both races and sexes and the young W.E.B. Du Bois mentions having attended meetings at her home during his years at Harvard.[11]

One of Mrs. Ruffin's reformer associates was an English woman, Laura Ormistion Chant. Mrs. Chant was an officer of the Anti-Lynching Committee of London, an organization which attempted to carry on in the British tradition of abolitionism that had flourished before the American Civil War. Her activities were criticized by an American newspaper editor, Jno. W. Jacks of Montgomery City, Missouri who sent her "a most indecent foul and slanderous letter" maligning Afro-American women and all who supported them. When Laura Chant forwarded a copy of the letter to Mrs. Ruffin, it was distributed to black women's clubs throughout the United States along with a call for a national conference of Afro-American women.[12] The conference met in Boston during the last days of July, 1895. Delegates from twenty-seven states representing regions as diverse as New England, the South and the Missouri Valley were in attendance. Regional factionalism was restrained, but nonetheless Richard T. Greener reported that "The South insisted on industrial training and practical housewifery; the West seemed heart and soul bent only on Temperance. . ." Despite regional factionalism, a degree of national unity was readily accomplished and an organization known as the National Federation of Afro-American Women had come into existence by the first of August. In the meantime, a similar federation was evolving, this was The Colored Women's League, organized in Washington, D.C. in 1893.[13]

At the time of the World's Fair and Columbian Exposition at Chicago in 1893, Mrs. Hallie Q. Brown of Wilberforce. Ohio was dismayed that black Americans were not substantially represented. She appealed to Mrs. Potter Palmer, who headed the Woman's Board of Managers, that she might be admitted to membership on the board as a representative of her people. Mrs. Palmer responded that membership on the board was by organization, not by individual. At this point—so the story goes—Hallie Q. Brown recognized the importance of a national black women's organization that could speak before the world as if with one voice. In her attempt to find sponsorship, Mrs. Brown travelled to Washington and addressed members of the League, asking them to allow her to be their representative. This, the League was not able to grant, but shortly thereafter, they did organize a federation of local clubs that came to be called the National League. The dispute as to which group originated the national union idea was eventually resolved by Mary Church Terrell, originally a member of the Washington group, but eventually president of the new association that came into existence with the two organizations' merger. "It would appear," Terrell said, "that while the Colored Women's League of Washington was the first to 'resolve that colored women of the United States associate ourselves together. . .' the group which assembled in Boston in 1895 at the Call of Mrs. Ruffin was the first secular, national gathering of colored women in the United States which actually met with the intention of becoming a permanent organization."[14]

Shortly after the first convention of the National League, the National Federation held its first annual convention in Washington, D.C.. where they promptly took up the question of unifying the two movements. Consolidation was effected by the convention's closing. The name of the new organization was to be the National Association of Colored Women (NACW). Its first president was Mary Church Terrell, a compromise candidate capable of appealing to the munerous factions. The purposes of the NACW varied as conceived by individual members, the major division being between those who favored agitation and a vigorous anti-lynching campaign, and those who emphasized racial uplift and domestic feminism.[15]

Josephine Ruffin stood with the more radically inclined reformers. Her native Boston had been a center of abolitionism, and some of its most respected families had been identified with the movement. A progressive approach to race relations was associated with the elite classes and political liberalism was eminently respectable in Boston. Mrs. Ruffin made good use of her contacts with New England liberals and feminists, some of whom became supporters of black causes due to initial contacts with Mrs. Ruffin. As a radical assimilationist, she seemed committed to the principle sometimes articulated by Frederick Douglass that racial pride is "silly" and she protested vigorously against the establishment of a separate "Negro Exhibit" at the Atlanta Expostition in 1895. She was conspicuous by her absence from the Atlanta Congress of Colored Women held in connection with the Atlanta Exposition.[16]

Likewise radically inclined was Victoria Earle Matthews, who did attend the Atlanta Congress and vigorously opposed its tendencies toward conservatism. She fought hard against a resolution condemning "the crime that provokes lynching," arguing that black men were no more quilty of any such crime than any other men. To have condemned the crime of rape in the same breath with a condemnation of lynching would have amounted to an admission that lynching was provoked by rape, and the radical faction were inclined to no such admission. Matthews was a person of relatively light complexion and thus was able to travel with some freedom throughout the South investigating the conditions under which black people lived. She made her home in New York, where she organized the Women's Loyal Union of New York and Brooklyn, and sponsored the White Rose Mission, which crusaded to save young women from the red light districts. Mrs. Matthews was a friend and supporter of the journalist T. Thomas Fortune, with whom she collaborated to produce an anthology of Booker T. Washington aphorisms. Like Fortune, she was committed to the term Afro-American, in preference to Colored or Negro, and she was bitterly dissapointed when the National Federation of Afro-American Women changed its name to National Association of Colored Women.[17]

The most radical personality associated with the NACW was Ida B. Wells-Barnett, the journalist and anti-lynching crusader. Her out-spoken-

966

ness earned her the open hostility of many whites, and even made it necessary for her to flee the city of Memphis where she had attempted to operate a newspaper called the *Free Speech*. Her militancy often made other blacks nervous and her relations with the NACW were sometimes strained. Along with her hasband, she worked against the Tuskegee forces in Chicago. Wells agitated for the rights of black soldiers during the First World War and during the post war decade lent her support to Marcus Garvey's movement.[18]

A more conservative group within the NACW was led by Margaret Murray (Mrs. Booker T.) Washington. She was, as her husband stated, one with him in his work. Much to the distaste of Mrs. Wells-Barnett, she crusaded for a two class system in the Jim Crow coached of the South.[19] Like her husband, she was a vocal nativist, and she criticized her white associates for paying too much atttention to the problems of white emigrants in the cities and not enough to those of rural blacks in the South.[20] She urged white women in the name of "common womanhood" to exert all possible pressure to combat segregationist legislation. The main thrust of her concern was for selfhelp, however, and she wrote in *The Woman's Era:*

> Our poor need to be clothed. Our women must be taught to study for their own advancement. They need inspiration and encouragement to keep a brave heart. Homemaking must be thought about, child rearing needs attention. Our girls need social purity talks. They must be warned of evil company. They must be brought in closer touch with more that is good and pure. They must be taught to realize that they have a vital part to enact in developing the womanhood of their country.[21]

A strong ally of the Washington's was Mrs. Fannie Barrier Williams, who, like Ida B. Wells-Barnett, was the wife of a Chicago barrister. Williams could fight aggressively for integration, when occasion demanded. This she demonstrated by her courageous fight to be seated among the membership of the Chicago Women's Club. Most of her energies, however, were expended upon image building; Williams published widely on the activities of the club women and was closely identified with the drive to help black women and men as well to feel that they were "something better than a slave or a descendent of an ex-slave" but units in "a great nation and a great civilization. . ." Other agents in the image-building process were Mrs. N.F. Mossell, and Mary Church Terrell.[22]

Mossell and Terrell were concerned about the peculiar "temptations" (that was Terrell's word) to which black women in the South were exposed due to their economic condition.[23] Mossell was committed to voluntaristic

967

self-help approaches to uplift. Like many of her contemporaries, she was committed to the idea of preaching black people up to a higher social ideal. Terrell's approach was somewhat more social scientific. She was committed to the domestic feminist approach—the idea that women should work in woman's sphere to upgrade the morality of home and family; however, she also supported the idea of political involvement for women. She recognized the importance of institutionalizing reform and proposing economic rather than moral solutions for problems that were essentially economic. Eventually, Terrell became president of the Association, serving several terms in that office. She was an ideal compromise candidate, for she was committed to domestic feminism and social purity, but still an advocate for the rights of the working mother. She was a college educated woman—a graduate of Oberlin, who spoke French and German—but sympathetic to the Tuskegee program for industrial training. She was a militant integrationist, but understood the ethnic basis of urban political power and was a tough in-fighting, machine politician. But Terrell and Ida B. Wells-Barnett were bitter enemies. Their problems would seem to be due to personality clash and matters of a personal nature and not wholly ideological.

A perusal of the extant primary sources: records of meetings and reports of local club activities leads one to believe that the rank and file membership of the turn to the century clubs was less radical than the leadership. The leaders, however, were by no means uniformly radical. Ruffin was a radical integrationist, to be sure, and showed some sympathy for issues of concern to white feminists. She believed that women could find a useful sphere of activity outside the home and her efforts in the line of political journalism clearly demonstrated this, but Ruffin had conservative ideas concerning sex roles for black women and believed in the development of home and hearthside as a top priority concern for black people. Terrell was personally a liberated woman, active in community affairs and the first black woman on the Washington, D.C. schoolboard, but she supported the Tuskegee program of domestic and industrial education for women. Ida Wells certainly represented a radical voice in the early stages of national organization, but the Terrell forces seemed dedicated to minimizing her role as the organization developed.[24]

Conclusion

The National Association of Colored Women was not a monolithic, centrally organized institution, but a free association of various types of local clubs. Some of these groups were highly political, radically integrationist, and given to sensational agitation. Others were accomodationist, and inclined

968

towards the philosophy that Christorpher Lasch refers to as pseudo-femininst. I would prefer to characterize them as domestic femininsts, rather than pseudo-feminists. They attempted to rationalize their desire for activism and social involvement in a manner consistent with their essentially conservative values. They were typical of black action groups in that they were not committed to radical changes in American society and culture— but committed rather to the idea that black people should change to render themselves more acceptable to society. They showed a genuine sympathy for the masses of black people, but at the same time a patronizing contempt. This was evident especially under the Washington administration, when the Association was more concerned with establishing a "first class" Jim Crow coach to separate upper and lower class blacks than with a frontal assault upon Jim Crow. Conservatism was also evinced by their lack of sympathy for the white urban poor. Although some of the more progressive leaders like Mary Church Terrell, Ida B. Wells, Josephine Ruffin, and Josephine S. Yates occasionally were concerned with re-defining the role of women, most of the leaders were clearly resolved that woman should best work in "woman's sphere". In short, the NACW in its early stages was typical of most black organizations since the end of reconstruction. It was conservative rather than radical; and its attitude towards fundamental American institutions was admiring, rather than critical.

969

NOTES

[1]The work of black literary societies, male and female, is described in Dorothy Porter's," The Organized Activities of Negro Literary Societies, 1828-1846," *Journal of Negro Education*, V., (October, 1936), pp. 556-576. For work of the Afric-American Female Intelligence Society of Boston, see Gerda Lerner, *Black Women in White America* (New York, 1972), pp. 437-439.

[2]Robert W. Fogel and Stanley Engerman, *Time on the Cross*, (New York, 1974), p. 138.

[3]E. Franklin Frazier, *The Negro Family in the United States*, (Chicago, 1966), pp. 36-37.

[4]Ibid, p. 39.

[5]Charles H. Nichols, *Many Thousand Gone*, (Bloomington, Ind., 1969). Stanley Feldstein, *Once a Slave*, (New York, 1970), pp. 52-60.

[6]Alexander Crummell, "The Black Woman of the South, Her Neglects and Her Needs," in Crummell's *Africa and America*, (Springfield, Mass.. 1890), pp. 64-66.

[7]Du Bois, "The Damnation of Women," in *Darkwater*, (New York, 1919), p. 171. E. Franklin Frazier's work on the black family was influenced by this book. See Frazier, op. cit. pp. 10-11. Du Bois also edited an Atlanta University Study on *The Negro American Family*, (Atlanta, 1909). See p. 21, passim, for the quoted lines.

[8]Charles S. Johnson, *Shadow of the Plantation*, (Chicago, 1934), pp. 49. 58, 80-83, 89-90, 208.

[9]Hortense Powdermaker, *After Freedom*, New York, 1939), pp. 144-145.

[10]Thomas Beer, *The Mauve Decode*, (New York, 1926).

[11]W.E.B. Du Bois, *Autobiography*, (New York, 1968), p. 137.

[12]Eleanor Flexner claims in *Century of Stuggle*, (New York,   ), that no copies of the letter exist. The present author found one in the Rare Books Room, Boston Public Library where

Flexner did her research.

[13]Richard T. Greener's typed manuscript report on the conventions is in the Rare Books Room. Boston Public Library.

[14]Mary Church Terrell, *A Colored Woman in a White World,* (Washington, D.C., 1940), p. 150.

[15]Details of the organizational meetings are given in *A History of the Club Movement Among the Colored Women of the United States of America,* (, 1902).

[16]Frederick Douglass, "The Nation's Problem," in Howard Brotz, ed. *Negro Social and Political Thought, 1850-1920.* (New York, 1966), p. 137. *The Women's Era,* II: 3:8, contain Mrs. Ruffin's protests against a separate Negro Exhibit.

[17]History of the Club Movement. . ., p. 45.

[18]*The Autobiography of Ida B. Wells,* (Chicago, 1970), pp. 25, 265, 280, 367-374, 380-382.

[19]The Women's Era, II: 10:9.

[20]Margaret Murray Washington to Edna Dow Cheney, letter in the Edna D. Cheney Papers, Rare Books Room, Boston Public Library.

[21]*The Women's Era,* November, 1895.

[22]Booker T. Washington, ed., *A New Negro For a New Century,* (Chicago, 1900), p. 904.

[23]Mary Church Terrell, "Club Work of Colored Women," *Southern Workman,* XXX, (August, 1901), p. 436, speaks of these "peculiar tempations," as does Mrs. Mossell in *The Work of the Afro-American Woman,* (, 1894), cf. Eleanor Flexner's statement that black women did not talk much about "temptations".

[24]The feud between Terrell and Wells-Barnett is chronicled in Ida B. Wells, op. cit. references are recurrent in the Mary Church Terrell Papers, Library of Congress, 1899-1900.

970

BLACK WOMEN IN THE ERA OF THE AMERICAN REVOLUTION IN PENNSYLVANIA

Debra L. Newman*

971

It is undeniable that the era of the American Revolution saw the passage of the Gradual Abolition law in Pennsylvania. It is also undeniable that this law made a significant difference in the lives of Afro-Americans even if the material aspects of freedom were worse for some. After all, who would argue that slavery was better than freedom? No other single law or action in this period would have a greater impact on the lives of Afro-Americans. One of the cogent reasons for the passage of this law was the effort of the Pennsylvania abolitionists to erase the contradiction that the institution of slavery caused in the American people's struggle for independence from England. Their pressure augured an era of experimentation, of change. In order to assess the changes that the American Revolution made for black women in Pennsylvania, it is necessary to study their lives during the decades before the war and in the period immediately after it.

Black women were a small but important segment of eighteenth-century Pennsylvania society. This is not a study about black women as victims of the social and legal system of the colony under the institution of slavery nor about the abolitionist movement but an attempt to provide some information about the fabric of these women's lives—information about what they could and did do in spite of slavery. Few records were generated by blacks themselves prior to the gradual abolition law, and only scattered records with information about individual blacks were kept: some baptism and marriage records, wills and deeds which mention blacks, newspaper advertisements for sale of blacks or for runaways, tax records, censuses, slave manifests and merchants' records, diaries of observers, court records and emancipation, indenture and other legal protection papers. None of these records alone provide a well-rounded view of the black woman; using some of them collectively only gives a sketch of their existence. There are enough records, however, for a statement to be made with an attempt to evoke the point of view of the women themselves.

The eighteenth-century Pennsylvania black women were fettered on all sides by behavioral constraints whether they were slaves, indentured servants, or free

*Debra L. Newman is an Archivist in the General Services Administration, National Archives and Records Service, Civil Archives Division in Washington, D. C.

Originally published in *Journal of Negro History*, Vol. LXI (July 1976).

persons. Lacking real freedom these women exersized limited personal liberty by rebelling against their masters, by running away, feigning sickness or being generally uncooperative. Finding futility in recalcitrance in many cases, black women could decide to work creatively in their limited spheres, act as wife and mother as effectively as they could, take advantage of a few legal rights and maintain a circumscribed social life. This statement does not imply that the treatment of the black women, slave or free, was benevolent or just rather that no matter what the intent of the builders of the peculiar institution, in order to survive the black women had to deal effectively with all phases of life. They could not be swept along by the social and legal proscriptions of slavery.

Most Afro-American women came to Pennsylvania in the eighteenth century when slavery was flourishing in the colony. Some were brought by ship from other colonies, especially South Carolina, and from Jamaica, Barbados, Antigua, St. Christopher, Nevis, Anguilla and Bermuda. From mid-century, blacks were forced immigrants to the colony directly from the African continent. Up to 1729 only a few blacks, about two or three, came on each ship. From the time of the Seven Years War, however, when the number of white servants was reduced because of the participation of white male servants in the fray, the numbers of blacks brought into the colony aboard ships increased until 1766 when the trade had slowed significantly but not completely.[1] Records of the Bureau of Customs indicate that blacks were imported and exported through the port of Philadelphia until the 1860s—often illegally. The schooner, *Prudence,* brought seventeen African men, women and children in 1800 and the ship, *Phoebe,* 100 Africans in the same year in defiance of the section of the Gradual Abolition law which expressly forbade the trade.[2] The ships' records for the eighteenth century generally yield some physical information about the individual women. Sometimes the records just indicate that there were black women aboard the ship, other times they give the individual's first name, (surnames are rare), sex, age, height, color and owner. For example, the description of Nelly states that her age is 13, her height 4'9'' and her complexion, yellow. Collectively the records describe most of the women as teenagers or in their early twenties with varied complexions represented as bright mulatto, mulatto, yellow, black or African. Their different hues point to the preference of Pennsylvanians for second generation Africans who they felt could better adapt to their society and to the climate.[3] Many of the women had smallpox marks. Of the thousands of blacks imported or smuggled into Pennsylvania, it is virtually impossible to determine the number of women or their proportion to the men because too many of the records give numbers of blacks aboard ship without giving specific numerical breakdowns by sex.[4]

972

[1]Darold Wax, "Negro Imports into Pennsylvania, 1720–1766," *Pennsylvania History,* 32, (July 69), pp. 254–87.

[2]Slave Manifests for Philadelphia, 1800 to 1860 in the Records of the Bureau of Customs, National Archives and Records Service, Washington, D.C. Hereafter, NARS.

[3]Darold Wax, "Quaker Merchants and the Slave Trade in Colonia Pennsylvania," *The Pennsylvania Magazine of History and Biography,* 86. (April 62), pp. 153–56.

[4]Slave Manifests, Nars; and Wax, "Negro Imports," pp. 254–87.

Black women came into Pennsylvania overland with their owners. Free blacks and runaways came to Pennsylvania of their own volition during the course of the century because the harsh work-gang plantation system of labor of the South was rare in this colony, because of the Gradual Abolition in 1780 and because of the limited opportunities for employment and for political and social life.[5] Most of the blacks in the colony were concentrated in six southeastern counties: Philadelphia, York, Bucks, Lancaster, Chester and Montgomery.[6] Any statement of the numbers of blacks in the colony made before the first federal census of 1790 represented an estimate since no comprehensive count was made before that time. Green and Harrington in *American Population before the Federal Census of 1790* give estimates of 2,000 to 30,000 Afro-Americans for various years between 1715 and 1775 based on views of contemporary observers and county tax records.[7] Some county tax records give information about the number of blacks taxable as property between 1772 and 1783: Bedford, 28; Berks, 164; Cumberland, 649; Lancaster, 439, Washington, 448; and York, 448.[8] Gary Nash explains that taxable blacks were generally between the ages of twelve and fifty.[9] Nash, in his article, "Slaves and Slaveowners in Colonial Philadelphia," estimates the size of the black population by using burial records, Philadelphia tax records and comparisons with censuses for the black population in New York.[10] The following is a chart of burial statistics in Philadelphia for the first half of the eighteenth century:

973

AVERAGE BURIALS PER YEAR

Year	White	Black	% Black
1722	162	26	13.8
1729–32	396	94	19.2
1738–42	418	51	10.9
1743–48	500	64	11.3
1750–55	655	55	7.7

[11]

[5]Leon Litwack, *North of Slavery*, (Chicago: University of Chicago Press, 1961), pp. 69, 80. W. E. B. DuBois, *The Philadelphia Negro*, (New York: Schocken Books, 1967), pp. 46–47. Edward R. Turner, *The Negro in Pennsylvania, 1639 to 1861*, (New York: Arno Press, 1969), pp. 83, 253.

[6]Bureau of the Census, *Heads of Families at the First Census of the United States Taken in the Year 1790. Pennsylvania.* (D.C.: Government Printing Office, 1908), pp. 9–11; Turner, p. 12.

[7]Evarts B. Greene and Virginia D. Harrington, *American Population Before the Federal Census of 1790.* (New York: Columbia University Press, 1932), pp. 114–19.

[8]*Ibid., p. 119.*

[9]*Gary B. Nash,* "Slaves and Slaveowners in Colonial Philadelphia," *William and Mary Quarterly,* 30, (April 1973), p. 232.

[10]*Ibid.,* pp. 223–56.

[11]*Ibid.,* p. 226.

The next table is Nash's estimate of the population for the latter half of the century:

BURIALS IN PHILADELPHIA 1756–1775

Year		Average Burials	
	White	Black	% Black
1756–60	917	91	9.2
1761–65	990	87	8.1
1766–70	856	87	9.2
1770–75	1,087	87	7.4

[12]

974

The latter table shows a decline in the black population of Philadelphia. Nash contends that the decline was caused by the inability of the slave population to reproduce itself because of limited familial contact, males outnumbered females, a high infant mortality rate and because many females were beyond the childbearing age. The slave population is estimated at 1,392 in 1767 and 673 in 1775. When slave importation slowed after the 1760s, it became more obvious that natural reproduction among the black population was limited.

According to the 1790 census the total number of blacks in Pennsylvania was 10,301—6,540 free and 3,761 slave. So many blacks throughout the colonies flocked to Pennsylvania in order to enjoy a life of freedom after 1780 that between 1790 and 1800 the black population of Philadelphia increased more than 176 percent.[14] The underground railroad which was at its inception directed to Pennsylvania and freedom became active in the last fifteen years of the eighteenth century, and blacks themselves were active directors and helpers during these dramatic flights to freedom which brought many more Afro-Americans into the colony.[15] Afro-Americans were still brought into Pennsylvania as slaves after the passage of the Gradual Abolition law but were sometimes freed and made indentured servants until the age of twenty-eight.[16] In 1800 the total black population was 16,270 with 14,564 free and 1,706 slave.[17] The 1820 census was the first one to enumerate the black population by sex. The number of black females was 15,398 while the number of males was 14,804 with most concentrated in the Philadelphia area. There were 6,671 black females and 5,220 males in Philadelphia County and 4,426 females and 3,156 males in the city.[18]

---

[12]*Ibid.*, p. 231.

[13]*Ibid.*, p. 238.

[14]1790 Census of Pennsylvania; *Second Census of the United States, Pennsylvania,* Records of the Bureau of the Census, microfilm, NARS.

[15]Turner, p. 241. Wilbur H. Siebert, *The Underground Railroad from Slavery to Freedom.* (New York: Macmillan Co., 1898), pp. 431–34.

[16]Stanley I. Kutler, "Pennsylvania Courts, the Abolition Act and Negro Rights," *Pennsylvania History,* 30, (January 63), p. 14.

[17]1800 Census of Pennsylvania.

[18]*Census for 1820,* compendium, (D.C.: Gales and Slaton, 1821), Table 11.

From 1700 to 1780 most black women in the colony were held as slaves. Those who were free were constrained by a web of laws woven with the intent of limiting the activities of all black people. The intent of the laws is easy to isolate. Duty acts and trade regulations relating to black people were directed to slave traders and owners. Restraining laws were addressed to blacks, slave and free. As the century progressed, the laws regarding blacks became more and more restrictive. In 1700 special courts were established for blacks who were from this time until abolition denied trial by jury. Blacks could not carry arms without special license, and Afro-American men received severe penalties for assaults on white women. In 1721 laws were passed stipulating that no liquors were to be sold to Afro-Americans without the permission of their masters and another prohibiting Philadelphia blacks from shooting guns without a license.[19]

A group of laws passed in 1726 provided that vagrant free persons could be bound out to indentured service, provided fines for free blacks who harbored slaves and forbade trade between free blacks and slaves who did not have their master's consent to do so.[20] These provisions suggest that the free black was sufficiently concerned with the plight of his enslaved brothers and sisters to make laws necessary to restrict conspiricies for freedom. The harboring of slaves by free blacks was less effective than trading because trading could provide the slave with money necessary to purchase his own freedom whereas the harbored slave could only change his status by eluding the authorities for a period long enough to pass as free.

975

A free black person could be sold into slavery for life for marrying a white person. The laws of 1726 also discouraged manumission. Although the laws of 1700 and 1726 forbade blacks to assemble in companies, in 1732, 1738 and 1741 the Philadelphia City Council passed acts prohibiting slave "tumults" on Sundays and in the court house square at night.[21] These "tumults" were generally social gatherings, parties, funerals, or church services which were led by self-appointed black religious leaders who wandered about the vicinity of Philadelphia and through the colony preaching to the black population.[22] Because black people became skilled in many areas of endeavor, white workers petitioned the Pennsylvania assembly in 1708 and 1722 to forbid the employment of black mechanics or skilled workers. In 1726 a law was passed forbidding masters to hire out their slaves.[23]

The major legal action of the century for blacks was the Gradual Abolition Act. The preamble to the act cites the tyranny of Great Britain as a moving force in Pennsylvania's efforts to reduce tyranny against blacks. The preamble also mentions that slavery cast blacks "into the deepest affliction by an unnatural separa-

[19]*Pennsylvania Statutes-at-Large*, Chapters 49, 56, and II, 250.

[20]*Ibid.*, IV, 59.

[21]DuBois, p. 414. (Appendix B. Legislation, etc. of Pennsylvania in Regard to the Negro, pp. 411–18.)

[22]Charles Wesley, *Richard Allen*. (D.C.: Associated Publishers, 1969), p. 9. Turner, p. 45.

[23]*Pennsylvania Statutes-at-Large*, IV, 59; and DuBois, p. 412.

tion and sale of husband and wife from each other and from their children. . . ."[24] The act provided that no child born after the passage of the act would be a slave; that black and mulatto children were to be servants until 28 years of age; that all slaves were to be registered; that owners of slaves, though not registered, were to be liable for their support; that blacks were to be tried in court like other inhabitants; that the jury would value a slave in the case of a sentence of death in order to pay the owner; that the reward for blacks who captured runaways would be the same as that for white servants; that none would be deemed slaves but those registered except runaways from other states; that slaves taken from the state could be brought back and registered and that no blacks or mulattoes other than infants could be bound to indenture for longer than seven years.[25] The law was later amended to provide for the forfeiture of ships employed in the slave trade, for a prohibition against masters separating husbands, wives and their children and for penalties against taking blacks or mulattoes out of the state.[26]

976

Unfortunately, so many people sought to evade the act that the act itself ushered in a new set of legal protection certificates which were absolutely necessary for freed blacks. Since slave states surrounded Pennsylvania and master and slave dealers saw free blacks as potentially valuable for reenslavement, it was necessary to find ways of protecting the expanding free black population. Emancipated blacks were given certificates; and indentured servants were provided with papers stating the terms of their indenture. These papers had no value to blacks, however, if they could be stolen from them or destroyed. The Pennsylvania Society for Promoting the Abolition of Slavery and for the Relief of Free Negroes served as a registry for the legal protection papers of free blacks in Pennsylvania and blacks in neighboring states.[27] The Society kept marriage and birth certificates, certificates of freedom, of identity, statements of character, certificates allowing blacks to seek employment, passes and passports, certificates to prevent impressment and indenture papers.

Certificates of freedom showed that blacks gained their freedom in many different ways such as birth, will, manumission, purchase by themselves, their family or by benevolent persons or groups and then freed. Some were freed when their masters left with the British. Others gained freedom through work agreements, through indenture or by attaining a certain age.[28] Some masters brought their slaves into Pennsylvania after the Gradual Abolition Law was passed so that the slave would be freed:

---

[24]Pennsylvania Society for Promoting the Abolition of Slavery, (Hereafter PAS), *The Constitution of the Pennsylvania Society for Promoting the Abolition of Slavery and the Relief of Free Negroes Unlawfully Held in Bondage and the Acts of the General Assembly of Pennsylvania for the Gradual Abolition of Slavery.* (Philadelphia: J. Ormrod Printer, 1800), pp. 8–15.

[25]*Ibid.*

[26]*Ibid.*, p. 26.

[27]PAS, Committee for Improving the Condition of Free Blacks (Hereafter, Committee), Minutes, 1790–93, p. 17, September 1790. Historical Society of Pennsylvania, Philadelphia, Pa. (HSP).

[28]PAS Papers, HSP.

The bearer, Nanny, with her daugher, Hagar, were brought by me to Philadelphia from Dover in June 1785 where they remained with me until this day, having by the laws of Pennsylvania become free in six months after they came into the state. When I brought them up it was my intention they should become free by their stay in Pennsylvania. Nanny received wages from me for the time she has been with me here.

May 14, 1788 Edward Telshman   [29]

Some were cruelly freed when they were obviously too old to take care of themselves for any extended period. Mercy Candwell was freed when she was 87 years old after "a servitude of the greater part of her life."[30] The certificates of freedom and manumission papers sometimes listed the possessions of their owners especially if they consisted of goods, livestock or property which were inconsistent with the material level of blacks during the period. The Society used these records to act as legal counsel for blacks who were wronged or kidnapped if the unfortunate victim could establish contact with the Sociey.[31]

977

Within the confines of slavery black women worked hard and suffered many trials. For some the English language was difficult, and diseases aggravated by the harsh Pennsylvania winters took many lives.[32] Blacks who were free were sometimes not given the opportunity of employment; so they fed, clothed and housed themselves with difficulty. Some women went to the poorhouse; others ended up in jail. The Pennsylvania Abolition Society petitioned for the release of Dinah Nevil and her children from the Philadelphia workhouse on May 29, 1775.[33] There was also the everpresent threat of being kidnapped and taken to the South, a practice which became alarmingly common after abolition. The Pennsylvania Legislature urged by the Abolition Society took a strong stand in the matter of kidnapping. In May of 1791 the Society sent a memorial to the Congress protesting the kidnapping of free blacks and asking for the relief of a man named John who was being unlawfully held as a slave in Virginia. In June of the same year the governor of the state sent a letter to his counterpart in Virginia protesting the seizure of John by three men who were attempting to sell John as a slave and requesting that the governor of Virginia help restore the man's freedom. This letter is followed a month later by a demand from the governor of Pennsylvania to the governor of Virginia to deliver the three men who forcibly seized John.[34]

The occupations of most Afro-Americans did not vary much after abolition. Most blacks in the colony worked on farms or as domestic servants. Often farmers utilized a slave or a free family along with their own for field and house work, but more often blacks worked in urban centers. In the era of the American Revolution

[29]Manumission Books, May 1788, PAS Papers, HSP.
[30]Character References for Blacks file, PAS, HSP.
[31]Case Files, PAS Papers, HSP.
[32]Wax, "Quakers . . .," p. 156.
[33]Minutes of the Society for the Relief of Negroes, p. 2. Cox-Parrish-Wharton Papers, HSP.
[34]Papers of the Continental Congress, Vol II, pp. 565, 575, 579, NARS, microfilm.

in Philadelphia about one in every five families owned a slave.[35] It was fashionable in the colony, especially in Philadephia, to employ black women as housekeepers and cooks. This is the principal reason why black women were more numerous than black men in the Philadelphia area. The women's tasks as housekeepers included washing, ironing, tending children and waiting table. Some women were skillful with needlework or spinning. Black women worked as laundresses, nurses, dressmakers, seamstresses and cooks. A few were employed outside the city in ironworks.[36] The 1790 census lists occupations for a few Philadelphia free black women: Miss Arthur and Jane Mullen were milliners; Susanna Hammil worked in a tavern; Ann McNeil was a housekeeper; Phoebe (no surname given) was a huckster or peddler and Margaret Woodby was a cake baker.[37] Another source lists Ann Poulson as a laundress and Terra Hall as a hatter.[38]

978

Newspaper advertisements tell even more about the various occupations of black women. Owners often stressed (and probably sometimes exaggerated) the areas in which a black women excelled in order to facilitate her sale. An advertisement from an owner in Carlisle, Pennsylvania reads, "To be sold, a strong, healthy mulatto wench, 16 years old, she has had the small pox, measles, can cook, wash and do most sorts of housework."[39] A Lancaster woman is described as a good cook and dairy worker and another younger woman in the same advertisement "about 27 years old is an excellent house servant and besides washing and ironing can spin wool and flax, knit, etc., understands the management of a dairy and the making of butter and cheese."[40] A 17-year-old girl is described as having had the smallpox and measles, as healthy, strong and lively, "would suit the country or town, she can do all sorts of housework, and might soon be made a good cook."[41] One women is advertised as a good cook "who can be recommended for her honesty and sobriety."[42]

Character references for blacks which are among the records of the Pennsylvania Abolition Society list the numerous household skills of black women.

Rachael Roy is a slave belonging to Dr. Gardener of Charleston, South Carolina. Sometime past her master went to England and left her with three children. . . . She has schooled them all and taught them all plain needlework.[43]

---

[35]Nash, p. 242.

[36]Some mention of women in ironworks is made in Darold Wax, "The Demand for Slave Labor in Colonial Pennsylvania," Pennsylvania History, 34, (1967), pp. 331–45.

[37]1790 Pennsylvania Census, pp. 208–45.

[38]Tom W. Shick, Emigrants to Liberia, 1820–43, An Alphabetical Listing, (Newark, Del.; Liberian Studies Assn., Inc., 1971), pp. 41, 77.

[39]The Pennsylvania Packet or General Advertiser, Lancaster, Pa. February 18, 1778.

[40]Ibid., Mar. 18, 1778.

[41]Dunlap's Pennsylvania Packet or the General Advertiser, Phila. Pa. January 24, 1774.

[42]Ibid., March 21, 1774.

[43]Character References for Blacks file, PAS, HSP.

This is to satisfy whom it may concern that Negro Tamer has leave to hire with whom she pleases and receive her own wages. She is a good weaver and spinner and knitter. She can wash and iron well, is acquainted with house business.[44]

Many women who were freed chose to become indentured servants, or were freed under the condition that they became indentured servants, or were indentured by their parents. The years of indenture varied greatly, but black women were usually indentured for "housewifery." January 27, 1786 Margaret, a mulatto free woman, indentured herself for three years, occupation, housewifery. Jane. Pernall with the consent of her father was indentured for nine years of housewifery including sewing, knitting and spinning. Phoebe, about 25 years old, was indentured to Adam Lantzinger for 16 years of housewifery.[45]

The eighteenth century found most black women doing various types of domestic work. Neither the Revolution nor the Gradual Abolition Law caused a significant change in occupation. By mid-nineteenth century there was still no meaningful change; women were effectively lodged in the same types of occupations. Of 4,429 women over 21 in 1848, 1,970 were laundresses, 486 were seamstresses and 786 domestic workers. The rest were in trades, housewives, servants, cooks and rag pickers.[46]

Although it was not uncommon for black families to be sold apart in Pennsylvania, the family structure remained strong and marriages were frequent. Among the archives of the colony a number of marriages of black men and women are recorded. Various churches listed marriages among Afro-Americans. A large number were registered in Swedes' Church, St. Paul's Church and St. Michael's and Zion Church, all of Philadelphia. The registration sometimes indicated whether blacks were slave or free, mulatto, black or African, or whether they had the consent of their masters and sometimes listed the masters' names. Two recorded marriages took place in January of 1756. William Derrham and Mary Waldrek both free mulattoes had their marriage registered in St. Michael's and Zion Church as did John, who was freed by John Sin Clear (St. Clair), and Mary Ann. The next year John, the servant of Mr. Bankson, and Jane, a servant of Mr. Master, were wed in the same church.[47] Forty-eight black marriages were recorded in this church's records between 1756 and 1794.[48] The only occupation given is servant or slave except for one man who is listed as a cooper.[49] The distinction between the meaning of slave and servant is often unclear.

There are thirty-nine marriages listed for St. Paul's Church between 1768 and 1792.[50] The record keeper for St. Paul's sometimes added an additional comment to the marriage records. For instance, in recording the marriage of Edward Tal-

979

---

[44]*Ibid.*

[45]Indenture Papers, PAS, HSP.

[46]DuBois, p. 143.

[47]*Records of Pennsylvania Marriages Prior to 1810, Pennsylvania Archives*, II, Vol. 8 and 9, (Harrisburg: Hart, 1878, 1880), Vol. 9, pp. 300, 324, 332.

[48]*Ibid,.* Vol. 9, pp. 300-411.

[49]*Ibid.,* Vol. 9, p. 370.

[50]Ibid., Vol. 9, pp. 453-92.

bert and Alice David, both free blacks, he wrote, "That is good." For another couple who he had probably forgotten to register right away, he gave the date "about April 23, 1791." For the marriage of Rebecca Wood and Samuel Berry he indicates that he gave them no certificate.[51] In these records the racial designation "African" seems to be distinct from that of "Negro." Samuel Carson and Sophia Hand, Africans, were married on February 8, 1795 and Jan Ellis and Samuel Robeson, Africans, were wed in May of 1793 while Thomas Yervis and Philis Cox, Negroes, registered on May 5, 1783.[52]

The Moravian Church in Bethleham, Pennsylvania married Magdalena Mingo and Samuel Johannes on April 20, 1757. Johannes was described as a "Malabar" presumably from eastern India.[53] Andreas, *ein Mohr,* and Maria, *eine Mohrinn,* were married in November of 1742 in Bethleham.[54] Other churches registered a few blacks. Some of the records do not indicate either the church or the place of the marriage. Cuff and Judith, two blacks belonging to Messrs. Mifflin and Elves, were married on November 2, 1764.[55] It is probably also true that many of the records were not kept or simply do not indicate race. Black churches under Richard Allen and Absalom Jones performed wedding ceremonies also in the last years of the eighteenth century. On July 1, 1798 Luke Johnson and Sabarah Smith were married by Absalom Jones, rector of St. Thomases Church.[56] Several resolutions passed in the last decade of the century by the Philadelphia Free African Society suggest that there was a number of people who did not bother with the marriage ceremony at all.[57] There are certainly enough records, however, to point out that the black women had a value for solidifying the family structure according to the laws of the colony especially since women held as slaves had to have the permission of their masters in order to wed.

Probably throughout the century women acted as family leaders alone. The 1790 census lists fifty black women family heads with a total of ninety-four dependents. Some of the women were widows; most had dependents; only eleven were listed as the only person in the family.[58] The 1800 census gives seventy-six black women as heads of families. It is rare that the same women who appear in the 1790 census as women alone show up again in the one for 1800.[59] This is an indication of either geographical or social mobility (or unfortunately, of the census takers mistakes). They probably had either moved out of the state, were married, or lived with another person, even a male minor over sixteen, who was considered head of a household.

[51]*Ibid.,* Vol. 9, pp. 463, 467, 483.

[52]*Ibid.,* Vol. 8, pp. 325, 340, 361.

[53]*Ibid.,* Vol. 9, p. 116.

[54]Ibid., Vol. 9, p. 120.

[55]*Names of Persons for Whom Marriage Licenses Were Issued in the Province of Pennsylvania Previous to 1790, Pennsylvania Archives,* II, Vol. 2, (Harrisburg: Hart, 187-), p. 63.

[56]Marriage Certificates, PAS, HSP.

[57]Wesley, *Richard Allen,* pp. 93, 95.

[58]1790 Census of Pennsylvania.

[59]1800 Census of Pennsylvania.

In most cases, the responsibilities accompanying marriage or heading a family had to be secondary for the black woman because she had other houses to maintain, other families to feed and other children to tend. Nevertheless, she persevered. A number of women, however, did strike out for freedom before and after the passage of the Gradual Abolition Law. Newspaper advertisements tell the stories of the numbers who ran away, which many probably did by melting into the crowds of Philadelphia.

Runaway on the night of the eighth of March [1778] from the subscriber, of Thornbury Township, Chester County, Pennsylvania, a mulatto woman named Rachel, of a middle size, about 30 years of age. . . . Took with her one black bonnet and four gowns.[60]

Some women married free men who purchased their freedom for them. Others married to slaves, like the wife of Absalom Jones, were bought out of slavery first since the children followed the condition of the mother.[61] Dinah Jones of Chester County was freed when her husband purchased his liberty.

Pennsylvania black women had their share of more daring escapes too. While some women waited for their husbands and sons to return from fighting the colonists' battle, others joined with the British during the occupation of Philadelphia in 1777 and in 1783 left with them to seek a better life in Nova Scotia, England or the West Indies. The British had promised freedom to all blacks who joined their ranks.[63] The Continental Congress demanded in 1783 that the British make a list of all of the Afro-Americans removed from the United States so that reparations could be made to the owners at a later date.[64] The British complies creating an "Inspection Roll" of blacks with information about their ships' destinations, and personal information such as age, description, indication of slave or free status and, if formerly enslaved, then to whom and how long separated from them, and, finally, whose possession they were in at the time of embarkation. A large proportion of blacks in Philadelphia left with the British. Some of the women who went were Tinah Leech, 25, who was formerly the property of George Leech of Philadelphia, and Catherine, 30, formerly the property of a doctor in Philadelphia from whom she had been separated for five years in 1783. Bellah Miles, 44, and Sally Miles, 10, were probably mother and daughter. Isaac Bush and Lucy Bush, both 35, and probably husband and wife, also left.[65]

It is obvious that during the time blacks lived within the British lines, and sometimes it was for as long as seven years of more, there was an active social

---

[60]*The Pennsylvania Packet*, March 18, 1778.

[61]Sidney Kaplan, *The Black Presence in the Era of the American Revolution*. (New York: New York Graphic Society, Ltd., 1973), p. 83. Wesley, p. 59.

[62]Certificates of Freedom, PAS, HSP.

[63]Papers of the Continental and Confederation Congresses, Vol. 68, p. 445. NARS.

[64]*Ibid.*, PCC 121, pp. 59–62.

[65]"Inspection Roll of Negroes Taken on Board Sundry Vessels at Staten Island, 1783," Papers of the Continental and Confederation Congresses, NARS.

existence. Couples were married and a number of children were born. The children are listed in the records as "born free within British lines." For example, Ralph and Nancy Henry had a daughter, Molly, who was 4 years old in 1784 and was described as a fine child. She had been born free behind British lines. Peter and Betsy Johnson had a son four and one two years old. Johnson had left Robert Morris of Philadelphia six years before; so both of the family's children were born out of captivity probably within British lines. John Jones left Virginia in 1776 with Lord Dunmore and Lucretia, Jones' wife, had left Philadelphia with the British troops. They had a daughter, Charlotte, who was three years old. Some mothers came with their children but no fathers. One father, Cato Cox of Frankford, Pennsylvania, came with his son to the British lines and married a New York woman there.[66]

982

Some women whose lives span part of both the eighteenth and nineteenth centuries opted to join with those who returned to Africa from 1820 to 1840. Mary Smith, Elizabeth Small, Ann Poulson, Elizabeth James, Jane Hawkins, Terra Hall, and Mary Butler, all of whom were literate, were among those who left. Other women were Matilda Spencer, Sarah Smith, Elizabeth Carey, Charlotte Cain and Charlotte Brown. Terra Hall was 55 and Charlotte Brown was 60 years old. Mrs. Black, Nancy Bantam and Nancy Augustine also made the trip. They went alone or with their families to face the inhospitable African climate. Most were destined for Liberia, but some went to Sierra Leone and many died of fever shortly after they had arrived.[67] These women were not escaping slavery for there were few slaves left in Pennsylvania by 1820; they wanted an alternative to being a free black women in a white-ruled land.

Not all women sought physical emancipation. Some tried to escape through education. By the last decade of the century the black church and black benevolent societies were sponsoring schools for blacks.[68] Earlier, in 1770, Anthony Benezet had provided for a school for free blacks and mulattoes. Other Quakers provided educational facilities for blacks and by 1797 had seven schools for them. A school for black women was established by the Society for the free instruction of blacks in 1792.[69] The school in Cherry Street was taught by Helena Harris, a black woman "of considerable parts, who had been for several years employed as a teacher of white children in England."[70]

[66]*Ibid.*
[67]Shick, passim.
[68]Committee Minutes, PAS, HSP; Wesley, pp. 91–2; Turner, pp. 129–30, 191–92.
[69]Turner, pp. 128–29.
[70]*Philadelphia City Directory, 1794.* (Philadelphia; Jacob Johnson and Co., 1794), p. 225.

A roll from the Society's Girl's School demonstrates some interesting facts about this early education.

LIST OF THE GIRLS IN THE BLACK SCHOOL UNDER THE CARE OF THE COMMITTEE OF EDUCATION OF THE ABOLITION SOCIETY
July 2, 1800

Name	Age	Sent by	Time	Subject
Charlotte Johnson	16 yrs.	John Richards	Half day	Reading and writing
Rebecca Harrison	16 yrs.	John Richards	Half day	Reading and writing
Sarah Lewis	16 yrs.	Parents	All day	Writing and arithmetic
Catherine Still	14 yrs.	D. Dupuy	Half day	Writing and arithmetic
Abby Macclan	16 yrs.	A. Howell	Half day	Spelling
Nancy Ellis	14 yrs.	M. Wilcocks	Half day	Spelling
Jane Nash	8 yrs.	J. Folwell	All day	Spelling
Mary Lewis	8 yrs.	Committee	All day	Letters
Minte Liston	6 yrs.	Committee	All day	Letters
Elizabeth Sewel	12 yrs.	Committee	All day	Letters
Elizabeth Still	16 yrs.	D. Dupuy	Half day	Spelling, reading and writing
Rebecca Lewis	17 yrs.	Parents	All day	Spelling and reading
Patty Pennington	3 yrs.	Parents	Half day	Letters[71]

983

Most of the young women were taught academic subjects rather than household skills although these skills were sometimes a part of the curriculum. The roll for the Girls' School was short in this year, but among the sponsors are three parents, (or two; perhaps Sarah Lewis and Rebecca Lewis were sisters), black parents who had the means to send their children to school. The roll for the Boys' School is about twice as long. Six of the boys were sent by their parents.[72]

The Society noted the enthusiasm the black community had for increased schooling and sometimes pooled their efforts with the free black community in Philadelphia in matters of education. Many women were later able to attend the Clarkson School. The roll for this school for the years 1820–23 list over fifty pages of women aged 16 to 50.[73]

The Society also helped the free black community with their efforts for employment. The Society's minutes report that they were able to find jobs for black adults and children and that they sometimes had more applications from the Afro-American community than they could fulfill.[74]

The most significant change accompanying abolition for Afro-Americans in Pennsylvania was that blacks finally had the legal right to organize. In November

---

[71]Roll of the Girls' School, PAS Papers, HSP.
[72]Roll of the Boys' School, PAS Papers, HSP.
[73]Committee Minutes, PAS, HSP.
[74]Wesley, *passim.*

1787 Richard Allen and Absalom Jones organized the Free African Society, which was a mutual aid association, and began their independent church movement.[75] Men and women joined together to start working to help take care of their own people. The society made special provisions for the support of widows and orphans of members. In addition to establishing churches, schools and benevolent societies, by the end of the century blacks in Philadelphia owned nearly one hundred houses.

The greatest transition for the black woman during the era of the American Revolution was the move from slavery to freedom. Economic improvement was practically nonexistent for all but a few of these women who were frugal enough to save a little money and to buy property or those who ran small establishments. Although abolition was gradual, by 1820, forty years after emancipation, there were only 211 slaves in the state of Pennsylvania and 150 of those were over 45 years old. Freed blacks tended to stay with their masters after emancipation. This seems especially true of York County where there were 847 free blacks listed in 1790 but none as heads of families. The occupation of black women in the eighteenth century, servant, was not one that they could leave behind with the coming of emancipation or the passage of more than a century. It was during the eighteenth century that the patterns of oppression of the black women were designed, a pattern which would continue into the twentieth century. It was also during the last two decades of this century that black women were first given opportunities for organizational leadership. These opportunities were provided by the church, benevolent societies and social groups. A few black women were given opportunities for basic education. Slavery did not devastate the black woman. She performed her occupational duties, played her role as mother and wife and interacted with other Afro-Americans inside and outside of the legal and social confines of slavery.

984

[75]Wesley, p. 58. Turner, p. 125.

"Custodians of a House of Resistance": Black Women Respond to Slavery

MARY ELLEN OBITKO

Undoubtedly, because black women belong as they do to two groups which have traditionally been treated as subordinates by American society—blacks and women—they have been doubly victimized by scholarly neglect and prejudicial assumptions. Bearing the weight of inferior status coupled with the burden of the prejudice derived from their sex as well as their color, black women have been portrayed by historians as occupying an obscure role in the shaping of American culture. Since the slave women are conspicuously absent from most discussions of slavery, one might simply infer that their role was minimal. Such an assumption is dangerous and incorrect. On the contrary, slave narratives indicate that women played a variety of roles in the efforts to combat the brutalizing forces of slavery. Yet, although these narratives make mention of the various roles that females played, historians have chosen to ignore the evidence and have continued to portray slave women as docile and accommodating.[1]

Originally published in *Women & Men: The Consequences of Power*, edited by Dana V. Hiller and Robin Ann Sheets (Cincinnati, Ohio: University of Cincinnati, 1977), pages 256-269.

1

Past scholars of American slavery have generally depicted slave women as the broad-bosomed, turban-topped, beaming-faced "Black Mammy." Moreover, some historians have asserted that all slave women possessed such qualities as self-respect, loyalty, gentleness, affection, warmth and compassion.[2] Such descriptions of black women are erroneous in that they lead one to believe that all slave women responded in the same manner to slavery—that is, in a docile and accommodating manner. Likewise, historians have tended to label all slave women as matriarchs. That characterization is equally misleading, for although women may have been extremely important in the slave family, that fact cannot be construed to mean that the typical

986   slave family was matriarchal in form.[3] In a matriarchy, the mother occupies the headship of the family, and all descent, kinship, and succession are reckoned through the mother (matrilineal). However, in the slave family, the female could not be the "head" because, in reality, the only "head" of the family was the white master who held the reins of power. It was the white master who decided which slaves from which families would be sold. It was the white master who determined which black men would marry which black women. Female slaves did not, therefore, have the kind of power or influence one generally associates with a matriarchy. Moreover, to label slave women as matriarchs is, as former University of California at Los Angeles Professor Angela Y. Davis contends,

> a cruel misnomer because it implies stable kinship structures wherein the mother exercises decisive authority. It ignores the profound traumas the black woman might have experienced when she had to surrender her childbearing to alien and predatory economic interests. Even the broadest construction of the matriarch concept would not render it applicable to black slave women. But it should not be inferred that she therefore played no significant role in the community of slaves. Her indispensable effort to ensure the survival of her people can hardly be contested.[4]

Likewise, Professor of Sociology Robert Staples argues that "the myth of a black matriarchy is a classical example of what Malcolm X called making the victim of the criminal."[5] The role of slave women cannot be explained in approbatory terms that falsely present the female slave's real contribution to the black struggle. Certain forces existed within the American slave system which warranted a particular role for the women. A careful analysis of those conditions is necessary in order to reconsider the response of black women to slavery.

Under slavery, the family life of black Americans was drastically altered. This alteration resulted in the reordering of the male and female roles. Eugene D. Genovese notes that the position of the black male slave was "precarious and frustrating since he was not a breadwinner in the usual sense."[6] In the slave family, the woman was independent of the male for support and, as Staples observed, assumed a type of leadership in her family not found in white society.[7] Therefore, black males were continually denied "the opportunity to obtain the economic interests wherewithal to assume the leadership in the family's constellation."[8] Under these circumstances, as Professor Stanley M. Elkins has pointed out, the plantation offered no really satisfactory father image other than the master. As a result, the black woman assumed prime authority in the household because it was she who controlled those activities—household care, preparation of food, and rearing of children—that were left to the slave family.[9] Apparently "in the plantation domestic establishment, the woman's role was more important than the husband's."[10]

987

Although the burden of slavery weighed heavily upon the black woman, she managed to maintain a measure of strength. "Because she was a worker and a free agent, mistress of the cabin and head of the family, she developed a spirit of independence and a keen spirit of personal rights."[11] She recognized her unique position and her value as a childbearer and used her higher status to become a strong, dependable, important figure in the family. As Professor Robert H. Abzug writes, black women under slavery "developed self-reliance" and played a major role in the decision-making process; however, as Abzug makes clear, "her maternal strength did *not* have to mean domination."[12] Clearly, the black woman had to possess the strength to respond to slavery in a variety of roles. Economically as well as sexually exploited, the female was thrust into the center of the slave community.[13] While the black woman was wholly integrated into the productive forces which allowed slavery to function, she was aware of the role she must play in order to promote resistance against the forces of dehumanization.[14] Indeed, many women not only played a significant role in obstructing and thwarting the wishes and plans of the slaveholders, they actively participated in all aspects of resistance to the forces of slavery.[15]

First of all, misconduct and general insolence to the slaveholder comprised a major part of the black woman's attempt at resistance. Bennet H. Barrow, a plantation owner in the Florida parishes of Louisiana, notes in his diary for the year 1840-1841 the misconduct and punishment of his slaves. Of the 47

3

slaves listed for misconduct, 21 were women, and of the 22 slaves who received whippings as a punishment, 7 were women who were cited mostly for not doing their jobs well, feigning illnesses, inattention to their work, and attempting runaways.[16] Georgia plantation mistress, Fanny Kemble, recalls this instance of an impertinent slave woman when the plantation overseer, Mr. O——, was questioned concerning the flogging of a slave woman, Harriet, who had sassed Mr. O——, the overseer:

988

> Mr. O—— then said it was not at all for what she [Harriet] had told me that he had flogged her, but for having answered him impertinently; that he had ordered her into the field whereupon she had said she was ill and could not work; that he retorted he knew better, and bade her get up and go to work; she replied: 'Very well, I'll go, but I shall just come back again!' . . . For this reply, Mr. O—— said, 'I gave her a good lashing; it was her business to have gone into the field without answering me, and then we should soon see whether she could work or not; I gave it to Chloe too for such impudence.'[17]

U. B. Phillips, in *American Negro Slavery*, related the tribulations of an overseer in Jefferson County, Georgia, Elisha Cain, who was angered by the activities of a slave woman, Darkey, who "shortly became a pestilent source of trouble."[18] As Phillips mentions, "Cain wrote in 1833 that her [Darkey's] termagant outbreaks among her fellows had led him to apply a 'moderate correction,' whereupon she had further terrorized her housemates by threats of poison."[19]

Insolence to her master and overseer comprised only one aspect of the black woman's resistance to slavery. Overt resistance to the frequent whippings meted out by master and overseers made up another form of her reaction to the system. The following reveals several incidents in which black women reacted rather violently to their slavery:

> There was Crecie, for example, who pulled up a stump and whipped an overseer with it when he tried to lash her; or Aunt Susie Ann, who pretended to faint while she was being whipped and then tripped the overseer so that he couldn't stand up; or Lucy, who knocked an overseer over and tore his face up so that the doctor had to tend to him; or the mammy who nursed a child but later, when he tormented her, did not hesitate to beat him until he wasn't able to walk; or Aunt Adeline who committed suicide rather than submit to another whipping; or Cousin Sally, who hit her master over the head with a poker and put his head in the fireplace.[20]

The Southern Plantation Overseer As Revealed in His Letters by John Spencer Bassett clearly reveals the genuine concern the overseers had for the insolence shown by the women and the threat to the harmony of the slave community these women posed:

> Testimony shows that the overseer had more trouble with slave women than with the men. Travelers in Africa have noticed that women there have a marked ascendancy over the men, that they keep them in awe of their sharp tongues and that they are in general of violent passions as compared with the men. These qualities appeared in the slaves in the South. As a result many plantations had women who kept the rest of the slaves in a state of unrest and thereby made it hard for the overseer to keep order.[21]

989

Slave women were tough, powerful, and spirited, and at times desperately resisted the floggings and the lashings meted out to them by the overseers and masters. Probably most remarkable among slave accounts which depict such resistance are the incidents involving the dramatic attempts of Silvia DuBois. Silvia, a slave for nearly all of her life, could withstand the cruelties of her mistress, who often beat her for any displays of sauciness or insolence, no longer. In the following passage, Silvia DuBois describes how she decided to return the abuse of her mistress in the form of a beating which resulted in the death of the mistress, and ironically, the emancipation of Silvia DuBois. Silvia remarks concerning her cruel mistress:

> But I fixed her—I paid her up for all her spunk. I made up my mind that when I had a good chance, when some of her grand company was around I fixed her. I knocked her down and near killed her. It happened in the barroom; there was some grand folks stopping there, and she sent me to scrubbing up the barroom. I felt a little grum, and didn't do it to suit her; she scolded me about, and I sassed her; she struck me with her hand. Thinks I, its a good time now to dry you out and damned if I won't do it. I set down my tools and squared for a fight. I struck her a hell of a blow with my fist. I didn't knock her entirely through the panels of the door, but her landing against the door made a terrible smash, and I hurt her so badly that all were frightened out of their wits, and I didn't know myself but that I'd killed the old devil. The master he scolded me much; he told me that as my mistress and I got along so badly, if I would take my child and go to New Jersey, and stay there, he would give me freedom; I told him I would go. It was late at night; he wrote me a pass, gave it to me, and early the next morning I set out for New Jersey.[22]

Another form of resistance practiced by women was the well-knwon phenomenon of malingering or feigning illness to avoid work.[23] Feigning

5

illness was a widespread occurrence, yet such flagrant abuses necessarily were tolerated by the slaveowners because the slaves were important economic investments, and if a sick slave were driven to work he or she might die.[24] Slave women, recognizing the economic importance they represented to their owners, resorted quite often to feigning illness as well as occasionally pretending pregnancy because then they were given lighter work assignments and were allowed extra rations of feed.[25] Phillips provided an excellent account of a young woman, Beckey, who had given pregnancy as the reason for a continued slackness in her work:

990

> Her master became skeptical and gave notice that she was to be examined and might expect the whip in case her excuse was not substantiated. Two days afterward a negro midwife announced that Beckey's baby had been born; but at the same time a neighboring planter began search for a child nine months old which was missing from his quarter. This child was found in Beckey's cabin, with its two teeth pulled and the tip of its navel cut off. It died; and Beckey, charged with murder but convicted only of manslaughter, was sentenced to receive two hundred lashes in installments of twenty-five at intervals of four days.[26]

Gerald W. Mullin's study of slave resistance, *Flight and Rebellion: Slave Resistance in Eighteenth-Century Virginia*, suggests that women who feigned illness were more effective than men, and notes that women who pretended to be pregnant were a constant source of trouble.[27] For example, plantation owner Landon Carter alerted his overseers to be particularly aware of such situations, and to have the slave women whipped if they practiced any form of deceit.

Women often found it to their advantage to pretend that they were victims of other disorders as well. In *The Cotton Kingdom*, Frederick Law Olmsted remarks:

> The liability of women, especially to disorders and irregularities which cannot be detected by exterior symptoms, but which may be easily aggravated into serious complaints, renders many of them nearly valueless for work, because of the ease with which they can impose upon their owners. "The women on a plantation," said one extensive Virginia slaveowner to me [Olmsted], "will hardly earn their salt, after they come to breeding age: they don't come to the field, and you go to their quarters, and ask the old nurse what's the matter, and she says, 'Oh she's not well, master; she not fit to work, sir,' and what can you do? You have to take her word for it that something or other is the matter with her and you dare not set her to work; and she lays up till she feels like taking the air again, and plays the lady at your expense." I was on

a plantation where a woman had been excused from any sort of labour for more than two years, on the supposition that she was dying of phthisis. At last the overseer discovered that she was employed as a milliner and dress-maker by all the other coloured ladies of the vicinity.[28]

Besides feigning illness, women contemplated and often resorted to self-mutilation in order to thwart the slaveowner's attempts to sell them on the auction block. Observe the following account of a young girl who cut off her finger in order to prevent her owner from selling her.

A young girl, of twenty years or thereabouts, was the next commodity put up. Her right hand was entirely useless—'dead'; as she aptly called it. One finger had been cut off by a doctor, and the auctioneer stated that she herself chopped off the other finger—her forefinger—because it hurt her, and she thought that to cut it off would cure it. 'Didn't you cut your finger off?' asked a man 'kase you was mad?' She looked at him quietly, but with a glance of contempt, and said: 'No, you see it was a sort o'sore, and I thought it would be better to cut it off than be plagued with it.' Several persons around me expressed the opinion that she had done it willfully, to spite her master or mistress, or to help her from being sold down South.[29]

991

Reacting to the institution of slavery in a fashion far more drastic than feigning illness or the mutilation of their bodies, some women committed suicide, and many times they actually murdered or took part in attempted murder plots. Phillips records that as early as 1774 in Georgia "six Negro fellows and four wenches" killed an overseer, murdered the overseer's wife, and "ran amok in the neighborhood until overpowered."[30] Also there is the story of a slave woman, Peggy, who would not submit to intercourse with her master and was provoked to a state of anger in which she murdered him. As a result of her act, Peggy was hanged.[31] Other acts of violence committed by females included arson and poisonings. "In 1754 a C. Craft of Charleston, South Carolina, had two of his female slaves burned alive because they set fire to his buildings," and in 1775 a black slave woman, Phillis, along with a slave man, Mark, both slaves of John Codman of Charleston, after learning that their master had by his will made them free, "poisoned him that they might expedite the matter."[32]

Running away, as well as organized slave rebellion, constituted another form of resistance to slavery for women. Gerald Mullin's study on slave resistance calls attention to the fact that 142 women were advertised as runaways from 1737 to 1801 in the newspapers he used in formulating his work.[33] Providing some explanation concerning the desire of these women

7

to run away, Mullin surmises that although women who ran away were fewer in number than men, "it should be remembered, however, that it would be extremely difficult for women to pass as free and live and work in a society in which women in general did not go about alone."[34] Yet apparently slave women were rather ingenious and clever in their attempts to escape. Mullin records the following descriptions which point out their skill and effort in such endeavors.:

> Milly with grey eyes and 'very large Breasts,' was also a 'sly subtle Wench, and a great Lyar.' Cicley's master, a wiser man after his slave woman ran off, warned: 'Beware to secure her well, for she is very wicked and full of flattery.' Another, a mulatto woman with some pretensions to freedom, somehow obtained a pass from a justice of the peace in order to seek for witness to support her claim and never returned. Her owner wrote: 'she was a sensible wench and may impose on the credulous as a free woman.'[35]

More convincing in analyzing the active role played by women, especially as runaways, is Mullin's conclusion that since such descriptive terms as "genteel," "neat," and "bold" recurred in runaway female slaves' notices, fugitive females were superior to males, and "that these women were exceedingly clever, aggressively resourceful slaves."[36]

Indeed, numerous accounts depict the determination with which women sought to resist the forces of slavery and eventually gain emancipation. For example, from the *North Carolina Standard*, July 28, 1838, comes this advertisement for a runaway woman and her two children:

> Twenty Dollars Reward.—Runaway from the subscriber, a negro woman and two children; the woman is tall and black and *a few days before she went off I burnt her on the left side of her face: I tried to make the Letter M, and she kept a cloth over her head and face, and a fly bonnet over her head, so as to cover the burn.*[37]

More dramatic is the story of a young woman who escaped in a box. In the winter of 1857, she was boxed up in Baltimore by a young man who had the package conveyed as freight to the depot in Baltimore, consigned to Philadelphia. Nearly all one night it remained at the depot with the living agony in it, and after being upside down more than once, it reached Philadelphia about ten o'clock the next day. The box was picked up by a Curtis in Philadelphia who then took it to the home of a Mrs. Myers at Seventh and Minster Streets, whereupon the box was opened and there

992

beneath a mustering of straw lay the young, nearly dead fugitive woman. Suffering from exhaustion, the woman was taken to an upstairs room in Mrs. Myers' house, put to bed, and in a few days displayed all the signs of recovery. Trying to describe her sufferings and fears while in the box, she remarked that her chief fear was that she would be discovered and sent back to slavery. Indeed, in this instance the utmost endurance was put to test; the black woman's accomplishment in many ways surpassed that of Henry "Box" Brown's.[38]

Organized rebellions or insurrections comprised another form of resistance to slavery, and the conspiracies led by Gabriel Presser in Richmond, Virginia in 1800; by Denmark Vesey in Charleston, South Carolina, in 1822; and by Nat Turner near Southampton, Virginia, in 1831, have received wide publicity and have become the subject of much historical controversy. Therefore, it becomes necessary to consider what role, if any, women played in such insurrections. They did participate. For example, there are the efforts of Lucy, female servant of a John T. Barrow, who held a woman hostage in the weeds for the Turner insurgents to kill. Later sent to the gallows for her action, Lucy was the only woman convicted and hanged as a conspirator. Convicted on the testimony of her mistress, Mrs. Barrow, whom Lucy held as hostage, Lucy was "remembered by the singular spectacle created when she boldly rode her own coffin to the place of execution."[39] However, a more complete discussion of female insurrectionists is hampered by the fact that available historical scholarship has neglected to present the role of women, just as in many of the slave narratives in which the role of women is frequently mentioned only in passing. Works on the subject of slave revolts, such as Herbert Aptheker's *American Negro Slave Revolts* and Joseph C. Carroll's *Slave Insurrections in the United States, 1800-1865*, only briefly mention that in certain insurrections a girl or a woman aided in the conspiracy and do not in any broad sense evaluate the contribution of black women in the successfulness of the plots.[40] The result, of course, is that the reader is left only to speculate as to what role black women did play in the insurrections. Furthermore, if more males than females participated in rebellions, then perhaps such a form of resistance presented the only successful manner in which the male could resist the forces of slavery. Also it should be noted that slave rebellions did not occur every day, but rather occurred usually as a result of certain intolerable social and economic conditions.[41] Black women, on the other hand, were constantly in a day-to-day manner resisting the conditions of slavery. That is, they could feign

993

pregnancy or illness or resist the sexual advances of their owners. Therefore, it cannot be said that females did not participate in slave insurrections, but that they simply found other means of resistance more effective, and in the long run they posed a greater threat to the stability of the slave community than their male counterparts who often waited until the opportunity presented itself before they openly resisted. In any event, historians must engage in a wider investigation of the role of women in these rebellions.

Finally, a discussion of the female slaves' participation in efforts aimed at resistance necessitates a discussion of their role in the Abolition and Underground Railroad movements.[42] Quite fascinating and vital to the functioning of the Underground Railroad was one of its most formidable conductors, Harriet Ross Tubman, often referred to as the "Moses" of her people. Born a slave in Maryland in 1820, Harriet Tubman bore the marks of the lash on her flesh, and from her early teens as a field hand, she sensed the importance of open resistance to slavery. On one occasion when Harriet was ordered by her overseer to help whip a fellow slave, she refused, and as the man ran away, Harriet placed herself in the door to stop pursuit. Running away in 1849, she went to Boston where in 1854 she was welcomed into the homes of leading abolitionists who listened intently to her stories of slave life. Absolutely illiterate, possessing no knowlege of geography, she personally led nineteen successful rescues of over three hundred fugitive slaves, all the while working under the dangers of the $40,000 reward offered for her head. But as Harriet Tubman remarked, "I nebber run my train off de track an' I nebber los' a passenger."[43] Always carrying a pistol, she spurred on despairing fugitives telling them, "You'll be free or die."

994

Virtually ignored by history are the efforts of the "African Sibyl," Sojourner Truth, who contributed much to America's enlightenment regarding slavery. Gaining her freedom by running away, this ungainly ex-slave made her mark in history by boldly speaking out for freedom for blacks and for women as well. In fact, "her pleadings, along with manpower shortages in factories, finally convinced Lincoln and Congress to enlist the Northern free men of color to help fight the Civil War."[44] Though illiterate, she spoke with pronounced natural talent on emancipation and many reforms. Traveling in the states of Indiana, Michigan, and Ohio, preaching the cause of Abolition, she finally met a few abolitionists and began working on an anti-slavery project which ultimately led her to Washington and a meeting with President Lincoln.

Certainly the courage displayed by Harriet Tubman and Sojourner Truth, as well as many lesser known black women, was truly extraordinary. Francis Ellen Watkins (1825-1911), a popular American Negro poetess and also active in the Underground Railroad and other reform movements, composed the following poem which depicts most vividly many of the hazards that confronted women who chose to seek freedom rather than submit to the degradation of slavery:

"Eliza Harris"

Like a fawn from the arrow, startled and wild,   995
A woman swept by us, bearing a child;
In her eye was the night of a settled despair,
And her brow was o'ershaded with anguish and care.

She was nearing the river—in reaching the brink,
She heeded no danger, she paused not to think;
For she is a mother—her child is a slave—
And she'll give him his freedom, or find him a grave![45]

Clearly then, by actively participating in the resistance to slavery, black women performed a significant task in developing and sharpening the thrusts toward freedom. Indeed, the women were "custodians of a house of resistance," and were, therefore, essential to the survival of the slave community. Why did slave women assume such a role? Evidence seems to indicate that the dehumanizing forces and conditions of slavery warranted the rebelliousness, as manifested in the resistance that black women displayed. Coupled with the deplorable conditions created by the system was the unique position of women among the slaves—that is, they were valued as economic assets and exploited as sexual objects—which placed them in higher regard than men, and in this manner initiated their desire to overtly resist slavery. In any event, the fact remains that women did actively resist the forces of slavery and were not confined, nor were they content to function in a docile and accommodating role like Butterfly McQueen in *Gone With The Wind*.

NOTES

1. Slave narratives are a most useful source since they are presumably written from the slaves' point of view. But a critical evaluation of each narrative is essential, as is a comparative approach. Most of the slave narratives were dictated to or ghost-written by white abolitionists who, consciously or unconsciously, imposed their own biases on the narrative. Furthermore, it must be kept in mind that since most of the slave narratives available are those written by males, the woman receives mention frequently only in passing, i.e., as a "loving wife," or a "devoted mother." Therefore, the slave narratives tend to reflect the conditions of slavery from a male-oriented point of view. As a result, one must be careful not to conclude that women played no particular role in slavery, but rather that in many cases a discussion of the role of women under slavery reflected the biases of the writer.

2. Jessie W. Parkhurst, "The Role of the Black Mammy in the Plantation Household," *Journal of Negro History*, XXIII, No. 3 (July, 1938), pp. 351-53.

3. E. Franklin Frazier, *The Negro Family in the United States* (Chicago: University of Chicago Press, 1966), p. 49, and Kenneth M. Stampp, *The Peculiar Institution: Slavery in the Antebellum South* (New York: Alfred A. Knopf, Inc., 1956), p. 344.

4. Angela Y. Davis, "Reflections on the Black Woman's Role in the Community of Slaves," *The Black Scholar*, III (December, 1971), p. 5.

5. Robert Staples, "The Myth of the Black Matriarchy," *The Black Scholar* (January, 1970), p. 17.

6. Eugene D. Genovese, "American Slaves and Their History," *The New York Review of Books*, XV, No. 10 (December 3, 1970), p. 37.

7. Staples, p. 19.

8. Staples, p. 19.

9. Stanley M. Elkins, *Slavery: A Problem in American Institutional and Intellectual Life* (Chicago: University of Chicago Press, 1959), p. 130.

10. Maurice Davis, *Negroes in American Society* (New York: McGraw-Hill, 1949), p. 207.

11. Frazier, p. 47.

12. Robert H. Abzug, "The Black Family During Reconstruction," *Key Issues in the Afro-American Experience*, Vol. II, ed. Nathan Huggins, Martin Kilson and David M. Fox (New York: Harcourt, Brace, Jovanovich, Inc., 1971), p. 38.

13. The white male found it necessary to impose on the black woman another stereotype—the myth of the "bad" black woman. This labeled the female slave as eager for sexual exploits. The white male would have liked society to believe that the female slave was "loose" in her morals and therefore deserved none of the consideration that white women received. For further discussion of the implications of this concern, see Chapter 4 of Winthrop D. Jordan's *White Over Black: American Attitudes Toward the Negro, 1550-1812* (Chapel Hill, 1968).

14. Davis, p. 7.

15. As early as 1942, Raymond A. and Alice H. Bauer, in an anthropological study, had challenged the widely-held belief that certain forms of behavior on

the part of the black slave inferred that the blacks possessed an inferior status. The Bauers maintained that all slaves, both *male and female*, responded to the institution of slavery with certain, persistent patterns of what they label, "day-to-day resistance." Furthermore, they maintained that this "day-to-day resistance" was carried out in such a manner that to stereotype the role of male and female slaves as docile and accommodating in response to slavery would be to present only a partial picture of the slave community's efforts aimed at emancipation. For further discussion, see Raymond A. and Alice H. Bauer's "Day to Day Resistance To Slavery," *Journal of Negro History*, XXVII (Oct. 1942).

16. Edwin Adams Davis, *Plantation Life in the Florida Parishes of Louisiana, 1836-1846 as Reflected in the Diary of Bennet H. Barrow* (New York: Columbia University Press, 1943), pp. 406-10.

997

17. Francis Anne Kemble, *Journal of a Residence on a Georgian Plantation in 1838-1839* (New York: Alfred A. Knopf, 1961), pp. 85-86.
18. U.B. Phillips, *American Negro Slavery* (New York: Appleton-Century Co., 1918), p. 236.
19. Phillips, p. 236.
20. B.A. Botkin, *Lay My Burden Down* (Chicago: University of Chicago Press, 1945), pp. 174-75, 176, 183-84.
21. John Spencer Bassett, *The Southern Plantation Overseer As Revealed in His Letters* (New York: Negro Universities Press, 1968), pp. 19-20.
22. C.W. Larson, *Silvia DuBois: A Biography of the Slave Who Whipt Her Mistress and Gained Her Freedom* (Ringos, New Jersey: C.W. Larson, 1883), pp. 62-65.
23. Bauer and Bauer, p. 406.
24. Bauer and Bauer, p. 408.
25. Bauer and Bauer, p. 407.
26. Phillips, p. 456.
27. Bauer and Bauer, p. 411.
28. Frederich Law Olmsted, *The Cotton Kingdom* (New York: G.P. Putnam, 1904), p. 94.
29. Bauer and Bauer, p. 413.
30. Phillips, p. 194.
31. James Hugo Johnston, *Race Relations in Virginia and Miscegenation in the South 1776-1860* (Amherst, Massachusetts: University of Massachusetts Press, 1970), p. 307.
32. Francis L. Hunter, "Slave Society on the Southern Plantation," *Journal of Negro History*, VII, No. 1 (Jan., 1922), p. 33.
33. Gerald W. Mullin, *Flight and Rebellion: Slave Resistance in Eighteenth-Century Virginia* (New York: Oxford University Press, 1972), p. 187.
34. Mullin, p. 103-104.
35. Mullin, p. 104.
36. Mullin, p. 105.
37. William Wells Brown, *The Narrative of Williams Wells Brown a Fugitive Slave* (Reading, Massachusetts: Addison-Wesley Publishing Co., 1969), p. 59.

38. James Williams, *Life and Adventures of James Williams* (Philadelphia: A.H. Sickler and Co., 1893), pp. 75-76.
39. F. Roy Johnson, *The Nat Turner Slave Insurrection* (Murfreesboro, N.C.: Johnson Publishing Co., 1966), p. 67.
40. See Herbert Aptheker, *American Negro Slave Revolts* (New York: International Publishers, 1943), Joseph C. Carroll's *Slave Insurrections in the United States 1800-1865* (New York: Negro Universities Press, 1971) and F. Roy Johnson, *The Nat Turner Slave Insurrection* (Murfreesboro, N.C.: Johnson Publishing Co., 1966) for a discussion of slave insurrections.
41. Carroll, p. 148.
42. In regard to historical discussions concerning the Abolition and the Underground Railroad, the role of black women is once again slighted. Historians have chosen instead to underscore the efforts of white women in these movements. Although many historians do attempt to provide accounts of Harriet Tubman and Sojourner Truth, the lack of a more complete analysis in apparent. A notable exception is Benjamin Quarles' *Black Abolitionists* (New York: Oxford University Press, 1969), which briefly mentions the unusual account of a black woman, Elizabeth Barnes, who hid fugitive slaves on vessels sailing for Boston and New Bedford. Quarles also provides some interesting discussion concerning the role of free black women abolitionists. Other attempts depicting the role of slave women and the Underground Railroad are more readily concerned with providing vivid accounts of the dramatic escapes of females slaves along the "liberty line." See William Still's *The Underground Railroad* (New York: Arno Press, 1968) for the most extensive of these accounts.
43. Gerda Lerner, *Black Women in White America: A Documentary History* (New York: Pantheon Books, 1972), p. 64.
44. Gwendolyn Cherry, Ruby Thomas, and Pauline Willis, *Portraits in Color: The Lives of Colorful Negro Women* (New York: Pageant Press, 1962), p. 16.
45. Mel Watkins and Jay David, *To Be a Black Woman: Portraits in Fact and Fiction* (New York: William Morrow and Co., Inc., 1970), pp. 236-37.

998

The Journal of Charlotte L. Forten:
The Salem-Philadelphia Years
(1854–1862) Reexamined

By GLORIA C. ODEN*

*T*HE *Journal of Charlotte L. Forten: A Free Negro in the Slave Era*, edited by Dr. Ray Allen Billington, has established itself in the literature of the Civil War. Published by Dryden Press in 1953, the *Journal* has since been reissued twice without revision, in 1961 by Crowell-Collier and in 1981 by W. W. Norton. This paper is based upon the latter publication. The *Journal* begins with the first entry in Forten's diary, 24 May 1854, when she was a sixteen-year-old school girl in Salem, Massachusetts, and the volume ends in May 1864 at the Olive Fripp Plantation, South Carolina, where Forten was concluding her mission as teacher to the newly freed slaves of the coastal Sea Islands.

999

Forten left five diaries, of which four were published as the *Journal*; the fifth was discarded inasmuch as it covers the years 1855 to 1892 and has no bearing on events in the first four. Billington explained his method of editing as follows:

> In preparing Miss Forten's *Journal* for publication I have taken certain liberties with the text. Large sections in the period between 1854 and 1862 have been deleted. These describe the weather, family affairs, the landscape, and other matters of purely local interest. Space limitations have also forced me to omit many of her comments on the books that she read. In each case, however, I have tried to retain enough of the original to impart the flavor of the *Journal*. All items dealing with public figures, abolitionism,

* Gloria Oden is an associate professor in the English department, University of Maryland Baltimore County. She is grateful to the University and to the National Endowment for the Humanities for funding to support the research for this paper. The unpublished quotations from Charlotte Forten's diaries are cited by the courtesy of Howard University, where the diaries are on deposit with the Francis J. Grimke Papers in the Moorland-Spingarn Research Center.

Originally published in *Essex Institute Historical Collections*, Vol. 199, No. 2 (April 1983).

and Miss Forten's intellectual development have been fully repro-
duced. The portions describing her experiences in South Carolina are printed in their entirety, with only a few lines on family
affairs omitted. Wherever omissions have been made the fact has
been indicated in the usual manner, and in no case has the sense or
meaning been distorted.[1]

Arthur Ponsonby, the distinguished critic of English diaries, has written, "It may often be found in the printed editions of diaries that editors
extract only those portions which deal with events of public, historic or
local importance, and a note will be found declaring that the rest is
omitted because it was only of a private character. Many a diary has
been emasculated in this way."[2]

In the case of *The Journal of Charlotte L. Forten*, research has proved
the truth of this astute observation. Billington's failure to pay attention
to Forten's family affairs and to those other families with whom she was
intimate has perpetuated tangled misidentifications and omissions of both
close and more distant family relationships which, added to those he
himself specified, inflicted distortions on Forten's life not only as she
lived it but as it illuminates the lives of that small population of free
blacks of which she was a part. The errors of fact that mar Billington's
Journal can be summarized under three headings: incorrect identifications and omissions of family members; incorrect identifications and
omissions of those with whom she lived in the Salem household; incorrect identifications and omissions of the small society which made up
her social ambience.

The significance of genealogy to black history perhaps needs to be
stressed. Black history *is* genealogy—that first sure step towards reconstruction of those human interrelationships which must be gathered,
sifted, and pieced together *before* the pattern of a living community can
be crudely resurrected. In the case of the *Journal*, this first step (further
complicated by Forten's habitual use of initials for names) cannot be
taken until the misidentifications are cleared away and the omissions
restored. In the process, however, for various reasons, one being keeping

1000

---

1. *Forten Journal*, p. 40.
2. Arthur Ponsonby, *English Diaries: A Review of English Diaries from the Sixteenth to
the Twentieth Century with an Introduction on Diary Writing* (1923; reprint ed., Freeport,
N.Y.: Books for Libraries Press, 1971), p. 30.

families intact, the researcher must record a goodly number of persons, adolescents and infants included, who, beyond their own families, seemingly have little relevance to the contemporary community. Some of these persons may take on significance as the years pass.

Charlotte Forten went to Salem from Philadelphia where, in 1850, free blacks made up less than 9% of the population. Even so, racial antagonism was so virulent that a visitor from abroad observed, "Nowhere is the prejudice against race stronger than in Philadelphia, the city of brotherly love."[3] Denied the rights and privileges of citizens, free blacks found their activities everywhere proscribed by law and custom; to find relief, they turned to their family, their kin, and their circle of friends.

So it was for Charlotte even though, as Billington's introduction amply instructs, she came from the upper economic stratum of the free black society. Indeed, she makes clear the importance of personal relationships in the first entry in her diary when she writes, "I feel that keeping a diary will . . . afford me much pleasure in after years, by recalling to my mind the memories of other days, thoughts of much loved friends from whom I may then be separated, with whom I now pass many happy hours, in taking delightful walks, and holding 'sweet converse'. . . ."[4]

With respect to "sweet converse" in her immediate family, Billington, in a footnote, asserts that Charlotte has a brother named "Henry" who lives in New York. In a previous footnote we have been told that Charlotte's "mother died when Charlotte was a small girl."[5] The latter was a fact, but the lengthy obituary in the Colored American, 29 August 1840, at the time of the death of Mary Virginia Forten in her twenty-fourth year, from consumption, makes no mention of any child of hers other than the "infant" brought to her bedside. The census for 1850 for Charlotte Forten's father, Robert Bridges Forten, does not list any brother named Henry. It does list other members of his family, namely, a second wife, also named Mary, and two sons, Wendell P., aged three, and

1001

---

3. A quotation of Alexander Marjoribanks in Ivan D. Steen, "Philadelphia in the 1850's," Pennsylvania History 33 (January 1966):48. See also Elizabeth M. Geffen, "Violence in Philadelphia in the 1840's and 1850's," Pennsylvania History 36 (July 1969):381–410.

4. Forten Journal, p. 42.

5. Footnote 19, Forten Journal, p. 263. For the most part, Charlotte used initial caps of names to designate people in her diaries. Billington supplied identification; footnote 65, Forten Journal, p. 252.

Edmund Q., one. Charlotte is listed as eleven, although by her count she was thirteen.[6]

Two other persons are listed as living in the Robert Bridges Forten household in Philadelphia: Thomas Forten, Robert's thirty-year-old brother, and Mary Lanigan, eleven. Robert Bridges Forten and Thomas Willing Forten had two other brothers, William Deas Forten and James Forten, Jr. These four brothers had four sisters, Margaretta, Sarah, Harriet, and Mary Isabella.[7] By 1850 when their mother, also named Charlotte and aged fifty-five, was alive (their father, wealthy sailmaker James Forten having died 24 February 1842 at age seventy-five), it is certain that three of the children remained unmarried and without issue: Thomas, William, and Margaretta.

That James is married with at least a son is inferred through the entry in Charlotte's diary relating to "*Cousin* James F." (italics mine), not "Uncle."[8] Sarah and Harriet married brothers: Joseph and Robert Purvis, the wealthy, transplanted South Carolinians. While the date of Sarah's wedding is unknown, Harriet was wed on Tuesday, 13 September 1831, Bishop Onderdonk officiating. According to the *Liberator*, Harriet and Robert Purvis first lived at 11 Jefferson Row, Lombard Street,[9] Philadelphia, before moving to Byberry (Bybury), the township fifteen miles away. Here, in 1850, the census shows Robert, thirty-nine, and Harriet, forty, to be the parents of six children: William P., seventeen; Harriett, eleven; Charles Burleigh, nine; Henry W., six; Grinnel (?), four; and Georgiana, one. A seventh and eldest child, Robert Purvis, Jr., whose death is noted in Charlotte's diary, does not appear in the listing.[10] For the same year, 1850, in Bensalem, Bucks County, Pennsylvania, the listing

1002

6. Manuscript Returns of the Seventh Census of the United States (1850), Population Schedule, Record Group 29, Microfilm Pub. 432, National Archives, Washington, D.C. The reels consulted for this paper, by state, are the following: Massachusetts: 312, 325; New York: 537; Pennsylvania: 759, 815, 817, and 824.

7. Esther M. Douty, *Forten The Sailmaker: Pioneer Champion of Negro Rights* (Chicago: Rand McNally & Company, 1968), p. 115. Douty states that the birthdates of all eight children are not known, but lists their names. Activities of seven are to be found in the literature, but not of Mary Isabella.

8. Entry for 1 May 1858. This entry is unpublished. All such unpublished entries are hereinafter indicated by an asterisk (*).

9. *Liberator*, 24 September 1831; 23 March 1833.

10. Entry for 22 June 1862, *Forten Journal*, p. 132. An eighth child was born later. See Charles B. Purvis's biography in *Men of Mark: Eminent, Progressive and Rising*, by Rev. William J. Simmons, D.D. (New York: Arno Press, 1968), p. 690.

shows that Joseph Purvis, thirty-eight and Sarah, thirty-six, were the parents of eight children: Joseph, Jr., eleven; James, ten; William, eight; Sarah, seven; Emily, five; Alfred, four; Harriett, two; and Alexander, five months. While Billington, in his introduction, gives an account of Robert Purvis, Sr., he never mentions Joseph Purvis, Sr., whose death is noted in the diary.[11]

Charlotte Forten was named for her grandmother, who in 1850 lived with her daughter, Margaretta, and son, William, in the family home at 92 Lombard Street, Philadelphia. Charlotte felt closest to her and her Aunt Margaret, and never more so than in the fall of 1855 when her father, Robert Bridges Forten, moved with his new wife and their children to Canada. A talented, sensitive, mercurial man, he had alienated his daughter. In an entry of 21 February 1856* Charlotte writes, "Only one letter this long winter! It worries and grieves me." On 23 July 1857* she continues in this vein: "Had a long talk with grandmother about father. His behavior is very unaccountable;—very saddening to me." Not long after that she has cause to write, ". . . I too have known but little of a father's love. It is hard for me to bear. To thee alone, my journal can I say with tears how very *hard* it is."[12]

We must be aware of how deeply Charlotte felt the inattention of her father. It was one of twin streams of disturbance that replenished the other. In her mother's obituary, cited earlier, headlined "The Triumphant End of Mrs. Mary Virginia Forten (signed by D.A.P.),"[13] which took up a full column of the paper, we learn that at the hour of Charlotte's mother's death, her husband, Robert Bridges Forten, her younger sister, two of her husband's sisters, her father-in-law, and two friends (husband and wife) were in attendance. "They brought her infant to the bed, which caused her to say, I have kissed my babe, put her away, the Lord will have mercy on her. He has promised to be a friend to the

11. Entry for 24 January 1857.* For information about Joseph Purvis, refer to William Whipper's letter in *The Underground Railroad* by William Still (Philadelphia: Porter and Coates, 1872), pp. 738-39; Martin Robison Delany, *The Condition, Elevation, Emigration, and Destiny of the Colored People of the United States: Politically Considered* (Philadelphia, 1852), p. 146.

12. Entry for 21 August 1857.*

13. Daniel Alexander Payne was a long-time family friend of the Fortens. As Senior Bishop of the African Methodist Church, later president of Wilberforce University, he wrote under his initials for the *Anglo-African Magazine*. He also was editor of the *Christian Recorder* to which Charlotte Forten sent her poetry on 16 May 1858,* and in return for which on 20 May 1858* she received a dollar in payment.

orphan and the fatherless children." What, if anything, Charlotte recollected of that intense event we cannot say, but a reader of her diaries will notice how often death is part of the day's entry. During the Salem-Philadelphia years (1854–1862) a dozen deaths, at least, are despaired of: Albert, Joseph, Mr. Smith, Mrs. Remond, Hugh Miller, Maria Brown, Lizzie Swan, Mr. Chew, Cousin William, Mr. Putnam, Mr. Hovey, and Cousin Robert.[14]

It is her mother's death, however, that surfaces repeatedly in Charlotte's writing. Accented to some degree because she is without any representation of her—sketch, painting, daguerreotype—Charlotte, nearly twenty-one, writes, "My mother! my loved lost mother! Thou are hovering near me now! Oh! bless and lead aright thy erring child, and let it not be long ere thou claimest her again for thine own! For I am very weary. I *long* for thee, my mother. Oh, take me, take me to thy arms, there to rest forever!"[15] Her death wish is the other stream of stress that affects her, underlying her friendships, her admirations. Bereft and keenly missing both a mother's and a father's care, she feels the lack all the more as she observes the large and loving families of her aunts Sarah and Harriet.

When Forten begins keeping a record of her life in Salem, Massachusetts, she is boarding in the home of Charles Lenox Remond, 9 Dean Street. This household, as Billington tells us, consists of Remond, his wife, their daughter Sarah, and his sister, Sarah Parker Remond.[16] However, Charles Lenox Remond is not the father of a girl named Sarah, nor does his sister, Sarah, live with them. The censuses for 1850 and 1860[17] show not only that Sarah Parker Remond lived at home with their father, John Remond, 5 Higginson Square, but that in August 1850 Charles, unmarried, also lived with them. Further, the *Salem Directories*, listing both father and son for 1842 through 1850, show that when John Remond changed residences, Charles Lenox Remond moved with his father, John, to the new address. Nor is there evidence that Charles

14. Entries for 20 June 1854*; 11 July 1854*; 25 May 1855*; 15 August 1856*; 16 January 1857*; 4 February 1857*; 11 April 1857*; 14 June 1857*; 1 September 1857*; 30 January 1859*; 7 May 1859*; and 22 June 1862, *Forten Journal*, p. 132.

15. Entries for 15 April 1858, *Forten Journal*, p. 118; 18 June 1858.*

16. Footnote 13, *Forten Journal*, p. 235; footnote 64, *Forten Journal*, p. 252.

17. Manuscript Returns of the Eighth Census of the United States (1860), Population Schedules, Record Group 29, Microfilm Pub. 653, Washington, D.C. The reels consulted for this paper, by state, are the following: Massachusetts: 497, 527; Rhode Island: 1204.

Lenox Remond ever married before 1850 or had any wife other than the woman we meet in Charlotte's diary.[18] Charles Lenox Remond and his wife had not been married long enough to have a daughter old enough to play the piano for Charlotte or for Charlotte to have given her a lesson in French.[19]

Since in the Remond household Sarah is neither daughter nor sister, we must look more deeply. When Charlotte writes of the illness and death of Mrs. Remond, Billington identifies her only as Amy Matilda Williams, the daughter of Rev. Peter Williams of New York.[20] In so doing, he neglects the opportunity to note that the Reverend Mr. Williams, an early activist in the National Negro Convention Movement,[21] was the first rector of St. Philips, the first and therefore the oldest black Episcopal church in the United States. Amy Matilda was the Reverend Mr. Williams's only child,[22] and before she married Charles Lenox Remond, she had married Joseph Cassey, a wealthy Philadelphia wig manufacturer, who died in January 1848 aged fifty-nine. As Cassey's widow, she is listed in the 1850 census along with their five children: Alfred, twenty-one, lawyer; Peter, nineteen, dentist; Sarah, seventeen; Henry, ten; and Francis, six. At this time, she lived on Lombard Street—no. 113 —a few houses up from the James Forten, Sr. family home.[23]

Joseph Cassey had been an early and vigorous supporter of black hopes and aspirations. A member of the Provisional Committee for the first and second National Negro Convention, along with Robert Douglass,

18. On 5 July 1858, in Newton, Massachusetts, Charles Lenox Remond married Elizabeth Magee. Charlotte, who knew Elizabeth well, did not look with favor on the wedding. By 1870 the Remonds were parents of three children: Amy M., eleven; Charles L., Jr., nine; and Ernest A., four months. Remond died on 21 December 1873. See *Liberator*, 16 July 1858; entry for 14 July 1858,* Manuscript Returns of the Ninth Census of the United States (1870), Population Schedules, Record Group 29, Microfilm Pub. 593, Washington, D.C., Reel 632; the *New York Times*, 26 December 1873; *Wakefield Citizen & Banner*, 27 December 1873.

19. Entries for 26 May 1854*; 9 April 1857, *Forten Journal*, p. 96.

20. Footnote 10, *Forten Journal*, p. 248.

21. Howard Holman Bell, ed., *Minutes of the Proceedings of the National Negro Conventions* (New York: Arno Press, 1969) (1831), p. 7.

22. Rev. J. B. Wakely, *Lost Chapters Recovered from the Early History of American Methodism* (New York: Carlton & Porter, 1858), p. 447; Sarah Williams, the Reverend Mr. Williams's widow and Amy Matilda's mother, appears in Charlotte's diaries briefly at the time of the final illness and death of Amy Matilda. The census of 1850 discloses that, in New York, Sarah and her husband's adopted sister, Mary, were living in the household of Dr. James McCune Smith. See entry for 19 July 1856.*

23. *Liberator*, 28 January 1848; *Philadelphia Directory* (1850), p. 65.

who authored a poem to Amy Matilda on her death, Cassey had been an early admirer of Garrison as well as the first agent for the *Liberator* in Philadelphia. Like her husband and her father, Amy Matilda Cassey was an activist, and her name can be found appended to a report of the Philadelphia Anti-Slavery Society of its Eleventh Annual Fair.[24]

Knowing the Fortens and the Casseys had lived so close to each other —and they had lived so before 1850[25]—it becomes clear why Robert Bridges Forten would permit his sixteen-year-old daughter to go from Warminster, Bucks County, Pennsylvania, to live with Amy Matilda Cassey Remond in Salem, Massachusetts. When we consider, moreover, that Charles Lenox Remond had been known to both families since 1834, when he, too, had become involved in the National Negro Conventions, it is clear why Billington should have paid more attention to passages about "family affairs" that he deleted. With the exception of Alfred Cassey, who remained in Philadelphia,[26] and Peter Cassey, who went to California,[27] all the other Cassey children moved with their mother to Salem. All turn up in Charlotte's diary. Much of her "sweet converse" is with them.

The "Sarah" that Billington misidentifies is Sarah Cassey. And he made more errors. The entry for 17 December 1854 reads, "This evening Sarah's husband arrived from California. . . ." Billington has previously identified this "Sarah" as Helen S. Putnam, the daughter of Caroline E. Putnam, whose marriage to Jacob D. Gilliard of Baltimore is celebrated early in Charlotte's diary.[28] The "Sarah" the entry refers to is Sarah Cassey Smith. Charlotte notes Smith's death at twenty-six in the entry of Friday 25 May 1855,*[29] and in the next published *Salem City Directory* under her married name, Sarah Smith, she can be found listed at 9 Dean Street, the address of Charles Lenox Remond.[30]

24. Bell, *National Negro Conventions* (1831), p. 7, and (1832), p. 25; *Liberator*, 26 September 1856; 28 January 1848; 29 January 1847.

25. Entry 7 July 1858.*

26. Bell, *National Negro Conventions* (1834), p. 8; (1855), p. 7.

27. Entry for 14 November 1856.* Peter Williams Cassey became an Episcopal pastor. In San Jose he established a boarding school. Additional information about his activities and letters by him can be found in the *Elevator*, the weekly newspaper published in San Francisco every Friday by Philip A. Bell, commencing 18 April 1865.

28. Entry for 1 June 1854, *Forten Journal*, p. 46; footnotes 18, 58, 50, *Forten Journal*, pp. 236, 240, and 245.

29. See also *Liberator*, 15 June 1855.

30. On 28 February 1861 she married Dr. Samuel C. Watson of Chatham, Canada.

With respect to the two remaining Cassey children, we learn that Francis, or Frank as Charlotte calls him, is enrolled in school at Hopedale, Milford, Massachusetts.[31] The Hopedale Community, the first of the Utopian enterprises, was founded by Adin Ballou and was originally called Fraternal Community No. 1. Formed at Mendon, Massachusetts, 28 January 1841, the community did not begin operations until April 1842 and by 1855 had a juvenile and collegiate Home School for both sexes.[32] Henry, the other Cassey boy, remained at home. Of a typical evening spent with the Cassey children, Charlotte writes, "Afterwards Sarah read aloud and Henry amused us with enigmas and conundrums. . . ."[33]

All this changed with the death of their mother, Amy Matilda Cassey Remond. The Casseys moved and Charlotte went with them. Her entry for Saturday, 12 December 1857, reads, "This eve. thoroughly tired bade the old house good-bye. . . . S[arah] and I are established at Mrs. P[utnam]." Billington explains: "The change in residence to the home of Mrs. Caroline E. Putnam was made necessary by Mr. Remond's growing unpleasantness." Previously Billington had identified Caroline E. Putnam as a "close friend of Miss Forten."[34] She was, but she also was the sister of Charles Lenox Remond, who had, besides Caroline E. and Sarah P., four other sisters: Cecelia, Susan H., Maritche J. (the correct spelling of the name is not known), and Nancy. Charles Lenox Remond also had a brother, John Lenox. These eight children of Nancy and John Remond, like the Forten eight sons and daughters, were the offspring of strong and successful parents.[35]

Nancy Remond was the daughter of Cornelius Lenox, Revolutionary War soldier, said to be a mulatto, and his wife, Susannah Toney. They were married 4 April 1780 and in 1783 settled near Watertown on a

1007

Watson had studied at Phillips Academy in Andover, Massachusetts, and later pursued medical studies at Michigan University before taking his degree from Western College of Homeopathy in Cleveland. See his biography in Simmons, *Men of Mark*, pp. 860–65. *Liberator*, 8 March 1861.

31. Entry for 19 November 1856.*

32. *Milford Directory* (1856), p. 122–23; *Liberator*, 26 December 1851 and 16 November 1855.

33. Entry for 12 January 1855.*

34. Footnote 30, *Forten Journal*, p. 256; footnote 58, *Forten Journal*, p. 240.

35. Francis Jackson, *History of the Early Settlement of Newton, County of Middlesex, Massachusetts: From 1639 to 1800 with a Genealogical Register of its Inhabitants, prior to 1800* (Boston: Printed by Stacy and Richardson, 1854), p. 362.

bank of the Charles River.[36] This area became the city of Newton, but on 16 April 1849 the part wherein the Lenoxes resided was annexed to Waltham. By 1850 only two of the grandchildren, John M., twenty-five, barber, and Cornelius, twenty-three, barber, still lived there, the only two blacks in the town.[37]

John Remond was a singular black man. He debarked at Beverly, Massachusetts, from Curaçao, aged ten, on 11 September 1798 from the brig *Six Brothers*, captained by John Needham.[38] While it is not clear what happened to Remond then and for some few years after, it is certain that by 2 May 1811 his career in Salem was that of hairdresser. It was on that date, through the personal appearances and sworn testimonies of Samuel Tucker and George Ingersoll, that he was admitted to citizenship in the United States.[39] Although through naturalization John Remond had achieved what the free black population exemplified by the Fortens desired, his good fortune did not stop him from identifying with the slave and his free brother. When *Freedom's Journal*, the first black newspaper in America, was published in New York City on 16 March 1827, John Remond was one of its authorized agents. Although his name was incorrectly spelled "Raymond" in the first issue, by the fifth issue, 13 May 1827, it had been corrected.

It was Nancy Remond who did the cooking for their catering ser-

1008

36. Secretary of the Commonwealth, *Massachusetts Soldiers and Sailors in the War of the Revolution: A Compilation from the Archives*, 17 vols. (Boston: Wright & Potter Printing Co., 1896), 9:680, 931; 10:43, 44. Miriam L. Usrey is incorrect in her attributions of the parentage of Nancy Remond. The distinction between John Lenox and John M. Lenox is clarified in this paper. *Essex Institute Historical Collections* 106 (April 1970):112–25. *A Volume of Records Relating to the Early History of Boston Containing Boston Marriages from 1752–1809* (Boston: Municipal Printing Office, 1903), p. 408. S. F. Smith, D.D., *History of Newton, Massachusetts: Town and City from Its Earliest Settlement to the Present Time, 1630–1880* (Boston: The American Logotype Company, 1880), p. 145.

37. Kevin H. White, *Historical Data Relating to Counties, Cities and Towns in Massachusetts* (Boston: Commonwealth of Massachusetts, 1966), p. 49.

38. Record Group 36, Preliminary Inventory of Records of the Bureau of Customs, NC 154, Entry Number 442: Report of Alien Passengers. 1798–1800. Note: "Passenger Arrivals at Salem and Beverly, Mass., 1798–1800" by Mrs. Georgie A. Hill, New England Historical and Genealogical Society, 106 (July 1952):203–9, incorrectly lists the captain as "Newham" and the second passenger as "Dongal" instead of "Dougal." The passenger listed as "Vonreman" is John Remond. See *Black Names in America: Origins and Usage Collected by Newbell Niles Puckett*, and Murray Heller, ed. (Boston: G. K. Hall & Co., 1975), pp. 1–8.

39. Record Group 59, General Records of the Department of State, Supreme Judicial Court of Essex County, Salem, Mass., vol. E, p. 365½.

vices and was long remembered as an excellent cook.[40] Nancy and John Remond catered the affairs at Hamilton Hall, that edifice erected by Salem's Federalist maritime wealthy, and by their catering established their niche in Salem's scheme of things. In time John Remond became an even more successful wine merchant and victualler. Like James Forten, he, too, maintained a deep interest in the causes of his people. In 1833 he became a life member of the New-England Anti-Slavery Society,[41] and in 1853 he applied for a passport at a time when secretaries of state were disinclined to validate a black man's citizenship. On 1 February 1854, not 1 January as incorrectly given by William C. Nell in *The Colored Patriots of the American Revolution*, Passport Application 3164 was approved. Remond had proposed to "go by the way of New Orleans to Cuba to Curraco and probably return home by way of France or England."[42] That was four months before Charlotte began her diary. There is no evidence in it, or in other sources, that such a journey was made.

1009

Of the Remond children, two remained home and never married. One was Susan H., the third oldest child, who was thirty-six in 1850. Little is known about her, although her name is listed as a contributor to the Massachusetts Anti-Slavery Society. Because her given name is not to be found in the diary, it is impossible to say whether she is ever referred to when Charlotte writes of "Miss Remond." The other daughter who remained at home, Maritche Juan, thirty-two, is mentioned once. But it is reasonable to assume that Charlotte saw Maritche Juan often, because Maritche was in the hairweaving business with her younger sister, Cecelia Babcock, and when Charlotte writes of working in Mrs. Babcock's store, it may be inferred that Maritche Juan was sometimes present.[43]

Cecelia Remond was married to James Babcock of Kingston, Rhode Island, on Sunday evening, 10 December 1843.[44] In 1850 they were aged twenty-six and twenty-eight and the parents of three girls: Ger-

40. M. C. D. Silsbee, *A Half Century in Salem* (Boston: Houghton, Mifflin and Company, 1887), p. 94.

41. *Massachusetts Anti-Slavery Society Annual Reports* (Westport, Conn.: Negro Universities Press, 1970) (1834), p. 49.

42. Record Group 59, General Records of the Department of State, Passport Application Letter to Charles W. Upham dated 28 January 1854.

43. *Liberator*, 15 March 1850; *Salem Directory* (1851), p. 127.

44. *Liberator*, 15 December 1843.

trude, Agnes, and Cecelia. Charles Babcock, twenty-three, a brother of James, lived with them. Both brothers were hairdressers. When Charlotte writes, "Spent the evening very pleasantly at Mrs. Babcock's," we are meeting another segment of that small society with whom she had "sweet converse."[45]

This brings us to Caroline Remond Putnam, who was twenty-four in 1850, her birthday anniversary falling on 26 February. Billington correctly noted that in the beginning of that year Caroline and Cecelia had been partners in the hairweaving business. Why Caroline established herself on her own in the same business is unknown. However, these two establishments, particularly Mrs. Putnam's, became a source of extra income for Charlotte.[46]

1010

Caroline Remond Putnam was not married to Israel Putnam as Billington informs us.[47] Joseph H. Putnam was Caroline's husband, and Charlotte notes his death in her entry for 10 January 1859.* William C. Nell, longtime friend of the Fortens, Remonds, and Putnams, wrote Putnam's obituary for the Liberator 28 January 1859 and tells us that Joseph H. Putnam at one time had served in Boston, where he was born, as "assistant School Teacher." Further, Nell writes that Putnam, two years before, had returned from a "successful business sojourn" in Australia. An entry in Charlotte's diary for 3 July 1856* does, indeed, document that return but reveals nothing more.

In 1854 Forten noted on 17 September, "I was much interested in a conversation between Mrs. P[utnam] and her grandson—little Eddie, about slavery and prejudice."[48] Billington did not identify little Eddie's parents, leaving the false impression that he is the son of Helen S. Putnam, previously identified as Caroline's daughter. Caroline and Joseph are the parents of Edmund Q. Putnam, three years old in 1850. The birth of his little sister—Louisa Victoria—Charlotte noted on 3 August 1858. Louisa Victoria is the "little girl" mentioned as "dangerously ill"

45. Gertrude died 22 August 1863. See Liberator, 18 September 1863. James and Charles were raised by their oldest sister, Sarah, after their mother Phebe died, along with an older brother, Henry, and younger sister, Ruth. Henry married Freelove Bowers on 14 May 1834; Sarah died 2 April 1851, and Ruth died, at age twenty-nine, on 21 June 1860. Liberator, 24 May 1834; 18 April 1851; 29 July 1860. Entry for 28 May 1854.*

46. Entries 26 February 1855*; 25 April 1857, Forten Journal, p. 97.

47. Footnote 60, Forten Journal, p. 259.

48. Entry for 17 September 1854, Forten Journal, p. 59.

in Charlotte's entry of 7 May 1859. One week later Louisa Victoria died.[49]

John Lenox Remond, Charles Lenox Remond's brother, is never mentioned in the diaries. On 2 February 1843 he married Ruth B. Rice at Newport, Rhode Island.[50] By 1850 they had one daughter, Sarah, six years old. Ruth Rice had three sisters, Susan C., Hannah, and Sarah.[51] Susan visited Salem on 11 March 1857,* Charlotte noted, for it touched off a round of celebrations. By August, however, Ruth and her daughter had returned to Newport, to the home of her father, Isaac Rice. It was in Newport that Charlotte encountered the daughters and their father and spent time with them.[52]

The Remond daughter of next concern is Nancy, the first and therefore the oldest of John and Nancy Remond's children. On 19 March 1834 she married James L. Shearman.[53] By 1850 they had nine children: Ellen E., sixteen; John, fourteen; Charles, twelve; William, nine; Sarah, eight; Remond, six; Caroline, five; George, two; and Cecelia, one month. By 1860 there was an additional child, Elizabeth D. James Shearman was an oyster dealer, and his brother George, who lived with the Shearmans, was also. According to the *Salem Directory* for 1850, the family lived in Hamilton Hall. Although she never comments on the Hall, Charlotte visited them often. It was in their company she learned to play whist, a card game seldom played in the household where Charlotte lived, as Mrs. Remond had an aversion to such games. It was either James or George who provided her with the ticket to the Thalberg concert, and it was Ellen, the eldest daughter, with whom Charlotte became close.[54]

The eighth and last Remond is Sarah Parker Remond. Billington's misidentification of Sarah in the Charles Lenox Remond household has supported the published assertion that she and Charlotte were close. Charlotte wrote, "Sometimes she talks to me earnestly and as if she thought I understood what she was saying; but this is not often. Generally, it seems to me as if she treats me as if I were a silly child, with care-

1011

49. Entry for 7 May 1859, *Forten Journal*, p. 129; *Liberator*, 20 May 1859.
50. *Liberator*, 24 February 1843.
51. Sarah married George Pell 25 November 1852. Susan married Silas Dickerson 12 July 1860. *Liberator*, 3 December 1852 and 20 July 1860.
52. Entry for 2 August 1857.*
53. *Liberator*, 22 March 1834.
54. Entries for 13 March 1856*; 9 January 1857, *Forten Journal*, p. 88.

less indifference. . . . How often do I wish that I had a sister my superior, yet who, despite her superiority and my unworthiness, would truly and fondly love me."[55]

Charlotte was just shy of eighteen when she wrote those words, still hungering for the affection the death of her mother and the remarriage of her father had denied her. That she admired Sarah Parker Remond, thirteen years her senior,[56] is understandable—Charlotte, herself, would have liked to have been an antislavery lecturer—but from another entry it is more likely that Sarah Parker Remond saw Charlotte primarily in the role of an adoring fan. Charlotte writes, for example, "Miss R. spent the night here. As usual we lay awake till morning talking about her lecturing experiences."[57]

1012

55. Dorothy B. Porter, "Sarah Parker Remond, Abolitionist and Physician," *Journal of Negro History* 20 (July 1935):287–93. Entry for 9 September 1855.*

56. According to the sketch in *Notable American Women* by Dorothy B. Porter, Edward T. James, and Janet Wilson James, eds. (Cambridge, Mass.: Harvard University Press, 1971), vol. 3, pp. 136–38, Sarah Parker Remond was born in 1826, thus making her thirty-one years old in 1857. That age agrees with her sworn passport application of 10 September 1858, when she declared herself to be thirty-two. However, the census of 1850 gives her age as twenty-six, making the year of her birth 1824. That same census describes Caroline, her sister, as being twenty-four, making Caroline's natal year 1826. Caroline, on 30 April 1865, accompanied by her son, applied for a passport stating her age as thirty-nine. This, again, would make the year of her birth 1826. Nowhere in the literature is there any mention of Sarah Parker and Caroline as being twins.

57. Entries of 28 July 1854, *Forten Journal*, p. 55; 9 April 1857.* If any of these experiences foreshadowed Sarah Parker Remond's becoming a physician (see footnote 95) it is not to be found in Forten's diary, published or unpublished. Although this assumption has been accepted and repeated (see Ruth Bogin, "Sarah Parker Remond: Black Abolitionist from Salem," *Essex Institute Historical Collections* 110 [April 1974]:120–50), the matter is not settled. In the *Elevator*, 20 August 1869, is found an item that asserts that Sarah Parker Remond "has been admitted as a practitioner of mid-wifery in Florence, Italy. . . ." The column that contains it, headed "Personals," habitually contained information that came to the editor as a result of his many and long associations on the east coast. Bell did not move to California until 1857. Before then he had been an energetic abolitionist, certifiably from 1831 when, with James Forten, Joseph Cassey, Charles Lenox Remond, William Nell, and George Downing, he was associated with the National Negro Conventions.

According to the article on Sarah Parker Remond in *Notable American Women*, it is stated that in 1866 Sarah Parker Remond went to Florence and was a student until 1868. Regulations for medical education as detailed by Ruggero Bonghi in his book *La facolta di medicina e il suo regalamento* (Florence, 1876) does not support the likelihood of Sarah's completing her medical education in those two years. It is certain, however, that by 9 July 1870, the date of the ninth census, Sarah declared herself to be a "physician." This declaration is to be seen in the context of the woman's movement which argued for more women to move into the medical field. In the *Journal* Charlotte repeatedly refers to

We have been dealing with Billington's errors for the years 1854 through 1862 concerning Charlotte Forten's family in Philadelphia and the Remond household in Salem. Now we turn to his misidentifications and omissions among her associates.

Previously mentioned is Billington's observation that life in the home of Charles Lenox Remond, after the death of his wife, Amy Matilda, became so unpleasant for Charlotte that she moved into the home of Mrs. Caroline Putnam. He also stated that Sarah Parker Remond made the same move.[58] If Billington had been correct, Charlotte's move with Sarah would seem simple enough—one sister (Sarah) moving to the home of another (Caroline) and bringing a friend.

It was not Sarah Parker Remond but Sarah Cassey Smith and brother, Henry, who moved with Charlotte into the house where Caroline E. Putnam lived with her husband, Joseph H. Putnam, and son, Edmund. That house, however, was the home of Jane and George Putnam, the parents of Caroline Remond's husband.[59] In 1846 Jane and George Putnam moved to Salem from Boston, where he had established himself as a successful hairdresser in 1826.[60] The 1850 census shows that besides Joseph H. Putnam, they were the parents of four girls: Helen, twenty; Georgianna, eighteen; Jane M., sixteen; and Adelaide, fourteen. Shortly after arriving in Salem, and before the census, their young son, George, aged three years, had died, and another son, Wendell Phillips Nell, born in Salem, had died at the age of ten months.[61] Jane Putnam is the "Mrs. Putnam" that is referred to when we read "Mrs. P[utnam] and her daughters" and "Mrs. P[utnam] and her grandson."[62] Those entries reveal why the move was so easily made by Charlotte: Jane Putnam,

1013

Louise Matilda Towne, who established the school where Charlotte taught in South Carolina, as "physician," although Towne's medical education was unorthodox. To quote Martin Kaufman, "By the mid-nineteenth century the practice of medicine was open to anyone who considered himself qualified, including outright quacks and frauds." *Homeopathy in America: The Rise and Fall of a Medical Heresy* (Baltimore: The Johns Hopkins Press, 1971), p. 23.

58. Footnote 30, *Forten Journal*, p. 256.

59. After the death of her husband, Caroline Remond moved back to live with her father at 5 Higginson Square. Only after 1876 did she move from this address, 1884 being the last time she appears in the *Salem Directory*. Thereafter she went to Italy to live with her sister, Sarah.

60. *Boston Directory* (1826–1850), passim.

61. *Liberator*, 11 December 1846; 18 June 1847.

62. Entries for 5 September 1854; 17 September 1854, *Forten Journal*, pp. 58–59.

like Amy Matilda Remond, had become surrogate for the dead mother whose love she longed for, and Mrs. Putnam's daughters were the sisters she did not have.

At the outset of the diary, 1 June 1854, Forten writes of the marriage of Helen Putnam to Jacob D. Gilliard of Baltimore. We hear next to nothing of him thereafter in the *Journal*. He is not a factor, but in terms of the relative paucity of that circle of friends which Charlotte had, it should have been noted as, indeed, she noted, that Gilliard died three years later. A ship's barber, he was lost at sea when, on 8 September 1857, the *Central America* sank off the east coast carrying with it 566 passengers and crew.[63]

Nothing about Georgianna Putnam is mentioned in the *Journal*. In an entry of 4 September 1857,* we read of Charlotte's having tea with Georgianna. Unexpectedly, in another unpublished entry written on New Year's evening, we read of Charlotte's writing to her. Had Billington clarified the Putnam family relationships, he would have discovered that Georgianna had left Salem to go to New York, and settling in Brooklyn as a teacher, progressed to become a principal of a grammar school. Georgianna died in 1914 in Worcester, Massachusetts, the city to which her parents had moved by 1860 with daughters Adelaide and Helen.[64]

Another person to be reckoned with is "Annie," whom Billington describes as "a sister of Miss Forten's father." Charlotte declares not once but twice that Annie is her *mother's* sister. It must also be noted that in the obituary of Charlotte's mother, previously discussed, the sister's name is given as "Anna."[65]

Not only because of her special relation and repeated mention in the diaries, Annie takes on additional significance when the reader realizes she is the sister-in-law of Mary F. Webb, the "Black Siddons," as sometimes Mrs. Webb was called. Annie is married to a "Mr. Webb," as Charlotte identifies him, and they are the parents of two small girls. In 1850, Mary, twenty-one, is married to Francis B. Webb, twenty-two, Annie's husband's brother. It is Mary who brings news of Annie to

63. Footnote 18, *Forten Journal*, p. 236; entry for 17 September 1857*; *The New York Times*, 18 September 1857; 19 September 1857; 21 September 1857; and 26 September 1857.

64. Hallie Q. Brown, ed., *Homespun Heroines and Other Women of Distinction* (Xenia, Ohio: Aldine Publishing Company, 1926), pp. 135–40.

65. Footnote 10, *Forten Journal*, p. 267; entries for 17 July 1857*; 8 May 1859.*

Charlotte, who had been rather caustic about Mary Webb's performance when first she heard her. Charlotte's impression changed, to some degree, because of Webb's improvement with experience and success abroad. It may also have changed because Charlotte had adjusted to an "outsider" marrying a home-town boy. The Webbs were Philadelphians, and Mary, the daughter of an escaped slave, came from Massachusetts.[66]

The last persons we speak of were omitted by Billington from the *Journal* but were mentioned directly or indirectly in Charlotte's diary. They are the children of Nancy Lenox Remond's brother, John Lenox.[67] Specifically, there is Charles, with whom Charlotte goes fishing, and a "Miss L.," specifically identified as a cousin, who accompanies Charlotte on her first horseback ride. Another nephew, mentioned earlier, is John M., who lives in Waltham (Watertown) where Charlotte visits.[68]

When Dr. Billington edited *The Journal of Charlotte L. Forten,* so anxious was he to trace her heritage and her contacts with the leading abolitionists of the day that he ignored her intimate world. He distorted that world to such a degree that one of his reviewers wrote, "The racial situation so dominated the mind of Charlotte Forten that she found little time to record other situations in her diary."[69] Another reviewer felt that readers would find Forten was "hypersensitive—almost to the point of being psychotic."[70]

It is probably more accurate to say, as Leonard P. Curry has written, that ". . . not one sentient black in antebellum America could escape the knowledge that he lived in a white land under a white government that administered white law for the benefit of a white population, and that in the eyes of all these he was a being inferior to all but the most base and degraded of the whites, and that no amount of conformity to white

66. *Liberator*, 11 May 1855; entries of 18 March 1858*; 9 August 1858*; 23 March 1858*; 26 March 1858*; 18 March 1858.* Entry for 19 November 1855, *Forten Journal*, p. 76. Entry for 22 March 1858*; *Liberator*, 22 August 1856.

67. Jackson, *History of Newton*, p. 362.

68. Entries for 20 August 1856*; 28 August 1854.* John M. Lenox married Louisa Caesar on 22 September 1851. She died 10 May 1852. He then married Lucretia Hilton. Their son, at age two months and thirteen days, died 13 March 1860. *Liberator*, 26 September 1851; *Liberator*, 14 May 1852; and *Liberator*, 16 March 1860.

69. Robert E. Riegel, "Book Review," *Social Education* 18 (1954):743–44.

70. Edwin Adams Davis, "Book Review," *Mississippi Valley Historical Review* 40 (December 1953):743–44.

mores and customs or acceptance of white values could change that reality."[71]

The hostility pervasive in Philadelphia was felt less in Salem. While not without racial antagonism, New England nourished and enriched Charlotte Forten's life as it did the lives of those within the small circle of her society. In their company she spent her free hours—in their homes and stores, at antislavery meetings, and at antislavery fairs. Not even when she wrote in her diary is there any evidence she was alone. To have edited those diaries as if she were a solitary person reflects a failure to perceive the confinement blacks—slave and free—everywhere felt.

1016

71. Leonard P. Curry, *The Free Black in Urban America, 1800–1850: The Shadow of the Dream* (Chicago: The University of Chicago Press, 1981), p. 940.

THE ROLE OF THE BLACK MAMMY IN THE PLANTATION HOUSEHOLD

The present generation of Americans, both white and Negro, are acquainted with the "Black Mammy" as she has been handed down in tradition. They are acquainted with her as she is represented on the legitimate stage, in the moving pictures, and in fiction. Newspapers and periodicals from time to time print stories about this character, and people living who came under her influence relate their experiences with the "Mammy" to their children, friends, and acquaintances.

Negroes and whites in the South held different attitudes toward what came out of slavery. To the majority of Negroes anything that savored of the period of slavery was objectionable. Even the spirituals once came under the ban. To whites the period of slavery has been sentimentalized and glorified. Because the "Black Mammy" originated in and came out of the period of bondage she is an acceptable symbol to whites and an unacceptable one to Negroes.

Never was this made more evident than it was by the controversy which was kept up for many months through the press by the suggestion made in 1923 by the Daughters of the Confederacy that Congress set aside in the National Capital a site upon which they would erect a monument to the memory of this group of Negro women. The monument proposal was generally opposed by Negroes, who said a better memorial would be to extend the full rights of American citizenship to the descendants of these Mammies."[1] The proposals made by the Negroes included the discontinuation of lynching, the inequality in educa-

---

[1] *Washington Tribune*, Washington, D. C., 2-3-23; *National Baptist Union Review*, Nashville, Tenn., 5-4-23; *Christian Index*, Jackson, Tenn., 2-22-23; *Birmingham Reporter*, Birmingham, Ala., 3-17-23; *New York Age*, New York City, 1-6-23.

Originally published in *Journal of Negro History*, Vol. 23 (July 1938).

tional facilities, all practices of discrimination, the humiliation of Negroes in public conveyances, and the denial to them of the rights of suffrage.

White people of the South generally thought that this memorial was an excellent way to perpetuate what was to them tender memories. Monuments to the old Negro had been erected in the South before[2] and monuments to the "Black Mammy" of the South also had been proposed before;[3] the National Capital had been one of the places proposed by Lucian Lamar Knight in 1910.[4] The bitterness of expression called out by this controversy illustrated the depth of feeling on both sides of the racial lines about this traditional character. So great, however, was the pressure brought to bear against the erection of the monument that the bill was finally killed in the House of Representatives. The purpose of this paper is to go back of the tradition and to show the actual rôle of the "Mammy" in the plantation household of the Old South.

The rôle of the "Mammy" in the plantation household grew out of the rôle of the Negro slaves on the plantation. Negro servants played an important rôle throughout the period of slavery. The washerwoman, the cook, the maid, the seamstress, the butler, the porter, the gardener, and the coachman functioned in the home life of the South. Early in the establishment of the plantation in America they became fixtures in the plantation economy. The work of the plantation called for a division of labor on the basis of work to be done within the house and without. The plantation was the economic unit in the South, and the division of labor there was as important as it is in any industrial plant today. The two main divisions into which slaves were divided were household servants and field hands.

1018

[2] Brewton, Ala., *Standard*, June 10, 1937; F. J. M. Murray, *The Emancipated and Freed in American Sculpture*, p. 129.

[3] Mary Polk Branch, *Memoirs of a Southern Woman Within the Lines*, pp. 46-47.

[4] Lucian Lamar Knight, *Memorials of Dixie-land*, p. 374.

Within the house the division of work to be done was on the basis of duties to be performed. The mistress was the central figure. Her rôle within the house was similar to that of the master without. The supervision of the household servants was her part of the job, and a strenuous job it was.[5]

The "Black Mammy" was a household servant who generally had specific duties to perform. These were mainly connected with the care of the children of the family, thus relieving the mistress of all the drudgery work connected with child care. When these duties were not pressing, which meant that the children were large enough to be able to help take care of themselves, she assisted the mistress with the household tasks. Her sphere of influence widened with the years of her service. She was next to the mistress in authority[6] and "bossed" everyone and everything in the household.[7]

The "Black Mammy" tradition in the Southern household became a plantation tradition, for it arose on the plantation, bloomed when the plantation was in its glory and so took hold of the imagination of the people of the South that the "Black Mammy" eventually entered the homes of the middle class and the poorer farmer. Here she was oftimes the only slave and became the maid of all work, caring for the children, washing, ironing, cooking, cleaning and helping in the fields as well. Eventually she became an imaginary figure created in the minds of those who had never possessed a "Mammy," for in order to be recognized as belonging to the aristocracy of the Old South it was necessary to be able to say that one had been tended by a "Black Mammy" in youth.

In the plantation household the "Black Mammy" was

1019

[5] Belle Kearney, *A Slaveholder's Daughter*, p. 3; Thomas Nelson Page, *Social Life in Old Virginia before the War*, pp. 59-60.

[6] Myrta Lockett Avary, *Dixie after the War*, pp. 196-197; Eliza F. Andrews, *The War-Time Journal of a Georgia Girl*, p. 32.

[7] Lucian Lamar Knight, *Memorials of Dixie-land*, p. 374.

considered as much a part of the family as the blood members were.[8] She occupied a lower status, but was included in the inner circle. She has often been referred to as a "unique type of foster motherhood."[9]

THE "BLACK MAMMY'S" POSITION IN THE HOUSEHOLD

The "Black Mammy" was in intimate contact with the members of the family of her owner and reflected the ideals of the family to which she belonged. Her interests and those of her owner were so inextricably one that she is associated in the public mind more with the members of the white group than with those of her own race. She is referred to as the "Black Mammy," a name probably given to distinguish her from the real mother and also from the "Mammy" of the slave children. Actually, she ranged all the way from black to an indistinguishable white,[10] for household servants were selected for their personal appearance as well as for their general adaptability for the duties to be performed.[11]

What we know of the "Black Mammy" has been recorded mainly by those whom she nursed as children. To the planter class of the Old South we are indebted for an insight into what she meant in Southern society. She was associated with the earliest recollections of the children and sentiments similar to those surrounding "home," "mother," and "country," have been built up around her.

The qualities and characteristics attributed to the "Black Mammy" indicate a first hand and personal knowledge of her, which became standardized and institutionalized by sentiment. The following are examples of the traits which were generally denied to slave women as a group but which were attributed to her. She was considered

[8] Myrta Lockett Avary, *Dixie after the War*, pp. 391-392.
[9] Sally McCarty Pleasants, *Old Virginia Days and Ways*, p. 43.
[10] T. P. O'Connor, *My Beloved South*, p. 6.
[11] F. D. Syrgley, *Seventy Years in Dixie*, pp. 293-294.

self-respecting, independent, loyal, forward, gentle, captious, affectionate, true, strong, just, warm-hearted, compassionate-hearted, fearless, popular, brave, good, pious, quick-witted, capable, thrifty, proud, regal, courageous, superior, skilful, tender, queenly, dignified, neat, quick, tender, competent, possessed with a temper, trustworthy, faithful, patient, tryannical, sensible, discreet, efficient, careful, harsh, devoted, truthful, neither apish nor servile.

In dress and in deportment the "Black Mammy" reflected the status of her owner. Generally she was neat and clean, wearing the type of dress best suited for her duties. When she considered herself "dressed up" she might be seen wearing "a bonnet and silk velvet mantle" which formerly belonged to her mistress,[12] and she might even possess a "Sunday black silk."[13]

Like most slaves the "Black Mammy" was unlettered, but she was intelligent. As among the slaves also, there could be found a mammy here and there who could read and write, having been taught by the young children or some member of the family. But most of her lessons were learned through contact and experience. These brought to her a certain dignity which was noticeable in manner and bearing. The "Black Mammy" of an aristocratic family could readily be distinguished by her air of refinement.

She was a diplomat and knew how to handle delicate situations with such a fine sense of appropriateness that her purpose was usually accomplished. If there was difficulty with the household servants, the "Black Mammy" could generally straighten out the matter. With children, master, mistress and slaves her methods were often equally efficacious. From being a confidential servant she grew into being a kind of prime minister. It was well known that if she espoused a cause and took it to the master it

1021

[12] Sally McCarty Pleasants, *Old Virginia Days and Ways*, p. 128.
[13] Eliza M. Ripley, *Social Life in Old New Orleans*, p. 210.

was sure to be attended to at once, and according to her advice.[14]

When the "Black Mammy" did not stay within the house of her master, sleeping in the room with her master's children, she lived with her husband and children in a cabin, distinguished in some way from those of the other servants either in size or structure.[15] Her home stood near the "big house" where the cabins of the house servants were located, and away from the "quarters" of the other slaves which were some distance from the master's house.[16]

Her work was less strenuous than the physical labor of the other slave women, but her hours were long, and there was little time for leisure. Servants outside of the household were almost always given Sunday as a day of rest, except in the harvest season when crops had to be gathered or in some other emergency, and many had Saturday afternoons off to care for their own needs. It was not until the "Black Mammy" became too old for active duties that she could be said to enjoy any home life of her own. She was too closely bound up with the home life of her master.

She, however, escaped many of the rigors of slavery, for generally she was exempt from sale.[17] It was only through some disaster that she passed into other hands. She and her descendants were kept as far as it was possible in the same family; that is, the sons and daughters of the master and those of the "Black Mammy" continued the relationship begun in the previous generation.[18] The "Black Mammy's" position represented more than the price as a piece of property which she might bring. Old

[14] Susan Dabney Smedes, *A Southern Planter*, p. 38.

[15] Fannie A. Beers, *Memories*, pp. 250-253.

[16] Nicholas Ware Eppes, *The Negro of the Old South*, p. 26; Fannie A. Beers, *Memories*, pp. 250-253; Victoria V. Clayton, *White and Black Under the Old Regime*, p. 23

[17] F. W. Olmsted, *A Journey in the Seaboard Slave States*, p. 58.

[18] *South Carolina Women in the Confederacy*, Vol. II, p. 122; Susan Dabney Smedes, *A Southern Planter*, p. 8.

ties and associations were very often the background of the intimate relations.

The "Black Mammy" was exempt from corporal punishment, and what in another slave might have been considered impertinence was thought of as her privilege. Mrs. Meade in her book, *When I Was a Little Girl,* tells of an overseer who complained to her uncle that the insolence of one of the old women slaves was becoming so unbearable that he needed advice about punishing her. When told that the old woman's name was "Mammy" her uncle replied, "What! What! Why I would as soon think of punishing my own mother! Why man you'd have four of the biggest men in Mississippi down on you if you even dare suggest such a thing, and she knows it! All you can do is to knuckle down to Mammy."[19]

There was a flexibility about the "Black Mammy's" duties that distinguished her from the ordinary nurse or the wet nurse, though she might perform either or both of these functions. In the wealthy households there were assistants to the "Black Mammy" or nurses who were "the children's guardian and companion when they went out for exercises, on visits, or to seek diversion and recreation" and were much younger than the "Mammy" was.

A young woman, however, might become a "Black Mammy" at an early age, even before she married. Mrs. Eppes in her volume, *The Negro of the Old South,* relates how the little slave girl whom the mistress had taken into the house to play with her two small daughters, became at the age of eighteen the "Black Mammy" of the youngest baby who refused her mother's breast, the bottle, and every other effort to feed her. When it began to be feared she would starve to death the young girl "bethought her of a small pitcher belonging to a doll's tea set" and from this the child allowed herself to be fed, and thus a new "Mammy" came into existence.[20]

[19] Anne H. Meade, When I was a Little Girl. Quoted from Dorothy Scarborough, *On Trail of Negro Folk-Songs,* p. 144.

[20] Nicholas Ware Eppes, *The Negro of the Old South,* pp. 77-79.

But the "Black Mammy" was usually of mature years and had established a fine reputation for responsibility and reliability. She is hardly remembered as being young or youthful, but as mature and experienced. She was usually the child of a favorite servant, perhaps of a "Black Mammy" herself, who had entered the house at an early age as playmate for the children, later became the maid and then the "Black Mammy"; or, a playmate for one generation, maid for the next and "Black Mammy" for the third."[21] The "Black Mammy" was at the top of the social hierarchy of slaves and occupied a position to be envied as well as to be striven for.

In the early days when there were no trained nurses these Negro women as practical nurses were of invaluable aid in the sick room. Not only did they nurse the children in their illness, but any other member of the family who became ill. They were in constant attendance and ready to grant any wish that the patient might express. Some of them became famous as nurses and were loaned to other families in cases of severe illness. One of the leading families of the South relates that there was among its members before the Civil War a physician who was noted for his success as an obstetrician, and that he always took the "Black Mammy" with him as an assistant.[22]

When the master and mistress travelled the "Black Mammy" went with them and by her care of the children and her own distinctive manner attracted much attention. Most often her real name was not known, it was a matter of no significance. She was known by all simply as "Mammy."[23]

Upon the death of the master or mistress or before the master remarried the "Black Mammy" might assume the responsibility of the children and the household. Srygley relates that for him a "Black Mammy" was a necessity

[21] Nicholas Ware Eppes, *The Negro of the Old South*, pp. 77-79.

[22] Case related to the writer.

[23] Eliza M. Ripley, *Social Life in Old New Orleans*, p. 210.

as his own mother died not long after his birth. This woman cared for him as a mother would and did not give up her tender care until he was eighteen years old at which time she died.[24]

The "Black Mammy" was always busy in her master's house, and she helped to keep her master's home comfortable and happy.[25] As a housekeeper she was dependable and could be relied upon to care for the supplies and give them out in their proper proportion. The "Black Mammy" filled any gap that occurred in the southern household. If she were needed in the parlor she could fill that place. If the cook "flared up and refused to do her duty in the way in which she was expected the 'Black Mammy' descended into the deserted kitchen.'"[26]

When she grew too old for active service visitors to the plantation came to see the old nurse who had been so active in the life of the family group. In fact, it would have been an insult both to the "Black Mammy" and to the family if they did not pay their respects to her. She was a personage not to be overlooked, however old she might become.[27]

The husband of the "Black Mammy" if he lived on the same plantation might be a person of importance in some capacity, such as butler, the driver, the gardener, a mechanic or a foreman. To his own worth was added the sentiment of good feeling that was attached to the "Black Mammy." The children were also fond of him, and he in turn was never happier than when granting some of their whims or those of the mistress. He was at everybody's service.[28]

If he belonged to another owner on a distant plantation his visits were looked forward to, and he was a wel-

1025

[24] F. D. Syrgley, *Seventy Years in Dixie*, pp. 41-42.

[25] Eliza Ripley, *Social Life in Old New Orleans*, pp. 212-214; T. P. O'Connor, *My Beloved South*, pp. 6-7.

[26] Eliza M. Ripley, *Social Life in Old New Orleans*, pp. 209-210.

[27] Porte Crayon, *Virginia Illustrated*, p. 257.

[28] F. D. Srygley, *Seventy Years in Dixie*, pp. 42-44.

comed visitor. Restrictions concerning visits were set aside and the difficulties which slaves usually had in seeing their wives who lived upon distant plantations were made less so in his case. As he grew older he was given lighter tasks and was placed in a sort of supervisory position with younger slaves to do the work. In severe sickness the "Black Mammy" herself might be excused from her duties to care for him.[29]

The "Black Mammy" often nursed her master's child at one breast and her own at the other. When old enough her children along with those of other plantation women were kept under the care of the plantation nurse while their mothers were at work. When the mothers came home they took their children to their own cabins. These plantation nurseries were in charge of a woman who was too old for work, or some of the young girls who were not yet old enough for work in the fields. They were the forerunners of the present-day nurseries where children of working mothers are cared for while the mother is away from home. And the wholesale precipitation of the plantation women from their cabins into house and field foretold the large numbers of American women who leave their homes daily for factory, office, classroom and other occupations. The plantation children were communally reared while the parents worked. Any grown person on the plantation could correct them.

A little later the "Black Mammy's" children might be brought to the "big house" as playmates, then as maids or houseboys, and in this way they benefited by their mother's position.[30] A kind mistress would often teach the "Black Mammy's" children certain skills along with her own, such as sewing and embroidering; and despite laws against it some were taught to read and write.[31]

[29] Susan Bradford Eppes, *Through some Eventful Years*, p. 87.

[30] Eliza Frances Andrews, *The War-Time Journal of a Georgia Girl*, 1864-1865, pp. 293-294.

[31] Joseph B. Cobb, *Mississippi Scenes or Sketches of Southern and Western Life*, pp. 83-86.

Though the children of the "Black Mammy" were not exempt from sale, the master was very hard pressed when he sold one of her children. It was either through debt, because of insolvency or because of property complications that such a sale took place. S. C. Rankin tells how his playmate, the son of his "Black Mammy," was sold for debt, a blow from which she never recovered and of which she died of a broken heart.[32] And Mrs. Smedes whose father was noted for his kindness to his slaves reveals that the son of his favorite slave was sold.[33]

Though not able to prevent her children from being sold, by her tact and prestige she could and did save them from punishment. The story is related by Mrs. Pleasants that "Mammy Lily," "six feet tall and possessed of a vigor of mind in keeping with the size of her body," hid in the closet under the mistress' staircase for a week her twin sons, who had been hired in the coal pits, and who, not liking it, had run away. Here they stayed until discovered, but they were not sent back to the pits.

1027

Relations Between the "Black Mammy" and the Children

The "Black Mammy" was the white children's nurse in the sense that they were placed in her charge, with general supervision from the mistress. She bathed them, dressed them, fed them, put them to bed, cared for their clothing, and added more than simply the satisfaction of all physical needs. She assisted the mistress in everything pertaining to the training of the children.[34]

She was the first person to whom children visiting the

[32] S. C. Rankin, *The Story of My Life*, p. 15.

[33] Susan Dabney Smedes, *A Southern Planter*, Chap. III.

[34] Thomas Nelson Page, *Social Life in Old Virginia before the War*, pp. 59-60; *The Old South*, pp. 165-166; F. D. Syrgley, *Seventy Years in Dixie*, pp. 41-42.

plantation ran to see, for she was amiable in her greeting, and it was she who saw to all their wants. She showered the children with attention and could be kind and indulgent or stern and exacting as the occasion demanded. "Such a thing as rebellion against her was almost undreamt of, for she was high in authority."[35]

The intimacy between the "Black Mammy" and the children of her owner was the closest of all the relationships that existed between her and the other persons in the household. Subsequent relationships found their origin here. It was during this period that the future master and mistress formed attachments to their "Black Mammy" which they retained all during their lives. She was usually with them at birth; she cared for them through childhood and early manhood and womanhood, and in turn became the "Black Mammy" for the second generation and perhaps the third. In a few cases she was known to ve to see the fifth generation. Beginning thus early in its contact with this slave woman, the child had opportunity to acquire nothing but favorable attitudes toward the woman who nursed it.

Mrs. Ripley states that they loved their "Black Mammy" "right along all the week until Saturday night" when with the big tub upstairs, two pails of hot water, a heavy hand, a searching eye and a rough wash rag full of soap suds she reached every fold and crease in their bodies—"then we hated her and were glad when we outgrew the need of her assistance at those dreaded Saturday night baths and she went to other little lambs in pastures new."[36]

One of the roles of the "Black Mammy" was definitely that of orienting the children into the culture of their group. At no time did she depart from the mores in her

[35] Minnie W. Myers, *Romance and Realism of the South Gulf Coast*, pp. 55-56.

[36] Eliza M. Ripley, *Social Life in Old New Orleans*, p. 212.

relations with them. So persistent was this that she has been charged with having a far greater affection for them than she had for her own children. And of the children she nursed that they looked upon her as a mother and in their very early years hardly knew the difference between her and their real mother. Some have thought that they cared for her more than they did for their own mother.

When the child began to become aware of its surroundings and the difference between white and black became apparent the color of the "Black Mammy" might be a matter of curiosity. As for example, the question of the child who asked, "Mammy, who made you black?" And the answer, "Child, who been puttin' notions in your curly haid? Gawd made mammy black and He made you and your ma white, for the reason that when Noah came out'n de Ark, Ham was disrespectful to his pa and laughed at him, and Gawd told Ham he and his children should be always servants; so He made him black, and dat's where we all black people come from."[37]

Here one finds in the "Black Mammy's "reply the orthodox answer as if it had come from the mouth of the mother herself. There is given also one of the chief arguments put forth by the slaveholders for keeping the Negro in bondage; no other reply could have been more in keeping with the accepted popular thought. There need be no fear that from her the child would not receive the sense of its status in the social world.

The myths of Harris' *Uncle Remus* were known and told by Negro nurses to white children all over the Southern States long before his artistry gave them to the public.[38] Through the "Black Mammy" the white children became acquainted with the same superstitions possessed by the Negroes. Such sayings as, "Don' yer neber lay

1029

---

[37] Mathew Page Andrews, *The Women of the South in War Times*, pp. 190-191.

[38] Jerome Dowd, *The Negro in American Life*, p. 283.

down on de flo, and let nobody step over yer, kase ef yer do yer won't gro' no mo",[39] or "You must always burn and not throw away your hair, because the birds will pick it up to make their nests, and that will make you crazy"[40] were not likely to be forgotten.

Mrs. Pickett remembers that it was the "Black Mammy" who tended her who pointed out the advantage of being "sociable with one's self."[41] Srygley was proud of the fact that his "Black Mammy" taught him how to count up to ten in an African dialect. This was the only recollection she had of her native language.[42]

If asked by the child which of two dresses it would be better to wear the "Black Mammy" likely as not would answer after this fashion: "Well, honey, let it be dis way. Dat plaid is mostly bright; ef de sun is a-shining, you wear de blue, an' ef it's cloudy you wear de plaid; so we'll all have suppin-nuther to mak' us feel warm an' good even ef it's raining."[43]

The "Black Mammy" taught the children the proper forms of etiquette,[44] of deportment to all of the people of the plantation, the proper forms of address and the proper distances to maintain. They knew that it was correct to address the older women on the plantation as "aunt" or "mammy" or "mauma"; and the older men as "uncle" or "daddy." No one was stronger for "yes, ma'am," and "no, ma'am," or for "yes, sir," and "no, sir," than she was.

In the Old South where much was made of chivalry and where great emphasis was placed upon form, manners in the life of the child meant much. The "Black Mammy" knew just what these manners were[45]—when to speak and

[39] Minnie W. Myers, *Romance and Realism of the South Gulf Coast*, p. 6.

[40] *Ibid.*, pp. 56-58.

[41] La Salle Corbell Pickett, *What Happened to Me*, p. 34.

[42] F. D. Srygley, *Seventy Years in Dixie*, pp. 44-50.

[43] Nicholas Ware Eppes, *The Negro of the Old South*, p. 24.

[44] Caroline Couper Lovell, *The Golden Isles of Georgia*, pp. 192-193.

[45] Minnie W. Myers, *Woman and Realism of the South Gulf Coast*, pp. 56-58.

when not to speak; what was best to say on the proper occasion and what was not; the proper deportment of boy and girl, of young men and young women. Says Mrs. Eppes, "Her child was taught all the points of good breeding, the polite salutations, the modest answer when spoken to, the quiet demeanor. When the child remained unnoticed was the rule not as now the exception. The reason for this is readily to be perceived; "Black Mammy" was there, looking on, and woe be to the unlucky one who dared to be pert, or forward, or as she would express it, "fergit yer manners."[46]

And to the "Black Mammy" herself the children did not put their orders in the form of demands but in the form of requests. This was a part of their training. It was a means of maintaining pleasant family relationships with each other and with the servants. A Southerner of the upper class delighted in saying that he was taught his manners by his "Black Mammy."

"The mammy disciplined the children[47] and maintained her attitude of authority toward them even after they were grown. They were always children to her even after they took their places as heads of households. When the mammy thought that the master or mistress was overstepping bounds or reprimanded her unjustly, or when she became offended that her infallibility was questioned she was not above letting them know it in such a naive manner that it could not be called insubordination."[48]

No one was more solicitous about the child when it was ill than was the "Black Mammy." She rested neither day nor night in her care and attention. Here as in other matters of the child's life, the master and mistress allowed her complete sway. In fact, she knew more about the care of children than they did, and the child responded to her care as to that of no one else. Mrs. O'Conner tells an in-

1031

[46] Susan Bradford Eppes, *Through Some Eventful Years*, p. 38.
[47] *Ibid.*, p. 38.
[48] Lily Young Cohen, *Lost Spirituals*, pp. 21-37.

teresting story of how the "Black Mammy" saved the life
of her master's child. The weather was so hot that the
physician stated nothing but a change in temperature held
any hope for its recovery. By means of a wide palm-
leaf fan dipped from time to time in a bucket of fresh
water she "evenly and continuously made a cool moist
breeze" from the baby's head to his feet for thirty-six
hours without stopping. When she finished the muscles of
her arms "stood out swollen and rigid," but she had saved
the child's life.[49]

1032

She rendered the young girls of the family all kinds of
services and went out of her way to show them attention.
She sat up at night and waited for them to return from
social functions in order to help them undress, even when
the mistress did not require it. On such occasions the
"Black Mammy" became the confidant of love affairs, and
was not above suggesting which young man would make
the better husband; as for example, "Young missis should
marry her cousin Marse Tom, and keep our family like-
ness in our family."[50]

When the boys and girls went off to school they often
took the "Black Mammy's" picture along with those of
the rest of the family to put on their bureaus and to show
to their schoolmates.[51] She was often sent with the girls
"to sew and wash for them and take motherly care of their
health and playful exercises."[52] As little children they
were accustomed to hanging on to her skirts and throwing
their arms around her neck and kissing her. When they
grew up the intimacy of contact was little changed. When
departing from and upon being reunited with her they embraced her. Page makes note of a young lieutenant in a
volunteer company who kissed his old "Black Mammy"

[49] T. P. O'Connor, *My Beloved South*, pp. 122-123.
[50] Mary Polk Branch, *Memoirs of a Southern Woman within the Lines*,
p. 12.
[51] Eliza M. Ripley, *Social Life in Old New Orleans*, p. 210.
[52] Henry R. Schoolcraft, *The Black Gauntlet*, p. 182.

on the parade ground in sight of the whole company.[53]

To the slave boys and girls with whom the whites played as children the attitudes of the young men and women changed when they grew up, but to the "Black Mammy" their attitudes were always the same. To the "black sheep" especially did she extend her protection, helped him out of his difficulties and often saved him from the anger of an irate parent.

When a son of the family married and brought home his bride, the first thing that he did after he had introduced her to his parents and other relatives was to go through the same ceremony with the servants and especially with his old "Black Mammy."[54] The bride's wedding was not complete unless the "Black Mammy" was present. She was given a place of honor at the ceremony. Miss Bremer tells of a wedding at which the "Black Mammy" sat "black and silent by the altar." This foster mother of the bride could not bear the thought of parting from her.[55] Thomas Nelson Page gives the story of a wedding in the executive mansion at Richmond, Virginia. At the last minute when the bride was about to appear it was discovered that the bride's "Black Mammy" had not come in. The Governor himself went out and brought her in on his arm to take the place beside the mother of the bride.[56]

1033

Relations Between the Mammy and the Mistress

Frequently the best friend the mistress on the plantation had was the "Black Mammy." The overseer's wife, when there was one, was often the only other white woman on the plantation outside of the immediate household, but between her and the mistress there was the widest gulf. The mistress was as exclusive in her relationships with the overseer's wife as George Washington advised the

[53] Thomas Nelson Page, *The Negro, the Southerner's Problem*, pp. 202-203.
[54] T. D. Ozanne, *The South as It Is*, p. 75.
[55] A. W. Calhoun, *A Social History of the American Family*, Vol. II, p. 284.
[56] Thomas Nelson Page, *The Negro, the Southerner's Problem*, pp. 202-203.

steward who was placed in charge of his several plantations to be with the overseers. Said he, "To treat them
kindly is no more than what all men are entitled to; but
my advice to you is, keep them at a proper distance, for
they grow upon familiarity and you will sink in authority
if you do not."[57] Nor was there any association but those
that were necessary between the mistress and the other
poor whites that may have lived near. As a benefactress in
times of crises she would assist the poor man's wife, but
as an associate she received none of the benefits from the
constant association which the "Black Mammy" received.

1034

The "Black Mammy" was to the mistress in the household what the overseer was to the master in the fields, with
the difference that in general the overseer could never
enter into the life of the master as the "Black Mammy"
did that of the mistress.

Besides taking complete charge of the children, the
"Black Mammy" was the mistress' assistant in all that
pertained to the household.[58] "Nothing but the presence
of that 'gift of the Gods,' the Southern 'Mauma,' could
render life less than a burden for the mistress," says Caroline C. Lowell.[59]

When guests arrived unexpectedly it was the "Black
Mammy" who was called into consultation as to the best
means of caring for them. In many instances some tech-
nique was required when too many came at the same time.
Her homely but adequate advice was usually equal to any
situation. Every guest and acquaintance of the family
knew her. In cases she even had a state-wide reputation.[60]
Mrs. Ripley states that as a child she often visited the
plantation of her cousin. Here if anything was required
everyone knew that "all applications were to be made to
mammy."[61] Mrs. Smedes notes that on rainy days when

---

[57] Sarah A. Rice Pryor, *My Day, Reminiscences of a Long Life,* pp. 60-61.
[58] Myrta Lockett Avary, *Dixie after the War,* p. 181.
[59] Caroline C. Lovell, *The Golden Isles of Georgia,* p. 109.
[60] Sarah A. Rice Pryor, *My Day, Reminiscences of a Long Life,* pp. 60-61.
[61] Eliza M. Ripley, *Social Life in Old New Orleans,* pp. 211-212.

all the plantation women were brought into the house, her "Mammy Maria" was a Field Marshall in the way she gave out work and taught them to sew. "By word and action she stimulated and urged them on, until there was not on the Burleigh plantation a woman who could not make and mend neatly her own and her husband's clothes."[62]

There was a freedom of intercourse between the "Black Mammy" and the mistress who had grown old together. This was a result of a comradeship born of spending many years under the same shelter and participating in a common life, so much so that there was no need for the "Black Mammy" to obey an order strictly or to obey it at all, if she saw a better way.[63] Each depended on the other. Says U. B. Phillips, "No prophet in early times could have told that kindliness would grow as a flower from a soil so foul, that slaves would come to be cherished not only as property of high value but as loving if lowly friends."[64] It was the "Black Mammy" who tactfully broke the news of some sad event to the mistress, attempting to soften the blow before it fell.[65]

At no period during slavery did the attachment between mistress and slave undergo a greater strain than that which was brought about by the Civil War. Here was a crisis such as neither had been called upon to face before. The mistress represented the group which was fighting to keep the slaves in bondage. The "Black Mammy" was a member of this enslaved group. But as history records the old bonds held the slaves faithful to their masters and to their masters' families.

The Civil War brought many perplexing problems to the southern household. Not the least important of which was what disposition was to be made of wives and children

1035

---

[62] Susan Dabney Smedes, *A Southern Planter*, p. 38.

[63] *Ibid.*, p. 151.

[64] U. B. Phillips, *Life and Labor in the Old South*, p. 214.

[65] Joseph B. Cobb, *Mississippi Scenes or Sketches of the Southern and Western Life*, p. 162.

of departing soldiers. They had to be left at home, and some provision had to be made for them and other dependents. The "Black Mammy" was one of the answers to this question. Children could be left in her care with the utmost confidence that they would be well cared for. The young mistress could see her husband depart and feel reassured by the presence of the "Black Mammy." Here was always one source of reliance.

The "Black Mammy" helped to keep up the morale of the women and children during the war. Cut off from many of the luxuries to which they had been accustomed by the need to conserve for the troops the best of everything, and inconvenienced in that the markets which formerly furnished them with necessities were now closed by reason of the blockade, these people needed much inventiveness to keep themselves in clothing and other commodities. Many of the old fashioned ways of doing things had to be revived. Manufactured goods to which they had been accustomed, such as shoes and hosiery, were impossibilities. Old spinning wheels and looms were brought out and the Negro women spun, dyed and wove the thread into cloth.[66] The "Black Mammy" was skilful in making old home remedies, and upon them the family had to depend when medicines gave out and no more were to be had. She knew the cure for many aches and pains, and her knowledge was of value.

In other ways she aided in keeping up the spirit of the mistress. She it was who told her mistress whether or not the federal officers who came to the house were "gentlemen" and whether she had anything to fear from them. Believing in the efficacy of a good meal, Mrs. Branch states that her "Black Mammy," who was a famous cook, did her many a good turn by serving to the invading soldiers a good lunch, ably assisted by the other servants. This sense of identification with the group who owned her made

1036

[66] United Daughters of the Confederacy, *South Carolina Women in the Confederacy*, Vol. II, p. 37.

the "Black Mammy" loyal to the point of sacrificing her own interests. Changed conditions brought no change in her behavior. Those whom she served marvelled at her steadfastness. She went about her duties as usual.

When anxious wives went forth to seek and to care for their wounded husbands it was the "Black Mammy" whom they took with them to help nurse them back to health.[67] Many a Confederate soldier was nursed by these "mammies" and by other Negro women who had been trained and taught thus to function.[68]

The "Black Mammy" was usually at the bedside of her mistress when her last hour came. And the mistress was the first person called when the "Black Mammy" was passing to the Beyond. In death the "Black Mammy" might be given a "respectable" burial. The services might even be conducted by the master himself, and instead of the home-made box provided for the ordinary slave, there might be a neat coffin, with interment in the family burial ground and a marker of some kind indicating her service to her owner.

There was hardly a person of importance or one who belonged to the old aristocracy of the South who did not come under the influence of one of these slave women, and they were proud of the fact. One of the boasts of the "old gentlemen of the South" was that they were reared by a "Black Mammy," and they attributed certain of their good qualities to this influence. Says Lucian Lamar Knight, "Nor can it be said that her influence was unfelt in the councils of the government when she held the hand of him who wrote the Declaration of Independence and rocked 'the forest-born Demosthenes' who kindled the fires of the Revolution."[69]

JESSIE W. PARKHURST

Tuskegee Institute

[67] Fannie A. Beers, *Memories*, pp. 254-274; United Daughters of the Confederacy, *South Carolina Women in the Confederacy*, pp. 212-216.

[68] Francis Hewitt Fearn, *Diary of a Refugee*, p. 3.

[69] Lucian Lamar Knight, *Memorials of Dixie-land*, p. 372.

Heed Life's Demands: The Educational Philosophy of Fanny Jackson Coppin

Linda M. Perkins, *Assistant Director, The Mary Ingraham Bunting Institute, Radcliffe College*

This article will discuss the educational philosophy and activities of Fanny Jackson Coppin, one of the most influential Black educators and community leaders of the late nineteenth century. During a period when discussions of women's education in the larger society embraced "ornamental" and "female" education, Fanny Jackson Coppin took the "gentleman's course" (the collegiate degree) at Oberlin College in 1865. Driven by a deep religious devotion to helping her race through education, Fanny Coppin by the end of the century, headed one of the most prestigious Black academic institutions in the nation, the Institute for Colored Youth in Philadelphia.

Born a slave in 1837 in Washington, D.C., Fanny Jackson's freedom was bought during her early childhood by a devoted aunt, Mrs. Sarah Orr Clark. Fanny Jackson moved to New Bedford, Massachusetts and later to Newport, Rhode Island, in the 1850s to live with relatives. Her desire to obtain an education took on greater urgency as a result of the statement of antebellum Senator John C. Calhoun who made the alleged intellectual inferiority of Blacks the justification of slavery. Thus, as a teenager, Fanny Jackson pledged, "to get an education and to teach my people." Although academic excellence became a goal for her, Fanny Jackson also viewed it as imperative that education be linked with service to the race.[1] She frequently commented that "knowledge is power."

The first steps toward a higher education for Fanny Jackson came in the late 1850s at the Rhode Island State Normal School.

[1] Fanny Jackson Coppin, *Reminiscences of School Life and Hints on Teaching* (Philadelphia: AME Book Concern, 1913), pp. 9–10, 17.

Journal of Negro Education, Vol. 51, No. 3 (1982)
Copyright © 1982, Howard University.

With the financial help of her aunt, Mrs. Clark, and Bishop Daniel Payne of the African Methodist Episcopal Church, she enrolled in Oberlin College in Ohio in 1860. Although no Black woman had obtained a collegiate degree when Fanny Jackson enrolled at Oberlin, she received not only encouragement but financial assistance from her family and the Black community. This assistance demonstrates an attitudinal difference of Blacks and Whites regarding the need for females to be college-educated. Black families, more than White families, saw the need.[2]

Early in her life, Fanny Jackson concluded that each Black person was a representative of the race. And, it was for her race that she attended college. In her reminiscences she recalled that at Oberlin, when she was called upon to recite, she felt as if she had the "honor of the whole African race upon her shoulders." If she had failed, Jackson wrote, "it would have been ascribed to the fact that I was colored."[3] This statement indicates that it did not occur to Jackson that her gender would be a deterrent, only her race. Far from failing, however, Jackson's academic record was outstanding and resulted in her being chosen the first Black student teacher in the Preparatory Department of Oberlin College. Her presence in the classroom at Oberlin was such an event that visitors were in daily attendance to view her and the London *Athenaeum* even carried an article on her appointment.[4] These expressions of surprise by Whites of Jackson's intellectual capabilities influenced greatly her educational philosophy. Fanny Jackson stressed that circumstances, not dull intellect, prohibited academic learning by most Blacks. Throughout her academic career, Jackson took great interest in "slow learners" and pupils who needed remedial courses.

During the Civil War years when freedmen poured into the city of Oberlin, Fanny Jackson voluntarily formed an evening class to help the illiterate men and women learn to read and write. Putting her philosophy to practice, Jackson's attentiveness and great skill as a teacher resulted in her pupils' rapid progress. These activities were chronicled in the newspapers.[5] By the time Fanny Jackson graduated from the College in 1865, with an A.B. degree, she was considered one of the most competent teachers and learned women of her time.

From Oberlin, Fanny Jackson moved to Philadelphia to put her knowledge and talents to work for her race at the Institute for

[2]*Ibid.*, p. 18.
[3]*Ibid.*, p. 15.
[4]See "A Fortnight in Oberlin," *National Anti-Slavery Standard*, March 11, 1865; "Sketches by the Wayside," *Christian Recorder*, August 26, 1865.
[5]*Lorain County News* (Ohio), February 4, 1864 and February 10, 1864.

Colored Youth, one of the first institutions of higher education foi Blacks. At the time of her arrival in September 1865, the Institute was in the process of being transformed into a full-fledged classica high school and normal school.[6] The Black community eagerly awaitec. Fanny Jackson's arrival. Her progress as an Oberlin student had been followed in the *Christian Recorder*, the organ of the AME Church.[7] After her appointment as Principal of the Female Department of the Institute, Fanny Jackson became a popular and important figure with the Philadelphia Black community. Her impact upon the schoo! as an outstanding teacher brought her repeated praise by the Quaker Board of Managers as well as by the community.

In 1869, Ebenezer Bassett, the principal of the Institute, was appointed U.S. Minister to Haiti. Upon his departure from the Institute Fanny Jackson was promoted to his position.[8] Her appointment was an unprecedented event for the Black race. Highly trained Black educators were few during this period. For Black women, they were fewer still. Yet, Fanny Jackson had been one of the few to escape enforced ignorance. Her position at the Institute resulted in her becoming the first Black woman to head an institution of higher learning in the nation.

1041

Jackson's appointment by the Quaker Managers was seen as a departure from their view that women should not become too educated. However, in the case of Fanny Jackson, the Managers found that she was the most qualified person to hold the post and stated that she was considered superior in qualifications even to Bassett.[9] She had, as a teacher, successfully demonstrated that the inability of a student to grasp a concept or understand a problem was usually the fault of the instructor, not the student. Thus, in her first four years at the Institute, the number of students had increased and there were fewer dropouts. In addition, the class of 1869, the first to complete the entire four years of study under Jackson's instruction, was the largest in the history of the Institute—eighteen students.[10] Convinced that Fanny Jackson was an asset, not only to the Female Department but to the Institute as a whole, the Managers set aside prior notions of the subordinate role of women and placed this outstanding teacher into the position of leadership.

[6]For details on the history of the Institute for Colored Youth see Linda M. Perkins's "Fanny Jackson Coppin and the Institute for Colored Youth: A Model of Nineteenth Century Black Female Educational and Community Leadership, 1837–1902." (Ph.D. dissertation, University of Illinois, 1978).

[7]*Christian Recorder*, August 26, 1865.

[8]Managers Minutes in *Institute for Colored Youth Papers*, hereinafter referred to as ICY Papers, April 13, 1869, Friends Historical Library, Swarthmore College.

[9]Alfred Cope to Octavius V. Catto, April 23, 1869, *Ocatvius V. Catto Papers*, Leon Gardiner Collection, Historical Society of Pennsylvania.

[10]*Institute for Colored Youth Annual Report of 1870*, ICY Papers.

The Institute for Colored Youth was at its zenith in 1869. Public interest in the school was so great that visitors averaged 30 per week. The Managers boasted that "highly educated and accomplished teachers" were employed in the Institute with the school offering academic subjects similar to those taught in other liberal high schools of the late nineteenth century. Noting the demand for Black teachers after Emancipation, Fanny Jackson developed a normal school at the Institute and had tuition abolished to ensure the enrollment of poor students. Remembering the educational benefits she derived as a "student teacher" while enrolled at Oberlin, she instituted student teaching in the Preparatory Department for the Institute's normal students. It was Jackson's philosophy that "it is a good rule, if one wants to learn a thing, to teach it to another."[11]

1042

After getting the Institute on firm ground, Fanny Jackson began to focus on community activities. By the 1870s, race relations in Philadelphia were strained due primarily to the increase of Black emigrants from the South coupled with the huge migration of immigrant groups into the city. These new residents added to the growing job competition and their arrival coincided with an economic depression. To add to these problems, racial hostilities escalated as a result of the increased political power given to Black men with the ratification of the Fifteenth Amendment. Racial conflicts resulted in the death of Institute teacher O. V. Catto and two other Black men when they attempted to vote. In 1870, Fanny Jackson became a contributor to the *Christian Recorder* to discuss these problems.[12]

Jackson was particularly concerned with the lack of training and employment opportunities for Blacks in the skilled trades. Inspired by the industrial exhibits of the Centennial Exhibition of the nation held in Philadelphia in 1876, and aware that the nation was becoming increasingly industrial, she set out to educate the masses of Blacks of the need for industrial and technical education and sought to have such training offered at the Institute.

Lecturing throughout the Northeast and writing under the pen name of Catherine Casey in the *Christian Recorder*, Fanny Jackson's message was repeated again and again—industrial training and self-help.[13] She had been optimistic regarding interracial cooperation as a result of her positive Oberlin experience. But, life in Philadelphia, the murder of O. V. Catto in his attempt to vote, and her futile attempts to obtain jobs for Blacks in the city led her to

---

[11]*Institute for Colored Youth Annual Reports of 1869 and 1871; Monthly Report of the Boys' High School* (hereinafter referred to as Monthly Report), February 17, 1890. ICY Papers.
[12]Institute for Colored Youth *Committee on Discipline and Instruction Minutes*, October 7 and 26, 1871, ICY Papers.
[13]*Christian Recorder*, July 18, 1878.

conclude that Black solidarity and economic independence were the answers to race improvement. Thus, she began to focus on economic issues, as well as on educational matters, in her speeches and discussions.

Jackson's column in the *Christian Recorder* frequently addressed Black women. She informed them of the various new avenues of employment for women and gave them advice on educational opportunities. To illustrate her point on Black economic independence, Jackson organized an effort to save the *Christian Recorder* from bankruptcy in 1879. Planning a fair with articles made by the readership of the paper nationwide, she explained in her column what the death of the *Recorder* would mean, not just to the AME Church but to the race. She urged Blacks to ignore religious denominational loyalties and stressed that the *Recorder* was a *Black* newspaper which employed *Black* printers. She argued, "this paper finds its way into many a dark hamlet in the South where no one ever heard of the Philadelphia *Bulletin* or the *New York Tribune*."[14] This was, of course, a logical argument. The *Christian Recorder* was widely circulated throughout the Black communities of the nation and provided news of special interest to Blacks. Further, as Fanny Jackson noted, the paper employed Blacks. The fundraising event was a great success with articles being contributed from twenty-four states, thus clearing the paper's indebtedness.[15]

1043

At the Institute, race obligation and charity were thoroughly ingrained in the students. Each week, pupils voluntarily gave one cent each to a charitable society within the school. Thus, at the year's end, the treasuries amounted to $75 to $100. The money was contributed to various Black organizations.[16]

Because children of prominent Black Philadelphians attended the Institute and it carried great prestige to be associated with the school, Fanny Jackson strove earnestly to avoid elitism and snobbery on the part of her students. As mentioned earlier, immediately after she became principal, she had tuition abolished to ensure the enrollment of poor children. In addition, she encouraged and even sought the attendance of southern Blacks who were frequently looked down upon even by Black Philadelphians. Understanding well the social structure of the Philadelphia Black community, Jackson frequently lectured on the importance of humility, character, self-denial, and dedication to the race.

[14]Fanny Coppin, *Reminiscences*, pp. 29–31.
[15]*Ibid.*
[16]*Ibid.* p. 60.

In a March 1876 article eulogizing William Whipper, a prominent Black Philadelphia citizen, Jackson wrote the following:

> Mr. Whipper was unsparingly severe upon the extravagance. . . . He gave generously but not prodigally, widely but not ostentatiously. . . . He was a staunch and loyal friend to his race, and his purse, his tongue, and his pen, a weighty triumvirate, did them good service in the dark and terrible days of slavery.[17]

Jackson's comments were but another indication of her attempt to educate the community to the important philosophy of race obligation and self-help. She also used the occasion of commencement to draw immense audiences, to further stress this philosophy to both community and students. To a capacity crowd at the Institute's 1877 commencement, Jackson reminded the graduates that despite their education they should respect those who had not been educated by books, but by the experience of life. She told the group:

> Many of you will probably teach in obscure towns and villages, where you will be surrounded by persons who make no pretense to "booklearning." You will not, I feel assured, on this account overrate your own ability or acquirements; you will preserve a teachable spirit, and defer to the opinions of worthy persons older than yourselves, whose knowledge, gained from observation and experience and ripened by age, will excellently supplement what you have learned from books.[18]

Her address to subsequent classes were similar. In 1879, she closed her address by stating:

> You can do much to alleviate the condition of our people. Do not be discouraged. The very places where you are needed most are those where you will get least pay. Do not resign a position in the South which pays you $12 a month as a teacher for one in Pennsylvania which pays $50.[19]

Strange as this advice may appear today, during the period in which it was given the words had a profound effect upon the Institute's pupils. Fanny Jackson was a living example of self-denial. It was well known in Philadelphia that she financed the college education of many Institute pupils. When Jackson unsuccessfully attempted to have the Quaker Managers build a dormitory to accommodate students from the South, she rented a house next door to her home for them and paid the rent herself.[20] Even when Fanny Jackson paused during the Christmas holidays, in 1881, to marry Levi Jenkins Coppin, an AME minister, she refused to relinquish her position at the Institute. Although Reverend Coppin was transferred to Baltimore the year of their marriage, she remained

[17]The *Philadelphia Press*, June 1877, clipping in unclassified scrapbook at Cheyney State College (Pa.) Archives.
[18]Ibid, June 1877 clipping.
[19]*Ibid.*, July 1, 1879 clipping.
[20]*Monthly Report*, May 19, 1884, ICY Papers.

1044

in Philadelphia. In 1885, Levi Coppin returned to Philadelphia to become pastor of Mother Bethel Church.[21]

By 1889, Fanny Jackson Coppin was successful in having an industrial department added to the Institute. By the end of the century, the department offered ten trades, which included printing, plastering, tailoring, typing and stenography, bricklaying and sewing. The industrial department was independent from the academic department and offered its classes at night to accommodate working adults. Although Coppin believed that Blacks should be prepared to meet the industrial challenges as the nation grew, she remained committed to classical education. The courses offered in the industrial department fell short of those she envisioned for the school. Fanny Coppin had hoped to expand the Institute to offer pre-med as well as engineering courses; however, limited funds and interest by the Quaker Managers resulted in trade education.[22]

1045

Despite the limited course offerings of the industrial department, Fanny Coppin was able to encourage her students of the high school to aspire to the professions and technical fields. One former graduate of the Institute, John Durham, a civil engineer and later U.S. Minister to Haiti, remembered that Fanny Coppin suggested engineering to him as a career. Durham stated: "She [Fanny Jackson Coppin] pictured to me the great work to be done by specialists in the learned professions, great cures to be made by great colored doctors, cases to be won by colored lawyers, books to be made by colored writers.[23] Pointing out to Durham that he was an outstanding math student, Coppin suggested that he become an engineer. Durham recalled that his experience was not unique; the same type of story could be retold by "scores, hundreds, of other pupils."[24]

Employment opportunities for uneducated Black women also consumed much of Fanny Coppin's time. By 1886, only 32 percent of Blacks in the city were native-born Philadelphians; the majority of the black residents had migrated from the South. Of the latter group, there was a large number of single women. Due to limited employment and low wages, they were particularly vulnerable to vice. Coppin sought to aid these women. In 1888, with a committee of women from Mother Bethel, she opened a home for destitute young women after other charities had refused them admission.

[21]Levi Coppin, Unwritten History (New York: Negro University Press, reprinted in 1968), p. 333.
[22]For an extended discussion of the industrial department of the Institute see Perkins' "Fanny Jackson Coppin and the Institute for Colored Youth," pp. 168–306.
[23]New York Age, November 8, 1890.
[24]Ibid.

The three-storied home was staffed with a matron and a visiting Black physician, and courses in nurse training were offered.[25]

By 1894, Fanny Coppin opened the Women's Exchange and Girl's Home on Twelfth Street. In addition to providing housing for students and working females, the home gave instructions in cooking, dressmaking, and domestic economy. Coppin's philosophy was that if the women could not go to school, the school should be brought to them. On the days off of the women of the home, Mother Bethel held small receptions for the working women and conducted literary exercises. In his 1897 study of the Philadelphia Negro, W. E. B. Du Bois cited this home as one of the chief Black institutions of the city.[26]

As the nineteenth century came to a close, Fanny Coppin suffered frequent illnesses as a result of the decades of hard work at the Institute and within the Black community. By 1900, the new Quaker Managers of the Institute became more and more influenced by the education ideology of Booker T. Washington and made industrial education the primary focus of the Institute. In June 1902, Fanny Coppin retired from the Institute.[27]

"Heed life's demands" had been Fanny Jackson Coppin's motto, which she had imparted to her students and to the Philadelphia Black community throughout the latter half of the nineteenth century. These demands included developing competence in skilled trades, teacher training, and the professions, as well as establishing independent Black businesses, newspapers and banks. Such demands were equally as compelling in the urban North as in the rural South, in Coppin's views. She made these views known through her column in the *Christian Recorder*, as well as through her lectures in the Black communities of the North.

Firmly believing in the ability of Blacks to aid themselves, Coppin had constantly lectured on "The Power of Ourselves to Help Ourselves." One of her favorite lecture circuit stories was the one that pointed out that "the gods help those who help themselves." She told her audiences of a farmer whose wagon had gotten stuck in the mud. Frightened, the man called to the god Hercules for help. The god replied to the farmer: "Whip your horses and put your shoulder to the wheel." Thus, said Coppin, "unless Black

1046

---

[25]W. E. B. Du Bois, *The Philadelphia Negro* (New York: Schocken Books, reprint of 1899 edition, 1970), p. 78: unidentified Philadelphia newspaper clipping entitled "New Home for Fallen Women" in 1888 scrapbook at Cheyney State College Archives.

[26]*Ibid;* Unidentified Philadelphia newspaper clipping dated December 21, 1894 entitled "The Industrial Exchange" in scrapbook at Cheyney State College Archives; Coppin lived at 754 South 12th Street from 1893 to 1901 (Godpill's *Philadelphia City Directory,* 1893–1901).

[27]*Managers Minutes,* September 17, 1901, ICY Papers.

people learn to whip their horses and put their shoulders to the wheel, they would be forever stuck in the mud."[28]

This philosophy had been her theme throughout her industrial crusade. Fanny Coppin's plans for her race were never small. As she continued her efforts to increase employment opportunities for Black women in the 1890's, Coppin told a group of Blacks that they must learn to help themselves. She said, "A hundred men can lift a log together very easily, but when only a few take hold at a time very little is accomplished. So no one of us can promise to find employment for our young women, but when we combine our forces it becomes an easy matter."[29] This was not an easy lesson to get across to her audiences.

Yet, Coppin refused to be discouraged and continued her lectures on this topic. She well understood the strength that Blacks as a race possessed but realized that many of the race were not aware of this strength. On this point, Coppin stated:

1047

> We must know what strength we possess. The proposal to uniform Roman slaves was once rejected because, said a philosopher, they would thus learn their numbers and know their strength. When people are conscious of possessing strength, they rapidly grow stronger.[30]

Even the poor, the elderly, and the weak had an important role in the liberation of the race.

Fanny Coppin served on the Board of Managers of the Home for the Aged and Infirmed Colored People in Philadelphia for over twenty years (1881–1913). The home was founded in 1864 as a result of an elderly Black woman being rejected from the segregated homes for the elderly in that city. The first donations toward the institution were given by two poor Black women, one giving fifty cents, the other giving ten cents. Later, Stephen Smith, a wealthy Black lumber merchant, donated $100,000 to the establishment of the home. With this example, Coppin often reminded her audiences that great institutions were a result of small and humble beginnings.[31]

Coppin's continuing association with the poor and elderly Blacks of Philadelphia endeared her to them. She had often lectured at the churches and organizations of the poorer Blacks as well as the more prestigious literary societies and churches of the more affluent Blacks. John Durham remembered: "no so-called literacy society or church festival was too humble to command her [Fanny Jackson Coppin's]

---

[28]*Christian Recorder*, November 21, 1878, and January 5, 1881; quoted in M. A. Major, *Noted Negro Women, Their Triumphs and Activities* (Chicago: n.p., 1893), pp. 173–4.

[29]Majors, *Noted Negro Women*, pp. 174.

[30]*Ibid*.

[31]*28th Annual Report of the Board of Managers of the Home for Aged and Infirmed Colored People* (1892). The Home for Aged and Infirmed Colored People had an interracial Board of Managers which included many members of the Society of Friends. The institution still exists and has been renamed the Stephen Smith Home.

attendance." And, William C. Bolivar, also an Institute for Colored Youth graduate, noted that "even with her [Coppin's] rare learning, she never made even the humblest appear uncomfortable."[32]

But as Coppin would remark at a retirement party in her honor, she had always taught two schools—the students of the Institute and the Black community.[33] Education was not confined to academic institutions, as Coppin frequently reminded her pupils. Those educated by the experience of life had much to offer. And, it was the duty of Blacks formally educated or otherwise to aid one another. Writing to Frederick Douglass in 1877 on the purpose of education as she viewed it, Coppin stated that she was not interested in producing "mere scholars" at the Institute, but rather students who would be committed to race "uplift."[34] Continuing, Coppin wrote:

1048

> I need not tell you, Mr. Douglass, that this is my desire to see my race lifted out of the mire of ignorance, weakness and degradation: no longer to be the fog end of the American rabble; to sit in obscure corners in public places and devour the scraps of knowledge which his superiors fling him. I want to see him erect himself about the untoward circumstances of his life. I want to see him crowned with strength and dignity; adorned with the enduring grace of intellectual attainments and a love of manly deeds and downright honesty.[35]

For nearly forty years Fanny Jackson Coppin combined academic excellence and positive race values to thousands of students of the Institute for Colored Youth and the Philadelphia Black community. The impact of her contributions to education, however, extended far beyond the confines of that community, as attested to by her former students. In 1909, a normal school in Baltimore, now known as Coppin State Teachers College, was named in her honor. In the year of her death, 1913, she published her autobiography, *Reminiscences of School Life*, and *Hints on Teaching*.

---

[32]*New York Age*, November 8, 1890; *Philadelphia Tribune*, February 1, 1913.
[33]*Christian Recorder*, October 22, 1902.
[34]Fanny Jackson to Frederick Douglass, March 30, 1877, *Frederick Douglass Papers*, Library of Congress.
[35]*Ibid*.

4. The Black Female American Missionary Association Teacher in the South, 1861–1870

Linda M. Perkins

The efforts of the northern black female in the education of her race in the South during and after the Civil War have frequently been overlooked in educational history. Motivated primarily by the philosophy of self-help and race solidarity espoused within the black communities of the North, hundreds of black women journeyed south after the outbreak of war in 1861. This philosophy of "race uplift" was a compelling force in the lives of pre–Civil War blacks. Because black men and women were relegated to the lowest strata of American society, the efforts of members of both groups were necessary for the "elevation" of the race.

Although blacks also taught through the sponsorship of various private benevolent organizations and the federally funded Freedmen's Bureau, this discussion will be limited to the efforts of black women within the American Missionary Association (AMA) from 1861 to 1870. During this period, several thousand New England and northern women migrated to the South to teach the newly freed slaves. Most studies that examine these efforts overlook the small number of black women who were part of this educational crusade. An examination of black women's activities within the AMA provides greater insight into the educational philosophy of "race uplift" held by blacks, regardless of gender. In addition, as will be discussed, despite their common gender black and white women teachers differed in their desires and motivations and in the experiences they encountered.

Established in 1846 by a group of Congregationalist abolitionists, the AMA was a pioneer in the education of blacks. The association was the first and largest benevolent group to establish

Originally published in *Black Americans in North Carolina and the South*, Jeffrey J. Crow and Flora J. Hatley, eds. (Chapel Hill: University of North Carolina Press, 1984).

1050

Fig. 4-1. Northern white females under the auspices of the American Missionary Association traveled south to teach emancipated slaves after the Civil War. Northern black females also sought affiliation with the AMA in the work of educating their race. From J. T. Trowbridge, *The South: A Tour of Its Battle Fields and Ruined Cities; a Journey through the Desolated States, and Talks with the People* (Hartford, Conn.: L. Stubbins, 1866), facing p. 338.

formal educational institutions in the South for blacks, and it has been the focus of numerous studies.[1] The lack of knowledge about the activities, observations, and motivations of blacks within the AMA, however, has resulted in a skewed and unbalanced perspective on the group's educational efforts on behalf of blacks.[2]

The great majority of women who answered the call to go south under the auspices of the AMA were white, from New England or other parts of the North, and upper or middle class. The contributions of these women are well known. While traditional studies consistently cite altruism and abolitionist zeal as the forces that impelled these women to undertake this activity, a close examination of their letters, testimonies, and reports suggests a different interpretation.

Upper- and middle-class New England white women were constrained by the Victorian concept of "true womanhood." These women were educated for their "proper sphere"—to become

wives and mothers—and not expected to work except in the event
of financial necessity. Consequently, many young, well-educated
New England women saw teaching in the South primarily as an
escape from their idle and unfulfilled lives.[3]

The letters of application from white females to the AMA national office in New York often reflected the need to obtain refuge
from the entrapment of New England life. One writer, in what
was a common theme, stated, "My circumstances are such that it
is necessary for me to be doing something." Frequently, fathers
would write the AMA requesting employment for their daughters.
One such father declared that his family was financially comfortable and that his daughter had completed high school and three
years at Mt. Holyoke Seminary. She had traveled in Europe, was
twenty-seven years old, and was living at home. The daughter had
never worked because there was no reason for her to do so; however, she wished to go south "to do more good than she thinks she
is doing at home." Many widows also applied. One applicant was
brief and to the point: "I am a soldier's widow—left alone. I
desire to be busy—useful."[4]

1051

In a study of female teachers of the AMA who served in Georgia from 1865 to 1873, Jacqueline Jones concurs with the above
thesis and also finds white females "joined the cause in order
to liberate themselves from the comfort and complacency of a
middle-class existence. . . . The work fulfilled some of their
needs and enabled them to understand their own situation more
clearly."[5]

Many of the letters of application from New England women no
doubt came from the AMA's active recruitment efforts. Capitaliz-
ing upon the Victorian socialization of women to be self-sacrificing and dutiful, the AMA issued a pamphlet entitled *Woman's
Work for the Lowly*. The publication urged females to fulfill their
proper sphere, rather than remain "merely ornaments in their fathers' parlors, dreaming, restless, hoping, till some fortunate mat-
ing shall give them a home and a sphere."[6] Because of the eagerness of many women to go south, it was economical for the AMA
to employ them. Not only were women paid less than men, but on
occasion the women paid their own travel south and donated their
entire salaries to the organization.[7] Few, however, envisioned

their adventure south as anything other than a temporary one. Between 1860 and 1870 the average tenure of the white female educator was two to three years.[8]

As women of the larger society sought ways to improve the quality of their lives during the mid-nineteenth century, free black men and women struggled together to obtain freedom for their enslaved race. By the Civil War the shared experience of racial oppression had imbued these blacks with a deep sense of responsibility for members of their race. Thus, when war commenced in 1861, black men and women eagerly volunteered their services in the Union army.[9]

Many exiled southern black women living in the North returned to their homeland. For example, the legendary Harriet Tubman offered her services as a spy, nurse, and scout for the Union army. Mary Shadd Cary, who migrated to Canada in the 1850s, rushed back to the States after the outbreak of the war to serve as a scout for the Union army. And Louise De Mortie, a noted lecturer who had migrated from Virginia to Boston in the 1850s, moved to New Orleans in 1865 to open that city's first orphanage for black youth.[10]

Black women of the South also contributed greatly in the "uplift" of their race. Mary S. Peake, a prosperous woman from Hampton, Virginia, was found teaching in Fortress Monroe when the first AMA missionary, Lewis C. Lockwood, arrived to establish a school in September 1861. The association designated Peake's school its first institution in the South.[11]

The AMA soon established other schools in Virginia for the thousands of abandoned slaves. Although from the beginning the association employed black monitors within the schools, by 1863 officials had begun to seek black teachers. Missionaries had observed that blacks had more influence over the freed slaves than whites. On this point William Woodbury, AMA superintendent of schools, wrote George Whipple, AMA secretary, "It is a fact, that with the requisite culture, the colored teachers will get nearer to their own race in a thousand and one ways, than can the same grade of white talent."[12]

Woodbury's reference to "culture" reflected the AMA's belief in the superiority of New England culture. More than any other

1052

benevolent association the AMA sought teachers of New England
and northern education, "culture and refinement." These qualifications, of course, limited the number of black women who
sought employment with the AMA in the Civil War years. While
certain normal schools admitted an occasional black woman,
Oberlin College in Ohio was the only institution that admitted
them on a regular basis.

Yet from this small number of educated black women of the
North letters of application were received in the AMA's national
office. According to their applications, these women, like most
women of their race, were employed and financially supporting
family members. The presence of dependent children normally
prevented otherwise qualified black women from receiving positions with the AMA. For example, Lucie Stanton Day, the first
black woman to complete the Ladies Department at Oberlin College (1850), was rejected by the association for a teaching post
because she supported a seven-year-old daughter. Likewise, a
widow, Mary S. Leary of Oberlin, was also refused by the AMA
because she had a child. While these conditions disqualified black
women for AMA employment, they did not necessarily exclude
white women. White females with children frequently received
appointments as matrons of AMA mission houses.[13]

The double standard utilized in the selection of black and white
AMA employees reinforced Afro-American suspicions about the
prejudice of abolitionists. Because the black women were not
financial assets to the AMA and were burdened with having to
demonstrate their "culture and refinement," their applications received greater scrutiny from the organization. From the outset the
AMA viewed the black female applications with caution and regarded the initial black educators as "experiments."

The meager AMA salary of fifteen dollars per month seemingly
would have deterred poor black women from applying. The deep
conviction of duty to race frequently mentioned in the women's
applications, however, overshadowed possible monetary gain as a
motivation. The statement of one black woman applicant who
characterized herself as "possessing no wealth and having nothing
to give but my life to my work" reflected the level of poverty and
depth of commitment of most of the women.[14]

1053

The theme of "race uplift" characterized the letters of the women. A black woman from Rhode Island wrote, "Sir, I have a great desire to go and labor among the Freedmen of the South. I think it is our duty as a people to spend our lives in trying to elevate our own race. Who can feel for us if we do not feel for ourselves? And who can feel the sympathy that we can who are identified with them?" Lucie Stanton Day of Ohio also noted, "My sense of duty urge me to write. . . . I wish to engage in this work because I desire the elevation of my race." And Sara G. Stanley of Ohio, but originally from New Bern, North Carolina, reiterated "duty" as the motivation in applying for a teaching post. She wrote, "I have felt a strong conviction of duty. . . . I am bound to that ignorant, degraded, long enslaved race, by the ties of love and consanguinity; they are . . . my people."[15]

The black women emphatically expressed the belief that blacks should aid in the massive educational efforts of the South. Further, because of the kinship of northern blacks to the freed blacks, the women believed they were better equipped to serve their people than whites. Although AMA officials also recognized the tremendous influence of black teachers upon the freedmen, they viewed the black teachers primarily as cultural role models and not as potential authority figures within the organization.

Five black women were selected to go to Virginia in 1863 and 1864. Three of the women were from Oberlin College: Blanche Harris, a native of Michigan; Clara Duncan of Pittsfield, Massachusetts; and Sara G. Stanley. The other two were Sallie Daffin, a native of Philadelphia and a graduate of the Institute for Colored Youth of that city, and Edmonia G. Highgate of Syracuse, New York, a graduate of a normal school of her state.[16]

In a study of the AMA, Clara DeBoer states that the organization was "color-blind" in its treatment of black employees. The treatment of these five black women, however, contradicts that statement. Upon their arrival in Norfolk they quickly encountered conditions quite unlike those of their white colleagues. First, they were housed separately from the white teachers. Then when it was discovered that the school held in the Methodist church was to have an all-black staff, the trustees quickly moved the classes to the small, unventilated basement of the building.[17]

1054

The all-black school staff was successful, nonetheless, until the illness of Harris and the transfer of several of the black women teachers ended the "experiment" after only several months. Although the women remained in the area and taught in other localities, their original school continued with an interracial staff.[18]

By the summer of 1864 the women had moved into the mission house with the other white teachers. No open arms greeted them there. Throughout the summer the women sent letters complaining about their treatment to Superintendent Woodbury, who had returned north. Stanley and Highgate reported that the white teachers commented constantly on the alleged inferiority of blacks and observed sharp social distinctions toward blacks. Daffin and Duncan wrote that the white matron of the mission house had "no interest in the cause" and requested her dismissal.[19]

By fall conditions had worsened. Another mission house director, a Miss Gleason, objected to having black teachers board at the house. This indignity prompted Stanley to write two letters regarding "prejudice against complexion." Stanley pointedly wrote AMA Secretary Whipple that she refused to move and was "much pained" that the association would place in such a position of authority a person who was "a very serious obstacle in the way of the advancement of the work." Moreover, in Stanley's estimation the woman lacked "thorough" intellectual training compared to many of the other teachers. Despite Stanley's letters Gleason remained in her position.[20]

The expectations of the black teachers and of the AMA regarding those who educated the freed blacks differed widely. The women expected competent, race-sensitive, and dedicated whites to be affiliated with the AMA. Never neglecting an opportunity to speak on behalf of the former slaves, Stanley wrote the national office in 1864 expressing her opinions about the teaching staff. She explained in her letter that racist and insensitive teachers would have "delerious effects [*sic*]" upon the black community. Although not visibly black, Stanley strongly identified with her race and suffered all the distinctions that racism placed on blacks. Explaining that she mingled constantly and freely with the blacks of all classes and knew their feelings, Stanley wrote, "My motive is to utter a plea for those who have no voice to plead for them-

1055

selves." In closing she candidly declared that blacks preferred black teachers and recognized their true friends not through "*word* but *deed*."[21]

Recent research in black educational history suggests that a large majority of blacks preferred black teachers for their children during the nineteenth century. This conviction resulted not from ethnic chauvinism, as some have argued, but rather from a situation Stanley identified—racist teachers had a deleterious effect upon black pupils.[22] In addition, black parents doubtless understood the importance of a former slave child's having a black person as an authority figure.

Despite the letters to the national office the racial climate did not improve. By the spring of 1865 all of the black teachers who had arrived in Norfolk in 1864 had relocated to other parts of the country. There the women discovered that the racism they had experienced in Virginia was not an aberration but the norm with the AMA. For example, Blanche Harris and her sister were assigned posts in Natchez, Mississippi, in 1865. She reported in her first letter to the national office of the AMA the "marked" distinctions made between the black and white teachers by the local AMA. The Harris sisters were not assigned schools, were housed with the servants of the AMA, and received repeated insults. Even though the women refused to leave Mississippi, Harris admitted she and her sister often thought of resigning. When they remembered the work to be done, however, they were "willing to sacrifice much to see [their] race elevated."[23]

Edmonia Highgate was far less tolerant of discrimination and rarely apologized when she criticized the AMA. Prior to the Civil War she served as an agent for the National Freedmen Relief Association of New York City. When she applied to the AMA in 1863 at the age of twenty, she had taught two and a half years and was principal of one of the public schools for blacks in Binghamton, New York. For Highgate to go south required her relinquishing a position of prestige and money. In her initial letter of application to the AMA, Highgate stressed her commitment to blacks in the South and stated she was resigning a job that paid twice as much as the one offered by the AMA.[24]

In March 1865, Highgate was assigned to teach in Darlington,

1056

Maryland. From the day of her arrival she was disappointed in the position and immediately informed the AMA of her intention to resign as soon as she organized a school and found a replacement. Because the area had only two hundred black residents, Highgate had to make laborious climbs over difficult terrain to reach only a handful of pupils. She often articulated the belief to the AMA that first-rate black teachers should receive maximum exposure among blacks. Highgate frankly informed the AMA officials that with her qualifications she should be in the "front ranks" as a "first teacher." Why, she asked, should she stay in the woods teaching thirty-four pupils when she could be reaching hundreds? Less than two months later she left to accept a post in Richmond, Virginia, with the Freedmen's Bureau.[25] Not committed to any benevolent organization but only to the "uplift" of her race, Highgate taught in Louisiana and Mississippi during the 1860s through the sponsorship of several organizations. In these locations Highgate narrowly escaped death by yellow fever and was shot at twice in her Mississippi school.[26]

1057

The AMA began to focus on normal and collegiate training once its elementary schools were absorbed into the public school system after 1870. At this time Highgate wrote AMA officials of her decision to spend the rest of her days as a teacher at the recently established AMA normal school at Tougaloo, Mississippi (1869). Confidently informing the men of her qualifications, Highgate cited her experiences and noted her certificate of normal training from the Syracuse Board of Education. She remarked, "Only caste prevents me from occupying" a teaching position in Syracuse.[27] Unfortunately, the decision to teach at Tougaloo was not entirely in the hands of Highgate. With the AMA, as with the Syracuse Board of Education, caste would prevent her from obtaining the post. Even by 1895 of the 110 faculty members at the five AMA colleges, only 4 were black. And at the seventeen AMA secondary schools at this time, only 12 of the 141 teachers were black.[28]

Although DeBoer has asserted that "efficiency and economy rather than race dictated the placement of the AMA teachers," the experiences of Highgate and the other black women refute this statement.[29] It was a common practice of the association to send blacks to the most undesirable locations, assign them to teach only primary grades, and place them in small schools. Even though 105 of the 533 employees commissioned by the AMA before 1870 were black, most were student or assistant teachers and ministers. Because of the low positions of the black AMA employees and the stringent requirements of the association that blacks had to meet in order to become regular teachers, only 34 of the 105 were from the North.[30]

The desire of the AMA to dominate black education frequently sabotaged black efforts. Jacqueline Jones found in Georgia that the AMA not only had great contempt for independent black teachers but was also "perverse in [its] attempt to thwart efforts at black self-help in education." Jones's research further suggests that the association attempted to limit the influence of black teachers on black students by frequently denying teaching commissions to literate blacks.[31]

Revisionist historians have concluded that New England ethnocentrism and the refusal of the AMA administration to employ blacks in prominent positions had a negative impact upon the education of blacks. On this point historian Carter G. Woodson observed in 1933 that the missionary educators sought to "transform and not develop" blacks. In a study of student rebellions on black college campuses in the 1920s, Raymond Wolters has traced the source of the students' protests to the condescension of the nineteenth-century missionary educators.[32]

Although traditional studies in educational history have often indicated that blacks welcomed the missionary efforts with "open arms," evidence suggests that this belief is greatly overstated. Frederick Douglass, a critic of benevolent societies, expressed his apprehensions regarding such groups in 1865, when he observed that these groups tended to give blacks pity and not justice. In 1865 the *Christian Recorder*, the organ of the African Methodist Episcopal church, did not let the disparity between the principles and practices of some missionaries go unremarked. In an editorial the paper condemned those missionaries "who, while in the North make loud pretension to Abolition, when they get South partake so largely of that contemptible prejudice that they are ashamed to be seen in company with colored men."[33]

1058

The efforts of the black teacher in the South during and after the Civil War demand further examination. Oppressed themselves by racism but genuinely committed to assisting the advancement of their race, northern black females possessed different motivations from and endured experiences in sharp contrast to those of white educators. Few of the black women saw their task as a temporary one. In a letter to the AMA, Clara Duncan wrote that in spite of hardships, "I am prepared to give up everything even life for the good of the cause, and count it not a hardship but an honor and blessing to me." Similarly, Sallie Daffin received numerous offers of higher salaries and better facilities for teaching posts in and near her home of Philadelphia, but wrote the AMA that she could never teach in the North again after realizing the needs of her race in the South. Edmonia Highgate relinquished a comfortable position in the North and pledged her life to work in the South. Braving, among other things, bullets and yellow fever, Highgate wrote, "I must do or die for my freed brethren." And Blanche Harris's statement from Mississippi that she had to "suffer many things" to see her race elevated expressed the attitude of the many black women who decided to devote their lives to the "cause."[34]

1059

While current scholarship is reviewing more closely the dynamics of intraracial class, color, and cultural differences, the earliest black female teachers insisted that they did not see themselves as distinct from the freed blacks. One such black New England female teacher of a Freedmen's Bureau school in Mississippi wrote in 1866: "I class myself with the freedmen. . . . Though I have never known servitude they are . . . my people. Born as far north as the lakes, I have never felt no freer because so many were less fortunate."[35]

It is probable that the black women educators saw little difference between themselves and their southern kin, for in reality they were not treated differently. In spite of their light skin and privileged education the women were not strangers to racism. When on her voyage to her post in Virginia in 1864 it was discovered that Clara Duncan was black, she was refused meal service, was referred to as a "nigger wench," and was forced to ride in a separate compartment. All of the women had similar experiences.[36] Even within the AMA black women were often treated as servants.

Consequently, these women understood that the typical criterion for their treatment was normally color and not class or culture.

Despite the many acts of discrimination toward blacks by the AMA, the women sometimes found within the organization persons of goodwill and genuine friendship. Several of the white female teachers wrote letters of protest to the New York office when they observed that the black female teachers were housed in a separate residence in Norfolk in 1864. Martha L. Kellogg, a white teacher in Wilmington, North Carolina, wrote the AMA of her indignation at the treatment of black teachers and asked to be transferred.[37]

Except for the white females who taught in the AMA normal schools and colleges in the South, most whites returned north after 1870. For the black female teacher, however, the mission of "uplifting" her race remained an important and unfinished task. Barred from employment within the AMA schools, black women became the backbone of the public schools for blacks in the South by the end of the century.

Remembering these efforts, black scholar W. E. B. Du Bois wrote in 1920, "After the [Civil] War the sacrifice of Negro women for freedom and uplift is one of the finest chapters in their history."[38] The black women AMA teachers were an important force in this history.

1060

NOTES

1. Literature on the subject includes: Richard B. Drake, "The American Missionary Association and the Southern Negro, 1861–88," Ph.D. diss., Emory University, 1957; Elizabeth Jacoway, *Yankee Missionaries in the South: The Penn School Experiment* (Baton Rouge: Louisiana State University Press, 1980); Clifton Herman Johnson, "The American Missionary Association, 1841–61: A Study of Christian Abolitionism," Ph.D. diss., University of North Carolina, 1958; Jacqueline Jones, *Soldiers of Light and Love: Northern Teachers and Georgia Blacks, 1865–73* (Chapel Hill: University of North Carolina Press, 1980); James M. McPherson, *The Abolitionist Legacy: From Reconstruction to the NAACP* (Princeton: Princeton University Press, 1975); James M. McPherson, *The Struggle for Equality: Abolitionists and the Negro in*

the Civil War and Reconstruction (Princeton: Princeton University Press, 1964); Willie Lee Rose, *Rehearsal for Reconstruction: The Port Royal Experiment* (New York: Oxford University Press, 1964); Henry Lee Swint, *The Northern Teacher in the South, 1862–70* (New York: Octagon Books, 1941); Elizabeth Botume, *First Days amongst the Contrabands* (Boston: Lee and Shepard, 1893); Laura M. Towne, *Letters and Diary of Laura M. Towne, Written from the Sea Islands of South Carolina, 1862–84*, edited by Rupert Sargent Holland (Cambridge: Printed at Riverside Press, 1912).

2. Men represented a large percentage of black AMA employees by Reconstruction. Most, however, were from the South, as were the women by this time. For statistics on black AMA teachers see Clara Merritt DeBoer, "The Role of Afro-Americans in the Origin and Work of the American Missionary Association, 1839–77," Ph.D. diss., Rutgers University, 1973, p. 492.

3. For a discussion of "true womanhood" see Barbara Welter, "The Cult of True Womanhood, 1820–60," *American Quarterly* 18 (Summer 1966): 151–74. Similar reasons accounted for the proliferation of women in the abolitionist movement. See Barbara Berg, *The Remembered Gate: Origins of American Feminism, the Woman, and the City, 1800–1860* (New York: Oxford University Press, 1978), p. 161.

4. Jones, *Soldiers of Light and Love*, p. 42.

5. Ibid., p. 8; Kate Mattison, Mt. Vernon, Ohio, to Reverend S. S. Jocelyn, March 1864, in American Missionary Association Papers, Amistad Research Center, Dillard University, New Orleans, La.

6. As quoted in McPherson, *Abolitionist Legacy*, p. 165.

7. Jones, *Soldiers of Light and Love*, p. 37.

8. McPherson, *Abolitionist Legacy*, p. 165.

9. James M. McPherson, *The Negro's Civil War: How American Negroes Felt and Acted during the War for the Union* (New York: Vintage Books, 1965), pp. 173–244; Susan King Taylor, *Reminiscences of My Life in Camp* (1902; reprint ed., New York: Arno Press, 1969).

10. Sarah Bradford, *Harriet Tubman: The Moses of Her People* (Secaucus, N.J.: Citadel Press, 1974), pp. 31–32; biographical folder and Martin Delany to Mary Shadd Cary, 7 December 1853, Mary Shadd Cary Papers, Moorland-Spingarn Research Center, Howard University; John W. Blassingame, *Black New Orleans, 1860–80* (Chicago: University of Chicago Press, 1973), p. 170; George Washington Williams, *A History of the Negro Race in America*, 2 vols. (New York: Bergman Publishers, 1883), 2:449.

11. Lewis C. Lockwood, *Mary S. Peake: The Colored Teacher at*

1061

Fortress Monroe (Boston: American Tract Society, 1863), pp. 5, 14; Lewis C. Lockwood, Fortress Monroe, to AMA Executive Committee, 24 February 1862, AMA Papers.

12. William H. Woodbury, Norfolk, Virginia, to George Whipple, 7 November 1863, AMA Papers.

13. Lucie Stanton Day, Cleveland, Ohio, to George Whipple, 26 April 1864; Mary S. Leary, Oberlin, Ohio, to George Whipple, 17 September 1867, AMA Papers. During the period that Day sought a position with the AMA the organization employed a white female with four children to serve as matron of the mission house in Norfolk. See Clara C. Duncan, Norfolk, to William Woodbury, 29 August 1864, AMA Papers. The author wishes to thank Ellen Henle for directing her to the references on Day and Leary.

14. Sara G. Stanley, Cleveland, Ohio, to George Whipple, 19 January 1864, AMA Papers.

15. Mrs. E. Garrison Jackson, Newport, Rhode Island, to S. S. Jocelyn, 13 June 1864; Lucie Stanton Day, Cleveland, Ohio, to George Whipple, 26 April 1864; Sara S. Stanley, Cleveland, Ohio, to George Whipple, 19 January and 4 March 1864, AMA Papers.

16. Ellen Henle and Marlene Merrill, "Antebellum Black Coeds at Oberlin College," *Women's Studies Newsletter* 7 (Spring 1979): 10. Mrs. M. P. Dascomb, Oberlin, Ohio, to George Whipple, 2 March 1864; Edmonia Highgate to the Reverend E. P. Smith, 23 July 1870, AMA Papers. Fanny Jackson Coppin, *Reminiscences of School Life and Hints on Teaching* (Philadelphia: AME Book Concern, 1913), pp. 147, 184.

17. DeBoer, "The Role of Afro-Americans," p. viii.

18. Edmonia G. Highgate, Portsmouth, Virginia, to George Whipple, 30 April 1864; Sara S. Smith, Norfolk, to George Whipple, 15 March 1864, AMA Papers.

19. Sara G. Stanley and Edmonia Highgate, Norfolk, to William Woodbury, 21 July 1864; Sallie Daffin, Norfolk, to William Woodbury, 29 August 1864; Clara Duncan, Norfolk, to William Woodbury, 29 August 1864, AMA Papers.

20. Sara G. Stanley, Norfolk, to George Whipple, 6 October 1864, AMA Papers.

21. Sara G. Stanley, Norfolk, to William Woodbury, 21 July 1864, AMA Papers.

22. Carlton Mabee, *Black Education in New York State* (Syracuse: Syracuse University Press, 1979), p. 97; see also chapter 15, "The Struggle for Black Control," in McPherson, *Abolitionist Legacy*.

23. Blanche Harris, Natchez, Mississippi, to George Whipple, 23 January and 10 March 1866, AMA Papers.

24. Edmonia Highgate, Binghamton, New York, to George Whipple, 18 and 30 January, 17 February 1864, AMA Papers.

25. Edmonia Highgate, Darlington, Maryland, to George Whipple, 13 April 1865, AMA Papers.

26. Edmonia Highgate, Lafayette Parish, to Michael E. Strieby, 8 February 1866, and same, New Orleans, to Strieby, 24 September 1867, AMA Papers.

27. Edmonia Highgate, Cortland, New York, to the Reverend E. P. Smith, 23 July 1870, AMA Papers.

28. McPherson, *Abolitionist Legacy*, p. 273.

29. DeBoer, "The Role of Afro-Americans," p. 493.

30. Ibid., p. 326.

31. Jones, *Soldiers of Light and Love*, p. 206.

32. Raymond Wolters, *The New Negro on Campus* (Princeton: Princeton University Press, 1975), pp. 340–41; Carter G. Woodson, *Mis-education of the Negro* (Washington, D.C.: Associated Publishers, Inc., 1933), p. 17.

33. See Joel Williamson, "Black Self-Assertion before and after Emancipation," in Nathan I. Huggins, Martin Kilson, Daniel M. Fox, eds., *Key Issues in the Afro-American Experience* (New York: Harcourt, Brace Jovanovich, 1971), p. 225; *Christian Recorder*, 2 December 1865, as quoted in McPherson, *The Struggle for Equality*, p. 397.

34. Clara C. Duncan, Norfolk, to William Woodbury, 29 August 1864; Sallie Daffin, Norfolk, to George Whipple, 20 February 1865; Edmonia G. Highgate, New York, to Michael E. Strieby, 26 October 1864; Blanche Harris, Natchez, Mississippi, to George Whipple, 10 March 1866, AMA Papers.

35. As quoted in Leon F. Litwack, *Been in the Storm So Long: The Aftermath of Slavery* (New York: Knopf, 1979), p. 512.

36. Marie Bassette, Norfolk, to George Whipple and S. S. Jocelyn, 24 March 1864; Samuel H. Walker, Norfolk, to Whipple, 28 March 1864; Clara C. Duncan, Norfolk, to George Whipple, 30 March 1864, AMA Papers.

37. DeBoer, "The Role of Afro-Americans," p. 278; Martha L. Kellogg, Wilmington, North Carolina, to AMA, 5 November 1866, AMA Papers.

38. W. E. B. Du Bois, *Darkwater: Voices from within the Veil* (New York: Schocken Books, 1969), p. 178.

1063

Journal of Social Issues, Vol. 39, No. 3, 1983, pp. 17-28

The Impact of the "Cult of True Womanhood" on the Education of Black Women

Linda M. Perkins   1065

Mary Ingraham Bunting Institute of Radcliffe College

This paper compares the primary purposes and functions of educating black and white women in the 19th century. For white women, education served as a vehicle for developing homemaker skills, for reinforcing the role of wife and mother, and a milieu for finding a potential husband. For black women education served as an avenue for the improvement of their race or "race uplift." The economic, political and social conditions which contributed to these purposes are discussed within a historical context.

To better understand the education of black women vis-a-vis the education of women of the larger society, it is important to place black women within a social and historical context. This essay examines the impact of the "true womanhood" philosophy on the education of white women, and the black philosophy of "race uplift" on the education and development of black women in the nineteenth century. Although blacks considered the women of their race "women" in the early and mid-nineteenth century, by the end of the century they began to place more emphasis on them being "ladies". This shift in attitudes toward women by many educated male blacks will also be discussed.

THE NINETEENTH CENTURY CONTEXT: THE ANTEBELLUM PERIOD

Observers of the early nineteenth century frequently cite the emergence of the 'cult of true womanhood' as significantly shaping women's education during this

This paper depends on two collections of papers at Howard University's Moorland-Springarn Research Center: the *Mary Shadd Cary Papers* and the *Anna J. Cooper Papers*.

Correspondence regarding this issue should be addressed to Dr. Linda M. Perkins, The Mary Ingraham Bunting Institute, Radcliffe College, 10 Garden Street, Cambridge, MA 02138.

period. This concept of the "true woman" emphasized innocence, modesty, piety, purity, submissiveness and domesticity. Female education was necessary for the molding of the "ideal woman". Such education reinforced the idea of women's natural position of subordination and focused upon women being loving wives and good mothers. Literacy was deemed important for the reading of the Bible and other religious materials. And needlepoint, painting, music, art, and French dominated the curriculum of "female" education (see Cott, 1977, Rosenberg, 1982, Rothman, 1978; Welter, 1966).

This "true womanhood" model was designed for the upper and middle-class white woman, although poorer white women could aspire to this status. However, since most blacks had been enslaved prior to the Civil War and the debate as to whether they were human beings was a popular topic, black women were not perceived as women in the same sense as women of the larger (i.e., white) society. The emphasis upon women's purity, submissiveness and natural fragility was the antithesis of the reality of most black women's lives during slavery and for many years thereafter.

Not surprisingly whites of the early nineteenth century developed an educational philosophy to correspond with their attitudes towards women. At the same time, blacks espoused a philosophy of education for "race uplift". This education was for the entire race and its purpose was to assist in the economical, educational and social improvement of their enslaved and later emancipated race (For a detailed discussion see Perkins, 1981). Unlike their white counterparts, blacks established coeducational schools and similar curricula for both males and females.

The early decades of the nineteenth century witnessed a dramatic shift in the social and economic fabric of the nation. The growth of factories and increased industry provided employment outside homes and altered the colonial self-sustaining family. With the coming of urbanization and industrialization a new role for women emerged. Unlike the colonial period, when single and married white women worked without stigma, the early nineteenth century emphasized women's "proper sphere" as being within the home (See Rothman, 1978). Throughout the antebellum years, white women were deluged with sermons and speeches which stressed the "duty" of a "true woman". These speeches and sermons were reinforced by a proliferation of magazines, journals and other printed materials that focused upon instructing women of their proper sphere (Cott, 1977).

During the period of the development of the norm of "true womanhood", antebellum blacks struggled to abolish slavery and obtain equality in the nation. The theme of "race uplift" became the motto within the black communities of the nation. It was expected that blacks who were able to assist, i.e. "uplift", other members of their race, would do so (Perkins, 1981).

Although white society did not acknowledge the black women as female, the black race did. During the first half of the nineteenth century, black women's educational, civic and religious organizations in the north bore the word "ladies" in their titles, clearly indicating their perceptions of self. One of the earliest black female educational societies, the Female Literary Association of Philadelphia, combined educational and civic objectives for the group's purposes. The Preamble of the organization's constitution reflected the women's commitment to the philosophy of race "uplift". They wrote, it was their "duty . . . as daughters of a despised race, to use our utmost endeavors to enlighten the understanding, to cultivate the talents entrusted to our keeping, that by so doing, we may in a great measure, break down the strong barrier of prejudice, and raise ourselves to an equality with those of our fellow beings, who differ from us in complexion." (reported in the *Liberator,* December 3, 1931.). Clearly the woman spoke of their oppression as a result of their race and not sex.

1067

Unlike women of the white society, black women were encouraged to become educated to aid in the improvement of their race. An 1837 article entitled "To the Females of Colour" in the New York black newspaper, *The Weekly Advocate,* (Jan. 7, 1837) urged black women to obtain an education. The article stated, "in any enterprise for the improvement of our people, either moral or mental, our hands would be palsied without woman's influence." Thus, the article continued, "let our beloved female friends, then, rouse up, and exert all their power, in encouraging, and sustaining this effort (educational) which we have made to disabuse the public mind of the misrepresentations made of our character; and to show the world, that there is virtue among us, though concealed; talent, though buried; intelligence, though overlooked." (To the Females of Colour, 1837). In other words, black females and males would demonstrate the race's intelligence, morality, and ingenuity.

It should be understood that during the antebellum period, free blacks lived primarily in an occupational caste. The men were relegated to menial positions while women were primarily domestic workers. Although blacks perceived education as "uplifting", most whites viewed education of blacks as threatening to their position of dominance.

By the time of emancipation in 1863, every southern state had laws that prohibited the education of slaves, and in many instances free blacks as well (Woodson, 1919/1968). There were scattered opportunities for both free blacks and slaves to become literate prior to the 1830s in the nation. However, education for blacks was viewed as dangerous after the fiery *Appeal* of David Walker in 1829 and the 1830 slave revolt of Nat Turner—both literate men. After the 1830s, all southern states instituted laws prohibiting the education of blacks, and such activities were thereby forced underground (Woodson, 1919/1968).

The decades of the 1830s and 1840s in which free blacks sought access to educational institutions in the North paralleled the founding of seminaries for white women. Historian Ann Firor Scott (1979) points out in her study of Troy

Female Seminary, the first such institution to open, that the school combined the "true womanhood" ideal with feminist values from its opening in 1822. Under the direction of Emma Willard, the institution sought to preserve the traditional social and political status of women while challenging the notion of women's inferior intellectual status. Despite this challenge to society's view of the intellectual inferiority of women, Troy instilled within its students that "feminine delicacy . . . was a primary and indispensable virtue."

Other such seminaries proliferated in the nation prior to the Civil War. These institutions began the professional training of female teachers. However, few opened their doors to black women on a continuous basis. The lone exception was Oberlin College, which received notoriety in 1833 when it decided to admit both women and blacks on an equal basis with white men. As a result, most of the earliest black college graduates, male and female, were Oberlin graduates (DuBois, 1900). It was not atypical for black families to relocate to Oberlin for the education of their daughters. For example, when Blanche V. Harris was denied admission to a white female seminary in Michigan in the 1850's, her entire family moved to Oberlin (Henle & Merrill, 1979). Similarly, Mary Jane Patterson, who in 1862 became the first black woman to earn a college degree in the United States, moved from North Carolina in the 1850s to Oberlin with her family because of the educational opportunities at the College. Three Patterson females and one male graduated from Oberlin. Fanny Jackson Coppin, the second black woman to earn a college degree in the nation, was sent from Washington, D.C. to Newport, Rhode Island, where her educational opportunities were greater. After completing the Rhode Island State Normal School, she also went to Oberlin and graduated in 1865. Bishop Daniel Payne of the African Methodist Episcopal Church was so impressed with the ambition of Fanny Jackson Coppin that he aided her with a scholarship to Oberlin (see Coppin, 1913). This financial assistance is not insignificant when one remembers that when Fanny Jackson Coppin entered Oberlin in 1860, no black women in the nation had a college degree and very few black men attempted higher education. Bishop Payne's enthusiasm and support for Coppin's education contrasts with the debates on the danger of higher education that surrounded the question of education for white women. These arguments stated that higher education not only reduced a woman's chance of marriage but also resulted in physical and psychological damage (Woody, 1929).

As early as 1787 Benjamin Rush in his publication, *Thoughts on Female Education,* stated that women should be educated to become "stewards, and guardians" of the family assets. And Noah Webster warned that "education is always wrong which raises a woman above her station." Even as high schools for women became available after the Civil War, historian Thomas Woody, in his seminal history of women's education (1929) notes that the primary purposes of such institutions were to (1) extend the scope of "female education", (2)

1068

increase the social usefulness of women, and (3) train teachers for the lower grades as opposed to the preparation for college which was the primary aim of the male high school.

Studies of the students and graduates of white female high schools and seminaries confirm that marriage usually terminated employment of the women. Teaching, the predominant profession of these women, was merely a way-station until matrimony. Scott's work on Troy women students and graduates during the period 1822–1872 indicates that only 6 percent worked during marriage and only 26 percent worked at any time during their life. David Allmendinger's (1979) research on Mt. Holyoke students from 1837–1850 is consistent with Scott's data. Although the majority of the student population taught at some point in their lives, most did so for less than five years. Only 6 percent made teaching a lifetime profession. Although data on black women for these periods are inconclusive, the literature on black attitudes towards education strongly takes the view that educated black women and marriage were not incompatible. W. E. B. DuBois' study of 1900 of the black college graduates indicates that 50 percent of the black women college graduates from 1860–1899 were married. Similarly, census statistics in 1900 report that ten times as many married black women than married white women were employed. (DuBois, 1900) This disproportiate ratio is no doubt a reflection of the economic necessity of black women to their families.

1069

AFTER THE CIVIL WAR

For several thousand New England white women who journeyed South to teach after the Civil War, it appears that the "cult of true womanhood" was a significant impetus. The women were overwhelmingly single, upper and middle-class, unemployed and educated in New England seminaries and Oberlin College (McPherson, 1975). Their letters of application to the missionary societies sponsoring teachers to the South often reflected a deep need to escape idleness and boredom. A letter stating, "my circumstances are such that it is necessary for me to be doing something" was the common theme (Jones, 1980). In contrast, black women who applied were overwhelmingly employed and financially supported families. Their letters of application consistently reflected a theme of "duty" and "race uplift". While the tenure of the white female educator in the South was normally two to three years, the black female expressed a desire to devote their entire lives to their work and most did (Perkins, in press).

Although conscious of their gender, the earliest black female college graduates repeatedly stated their desire for an education was directly linked to aiding their race. Fanny Jackson Coppin expressed in her autobiography of 1913 that, from girlhood, her greatest ambition was "to get an education and to help [her] people." Anna J. Cooper (1882), an Oberlin graduate of 1884 whose papers are housed at Howard University, stated she decided to attend college while in kindergarten and devoted her entire life to the education of her race. Affluent Mary Church Terrell, also an Oberlin graduate of '84, jeopardized her inheritance when her father, who wished her to model her life on the upper-class white "true womanhood" ideal, threatened to disinherit her if she worked after graduating from Oberlin. Terrell wrote years later (1968) of this dilemma: "I have conscientiously availed myself of opportunities for preparing myself for a life of usefulness as only four other colored (women) had been able to do . . . All during my college course I had dreamed of the day when I could promote the welfare of my race." Although she was forced by law to forfeit her public school teaching post after marriage, she taught voluntarily in an evening school and became a widely known lecturer and women's club leader.

"Race uplift" was the expected objective of *all* educated blacks; however, after the Civil War, the implementation of this philosophy was placed primarily on the shoulders of black women. Women were prominent among the many educated blacks who migrated or returned south after emancipation to aid in the transition of emancipated blacks from slavery to freedom. For example, Louise DeMontie, a noted lecturer who migrated from Virginia to Boston in the 1850's, moved to New Orleans in 1865 to open the city's first orphanage for black youth. Mary Shadd Cary, who migrated to Canada in the 1850's, returned to the United States after the outbreak of the War to serve as a scout for the Union army. Scores of other black women went South to engage in the massive effort to educate the newly emancipated blacks (Blassingame, 1973; Williams, 1883).

Throughout the War and afterwards, northern black women raised money and collected clothes to send South. On one occasion the Colored Ladies Sanitary Commission of Boston sent $500 to blacks in Savannah. Similarly, in Washington, D.C., Elizabeth Keckley, the mulatto seamstress of First Lady Mary Lincoln organized the Contraband Relief Association of Washington in 1862. With forty other black women, in its first two years of existence, the group sent nearly one hundred boxes and barrels of clothing to southern blacks and spent in excess of $1600 (McPherson, 1965).

Perhaps more impressive were the efforts of black women in the South to aid themselves. Viewing charity primarily as an activity for the fortunate to aid the unfortunate, white missionaries frequently recorded with astonishment the establishment of black self-help groups. One such report in *The National Freedmen* in 1865 (May 1, 1865, Number 4) cited a group of poor black women in Charleston who formed an organization to aid the sick. After working all day, members of the group devoted several hours to duty in the hospitals. In fact, *The National Freedmen*, the organ of the National Freedmen Relief Society, often reported the general charity among blacks in general and black women in particular. One such missionary report stated:

> I have been greatly struck with the charity of these colored people. There are few of them even comfortably situated for this world's goods. Yet, their charity is the most extensive,

hearty, genuine thing imaginable. They have innumerable organizations for the relief of
the aged, the helpless or needy from whatever. (*The National Freedmen,* December 15,
1865, Number 11).

The observer was greatly impressed by the work of black women. He wrote that
he witnessed black women "past the prime of life and with no visible means of
support" who took in whole families of orphaned children. These stories were
found repeatedly in missionary letters.

Despite the significant contributions of black women to the economic,
civic, religious, and educational improvement of the race, after emancipation
there was a noticeable shift in the attitudes towards the role of women by many
members of the race.

Schools for blacks in the South proliferated after the close of the Civil War   1071
and, by the 1870's, those founded by northern missionaries and the federal
Freedmen's Bureau became the backbone of the public schools for blacks (Bullock, 1970). DuBois, in his 1900 study of the *Negro Common School,* reports
that in 1890 there were over 25,000 black teachers. Half of this number were
women. With education being placed at the top of the race's agenda for progress,
a huge number of black teachers was necessary. By 1899, more than 28,500
black teachers were employed in the nation.

While public schools for blacks were overwhelmingly coeducational, and
girls received primarily the same instruction as boys, the black men greatly
outnumbered black women in higher education. By 1890, only 30 black women
held baccalaureate degrees, compared to over 300 black men and 2,500 white
women. In this same year, white women constituted 35 percent of the undergraduate collegiate student bodies (Cooper, 1892; Graham, 1975). Whereas prior
to the Civil War education was viewed as important for all members of the race,
during and after Reconstruction, those black women who were educated were
trained almost exclusively to become elementary and secondary school teachers.
In contrast, the small number of educated black men had more encouragement
and access to institutions of higher education. Further, employment options of
black men were greater than those of black women (Johnson, 1938).

The issues of sexism and racism were confronted head on in 1892 by Anna
Julia Cooper in her book, *A Voice from the South.* Citing all of the well known
arguments against higher education of women promulgated by whites in the past,
Cooper stated that most black men had accepted these arguments and also believed women to be inferior to men. Cooper wrote, on the women question:
"[Black] men drop back into sixteenth century logic." These men, according to
Cooper ascribed to the view that "women may stand on pedestals or live in doll
houses . . . but not seek intellectual growth." Cooper continued, "I fear the
majority of colored men do not yet think it worth while that women aspire to
higher education." (Cooper, 1892, p. 75).

Cooper's observations were correct concerning the view of many educated
black men. The passage of the fourteenth amendment in 1870 which granted

black men the right to vote, signaled the first major gender distinction acknowledged by society towards them. As a result, black men during the latter decades
of the nineteenth century moved temporarily into high political offices. Twenty-
two black men served in the nation's Congress by 1900 and scores of others held
local and state political positions (Franklin, 1969). As black men sought to
obtain education and positions similar to that of white men in society, many
adopted the prevailing notion of white society, of the natural subordination of
women.

SEXISM AND THE EDUCATION OF BLACK WOMEN

1072 Given the unique history of black women in their race, to view them as less than
men was not only retrogressive but absurd. Even though the prevailing economic
deprivation of blacks at the end of the nineteenth and early twentieth centuries
demanded that black women work, many elite blacks nevertheless embraced the
Victorian "true womanhood" ideal of the 1820's and 1830's (see Williamson,
1971). As were New England white women of the antebellum period, black
women were expected to be self-sacrificing and dutiful. (Prior to emancipation,
all blacks were expected to do so.). Speeches and articles abound citing black
women as the nurturers and the guardians of—not the thinkers or leaders of the
race. Most black women educators accepted that charge. (See Laney, 1899)

By the end of the nineteenth century, sexism had increased significantly
among educated blacks. When the first major black American Learned Society
was founded in 1897, by a group of well known black men, the constitution of
the organization limited membership to "men of African descent". The issue of
female membership was debated by the group and they resolved that the male
stipulation would be rescinded; however, this was never done (Moss, 1981). It
was clear by the end of the nineteenth century that many black men viewed
women as their intellectual subordinates and not capable of leadership positions.
When Fanny Jackson Coppin eulogized Frederick Douglass in 1896 (included in
In Memoriam: Frederick Douglass) she praised him for "his good opinion of the
rights of women . . . that women were not only capable of governing the household but also of elective franchise." The fact that she made this the point of her
praise for Douglass indicates that his view of women was the exception rather
than the rule.

Fanny Coppin headed the prestigious Institute for Colored Youth in Phila-
delphia, the oldest black private high school in the nation from 1869–1901. After
she was forced to retire in 1901, the school was henceforth headed by black men.
(For details on Coppin's years at the Institute for Colored Youth, see Perkins,
Note 1.) Likewise, the prestigious, oldest black public high school in the nation,
M Street School in Washington, D.C. was initially headed by a black woman,
Mary Jane Patterson. Patterson served as Assistant Principal to Coppin at the

Institute for Colored Youth from 1865–1869 and was appointed principal of M Street in 1869 (Perkins, Note 1). She was removed several years later so that a male could head the institution. Anna Julia Cooper also served briefly as Principal of M Street from 1901–1906 but was dismissed for her refusal to adhere to the inferior curriculum prescribed for black students. Like the Institute for Colored Youth, by the turn of the century, and thereafter M Street was headed by black men (Anna J. Cooper Papers, Howard University).

As the century came to a close, "race uplift" was synonymous with black women. With the formation of the National Association of Colored Women 1896, educated black women focused their activities on community development. Reflecting the century old race philosophy, the group chose as their motto "lifting as we climb". Throughout the South, the organization founded orphanages, homes for the elderly and educational institutions, and supported religious programs. The crusade against lynching of this period was also spearheaded by a black woman, the fearless Ida B. Wells-Barnett.

1073

In 1894, the black Senator John Mercer Langston from Virginia recalled his visits in the South after Emancipation and noted:

> They (black women) were foremost in designs and efforts for school, church and general industrial work for the race, always self-sacrificing and laborious . . . Through all phases of his advancement from his Emancipation to his present position of social, political, eduational, moral, religious and material status, the colored American is greatly indebted to the women of his race. (Langston, 1894, p. 236)

Later, black scholar W. E. B. DuBois (1969) would also write, "after the war the sacrifice of Negro women for freedom and black uplift is one of the finest chapters in their history." Yet, today this chapter is rarely found in black, women's or educational histories.

Even into the twentieth century, the focus on educating black women to "uplift" and primarily to educate the race continued. In 1933, dean of women at Howard University, Lucy D. Slowe wrote a piece entitled "Higher Education of Negro Women" which addressed many of the same issues raised by Anna J. Cooper in 1892. Slowe voiced concern for the lack of opportunity for college educated black women to get leadership training within black colleges. Noting that while black men college graduates were found in the fields of ministry, law, medicine and other professions, teaching constituted the largest occupation of black women college graduates. After surveying the responses of forty-four black coeducational institutions, Slowe found that black women received little in courses, activities or role-models to aid them in leadership development. Slowe conceded that many black families were conservative when it came to the issue of independent and assertive women; however, black colleges aided in fostering this paternalistic and conservative view of women. She wrote: "The absence of women or the presence of very few on the policy-making bodies of colleges is also indicative of the attitude of college administrators toward women as responsible individuals, and toward the special needs of women (Slowe, 1933, p. 357).

Despite the feminist writings of Anna J. Cooper and Lucy Slowe, the education of black women into the twentieth century continued to be focused towards teaching and "uplifting" the race. In a 1956 study of the collegiate education of black women, Jeanne L. Noble observed that the education of black women continued to be basically utilitarian- to provide teachers for the race. One of the 412 women in her study commented on this professional isolation.

> There are entirely too many fine Negro women in the teaching profession. There should be vocational guidance to encourage them into new fields. Around this part of the country middle-class women go into teaching because this is the highest type of position for them (Noble, 1956, p. 87).

1074

Unlike black women of the mid and late nineteenth century who consciously prepared themselves for leadership positions, as Lucy Laney stated in 1899, to many black women in the twentieth century such a role had become a burden. Rhetaugh Graves Dumas indicates in her (1980) essay "Dilemmas of Black Females in Leadership," that their leadership has been 'restricted to primarily female and youth organizations most often surrounding the black community. Recent work by sociologist Cheryl Townsend Gilkes also confirms that the education of black women leaders has been focused to meet the black community needs (Gilkes, 1980).

The shift in attitude towards women in the black community and the role they were expected to assume vis-a-vis men paralleled the acceptance by black men of the dominance of man after Emancipation. Although black women have worked far out of proportion to their white counterpart, out of economic necessity, sexism and paternalism among the men of their race have resulted in relegation of black women to the roles of nurturer and "helpmate." The recognition of sexism within the black community has been slow. Recently (Summer, 1982, Volume 51) the *Journal of Negro Education* (1982) devoted a special issue to the Impact of Black women in Education—the first such issue in the journal's fifty-one year history.

Although the shift from egalitarian to sexist views of black women can be explained historically, sociologically, and psychologically, the continued depressed economic and educational status of blacks demands that race "uplift" return to its original meaning to include both men and women.

REFERENCE NOTES

1. Perkins, L. M. *Fanny Jackson Copping and the Institute for Colored Youth: A model of nineteenth century black female educational and community leadership, 1837–1902.* Unpublished dissertation, University of Illinois, Champaign-Urbana, 1978.

REFERENCES

Blassingame, J. W. *Black New Orleans, 1860–80.* Chicago, IL: University of Chicago, 1973.

Bullock, H. A. *A history of negro education in the South: From 1619 to the present.* Cambridge, MA: Harvard University Press, 1970.

Cooper, A. J. *A voice from the South.* Xenia, OH: Aldine, 1892.

Coppin, F. J. *Remininscences of school life and hints on teaching.* Philadelphia, PA: African Methodist Episcopal Church, 1913.

Cott, N. *The bonds of womanhood: "Woman's sphere" in New England, 1780–1835.* New Haven, NJ: Yale University Press, 1977.

DuBois, W. E. B. The college bred Negro. In *Proceedings of the fifth conference for the study of the negro problems.* Altanta, GA: Atlanta University Press, 1900.

Dubois, W. E. B. *Darkwater: Voices from within the veil (1920).* New York: Schocken, 1969.

Dumas, R. G. Dilemmas of black females in leadership. In L. F. Rodgers-Rose, (Ed.), *The black woman.* Beverly Hills, CA: Sage, 1980, 203–215.

Franklin, J.H. From slavery to freedom. New York: Vintage, 1969.

Gilkes, C. T. Holding back the ocean with a broom: Black women and community work. In L. F. Rodgers-Rose (Ed.) *The black woman.* Beverly Hills, CA: Sage, 1980, 217–231.

Graham, P. A. Expansion and exclusion: A history of women in American higher education. *Signs,* 1978, *3,* 766.

Henle, E., & Merrill, M. Antebellum black coeds at Oberlin College. *Women's Studies Newsletter,* 1979, *7,* 10.

In memoriam: Fredick Douglass. Philadelphia, PA: John C. Yorston, 1895.

Johnson, C. S. *The negro college graduate.* College Park, MD: McGrath, 1938.

Jones, J. *Soldiers of light and love: Northern teachers and Georgia blacks, 1865–1873.* Chapel Hill, NC: University of North Carolina Press, 1980.

Journal of Negro Education. Special Issue on the Impact of black women in education, Vol. 51, Summer, 1982.

Laney, L. The burden of the educated colored woman. In *Hampton Negro conference,* No. 3. Hampton, VA: Hampton Institute Press, 1899.

Langston, J. M. *From the Virginia plantation to the national capital.* Hartford, MA: Hartford, 1894.

McPherson, J. M. *The negro's Civil War: How American negros felt and acted during the war for the Union.* New York, NY: Vintage, 1965.

Moss, A. A. *The American negro academy: Voice of the talented tenth.* Baton Rouge, LA: Louisiana State University Press, 1981.

Noble, J. L. *The negro woman's college education.* New York: Teachers College, Columbia University, Bureau of Publications, 1956.

Perkins, L. M. Black women and racial "uplift" prior to emancipation. In F. C. Steady (Ed.), *The black woman cross-culturally.* Cambridge, MA: Schenkman, 1981, 317–334.

Perkins, L. M. The black female American missionary association teach in the South, 1860–70. In, *The history of blacks in the South.* Chapel Hill, NC: The University of North Carolina Press, in press.

Rosenberg, R. *Beyond separate spheres: Intellectual roots of modern feminism.* New Haven, CT: Yale University Press, 1982.

Rothman, S. M. *Woman's proper place: A history of changing ideals and practices, 1870 to the present.* New York: Basic Books, 1978.

Rush, B. *Thoughts upon female education, accommodated to the present state of society, manners and government in the United States of America.* Philadelphia, PA: Prichard & Hall, 1787.

Scott, A. F. The ever widening circle: The diffusion of feminist values from the Troy female seminary, 1822–1872. *History of Education Quarterly,* Spring, 1979, 3–25.

Slowe, L. Higher education of negro women. *Journal of Negro Education,* 1933, *2,* 352–358.

Terrell, M. C. *A colored woman in a white world.* Washington, DC: National Association of Colored Women's Clubs, 1968.

Welter, B. The cult of true womanhood: 1820–1860. *American Quarterly,* 1966, *18,* 151–174.

1075

Williams, G. W. *A history of the negro race in America.* New York: Bergman, 1883.
Williamson, J. Black self-assertion before and after emancipation. In N. I. Huggins, M. Kilson, &
      D. M. Fox (Eds.), *Key issues in the Afro-American experience.* New York: Harcourt Brace &
      Jovanovich, 1971.
Woodson, C. G. *The education of the negro prior to 1861 (1919).* New York: Arnon, 1968.
Woody, T. *A history of women's education in the United States.* New York: Science Press, 1929.

Black Women and Racial "Uplift" Prior to Emancipation*

Linda Perkins

The efforts of whites, both male and female in the abolitionist and antislavery movement have been well documented. And, while numerous studies and biographies provide some information concerning black male involvement in the pre-Civil War era, with the exception of Harriet Tubman and Sojourner Truth, little is known of the important role that black women played in improving the condition of their race during the antebellum period.[1]

In view of the dual oppression of blacks and females, an assessment of black women's efforts in the early and mid-nineteenth century sheds light not only on their significance to the race but also reveals the difference in the perception of a woman's "place" and role within the black community from that of the larger American society.

This essay examines the role of the black female prior to emancipation and highlights some of her activities in the "uplift" (as it was then termed) of the black race. Particular focus shall be given to the attention placed upon self-help, aiding improverished members of the race in the North, as well as the ardent efforts made by black women to abolish slavery. Throughout the nineteenth century, the threads that held together the organizational as well as individual pursuits of black women were those of "duty" and "obligation" to the race. The concept of racial obligation was intimately linked with the concept of racial "uplift" and "elevation".

Although slavery had been legally abolished in the North by the 1830s, racism remained. In the aftermath of Northern slavery, free

*The author would like to thank the National Institute of Education for support given during the preparation of this article.

317

Originally published in *The Black Woman Cross-Culturally*, Filomina Steady, ed. (Cambridge: Scheckman Publishing, 1981).

blacks were subjected to severe economic, occupational, and educational restrictions. Particularly destitute were black women, who outnumbered black men and were often widowed or single with dependent children. A report at the beginning of the nineteenth century illustrated the occupational caste into which most blacks were placed. It noted that while some black men in the North were employed as mechanics or mariners, most were day laborers. Black women, the report continued, "generally, both married and single, wash clothes for a livelihood."[2]

Northern blacks often voiced the opinion that the activities of white abolitionists were more theoretical than practical and tended to stress merely the abolition of Southern slavery while overlooking the dire needs of Northern blacks. Further, many blacks complained of the prejudice and condescension they experienced in their associations with the white abolitionists. One black stated, "whatever they [white abolitionists] do for us savors of pity, and is done at arm's length," while another commented that white abolitionists were only interested in the emancipation of blacks and not their "elevation."[3]

Thus, in an attempt to "elevate" themselves economically, educationally politically, and socially, blacks formed societies and organizations to work towards that end. The 1827 premier issue of the first black newspaper, Freedom's Journal, stated its purpose, reflecting the attitude of many blacks of the North: "we wish to plead our own cause. Too long have others spoken for us."[4]

Pooling their financial resources, blacks organized mutual aid and benevolent organizations as early as the 1780s. The African Union Society of Newport, Rhode Island was the first such organization to appear in 1780. Consisting of both black men and women, the group formed "to promote the welfare of the colored community ... by helping apprentice Negroes, and by assisting members in the time of distress." Similar societies such as the African Society of Boston and the Friendly Society of St. Thomas in Philadelphia also appeared by the 1790s with the focus of their beneficence being widows and orphaned children.[5]

By the 1820s, Philadelphia maintained the largest population of blacks in the North, two-thirds of which were female. This statistical imbalance within the black community resulted in a proliferation of mutual aid societies to assist women. By 1838, two-thirds of

1078

the 100 black mutual aid societies of the city with memberships totaling 7,600 were female. In addition, the poor black women in these societies provided two-thirds of the $20,000 raised by the groups in 1838 to help support themselves as well as others. Paying normally 12 1/2 cents a month or $1.00 quarterly to organizations such as the Dorcas Society, the Sisterly Union, the United Daughters of Wilberforce, or the African Female Union could provide a poor black woman assurance that she would be taken care of if she became ill, would receive a decent burial when she died, and that her children would be provided for by the funds from the societies. Because the societies had various foci, many women joined several of the groups. The Dorcas Society, for example, provided clothing and funds for the sick or infirm of any age while membership in the Daughters of Absalom was restricted to women over forty-five years of age.[6]

The above societies were testimonies to the ability of blacks to aid themselves. Throughout the pre-Civil War years, self-reliance was stressed. At a black national convention in 1848, the body stated, "to be dependent, is to be degraded,". Thus, as Benjamin Quarles noted in hist study of black abolitionists, the formation of black mutual socieites demonstrated that "a Negro family, no matter how poor, was determined that no town hearse would ever drive to its door." The predominatly Quaker Pennsylvania Abolition Society also commented upon the significance of the mutual aid societies in 1837 stating the groups had "a powerful influence in preventing pauperism and crime."[7]

As antislavery activities increased in the 1830s, black women, despite their poverty, were among the forerunners in such endeavors. When William Lloyd Garrison, famed abolitionist and editor of *The Liberator*, lectured in Salem, Massachusetts during the fall of 1832, and commented that there were no black antislavery socieites, a letter to the editor appeared in the paper shortly thereafter informing him that there was indeed such a society formed by "females of color" in February of that year. The letter enclosed a copy of the constitution of the Female Anti-Slavery Society of Salem, the first such organization by American women. In common with all black organizations formed during this period, the women stated that their purpose was to work for "mutual improvement" and "to promote the welfare of our color". Also, the writer

1079

informed the readers that there was still another black female organization established for over fifteen years—the Colored Female Religious and Moral Society of Salem formed in 1818. In a subsequent issue of *The Liberator*, a copy of the organization's constitution was also published. Although the group termed itself "religious and moral," the constitution revealed that the group was also an educational and benvolent organization. Membership was open to any female agreeing to conform to the bylaws of the constitution and pay the annual 52 cents dues. The group resolved to keep "a charitable watch over one another; to aid the sick and destitute members, and to meet weekly to study history, read interesting and useful books, and write and converse upon the sufferings of our enslaved sisters," and requested that "any plan that may be suggested for their melioration" would be welcomed.[8]

Predominantly white female antislavery societies such as the Boston Female Anti-Slavery Society and Philadelphia Female Anti-Slavery Society were subsequently formed in the 1830s and received greater prominence because of the membership of leading personalities such as Maria Weston Chapman and Lucretia Mott. Although blacks were with few exceptions barred from membership in the white antislavery societies, the Salem Female Anti-Slavery Society and the Colored Female Religious and Moral Society which were organized prior to the establishment of their white counterparts, indicated black women's desire to control and head their own socieites as well as demonstrate self-help. The above two black societies along with many others during and after the antebellum period raised money and supported a range of abolitionsts' activities.[9]

While many Northern black women were active participants on the underground railroad, the most famed being Harriet Tubman, Southern black women such as Ellen Craft and Anna Murray Douglass, wife of Frederick Douglass, aided in the escape of slaves and participated in slave revolts. Organizing with black men, the women of the race established and held positions on vigilance committees that aided runaway slaves by providing food, clothing, and money as well as finding employment for them. For example, two of the seven black directors of the New England Freedom Association whose function was to "extend a helping hand to all who may bid adieu to whips and chains" were females. Similarly,

1080

four of the nine members of the black vigilance committee of Cleveland were also women.[10]

Cooperative efforts between black females and males were common during the early nineteenth century. The disenfranchisement and oppression of all blacks left little room for male chauvisnism. Because the institution of slavery forced black women into work situations alongside the black male, having to endure the same punishments and hardships, sex role differentiation was minimized to a large extent within the slave community. Thomas Webber in his study of education of the slave quarters found this aspect of the slave community the most startling. He wrote, "one is struck by the absence of the familiar theme of male superiority and by the lack of evidence to support the view that the quarters was a female-dominated society." Although the traditional sex roles of cooking for females and hunting for men were prevalent,. It was not uncommon to find slave narratives depicting men as sewing, caring for children, or cooking. By the same token, women were frequently found as preachers, doctors, conjurors, storytellers, champion cotton pickers and respected leaders within the slave community. Since liberation of the race was the immediate goal of blacks, the men attached great importance to the females' roles in this effort. While sexism was not completely absent from the black community, black men became some of the earliest advocates of women's rights. In 1869 when black men formed the Colored National Labor Union, they admitted black women and elected a female to the executive committee of the group. The body voted to uphold equal rights for women and further stated that they were "profiting by the mistakes heretofore made by our white fellow citizens in omitting women."[11] Even by the turn of the century, John Daniels in his study of blacks in Boston observed that "with the Negroes there is a closer approximation to equality between the sexes than is yet the case among those of the other race." He concluded that this was due to the economic condition of blacks and further commented, thus,

> they [black women] have made a relatively greater economic contribution within their race than have white women in theirs, and so they have attained a place of relatively greater importance in the social order of their own community. Negro women manifest a marked independence, coupled with a sober realization of the extent to which the welfare of the race is in their hands. Negro men recog-

1081

nize and respect their position. The women take and are given a very important share in race affairs.[12]

The reality that a free black woman and later her emancipated sister would often become the primary, supplemental, or sole breadwinner, resulted in black men speaking out for women's economic and educational improvement as well as their own. Black abolitionist Martin Delaney wrote in 1852 of the menial occupations of black women and how black men lamented that the women were forced to perform "the drudgery and menial offices of other men's wives and daughters." And, while white females were found employed in more than a hundred industrial occupations during the first half of the nineteenth century, prejudice by this group barred black women from similar occupations—the same prejudice by that barred black men from jobs. Thus, race and not sex solidarity was the priority among blacks.[13]

And, while white females were found employed in more than a hundred industrial occupations during the first half of the nineteenth century, prejudice by this group barred black women from similar occupations—the same prejudice by that barred black men from jobs. Thus, race and not sex solidarity was the priority among blacks.[13]

Although a few white female abolitionists such as Abby Kelly Foster, Lucretia Mott, and the Grimke sisters were staunch advocates of social as well as political equality for blacks, they held a minority opinion even among abolitionists. For example, members of the Female Anti-Slavery Society of Fall River, Massachusetts vehemently opposed black female membership and threatened to dissolve when the issue was raised. The women argued that if admitted, black women would be perceived as being "on an equality with ourselves."[14] This view was no different than that of their male counterparts. In fact, many of the white female abolitionists were the nonworking daughters, wives, and sisters of prominent men and involved themselves in the antislavery movement because of the availability of leisure time rather than a great sympathy to the cause. Making this observation, in 1839 abolitionist Hannah Smith wrote Abby Kelly of her apparent displeasure with many of the white female anti-slavery workers:

> . . . they [white females] appeared to join [antislavery societies] more because their husbands were abolitionists than they themselves felt

1082

interested, and hardly seemed to understand the principles of the cause they were advocating—Indeed, I do not know of one anti-slavery women of the right stamp in Connecticut of sufficient information and energy to organize a Society or manage its concerns.[15]

In contrast, black female antislavery activites included poor working women as well as the middle class. Many had been former slaves and were intimately linked to the abolitionist as well as other self-help activities not as a social outlet or to please a husband, but out of a lifetime commitment to not only emancipate but "elevate" the race.

Continuing their separate activities, black women frequently received praise for their endeavors from abolitionist newspapers. When the Colored Female Produce Society was established in early 1831 for the purpose of boycotting slave made products, the *Genius of Universal Emancipation* reported that: "their [black women's] promptness and numbers are a reproach to the inactive carelessness of their white sisters and we sincerely hope they will persevere undiscouraged in the noble course they have commenced."[16]

1083

Of the many contributions made by black women during the antebellum period, their role in education was one of their most salient. Since the intellectual inferiority of the race was the primary justification for slavery, central to their mission of "uplift", blacks sought as a central goal in their mission of uplift to improve their education to help dispel the widespread myth of the dull black intellect. In the 1829 *Appeal* of the militant David Walker, he told the members of his race:

I would crawl on my hands and knees through mud and mire, to sit at the feet of a learned man, where I would sit and humbly supplicate him to instill into me, that which devils nor tyrants could remove, only with my life—for coloured people to acquire learning in this country, make tyrants quake and tremble on their sandy foundation...the bare name of educating the coloured people, scares our cruel oppressor almost to death.[17]

The need for the education of the race was again voiced at a black national conference in 1832 with the body resolving that "if we [black people] ever expect to see the influence of prejudice decrease and ourselves respected, it must be by the blessings of an enlightened education."[18] This emphasis upon education was directed to the black female as well as the male.

As in other activities during the period, black women were among the earliest educators of the race. In 1793, Caterine Ferguson purchased her freedom and opened "Katy Ferguson's School for the Poor" in New York City for both black and white pupils. In the same year "the Committee for Improving the Condition of Free Blacks in Pennsylvania" opened a school and recommended "a well qualified" black female teacher.[19]

And, while the dangers of education for women were constantly being debated in the larger society, and articles proliferated regarding a "womens sphere" and the "cult of true womanood"—all stressing the servility and submissiveness expected of females—blacks encouraged the women of their race to become educated to aid in race improvement. In the black newspaper *The Weekly Advocate,* an 1837 article entitled "To the Females of Colour" urged black women to seek an education for the benefit of the race. The article stated, "In any enterprise for the improvement of our people, either moral or mental, our hands would be palsied without woman's influence." Thus, the article continued, "let our beloved female friends, then, rouse up, and exert all their power, in encouraging, and sustaining this effort (education) which we have made to disabuse the public mind of the misrepresentations made of our character; and to show to the world, that there is virtue among us, though concealed; talent, though buried; intelligence, though overlooked."[20]

Prior to and after the Civil War, it was not uncommon for black families to relocate in areas where their daughters could receive a better education or to send their daughters away to be educated. For example, when Blanche V. Harris was denied admission to a white female seminary int he State of Michigan where she lived in the 1850s, her entire family moved to Oberlin, Ohio where she and her four brothers and sisters could receive an education. She graduated from the Ladies' Department of Oberlin College in 1860 as a sister did ten years later. Similarly, the parents of Mary Jane Patterson, who in 1862 became the first black female to earn a college degree in America, also moved to Oberlin from North Carolina in the 1850s to educate their children. Four of the Patterson children graduated from Oberlin College (three were female).[21]

Furthermore, as arguments in the larger society continued regarding coeducation, black females were included in schools for

1084

males from the beginning. An advertisement such as "the B.F. Hughes School for Coloured Children of Both Sexes" found in an 1827 issue of the *Freedom's Journal* was typical.[22]

The largest black literary society of New York, the Pheonix, organized in 1833 provided lectures, evening schools, and a high school that was available to both male and female students and employed both black men and women as teachers. When a Philadelphia Quaker, Richard Humphreys, bequeathed $10,000 for the establishment of a trade school for blacks in that city, a group of black men approached the Quaker Managers and persuaded them to establish instead a school of "higher learning" that taught "literary subjects" to females as well as males. The men agreed and the Institute for Colored Youth of Philadelphia was opened in 1852 and became one of the leading educational institution for blacks during the nineteenth century. The Institute always maintained an all-black faculty that included the most educated black men and women of the times. Sarah Mapp Douglass, a black Quaker and abolitionist who had been trained in physiology at the University of Pennyslvania, was Principal of the Preparatory Department of the school and in 1865, Fanny Jackson Coppin and Mary Jane Patterson, the first two black women to receive college degrees in the nation, were appointed Principal and Assistant Principal, respectively.[23]

1085

Literary and educational societies for the expressed purpose of mental improvement came into being during the early nineteenth century. Philadelphia was the leader in such organizations. In 1831, three years after the first black male literary society was established, a group of black women formed the Female Literary Association of Philadelphia. This group viewed their efforts not only as a means of self-improvement but also as a means of race improvement. In the preamble of the group's constitution, the women stated, "it therefore becomes a duty incumbent upon us as women, as daughters of a despised race, to use our utmost endeavors to enlighten the understanding, to cultivate the talents entrusted to our keeping, that by so doing, we may in a great measure, break down the strong barrier of prejudice, and raise ourselves to an equality with those of our fellow beings, who differ from us in complexion." Upon election into the organization, a $1.50 annual fee was required. Poems, essays, and short stories were submitted unsigned to be critiqued by the group. To counteract charges against the intellectual capabilities of blacks, *The Liberator* often published samples of the women's literary works. After visiting a meeting of the organization, William Lloyd Garrison reported, "if the traducers of the colored race could be acquainted with the moral worth, just refinement, and large intelligence of this association, their mouths would hereafter be dumb."[24]

One year after the formation of the Philadelphia association, the Afri-American Female Intelligence Society was established in Boston "to associate for the diffusion of knowledge, the suppression of vice and immorality, and for cherishing such virtues as will render us happy and useful to society." An initial fee of twenty-five cents was required to join the organization and 12 1/2 cents was charged thereafter. The funds were used for the purchasing of books and newspapers and for the renting of a room for their meetings. Regular attendance was strictly enforced with a fine imposed for absenteeism. Although educational in purpose, the organization also had a charitable component providing one dollar a week to any member of one year's standing who became ill. Despite the year's qualification for aid, the group agreed to aid any number "in case of unforeseen and afflictive event," stating "it shall be the duty of the Society to aim them as far as in their power . . . " This was the first such society among blacks in Boston.[25]

A black female, Maria W. Stewart, lecturing before the Afric-American Society became the first American female to speak in public in 1832. Less than six weeks of education in her background, the deeply religious Stewart had been inspired by the words of David Walker in his *Appeal* and urged black women to improve their education and aid in the struggle for racial "uplift." She told the women: "Oh, daughters of Africa, awake! arise!, show forth the world that yea are endowed with noble and exalted faculties . . . let us promote ourselves and improve our own talents." She expressed the importance of higher education and academies for black women and suggested that the women pool their resources to establish a high school. Informing her audience that "knowledge is power", she also told them to establish businesses and become economically independent. "Don't say I can't, but I will" was her challenge to her fellow sisters. Giving four lectures in Boston in 1832-33, Stewart continued to impress upon blacks their duty and obligation to the race. In the 1830s she moved to New York City, was educated through membership in the black female literary societies of the city, and subsequently became a teacher.[26]

Not only was Maria Stewart's public speaking viewed as radical, but the message that she provided her mixed audience, during an age when women, like children, were expected to be seen and not heard, was viewed as being quite "promiscuous". Yet, she paved the way for many other black women who would take the public platform to plead for the rights of their race.

The literary societies established by blacks prior to the Civil War performed great services with their communities in the education of their race by providing lectures, libraries, and reading rooms as well as instruction. In 1849, over half of the black population of Philadelphia belonged to one of the 106 literary organizations of the city. And, by the 1840s, the Ohio Ladies Education Society, formed by black women in 1837, was reported to have done "more towards the establishment of schools for the education of colored people at this time in Ohio than any other organized group."[27]

1087

While most of the literary associations greatly aided adults in obtaining or increasing their literacy, the black communities during the antebellum period frequently voiced concerned regarding the lack of educational institutions available to their female youth. *The Colored American*, a black newspaper of the 1830s appealed to white females to admit black females into their seminaries, and when these appeals went unheard, again in 1839 wrote that there was only one seminary available for black females to attend. The article stated, "the culture of the black female's minds require more care and attention, and it should not be neglected."[28]

Though there were scattered opportunities for black females to receive a common school education in the North prior to the Civil War, a secondary education was far more difficult to obtain. Thus, the founding in 1829 of the St. Frances Academy for Colored Girls in Baltimore, a boarding school, was an important event for the race. The institution was established by a group of black nuns (the Oblate Order) who had migrated to Baltimore from Santo Domingo. Most of the women had been educated in France and were of financial means. Elizabeth Lange, who became the First Superior of the Order and head of the school, had operated a free school for poor black children in her home prior to the opening of the St. Frances and conducted her classes in French and Spanish. Because the St. Frances Academy was the only institution that was available to black females that offered courses above primary level, the school was well known. Black females from across the nation and Canada were sent there to study. To perserve their native language, the Sisters conducted classes at the Academy on alternate days completely in French. By 1865, the school was coed and known simply as the St. Frances Academy.[29]

The Institute for Colored Youth in Philadelphia, established in 1852 by Quakers as the first classical high school for blacks (both male and female), produced, along with the St. Frances Academy, some of the first formally trained black female teachers in the North prior to emancipation.

Although opportunities for the education of blacks were located overwhelmingly in the North prior to the Civil War, many clandestine schools existed in the South during this period. For example, numerous such schools were reported in Savannah, Georgia. Julian Froumountaine, a black woman from Santo Domingo, openly conducted a free school for blacks in Savannah as early as 1819 and continued secretly after the 1930s when education of blacks in the South became illegal. Another black woman, known only as Miss Dea Veaux, opened an underground school in 1838 and operated it for over twenty-five years without the knowledge of local whites. Susan King Taylor, who served in the Union Army during the Civil War as a nurse and teacher, was educated in several of the "secret" schools of Savannah and in her *Reminiscences* recalled the methods devised by the black pupils to deceive the unsuspecting whites as they went to school. Similar schools were in other areas of the South. In Natchez, Mississippi, Milla Granson became literate through the teachings of her master's children and taught hundreds of slaves to read and write in what they termed her "midnight" school because the classes were held after midnight. These educational activities reveal not only the importance that blacks placed upon education but indicated the risk that black women took to ensure that members of their race obtained it.[30]

Oberlin College in Ohio gained notoriety in 1833 when it announced that it would admit blacks and women on an equal basis with white men and became the only collegiate institution available to black women prior to the Civil War. By 1865, 140 black women had attended the College. But it was not until the 1860s that the

1088

first baccalaureate degrees were received by black women—three by the end of the Civil War. This small group of Oberlin trained black women along with those trained in other Northern high schools would contribute greatly to the formal schooling of blacks after emancipation.

One such example is Fanny Jackson Coppin. Born a slave in 1837 in the District of Columbia, her freedom was purchased by an aunt who earned only 6 dollars a month but saved until she had the necessary $125 for Fanny's manumission (by the time she was twelve). She was sent to New Bedford, Massachusetts and later to Newport, Rhode Island to live with relatives where they believed her educational opportunities would be greater. Surrounded by the mutual aid and other self-help groups, as a young girl Fanny decided her life's goal was "to get an education and teach my people." While working as a domestic in Newport, her employers allowed her to hire a tutor for one hour, three days a week. She later attended the segregated schools of Newport and by 1859 had completed the normal course at the Rhode Island State Normal School. By this time, Fanny's life's goal had expanded to meet the challenge of the antebellum Senator John C. Calhoun who stated that if he could find a black who could conjugate a Greek verb, he would change his opinion regarding the inferior intellect of blacks. Thus, deciding to continue her education, she learned of a college in Ohio whose cirriculum was the same as Harvard's and that admitted women as well as blacks. With financial assistance from her relatives and a scholarship from Bishop Daniel Payne of the African Methodist Episcopal Church, she enrolled in Oberlin College in 1860.

Recalling her days at Oberlin, Fanny Jackson stated that although Oberlin in theory offered the "gentleman's course" (as the collegiate department was termed) to females, in practise they did not encourage it. But it was the belief in racial inferiority and not sexism that most concerned her while pursuing her studies. Remembering her Oberlin days, she stated that when she rose to recite in her classes she felt as if she carried the weight of the entire African race on her shoulders for if she failed, it would have been attributed to the fact that she was black. Far from failing, she distinguished herself as an outstanding student at the College and became involved in all fascets of campus life. However, when the freedmen began pouring into Oberlin during the Civil War years, despite her

1089

studies, Fanny established a free evening school to teach them. This experience had a profound effect upon her as she witnessed black elderly working men struggling to learn simple words. She remarked, "I rejoiced that even then I could enter measurabely upon the course of life which I had long ago chosen."[31]

Another black female of the North, Charlotte Forten, was also eager to help her race through education. Born free in 1837, Charlotte was the granddaughter of the wealthy John Forten and grew up in material comfort in Philadelphia. She spent her days as other affluent females did by reading classics and poetry and attending lectures and concerts. Despite the Forten's wealth, they had suffered discrimination as blacks and the entire family was actively involved in antislavery and abolitionist organizations. Charlotte studied with a private tutor as a girl because her family refused to send her to the segretated schools of Philadelphia. As an adolescent she was sent to Salem, Massachusetts to attend the integrated schools there. While in Salem, Charlotte submerged herself in the various abolitionist activities of the black women and became a member of the Female Anti-Slavery Society of Salem. These activities impressed upon her the role that black women could have in race improvement and in her journal of 1854, Charlotte wrote that she would improve her intellect to enable her "to do much towards changing the condition of my oppressed and suffering people." Deciding to become a teacher, by 1856 she had completed the normal course at Salem Normal School. Afterwards, she was appointed the first black teacher in the Salem Public Schools where she taught for two years, resigning due to poor health.

The Civil War years brought Charlotte, like Fanny Jackson, her first opportunity to teach her race. When the call came for teachers to take part in the social experiment at Port Royal, South Carolina in 1861, Charlotte enthusiastically volunteered to teach the contrabands. Arriving on St. Helena Island in October of 1861, she chronicled in detail the successes of the black pupils in her diary. While on the island she published articles in various magazines testifying to the great progress being made and the eagerness of the students of all ages to learn. She returned North in May, 1864 because of ill-health, and as Ms. Forten's biographer, Ray Billington, commented, her greatest reward in leaving "was the knowledge that the social experiment was successfull ... and that Negroes were as capable of progress as whites."[32]

1090

Working in the Sea Islands during the same period as Charlotte Forten was Susan King Taylor. With a background vastly different from Forten's, Taylor was born a slave in the Georgia Sea Island and grew up in Savannah where she was educated in several of the clandestine schools of the city. When only fourteen years old, she volunteered to teach in one of the freedmen schools on St. Simon Island. While there she joined the first black military regiment, Company E, serving as a laundress and nurse in the day and a teacher at night. Remaining on the island for over four years, she taught most of the men in the Company to read and write, never receiving pay the entire time. Her only compensation was to view a once illiterate slave read from a primer or Bible. In her *Reminiscences* published in 1902 Taylor stated that she was simply happy to know that her efforts had been successful and that her services had been appreciated. She did note, however, concern that by the turn of the century little attention or credit had been given to the great sacrifices and courageous acts that black women had made during the War. She noted that black women had assisted the Union Army, even at the price of death. She wrote,

1091

> There are many people who do not know what some of the colored women did during the war. There were hundreds of them who assisted the Union soldiers by hiding them and helping them to escape. Many were punished for taking food to the prison stockades ... Others assisted in various ways the Union army. These things should be kept in history before the people. There has never been a greater war in the United States than the one in 1861, where so many lives were lost, not men alone but noble women as well.[33]

As the Civil War came to an end, black women for over half a century had sought to "uplift" themselves and the race. And, although as Susan King Taylor noted, history has overlooked their efforts, their contributions have been vast and noteworthy. Mindfully aware of their poverty, they pooled their resources to aid one another financially; with educational resources limited to them, they educated themselves as well as others; spiritually they supported each other and prayed together for a better day for black people; abhorring the insitution of slavery, they banded together to initiate and support abolitionist causes, and aided, in untold ways, to ensure the victory of the Union Army.

The early involvement of black women in the struggle for racial equality was not barred by geographical, class, educational, or age boundaries as the above examples of Coppin, Forten, and Taylor exhibit. Poor black women, throughout the pre-Civil War era, literally gave the widow's mite to support the "uplift" of their race.

And, after emancipation was finally obtained by 1865, black women were left with the arduous task of seeking elevation not only with their men but for their men. Continuing in the footsteps of their mothers and gradmothers, black women's efforts during and after Reconstruction would result in DuBois characterizing their work as the "finest chapter" in the history of black women.[34]

In assessing the role of blacks in the pre-Civil War period, it is imperative, as Susan King Taylor commented, that the efforts of black women are "kept in history before the people."[35]

1092

NOTES

1. Standard works on white abolitionists are Alice D. Adams, *The Neglected Period of Anti-Slavery in America, 1808-31* (Boston, 1908); Louis Filler, *The Crusade Against Slavery, 1830-60* (New York, 1960); Alma Lutz, *Crusade For Freedom: Women of the Anti-Slavery Movement* (Boston: Beacon Press, 1968); Blanche G. Hersh, *The Slavery of Sex: Feminists-Abolitionists in America*, (Urbana: University of Illinois Press, 1978); Gerda Lerner, *The Grimke Sisters From South Carolina: Pioneers for Woman's Rights and Abolition*, (New York: Schocken Books, 1975); for information regarding black abolition: Herbert Aptheker, *The Negro in the Abolitionist Movement*, (New York, 1941); Frederick Douglass, *My Bondage and My Freedom* (New York, 1855); Leon F. Litwack, *North of Slavery: The Negro in the Free States, 1790-1860*; Jane H. and William H. Pease, *They Who Would Be Free: Blacks' Search for Freedom, 1830-1861*, (New York: Atheneum, 1974): for an excellent description of black male and female abolitionists' activities see Benjamin Quarles, *Black Abolitionists* (London: Oxford University Press, 1969).

2. Litwack, *North of Slavery*, p. 14; *Minutes of the Committee for Improving the Condition of Free Blacks*, Pennsylvania Abolition Society, 1790-1803, Historical Society of Pennsylvania, p. 112.

3. *Douglass's Paper*, April 13, 1855; quoted in Angelina Emily Grimke to Abby Kelley, April 15, 1837 in *Abby Kelley Foster Papers*, American Antiquarian Society.

4. *Freedom's Journal*, March 16, 1827.

5. Quoted in Irving H. Bartlett, *From Slave to Citizen: The Story of the Negro in Rhode Island* (Providence, Rhode Island, 1954), p. 35; Dorthorty Porter (ed.), *Early Negro Writings, 1760-1837* (Boston: Beacon Press, 1971), pp. 5-78.

6. Edward Needles, *An Historical Memoir of the Pennsylvania Society for Promoting the Abolition of Slavery*, (Philadelphia, 1848), p. 86; *Facts on Beneficial Societies*,

1823-1838 in Minutes of Pennyslvania Abolition Society, Historical Society of Pennsylvania.

7. *North Star*, September 22, 1848; Quarles, *Black Abolitionists*, p. 100; Needles, *An Historical Memoir*, p. 96.

8. *The Liberator*, November 17, 1832; February 16, 1833.

9. See for example Lutz's, *Crusade for Freedom*, Ira V. Brown's "Cradle of Feminism: The Philadelphia Female Anti-Slavery Society, 1833-1840" in *the Pennsylvania Magazine of History and Biography*, vol. CII. number 2, April 1978, pp. 143-166; Quarles, *Black Abolitionists*, p. 20.

10. For Ellen Craft's role in the escape of her husband and herself from slavery see William Craft's "Running a Thousand Miles for Freedom, or the Escape of William and Ellen Craft from Slavery", reprinted from the 1860 edition in Arna Bontemps (ed.), *Great Slave Narratives*, (Boston: Beacon Press); for Anna Murray's role in aiding Douglass escape see Sylvia Lyons Render's, "Afro-American Women: the Outstanding and the Obscure" in *The Quarterly Journal of the Library of Congress*, vol. 32, no. 4, October, 1975, pp. 306-321; quoted in Quarles, *Black Abolitionists*, p. 153.

11. Thomas Webber, *Deep Like the Rivers: Education in the Slave Quarter Community, 1831-1865* (New York: W. W. Norton and Company, 1978), p. 149; *Proceedings of the Colored National Labor Convention Held in Washington, D.C. on December, 6, 7, 8, 9, 10, 1869*, (Washington, D.C., 1870).

12. John Daniels, *In Freedom's Birthplace: A Study of the Boston Negroes* (reprint of the 1914 edition, New York: Arno Press, 1969), pp. 212-13.

13. Martin R. Delaney, *The Condition, Elevation, Emigration and Destiny of the Colored People of the United States* (Philadelphia, 1852), pp. 41-45; Eleanor Flexner, *Century of Struggle: The Women's Right Movement in the United States*, (Cambridge, Massachusetts: The Belknap Press of Harvard University, 1976), p. 52.

14. quoted in Litwack's, *North of Slavery*, p. 221.

15. Hannah H. Smith to Abby Kelley, July 25, 1839 in *Abby Kelley Foster Papers*, American Antiquarian Society.

16. *The Genuius of Universal Emancipation*, August, 1831, p. 57.

17. *David Walker's Appeal to the Coloured Citizens of the World* (reprint of the 1828 edition, New York: Hill and Wang, 1965), pp. 31-32.

18. *Minutes and Proceedings of the Second Annual Convention for the Improvement of the Free People of Color in these United States*, (Philadelphia, 1832), p. 34.

19. Gerda Lerner, (ed.), *Black Women in White America: A Documentary History, (New York: Vintage Books, 1973), p. 76*; Needles, *An Historical Memoir*, p. 43.

20. *The Weekly Advocate*, January 7, 1837.

21. Ellen Henle and Marlene Merrill, "Antebellum Black Coeds at Oberlin College," *Women's Studies Newsletter*, VII, number 2, (Spring, 1979), p. 10.

22. *Freedom's Journal*, March 23, 1827.

23. *The Colored American*, January 14, 1837; see Linda Marie Perkins', "Quaker Beneficence and Black Control: The Institute for Colored Youth, 1852-1903" in Vincent P. Franklin and James D. Anderson, (eds.) *New Perspectives in Black Educational History*, (Boston: G. K. Hall, 1978), pp. 19-43.

24. *The Liberator*, December 3, 1831; November 17, 1832.

25. *Genius of Universal Emancipation*, March, 1832, pp. 162-163.

26. *The Liberator*, November 17, 1832; April 27, 1833.

27. Leslie H. Fishel, Jr. "The North and the Negro, 1865-1900: A Study in Race Discrimination"(Ph. D. dissertation, Harvard University, 1953). p. 49; Dorothy B. Porter, "The Organized Educational Activities of Negro Literary Societies, 1828-1846", *The Journal of Negro Education*, volume 5, October, 1936, pp. 555-576.

28. *The Colored American*, March 18, 1837; November 23, 1839.

29. Grace H. Sherwood, *The Oblates' Hundred and One Years*, (New York: The MacMillian Company, 1931), pp. 5, 29, 34, passim.

30. Henry Allen Bullock, *A History of Negro Education in the South from 1619 to the Present*, (New York: Praeger Publishers, 1970), p. 25; J.W. Alvord, Bureau of Refugees, Freedmen and Abandoned Lands, *Fifth Semi-Annual Report on Schools for Freedmen* (Washington, D.C., 1868); pp. 29-30; W.E.B. DuBois, *The Negro Common School*, (Atlanta: University Press, 1901), p. 21; Susan King Taylor, *Reminiscences of My Life in Camp*, (reprint of 1902 edition, New York: Arno Press, 1969), pp. 7, 11; Laura S. Haviland, *A Woman's Life-Work: Labors and Experiences of Laura S. Haviland*, fourth edition, (Chicago: Publishing Association of Friends, 1889), pp. 300-311.

31. Fanny Jackson Coppin, *Reminiscences of School Life and Hints on Teaching*, (Philadelphia: AME Book Concern, 1913), passim.

32. Charlotte Forten, *Journal of Charlotte Forten*, (New York: The Dryden Press, 1953), passim.

33. Taylor, *Reminiscences*, p. 67.

34. W.E.B. DuBois, *Darkwater*, (New York: Harcourt, Brace & Howe, 1920, p. 178.

35. Taylor *Reminiscences*, p. 67.

1094

ELIZABETH H. PLECK

THE TWO-PARENT HOUSEHOLD: BLACK FAMILY STRUCTURE IN LATE NINETEENTH-CENTURY BOSTON

O nce the most rural of American ethnic groups, Afro-Americans are now the most urban. Slavery, migration to the city and the adaptation to urban culture have had major effects on black life, yet we know little about the ways in which the most basic unit of black life, the family, was affected by these changes. Through research in the manuscript census schedules of the federal census for 1880 and other largely quantitative materials, I looked for answers to the following questions. What was the effect of migration on the black family? What was the occupational situation of black heads of household? How did urban and rural families differ in their adaptation to life in the city? How did literate and illiterate families differ? What family forms predominated? How frequent was "family disorganization," as reflected in an imbalanced sex ratio, frequent desertions by the head of household and large numbers of female-headed households?

1095

We can learn a great deal about black family life from an examination of Boston in the late nineteenth century. The Hub was a major northern metropolis, with a large and diversified economy, which should have offered opportunities for unskilled but willing black workers. As a result of the long efforts of blacks and whites in the abolitionist movement, the city had no segregated institutions and a widely respected system of free

Ms. Pleck is a graduate student in History of American Civilization at Brandeis University. A Ford Foundation Dissertation Fellowship in Ethnic Studies financed the research cited in this article. The author's ideas about the black family have been greatly influenced by the comments and work of Herbert Gutman, whose forthcoming book on the black family should greatly enlarge our knowledge of the subject. The revision of this paper has benefited from the criticism of Stephan Thernstrom. The author is especially indebted to Joseph Pleck for writing the computer programs employed in this study, and for his aid in data analysis and the use of statistical techniques. Useful comments and suggestions for changes in this article were made by Gordon Fellman, Allan Kulikoff, John Demos, Doug Jones and Peter Knights.

Originally published in *Journal of Social History*, Vol. 6 (Fall 1972).

public schools. Boston had acquired a reputation among blacks as "the paradise of the Negro," a city of unparalleled freedom and opportunity.[1] Since the black population was so small a percentage of the inhabitants of the city, the racial fears and animosities of the white population appeared, surfaced, but did not explode into major race riots like those in New York and Philadelphia during the Civil War. The large Irish and small black populations lived in an uneasy truce, with the two groups dwelling in close proximity in the west and south ends of the city. Unique in some ways, representative of major Northern cities in others, Boston is an interesting city in which to study many facets of black family life.

1096

The most typical black household in late nineteenth-century Boston included the husband and wife, or husband, wife and children. This predominant household form prevailed among all occupational levels and among families of both urban and rural origins. By enlarging the household to include boarders, families from all occupational strata augmented the family income and provided homes for the large numbers of migrants in the population. This evidence from the manuscript census contradicts the commonly held association between "the tangle of pathology," "family disorganization" and the black family.

Before examining the composition of the black household, I will indicate how inferences were made about the origins and literacy of heads of household and I will discuss three aspects of social life in Boston—the transiency of the population, the depressing occupational position of black heads of household and the physical circumstances of life—which severely constrained family survival.

Comparison of Rural and Urban, Literate and Illiterate Heads of Household

In the analysis of one- and two-parent households which follows, the foreign-born heads of household were excluded since they offer too few cases for valid comparisons.[2] Comparing the Northern- and Southern-born heads of household, I looked for possible differences in urban and rural family adaptation to life in Boston. Since the manuscript census schedules indicate the state of birth of an individual, but not the city or area where the individual was born or raised, the comparison is imperfect. Although a majority of Northern-born blacks lived most of their lives in urban areas, the Northern-born category also included farmers from New England, townspeople from western Massachusetts and settlers from the free black communities of Ohio. By further separating those born in Massachusetts (mostly natives of Boston) from the rest of the Northern-born, I was able to discern differences between that part of the population which was born in Boston and that portion of the population which migrated into the city.

1097

While most Southern-born blacks were rural folk, that category also includes city-dwellers from Richmond, Baltimore, or Washington, D.C. Even more difficult to distinguish are those Southern-born blacks who were urban in experience, if not in place of birth. But despite these qualifications, it seems useful to perceive the Northern-born as essentially an urban group, and the Southern-born as a rural group.[3]

The distinction between literacy and illiteracy may have been as important as the difference between urban and rural families. Seven out of ten black adults could read a few words and sign their names, the nineteenth-century standard of literacy. Even this minimal knowledge reflected a variety of skills which facilitated successful adaptation to urban life. Those without such skills—the illiterates—were more at a disadvantage than they were on the farm and more noticeable for their deficiency as well. Whole families headed by illiterates faced far greater difficulties in cities than those headed by literate parents.

In the South, illiterates tended to be ex-slaves.[4] (The equation of illiteracy and slave status would have been unneccessary had the Boston census takers directly enumerated the number of freedmen in the black population.) Under slavery, most blacks were not taught to read or write or were prevented from even learning. While there were exceptions, self-educated slaves (Frederick Douglass is the best-known example), the opportunities for literacy were much greater for free blacks than for slaves. But before equating Southern-born illiterates with ex-slaves, two important qualifications must be added. First, even the majority of free blacks like the slaves, was untutored. Second, the number of illiterates was very low, far below any estimate we might make of the number of ex-slaves in the population.[5] Thus, while illiteracy appeared in both Northern- and Southern-born families, its presence among the Southern-born, in addition, reflected the existence of ex-slaves in the population.

Geographic Mobility

From the 3,496 blacks living in Boston in 1870, the population grew ten years later to include 5,873 persons.[6] By 1910, the population had expanded three times to 13,654. In the same forty-year period, the white population grew over two and one-half times, and the foreign-born white population tripled. The metropolis was growing rapidly, and within the city the black population, although small in absolute number and in size relative to the white population—never more than two percent of the total population throughout the period—was growing at a rate faster than that of the foreign-born immigrants.[7]

In the late nineteenth century the black population absorbed a large number of migrants. Though a minority, 42 percent of Boston's blacks in 1880, had been born in the North, a majority were strangers to Northern life; 49 percent of the population was born in the South, while another 9 percent were born in foreign countries. Of the Northern-born population, especially those born in Massachusetts, the majority probably were natives of Boston. Other Northern-born blacks came from neighboring cities in the Northeast and a few were from rural areas in New England. For the foreign-born, their life in Boston was the culmination of the long journey from Nova Scotia, New Brunswick, or other parts of Canada, or the end of a long sea voyage from the West Indies. The largest group in the population, the Southern-born, included migrants from the Upper South, especially Virginia.

These Southern newcomers seem to contradict prevailing theories of migration to cities.[8] Rather than travelling short distances and settling at the first stop along the way, these migrants moved as much as five hundred miles from home, often passing through other urban centers. Why did these men and women make the long journey? The usual explanation of black migration to the North refers to Jim Crow segregation, racism and declining economic opportunities in the South, combined with the

expanding economy and promise of a freer life in the North.
Pushed out by Southern conditions, pulled to the North, the land
of golden streets and busy factories, the combination of push and
pull factors explain the Great Migration, the period during and
after the First World War. The earlier movement, described by
Carter Woodson as the migration of the Talented Tenth,
represented a period when blacks were more "pulled" to the
North than "pushed" from the South.[9] The absence of two
factors—widespread agricultural depression and active recruitment
of blacks by Northern employment agents—further distinguished
the earlier migration from the Great Migration of World War I.
Despite the propaganda of some of their brethren and the appeals
of some Southern whites, the black emigrant was above all looking
for a better life in the Northern city. One migrant was Ella Beam,
a young woman who left the South Carolina Sea Islands for
Boston:

1099

> She stated that she did not leave home on account of hard times. When she
> left, her father was doing well on the farm. There were several boys in the
> family, so she was rarely called upon to go into the fields. She felt, however,
> that she was not especially needed at home. The fact that she manifested
> sufficient initiative to take the course at the training school [domestic
> science] is perhaps indicative of the courage and energy of a young woman
> who wanted to better her condition. She had been in Boston only one year
> when she received a simple job caring for children in the home of a Melrose
> family.[10]

For the most part, the migrants included young adults above
the age of twenty, very few of whom came with their families. In
households headed by a Southern-born parent, 72.1 percent of the
oldest children in the family were born in the North. Among the
oldest children of a Canadian parent, 60.7 percent had been born
in the North. Six out of seven of the oldest children in West Indian
families had been born in the North. Thus the migration from the
South and from foreign countries included single individuals or
couples, but in very few cases did the whole family make the
move.

The story of migration does not end with the arrival of the
newcomer in Boston. Instead of settling down, the transient
frequently packed up and left. Evidence from several nineteenth-
century cities in the Northeast indicates a high rate of black

migration, generally higher than that of other groups. But in the South and West the rate of black out-migration was about the same or a little lower than among other groups. Assuming this pattern is substantiated in further research, it indicates the absence of job opportunities for black workers in nearby Southern areas, in contrast to the proximity of many cities in the urban Northeast where the transient could find employment.

An examination of Boston city directories reveals that only 25 percent of adult black males listed in the 1880 census were enumerated in the 1890 city directory, while 64 percent of a representative sample of adult white males in 1880 remained in the city ten years later.[11] The rate of persistence for blacks was very similar among all occupational levels, as Table 1 suggests, while the rate of persistence among white males decreased for lower status workers.[12]

1100

Table 1. Proportion of Adult Male Residents of Boston in 1880 Persisting There
to 1890, by Racial Group, Household Status and Occupational Level[a]

	Overall Persistence Rate	White Collar	Skilled	Unskilled and Service	N
White Residents[b]	64%	72%	63%	56%	1,809
All Blacks	25%	26%	25%	25%	1,992
Heads of household	31%	35%	28%	32%	1,066
Sons	21%	25%	33%	15%	63

[a] The white collar category includes professionals, clerical workers, and petty proprietors. Heads of household include black males in single member households, as well as the more prevalent one- and two-parent households. Adult males were defined as those 21 and over. Sons include adult males residing at home. Persistence rates for women were extremely difficult to estimate because of name changes due to marriage and the incomplete city directory coverage given to women who were not heading households. There was no statistically significant relationship between occupational level and persistence for all blacks, nor was there a significant relationship for heads of households or sons.

[b] Data for white residents is from Stephan Thernstrom and Elizabeth H. Pleck, "The Last of the Immigrants? A Comparative Analysis of Immigrant and Black Social Mobility in Late-Nineteenth Century Boston," unpublished paper delivered at the annual meeting of the Organization of American Historians (April, 1970), p. 12.

Among blacks heading households, the rate of persistence was 31 percent, compared with the 25 percent overall figure. Adult sons residing at home, although few in number, were more transient than their fathers, since only 21 percent of them remained in the city for the decade 1880-1890.

High rates of turnover were common in other Northeastern cities. In the depression years of the 1870s black out-migration occurred frequently among Poughkeepsie and Buffalo residents. Only one-third of the black workers in Poughkeepsie in 1870 remained in the city ten years later.[13] In a twenty year trace of black adult males in Buffalo from 1855 to 1875, only 12 percent could be found.[14]

The Northern pattern of high black out-migration and much lower out-migration for other groups is reversed in the South and West. In Atlanta, for example, blacks were much more likely to remain in the city than either foreign-born whites or native whites. Even more remarkable, within all occupational categories, the black departure rate was lower than that of native white and foreign-born immigrants.[15] For Birmingham, Alabama, the much higher rate of black persistence was the result of fewer opportunities elsewhere for black workers.[16] During the depression decade 1870-1880, in San Antonio, blacks, European immigrants and native whites had very similar rates of persistence—36 percent for blacks, 36 percent for European immigrants and 35 percent for native whites—while the Chicano population was the most transient, with only 25 percent of the male population remaining there ten years later.[17] The question remains whether this pattern of Southern black geographic stability was also reflected in long-lasting marriages and continuity of parental care for black children.

1101

Occupational Structure

The occupational position of black heads of household placed a great strain on the black family. While the children of white immigrants moved up the occupational ladder, the black child, like his parent, remained fixed in a world of menial and temporary jobs. Eight occupations—waiter, servant, cook, barber, laborer, porter, laundress and seamstress—accounted for 74 percent of all blacks at work in Boston in 1880. The largest group by far were the 858 servants who worked in white homes, hotels and institutions. Two occupations, laundress and seamstress, were largely the preserve of single women and women heading households. The last hired and the first fired, blacks in late nineteenth-century Boston formed a surplus labor force at the bottom of society.

The concentration of blacks in unskilled and service occupations is demonstrated in Table 2.

Table 2. Occupational Level of Black Male and Female Heads of Household,
Black Non-Heads of Household, and Irish, 1880

	Black Heads of Household[a]		Black Non-Heads of Household		All blacks at work	All Irish at work[b]
	Male	Female	Male	Female		
Professional	36	1	25	25	87	562
	3.4%[c]	.6%	2.3%	2.9%	3.2%	1.6%
White Collar	33	2	52	6	93	3,333
	3.1%	1.3%	4.8%	.7%	2.9%	9.6%
Skilled	72	31	54	84	241	6,880
	6.8%	19.4%	5.0%	9.7%	7.2%	19.8%
Unskilled and Service	925	126	950	751	2,752	23,970
	86.8%	78.8%	87.9%	86.7%	86.7%	68.9%
Total	1,066	160	1,081	866	3,173	34,745

[a] heads of household with no occupation were omitted from the head of household group

[b] derived from data in Carroll Wright, *Social, Commerical, and Manufacturing Statistics of the city of Boston* (Boston: Rockwell and Churchill, 1882), pp. 92-116.

[c] Column percentages sometimes do not add up to 100 due to rounding. The relationship between occupational level and household status (head of household vs. non-head of household) is significant at .030 with three degrees of freedom for males, significant at .002 with three degrees of freedom for females.

Overall, 86.7 percent of the total black work force consisted of unskilled and service workers, 7.2 percent of black workers held skilled positions, 2.9 percent performed clerical jobs or owned small shops and 3.2 percent were professionals. Table 2 also includes the percentage of Irish workers in 1880 in each of these occupational status groups. An immigrant group of peasant origins, the Boston Irish were the white ethnic group which ranked lowest in the Boston social order. Except at the top of the occupational structure, where there was a slightly higher percentage of professionals among the black work force than among the Irish, Irish workers had much larger percentages of white-collar

1102

and skilled workers and much smaller percentages of unskilled and service workers than the black labor force. While 68.9 percent of the Irish were laborers, teamsters, hostlers and other unskilled and service workers, 86.7 percent of blacks performed this low status work. The classification of menial labor, moreover, tends to obscure the wage differences between the two groups. The black waiter and the Irish cotton mill operative both worked long hours at low pay, but the rewards were somewhat greater for the Irish worker than for his black counterpart.

Of all wage earners, 7.2 percent of the blacks and 19.8 percent of the Irish were skilled workers. Such work, particularly in the building trades, required apprenticeship training which was generally closed to blacks; even buying tools could be an expensive proposition for a black worker. The white-collar group, over three times as large among the Irish as among blacks, owed their jobs to the expansion of record-keeping, paper work and sales in an industrial society. The new jobs in the Boston labor market—office personnel, sales clerks, even telephone and telegraph operators—employed some of the children of Irish parents, while job discrimination and lack of the proper educational qualifications closed this employment to the aspiring black worker. The figures for the white-collar group also reflected the larger proportion of petty proprietors among the Irish than among blacks.

For the black professionals, Boston deserved its reputation as the city of the "Talented Tenth." The relatively large number of black lawyers, doctors and other professionals, compared with the somewhat smaller Irish percentage, was the result of the attractiveness of the city to educated blacks from the South and other parts of the North, as well as the educational opportunities for the black elite in the New England area.

Even so, the black child and the black parent clearly faced more limited job opportunities than even the proletarian Boston Irish. How did the occupational situation of heads of household compare with that of the black worker with no family responsibilities? Although the head of household, in order to support dependents, needed to earn more money than the unattached black worker, Table 2 indicates that there were virtually no differences in occupational situation between blacks heading household and those not heading households. Among

1103

unskilled and service workers, one finds 86.8 percent of black heads of household and 87.9 percent of the unattached black workers.

Providing for a family was even more difficult for the widowed or deserted wife. Female-headed households included 22 women with no occupations and 105 women at work, most of them in unskilled and service jobs. The skilled category in Table 2, which includes 18 percent of female workers, is the result of the large number of black seamstresses among females heading households.

Black workers, including male heads of household, female heads of household and workers with no family responsibilities were concentrated in the lowest ranks of the occupational structure. While there were slight differences in occupational level for heads of household as compared with all other workers, heads of household, in general, were no more occupationally diverse than other black workers.

Conditions of Life

In the vast new areas of Boston, large frame houses with plenty of rooms, indoor plumbing and spacious backyards were being built for the middle class. But the streetcar suburbs of late nineteenth-century Boston were restricted to whites. In 1880, about 42 percent of the black population lived in the West End (sometimes referred to as "Nigger Hill"), a conglomeration of tiny alleyways and side streets on the seamy side of Beacon Hill. Tenement commissioners visiting the area described filthy streets, polluted air, overcrowded housing, dirty cellars, unsanitary water closets, poor drainage and unsafe buildings.[18]

At No. – Anderson Street is a little court. Here a single water closet in a small shed, the bowl filled and in abominable condition, was the only accommodation in this line for eight or ten families of colored people, besides the hands in a stable and a couple of little shops.[19]

Since the tenement rooms were crowded, poorly heated and ventilated, children played in the street. Playing stickball in the summer and using Anderson and Phillips streets as ski slopes in the winter, black children made the most of their urban environment.[20] But street play also resulted in children being crushed under the wheels of fast-moving teams of horses.

The poor physical conditions and the inability of parents to provide an adequate family income resulted in sickness and sometimes death for black children. Mission workers from a settlement in the West End found "a young girl, whose only bed was two broken chairs placed between the cooking stove and the door. She was dying with consumption and was left all day with the care of a two year-old child, tied into a chair beside her, while its mother was at work." In the same neighborhood, they found a poor black child "who shared the floor with the rats and mice on a cold winter's night."[21] These cases were probably the most dramatic, not the typical circumstances of black poverty in the West End. The mission workers, no doubt, chose examples which would underline the importance of their work and the need for hospital care for their clients.

Individual human tragedies like the deaths of these two children are hidden in the high death rates in the Boston black community. Although the birth rate for blacks was higher than for whites, the number of deaths was so great that deaths generally exceeded births. In fact, 1905-1910 was the first five-year period since the Civil War when the black birth rate was higher than the death rate.[22] Year after year, the city registrar reported more black deaths than births. In 1884, the registrar speculated that "there can be no question that, so far as the limited field furnished by this city affords the means of judging, were accessions from without to cease, the colored population would, in time, disappear from our community."[23] Arguing that the "colored" race was unsuited to Northern climates, he concluded: "In short, it would not be too much to say, that were all opposing obstacles of every kind, and in every direction, to the entire liberty of the colored race removed, and they were allowed to seek and occupy any position they were qualified to fill, they would instinctively and inevitably gravitate to southern and congenial latitudes as naturally as water seeks its own level."[24]

As a result of poor diet, extremely high rates of infant mortality and deaths for mothers in childbirth and the frequent incidence of tuberculosis and contagious diseases, the mortality rate for the black population in 1886 was 41 per 1000, almost twice the white rate.[25] A black person who grew up in the West End recalled that

1105

on Sundays after church his family discussed the number of deaths in the neighborhood and which of the neighbors were dying of consumption.[26] Diseases connected with childbirth accounted for the slightly higher death rate among black females than among black males. In 1890 the death rate per 1000 for white males in Boston was 15.86, for black males, 32. Among white females the mortality rate was 24 out of 1000, while black females died at the rate of 35 for every 1000.[27]

1106

The death rate was highest among children under one year of age, and higher still among male children. But significant reductions in infant mortality for both whites and blacks led to a sharp decline in the death rate in the first decade of the twentieth century. From 1900 to 1910, the white death rate for children under one year of age fell from 189 per 1000 to 185, while the black death rate dropped from 322 to 294.[28] These figures were comparable to the mortality rates in other Northern and Western cities.[29]

The high death rate among adults created a large number of widowed persons. About one-third of women aged 4l-50 and a little less than half of women aged 5l-60 lost their husbands. Either as a result of migration or in consequence of a higher rate of remarriage, the census takers found only about one-third as many widowers as widows. Some of the widows remarried, others went to live with relatives and the remaining women made up the bulk of one-parent households in the black community.

The death of both parents left about 17 percent of black children homeless in Boston in 1880. These orphans were a much larger part of the population in late nineteenth-century cities than were the one out of ten black youngsters in 1968 who were not living with one or both parents.[30] Homeless black children, in most cases, lived with relatives or friends, for few such children found their way into asylums and homes for foundling children. Discrimination by public institutions combined with the desire of black families to adopt black children meant that few black children without parents became wards of the state.

Family Structure

The high death rate and overcrowded, unsanitary tenements,

the transiency of the population and the low occupational position constitute the kinds of pressures often cited as the causes of family disorganization. But several quantitative indicators—the sex ratio, the small number of one-parent households, the infrequency of desertion and the adaptation of the household to include large numbers of migrants—suggest that the black family structure maintained its organization despite the many depressing aspects of life in Boston.

Several statistics are useful gauges of the nature of family life. One such statistic is the sex ratio, the number of males per one hundred females in the population. A western frontier area, with a ratio of males to females of ten to one, or even higher, would have little family life. For everyone who chose to marry, a stable ratio of males to females would theoretically insure the selection of a mate. Another arrangement of sex ratio, a small male population and a large female population, is said to produce a society with few stable marriages and high rates of illegitimacy, desertion, delinquency and female-headed households. These theoretical possibilities, reasonable in the abstract, have less meaning in concrete historical situations. Even in societies with quite similar sex ratios, great deviations can occur in patterns of sexuality, marriage and family life. Still, for a population on the move, such as the black population over the last one hundred years, the possibility of imbalanced sex ratios due to large numbers of migrants is an important consideration in assessing the framework of family life.[31]

In fact, among blacks in late nineteenth-century Boston, parity of the sexes existed, as the third column of Table 3 discloses.

1107

Table 3. Sex Ratios for Native Whites, Foreign-Born Whites, and Blacks, 1880[a] (Males per 100 Females)

	Native White	Foreign-Born White	Black
All Ages	95.7	79.4	102.9
25 44	95.9	83.8	121.0

[a] derived from data in Carroll Wright, *Social, Commercial, and Manufacturing Statistics*, pp. 94-95.

The overall sex ratio in 1880 was 102.9 though much higher—121—for the marriageable age group of those 25 to 44. In two other age groups, the very young and the very old, there were more females than males, reflecting the differential mortality of the sexes. The preponderance of males in the 25 to 44 age group stems from the relatively greater economic opportunities drawing adult migrants to the city. Many of these males were "beachhead" migrants, husbands who sent for their wives after they had established themselves in Boston.

When the black sex ratio is contrasted with the sex ratio of the foreign-born and native white populations, we find greater imbalances in the two white groups. For all native whites in 1880 the sex ratio was 95.7, while it was much lower—79.4—for foreign-born whites. Among young adults, Table 3 indicates that there were 96 native white males for every one hundred females, and 83.8 foreign-born white males for every one hundred females. The large number of adult females in the foreign-born white group reflects the presence of adult working women, usually employed as domestic servants and factory workers, some of whom were earning enough money to finance their dowries.

Throughout the last decades of the nineteenth century, there were slightly more males than females in the black population of Boston. Only in 1910 did the census takers find the reverse. Many young adult females, migrants to Boston, created this surplus of females in the population.[32]

The second important statistic for assessing the possibilities of family life is the number of married persons deserted by their spouse. Even though parity in the sex ratio suggests the necessary environment for stable family life, it is still quite possible that a high number of desertions would modify this conclusion. The number of desertions was determined by tabulating all those married persons in the census record who were not living with their spouse. Of those deserted by their spouses, there were 157 females, about 11 percent of all married women, and 167 males, about 13 percent of all married men in this category. The figures for males, as we noted earlier, were probably increased by the large number of men awaiting the arrival of their wives. In a middle-class district of the late nineteenth-century Chicago, where few of the desertions could be explained as the result of large numbers of migrants, about 11 percent of households included a deserted wife or husband.[33]

What seems impressive in these figures for blacks in Boston is the low rate of desertion and separation, given the extremely high rate of out-migration, even among heads of household, and the dismal occupational prospect that blacks faced. W.E.B. DuBois discussed some of the causes of desertion and separation among blacks in Philadelphia.

The economic difficulties arise continually among young waiters and servant girls; away from home and oppressed by the peculiar lonesomeness of a great city, they form chance acquaintances here and there, thoughtlessly marry and soon find that the husband's income cannot alone support a family, then comes a struggle which generally results in desertion or voluntary separation.[34]

1109

As a result of death, desertion or voluntary separation, 18 percent of black households came to be headed by one parent. In nine out of ten instances the one parent was a female. In assessing one- and two-parent households, I included households in which there were no children present as well as those with children. If childless couples were excluded, we would be unable to examine households of young couples, that is, future parents, as well as those households where grown offspring had moved away.

How did one- and two-parent households differ? Without substantial historical evidence it would be foolhardy to apply present-day, widely questioned theories about the "tangle of pathology" associated with one-parent households.[35] Regrettably, I have found no qualitative evidence which bears on the issue of how members of the black community viewed the one-parent household.

Nevertheless, there was an important economic difference between the one- and two-parent household. Although precise income figures are not available for black households, black males enjoyed higher wages than black females. In consequence, a family dependent on a woman's wages almost always lived in poverty. The yearly wage among female domestic servants, for example, was half the wage of male domestic servants.[36] Moreover, given the concentration of female heads of household in the most poorly remunerated occupations, overall income levels between male- and female-headed households were even more disparate. In many two-parent households, the husband's wage was supplemented by his wife's earnings from domestic services or laundry work and the rent money from the boarder. Without these several income sources, the one-parent household was at an even greater disadvantage. Lacking the wages or unpaid labor of a wife, even the one-parent household headed by a male suffered economically.

From an analysis of the manuscript census schedules, three important distinctions emerged among two-parent households in the black community. First, there were proportionately more two-parent households among migrants to Boston than among native Bostonians. Second, the proportion of two-parent households among rural blacks was greater than among urban blacks. Finally, literate blacks headed two-parent households more often than illiterate blacks.

As we observed above, the early movement of blacks to Boston brought persons especially attracted to the advantages of the Northern city. Both those heads of household from the rural South and those Northern heads of household from outside of Massachusetts revealed large and almost identical proportions of two-parent households, 83.3 percent and 83.4 percent respectively, while native Bostonians contributed fewer two-parent households. Given the many theories about the disruptive nature of migration, we might expect a higher percentage of one-parent households among the newcomers to the city than among the long-established urban blacks. But Table 4 reveals that the percentage of two-parent households among the two migrant streams of the population was significantly greater than among black Bostonians.

1110

Table 4. One and Two-Parent Households,
by Place and Birth of the Head of Household[a]

	Born in Massachusetts	Born in another Northern State	Total Northern Born	Born in the South	N
One-Parent	36	27	63	136	199
	27.1%	16.6%	21.3%	16.7%	18.0%
Two-Parent	97	136	233	676	909
	72.9%	83.4%	78.7%	83.3%	82.0%

[a] This table omits foreign-born heads of household, heads of household with no place of birth, and single-member households. The relationship between place of birth and household status is significant at .02, with two degrees of freedom.

Thus, the stereotype of disruptive migration does not fit the situation of blacks in late nineteenth-century Boston.

The combined effects of rural origins and long-distance movement away from family and friends made Southern-born, rural migrants to Boston a distinctive group. We can compare the effect of rural origins on the household by contrasting rural heads of household (the Southern-born) with urban heads of household (the Northern-born). As we note in Table 4, slightly more two-parent households occurred among rural than among urban heads of household, 83.3 percent as opposed to 78.7 percent. If we assume that a majority of the Southern-born blacks were freedmen, the large number of two-parent households among them is even more remarkable. The common argument, that the abrupt transition from rural to urban life created indelible strains on the black family, does not hold for late nineteenth-century Boston. If anything, we find the reverse of this common proposition. It is clear from column four of Table 4 that households in which both parents were present were more frequent among rural than among urban black heads of household.

Even greater than variations between urban and rural households were variations within these two types of households. Table 5 bears on this issue, differentiating urban and rural blacks according to the literacy of the head of household.

Table 5. One and Two-Parent Households, by Place of Birth
and Literacy of the Head of Household, 1880[a]

	Northern-Born			Southern-Born			N
	Literate	Illiterate	TOTAL	Literate	Illiterate	TOTAL	
One-Parent	52	11	63	77	59	136	199
	19.9%	31.4%	21.3%	13.5%	24.3%	16.7%	18.0%
Two-Parent	209	24	233	492	184	676	909
	80.1%	68.6%	78.7%	86.5%	75.7%	83.3%	82.0%
Total	261	35	296	569	243	812	1,108

[a] Table omits foreign-born heads of household, heads of household with no place of birth, and single-member households. The relationship between literacy and household status was significant at .180 with one degree of freedom for the Northern-born, significant at .001 with one degree of freedom for the Southern-born.

For both urban and rural heads of household, a literate black was more likely to head a two-parent household than an illiterate. The percentage of two-parent households dropped from 86.5 percent of Southern-born literates to 75.7 percent among illiterates from the same region, and from 80.1 percent among Northern-born literates to only 68.6 percent among illiterates born in the North. Although these Northern-born illiterate heads of household were a very small group, only eleven persons, nevertheless it is striking that a larger percentage of one-parent households was found among them than among any other group in the population.

If slavery permanently weakened family ties among blacks one would expect to find greater numbers of one-parent households among the ex-slaves. To be sure, there were fewer two-parent households among ex-slaves (Southern-born illiterates) than among Southern-born literates, but the freedmen had two-parent households more often than Northern-born heads of household who were also illiterate. Thus, among both Northern- and Southern-born heads of household, illiteracy was associated with higher proportions of one-parent households.

It is possible that the relationship between illiteracy and one-parent, generally female-headed households, is only a statistical artifact, the consequence of a higher rate of illiteracy among females than males.[37] In order to test whether Table 5 described a spurious relationship, I compared the number of illiterates among two groups of women, female heads of household and those females living with their husbands in two-parent households. If higher rates of illiteracy among one-parent households in both the North and the South were merely the result of the fact that one-parent households were mostly female, we would expect to find roughly similar proportions of illiterates among married women living with their spouses than among females heading households. Instead, female heads of household were much more commonly illiterate than women living with their husbands. Significantly more female heads of household than married females were illiterate; about one-fourth of married women were illiterate, while more than a third of females heading households could not read or write. Among the Southern-born women, most of whom were born into slavery, the rate of illiteracy was much higher. However, the general pattern remained the same; while about one-third of married women were illiterate, almost half of females heading households were illiterate.

Whether or not illiterates thought less of themselves than blacks who learned to read or write, the numbers will never tell us. What is clear, however, is that for both urban and rural heads of household there were significantly more one-parent households among the illiterates. Speculation might lead us to conclude that illiteracy was both a real handicap in an urban society and, in addition, a characteristic found among the most disadvantaged adults in the black community.

Migrants and native Bostonians, rural and urban adults, illiterate and literate persons differed significantly in the number of two-parent households they formed. Did differences appear as well in the composition of the household? A single individual, or that person and boarders lived in one out of seven black households in Boston. These solitary adults were excluded from the analysis of household composition. The great majority of black households, as Table 6 indicates, consisted of nuclear families—usually husband and wife, or a husband, wife and children, but occasionally a single parent and child.

1113

Table 6. Nuclear, Extended, and Augmented Households,
by Place of Birth of the Head of Household, 1880[a]

	Born in Massachusetts	Born in another Northern State	Total Northern-Born	Born in the South	N
Nuclear	68	93	161	462	623
	51.2%	57.1%	54.4%	56.1%	56.2%
Extended	16	15	31	80	111
	12.0%	9.2%	10.5%	10.6%	10.0%
Augmented	49	55	104	270	374
	36.8%	33.7%	35.1%	33.3%	33.8%
Total	133	163	296	812	1,108

[a] This table omits foreign-born heads of household, heads of household with no place of birth, and single-member households. The relationship between place of birth and family structure shown in this table is not statistically significant.

Families which added other relatives to the nuclear family, in what it termed an extended household, were 9.7 percent of all black households. Finally, about one out of three black households included boarders, and in a few cases, boarders and relatives, in addition to parents and children. DuBois discovered roughly the same number of augmented households—that is, households with boarders—in late nineteenth-century Philadelphia.[38]

Virtually the same patterns of family composition existed among rural and urban blacks, as columns three and four of Table 6 disclose. In both cases the majority of households were nuclear, although a significant minority—about one-third—included boarders. Only when native Bostonians are separated from the rest of the Northern-born do differences appear in the composition of the household. The household headed by a black person born in Boston was somewhat more likely to mix relatives or boarders in the home than a household headed by a migrant. However, the differences in household composition between blacks born in Massachusetts, other Northern states and the South are not striking. What is important, in fact, is the uniformity of household composition among migrant and stable, urban and rural heads of household.

It might be thought that relatives were more frequent among the poorest families, huddling together because they could not afford to live by themselves. The figures in Table 7 demonstrate that this was not the case.

Table 7. Nuclear, Extended, and Augmented Households,
by Occupational Level of the Head of Household, 1880[a]

	Professional	White Collar	Skilled	Unskilled	N
Nuclear	19	16	49	558	642
	52.8%	50.0%	57.6%	58.8%	
Extended	7	6	8	84	105
	19.4%	18.8%	9.4%	8.9%	
Augmented	10	10	28	307	355
	27.8%	31.3%	32.9%	32.3%	
Total	36	32	85	949	1,102

[a] This table omits persons with no occupation and single-member heads of household. Heads of household from all places of birth are included. The relationship between occupation and family structure is not statistically significant.

Controlling for the occupational level of the head of household, the proportion of relatives increased among higher status heads of household, while the proportion decreased among lower status households. Relatives may have been more welcome to join the family in higher status households which could afford to sustain additional members. The George Ruffins (he was lawyer and judge, she a prominent clubwoman and suffragist) absorbed into their homes Mrs. Ruffin's niece, Daisy Nahar. In other cases, the presence of additional adult family members may have financed the education or supported the family business, which, in turn, resulted in the higher status of the head of household.

Relatives were more common in higher status households, but lodgers appeared more often in lower status households. The number of augmented households, as summarized in line three of Table 7, shows that about one-third of blue-collar households included a boarder, while slightly fewer boarders resided in professional and white-collar homes. Among households headed by unskilled and skilled workers, just as in the female-headed household, the lodger's rent money was often an essential part of the family budget. In response to the influx of Southern migrants, the black family accommodated these lodgers, generally single women and men who worked as servants and waiters. The augmented household was a product of necessity, but it met the housing needs of the lodgers, as well as additional income requirements of black families.

Nineteenth-century observers often described the "demoralizing" influence of lodgers on the household. DuBois exemplified this attitude, fearing that "the privacy and intimacy of home life is destroyed, and elements of danger and demoralization admitted" when the lodger entered the black home.[39] Given the desperate economic circumstances of most black families, the boarder's rent money may have insured family survival rather than destroyed it. Moreover, boarders were common additions to higher status households. The boarder, in many cases, became a "relative" of the family, in function, if not in kinship. Richard Wright recalled that as a boarder he easily became a part of a Memphis home—more so than he liked, since a match-making mother was eager for the boarder to marry her daughter.[40]

Conclusion

This study of the black family in late nineteenth-century Boston views the black family structure at one point in time. Subsequent studies must trace the family over the years in order fully to comprehend changes in the household. If we want to learn

1115

about the acculturation of children in the black family, it is particularly important to employ a dynamic perspective. For example, while we know that about seven out of ten black children in Boston in 1880 lived in two-parent households, we do not know how many of these children spent their early years in such a household. Nor, for that matter do we know how the family situation of the minority of children in 1880 who were missing both parents affected their futures, for better or worse. This kind of analysis can only be pursued through the tracing of individuals, a method extremely arduous to undertake, given the mobility of the population.

1116

Any study of black family life largely employing quantitative information represents only a point of departure for further analysis of black families. While the high number of two-parent households, 82 percent of all black households in Boston, indicates the existence of much greater family organization than has been generally assumed, we need evidence about the cultural context in which the urban black family operated. How were one- and two-parent households viewed? Were different values placed on marriage, the family, even desertion in the black community than in other groups? Did the addition of boarders and relatives endanger the intimacy of the home or create additional adult models for black children? Except in the few instances of family diaries and personal accounts, these questions may prove difficult, if not impossible, to answer through literary materials.

While there are limitations to numerical analysis, it does allow for comparisons across time and space. How then did Boston compare with other cities? Perhaps one could argue that, despite the poverty-stricken condition of blacks in Boston, there was still some way in which Boston was, indeed, "the paradise of the Negro," if only because the situation of blacks in the South was so much worse. Although more studies need to be undertaken, overall figures from Southern urban, Southern rural and Northern urban centers in the late nineteenth century demonstrate a striking similarity in the percentages of two-parent households. Theodore Hershberg reports that in both 1880 and 1896 the two-parent household comprised 76 percent of all households among blacks in Philadelphia. He found roughly similar proportions of two-parent households in ante-bellum Philadelphia, where 77 percent of all black households were two-parent. Among a special group of about 87 slaves who had bought their freedom, 91 percent formed two-parent households.[41] From the major work of Herbert Gutman on the black family, the two-parent household in 1880 appeared among 81 percent of Adams County, Mississippi black households and 77 percent of Mobile, Alabama black households.[42] In three urban areas in 1896, Atlanta, Nashville and Cambridge, Massachusetts, Gutman found respectively, 77 percent, 85 percent and 90 percent two-parent households.[43] It would be tempting here to contrast the relative effects on the black household of Southern urban, Southern rural and Northern urban environments. But what we find in the few areas studied is greater variation within a single locale than between locales. All in all, the two-parent household was the prevailing family form in Southern rural, Southern urban and Northern urban areas.

1117

The figures cited above, except in the case of ante-bellum Philadelphia, do not distinguish between native-born city dwellers and rural migrants to the city. Such an analytic strategy is vital to the study of the effects of city and country origins and the migration from one area to another on the black household.

How did migration to the city affect the black family? The standard texts on black history scarcely mention the migration of blacks to Northern cities before the Great Migration of World War I. On the whole, the northward migration was a movement of single individuals or couples; in few cases did the whole family move north. After the migrants from the South or other parts of the North reached Boston, an incredible number of single individuals and families left the city. This movement out of Boston in some cases left behind deserted wives and husbands, but the rate of desertion was rather low given the lack of occupational opportunity for blacks in Boston and the general rootlessness of the black population.

In the work of DuBois and E. Franklin Frazier, migration to the city is viewed as a disruptive factor which weakened the family and produced large numbers of one-parent households. DuBois wrote that "as a whole, it is true that the average of culture and wealth is far lower among immigrants than natives, and that this gives rise to the gravest of the Negro problems."[44] What these writers generally meant by migration was the *transition* from rural

1118

to urban culture among Southern migrants to the city. This disruptive transition was said to have been the source of desertion, delinquency and female-headed households. Frazier, in his discussion of the "city of destruction," noted: "Family desertion among Negroes in cities, appears, then, to be one of the inevitable consequences of the impact of urban life on the simple family organization and folk culture which the Negro has evolved in the rural South."[45]

At least for late nineteenth-century Boston, quantitative evidence calls Frazier's thesis into question. Two-parent households were more frequent among both migrant *and* rural black heads of household. Such evidence can be interpreted in two ways. One explanation would reverse the Frazier argument: instead of migration and the transition from rural to urban culture weakening the black family, these influences strengthened it. Persons who had invested so much effort to leave family, friends and familar ways, had a greater stake in establishing households once they were settled in the city. Also, the limited expectations of rural blacks may have meant that city life in the North was, indeed, a significant improvement over life in the rural South. Finally, the special character of this early migration might have distinguished the early newcomers to the city (both in ante-bellum Philadelphia and in Boston about fifty years later) from more recent city-bound blacks.

A second explanation of the differences in the number of two-parent households, offered by Theodore Hershberg, is that neither slavery nor migration but the urban environment produced greater numbers of one-parent households. Tremendous differences in wealth, poor health conditions for blacks in cities, the destructiveness of urban culture—all these are cited as the causes of "family disorganization" among blacks. Without more knowledge of the internal workings of black culture, of the values blacks placed on different family forms, it is impossible to know whether the one-parent, female-headed household was viewed by blacks as "family disorganization." The use of this value-loaded term generally presupposes a hierarchy of family types, with the male-present, nuclear and patriarchal household representing the most-valued family form.[46]

Another danger in substituting one grand interpretation of "family disorganization" in place of another is that it may tend to obscure other important differences in family type and composition which do not appear between rural and urban, ex-slave and free-born blacks. Important differences between city-dwellers and rural blacks must be noted. But in late nineteenth-century Boston the composition of the black household was similar for both rural and urban black heads of household. Moreover, significantly more one-parent households occurred among illiterate blacks from both rural and urban origins. The social meaning of illiteracy for blacks in the city remains enigmatic, but the discovery that the illiteracy of the head of household significantly altered the proportion of two-parent households hints at the existence of other fundamental social characteristics differentiating black households.

While variations in household composition and percentage of two-parent household which are associated with place of birth, illiteracy and migration should be noted and considered, the similarities in two-parent households among diverse groups in the black population are even more striking. The evidence suggests a family pattern of nuclear, two-parent households which prevailed among migrant and rural black heads of household as well as among stable and urban black heads of household. Despite the existence of blacks at the lowest rung of the occupational ladder, most black children lived in homes where both parents were present, and black families generally included husband, wife and children.

The presentation of these raw statistics force us to challenge and revise previous conceptions about the black family. More lies hidden behind a high death rate, a transient population and a poverty-stricken black community than the phrases like "culture of poverty" or "family disorganization" convey. Our vision of the family as an institution which reacts to and reflects changes is oversimplified, while there seems little understanding of the family as an institution which itself produces changes in individuals and institutions. If the black family were merely the image of the social conditions of urban blacks, we would find a rootless, disorganized mosaic of families. Notions of "black matriarchy" and "the tangle of pathology" of the black family have captivated

1119

sociologists and historians alike, but now the task before us is to tell the rather different story of the complex organization and continuity of the black household.

FOOTNOTES

1. "Boston as the Paradise of the Negro," *Colored American Magazine*, Vol. VII, no. 5 (May, 1904), 309-17. For a similar view, see also W.E. Burghardt DuBois, *The Black North in 1901: A Social Study* (New York: Arno Press and the New York Times reprint, 1969), 10-19.

2. There were 139 households headed by a black person born in a foreign country. In 28 of the foreign-born households, the head of household was a single individual, living without kin or children. Excluded from all analysis concerning family were those inter-racial couples which included a white husband and a black wife. Inter-racial couples composed of a black husband and a white wife were included.

3. Marriage records, registered by the Division of Vital Statistics of the Commonwealth of Massachusetts, indicated race and exact place of birth for the bride and groom. Of the marriage partners listing Massachusetts as their place of birth in the 1870 vital records, five out of seven were born in Boston. Half of the remaining non-Bostonians were from Newburyport, Worcester, Cambridge, Lynn and Salem. The largest group of Southern-born brides and grooms were natives of Virginia; two out of five were from Petersburg, Richmond and Norfolk. In the period when these brides and grooms were growing up in Virginia, none of these three towns could be considered "urban" by Boston standards. The largest city in Virginia in 1860 was Richmond, which at the time was only one-fifth the size of Boston. James M. McPherson, *The Negro's Civil War: How American Negroes Felt and Acted During the War for the Union* (New York: Vintage Books, 1965), Appendix B, 320.

4. I am indebted to Peter R. Knights for suggesting this use of the literacy category.

5. At first glance, it seems possible to estimate the number of Southern slave migrants to Boston by taking the percentage of slaves in the states of the upper South just before the Civil War. Between one-half and two-thirds of the Southern migrants to Boston in the late nineteenth century were from Virgina, whose population in 1860 consisted for about ten slaves to every free-born black. If black migration operated randomly, the Southern black population in Boston consisted of about ten freedmen for every free-born black. But migration to the North after the Civil War was extremely selective. We cannot assume that freedmen and free blacks migrated in proportion to their numbers in the population.

If we make the assumption that literacy corresponds to free status for blacks in the South, we arrive at a probability that it was twenty-seven times as likely for a free-born person to move north as it was for an ex-slave. This proportion is derived by taking the proportion of free persons to slaves in the 1860 Virginia population, a ratio of one to nine, multiplied by the proportion of literates to illiterates in the black population of Boston in 1880, a ratio of three to one.

For the proportions of blacks from the upper South in Boston's black population, see John Daniels, *In Freedom's Birthplace: A Study of the Boston Negroes* (Boston: Houghton Mifflin, 1915), 141, 468. For the number of ex-slaves in the Virginia 1860 population, see U.S. Bureau of the Census, *Negro Population of the United States, 1790-1915* (Washington, D.C.: U.S. Government Printing Office, 1918), Table 6, 57.

6. The statistics used in this paper are based on a total of 5847 individuals found in the

manuscript census schedules for Boston in 1880. The discrepancy between this figure and the official figure, 5873, is due to mistakes I may have made in transcribing the manuscript schedules, as well as errors in the original tabulated figure.

7. Net migration increases indicate only a small part of the actual population turnover. Stephan Thernstrom estimated that nearly 800,000 persons moved into Boston between 1880 and 1890. Since the population streams of in-migrants and out-migrants tended to cancel out each other, the total Boston population only increased from 363,000 in 1880 to 448,000 in 1890. Stephan Thernstrom and Peter R. Knights, "Men in Motion: Some Data and Speculations About Urban Population Mobility in Nineteenth-Century America," Tamara K. Hareven, ed., *Anonymous Americans: Explorations in Nineteenth-Century Social History* (Englewood Cliffs, N.J.: Prentice Hall, 1971), 21, 25.

8. E.G. Ravenstein, "The Laws of Migration," *Journal of the Royal Statistical Society*, XLVIII (1885), 167-227; Samuel A. Stoffer, "Intervening Opportunities: A Theory Relating Mobility and Distance," *American Sociological Review*, V (1940), 845-67.

9. Carter Godwin Woodson, *A Century of Negro Migration* (Washington, D.C.: The Association for the Study of Negro Life and History, 1918), 162-66.

10. Clyde Kiser, *Sea Island to City* (New York: Columbia University Press, 1932), 170.

11. Thernstrom and Knights, "Men in Motion," 22.

12. These four-fold classifications of occupation were based on an eight-scale occupational code devised by Stephan Thernstrom for his study of occupational mobility in Boston. Since there were so few high status black workers, professionals, large-scale proprietors, managers and officials and semi-professionals were collapsed into one category called professionals. The white collar category included clerical and sales personnel, petty proprietors and minor managers and lower level government officials. I maintained a distinctive category of skilled workers as Thernstrom did, but the semi-skilled, service, unskilled and menial service groups were merged into one category called service and unskilled workers. I am indebted to Professor Thernstrom for providing me with this occupational code. For a more detailed explication of the code, see Peter R. Knights, *The Plain People of Boston, 1830-1960: A Study in City Growth* (New York: Oxford University Press, 1971), Appendix E, 149-56.

13. Clyde Griffen, "Making it in America: Social Mobility in Mid-Nineteenth Century Poughkeepsie," *New York History*, Vol. II, no. 5 (October, 1970), Table II, 498.

14. Data cited in Thernstrom and Knights, "Men in Motion," 46.

15. Richard J. Hopkins, "Occupational and Geographic Mobility in Atlanta, 1870-1896," *Journal of Southern History*, XXIV (May, 1968), Table 6, 207.

16. Paul B. Worthman, "Working Class Mobility in Birmingham, Alabama, 1880-1914," Hareven, ed., *Anonymous Americans*, 180-185.

17. Alwyn Barr, "Occupational and Geographic Mobility in San Antonio, 1870-1900," *Social Science Quarterly*, Vol. 51, no. 2 (September, 1970), Table 3, 401.

18. Horace G. Wadlin, *A Tenement House Census of Boston*, Section II (Boston: Wright and Potter, 1893), 89-93.

19. Dwight Porter, *Report upon a Sanitary Inspection of Certain Tenements-House Districts of Boston* (Boston: Rockwell and Churchill, 1889), 37-8.

20. Walter J. Stevens, *Chip on My Shoulder* (Boston: Meador Publishing Company, 1946), 22.

21. *New York Age* (June 15, 1889), 1.

22. Daniels, *In Freedom's Birthplace*, 472.

23. *Boston City Document No. 68* (1884), 7-8.

24. *Ibid.*, 8.

25. *Boston City Document No. 100* (1887), 11.

26. Walter J. Stevens, *Chip on My Shoulder*, 18.

27. Frederick L. Hoffman, *Race Traits and Tendencies of the American Negro* (Publications of the American Economic Association, 1896), 47.

28. U.S. Census Bureau, *Negro Population, 1790-1915*, 32.

29. *Ibid.*

30. U.S. Bureau of the Census, *Current Population Reports*, Series P-20, No. 187, Tables 4 and 9; and *U.S. Census of the Population: 1960, Detailed Characteristics, U.S. Summary*, Tables 181, 182, and 185, as quoted in Paul C. Glick, "Marriage and Marital Stability Among Blacks," *The Millbank Memorial Fund Quarterly*, Vol. XLVIII, no. 2 (April, 1970), Table 8, 113.

31. The sex ratio does more than reflect differing economic opportunities for females and males in the city. Jacquelyne Jackson in a recent article also maintains that the sex ratio is related to the number of female-headed families. In states with high sex ratios in 1970, she found few female-headed families, but in states with low sex ratios, she found large numbers of female-headed families. Massachusetts, with a sex ratio of 88.6 in 1970, had the highest number of black female-headed families of any state in the nation. Jacquelyne J. Jackson, "But Where are the Men?" *The Black Scholar*, Vol. 3, no. 4 (December, 1971), 30-41.

32. U.S. Census Bureau, *Negro Population, 1790-1915*, 156.

33. Richard Sennett, *Families against the city: Middle Class Homes of Industrial Chicago, 1872-1890* (Cambridge, Massachusetts: Harvard University Press, 1971), 115.

34. W.E.B. DuBois, *The Philadelphia Negro* (New York: Schocken Books, 1967), 67.

35. Robert Staples, "Towards a Sociology of the Black Family: A Theoretical and Methodological Assessment," *Journal of Marriage and the Family*, Vol. 33, no. 1 (February, 1971), 119-30 contains a comprehensive review of current sociological literature on the black family and maintains a critical stance towards views which associate "the tangle of pathology" with the black family.

36. DuBois, *The Philadelphia Negro*, 448. For related income figures, see also the same work, 173-8 and W.E.B. DuBois, *The Negro American Family* (Cambridge, Massachusetts: MIT Press, 1970), 111-13.

37. Carroll D. Wright, *The Social, Commercial, and Manufacturing Statistics of the City of Boston* (Boston: Rockwell and Churchill, 1882), 130-1.

1122

38. DuBois, *The Philadelphia Negro*, 164, 194.

39. *Ibid.*, 194.

40. Richard Wright, *Black Boy: a record of childhood and youth* (New York: Harper, 1937).

41. Theodore Hershberg, "Free Blacks in Ante Bellum Philadelphia: A Study of Ex-Slaves, Free-Born and Socio-Economic Decline," *Journal of Social History* (December, 1971), Table 1, and p. 186. Mr. Hershberg kindly sent me a manuscript copy of this paper.

42. Herbert G. Gutman and Laurence A. Glasco, "The Negro Family, Household, and Occupational Structure, 1855-1925, with special emphasis on Buffalo, New York, but including Comparative Data from New York, New York, Brooklyn, New York, Mobile, Alabama, and Adams County, Mississippi," (unpublished tables presented at the Yale Conference on Nineteenth Century Cities, November, 1968), Table XXI. Figures were computed from this table in order to derive a percentage of one- and two-parent households. Professor Gutman kindly allowed me to quote from his unpublished data.

1123

43. *Ibid.*, Table XXVI. Figures for one- and two-parent households were computed based on data in this table.

44. DuBois, *The Philadelphia Negro*, 80.

45. E. Franklin Frazier, *The Negro Family in the United States* (Chicago: The University of Chicago Press, 1966), 255.

46. For example, these paragraphs can be found in the Moynihan Report. "But there is one truly great discontinuity in family structure in the United States at the present time: that between the white world in general and that of the Negro American. The white family has achieved a high degree of stability and is maintaining that stability. By contrast, the family structure of lower class Negroes is highly unstable, and in many urban centers is approaching complete breakdown." Office of Policy Planning and Research, United States Department of Labor, *The Negro Family: The Case for National Action* (Washington, D.C.: U.S. Government Printing Office, 1965), 5.